A DOGGY DAY
IN
LONDON TOWN

LIFE AMONG THE DOG PEOPLE OF
PADDINGTON REC, VOL. IV

ANTHONY LINICK

authorHOUSE®

AuthorHouse™
1663 Liberty Drive
Bloomington, IN 47403
www.authorhouse.com
Phone: 1-800-839-8640

Published by AuthorHouse   09/24/2012

ISBN: 978-1-4772-2606-3 (sc)
ISBN: 978-1-4772-2607-0 (e)

Any people depicted in stock imagery provided by Thinkstock are models, and such images are being used for illustrative purposes only.
Certain stock imagery © Thinkstock.

This book is printed on acid-free paper.

Other AuthorHouse Books
by Anthony Linick

Strictly Come Barking (2007)—
Life Among the Dog People of
Paddington Rec, Vol. I

The Lives of Ingolf Dahl (2008)

Have I Got Dogs For You! (2010)—
Life Among the Dog People of
Paddington Rec, Vol. II

A Walker's Alphabet (2010)—
Adventures on the Long-Distance
Footpaths of Great Britain

DSI: Dog Scene Investigation (2011)—
Life Among the Dog People of
Paddington Rec, Vol. III

INTRODUCTION

When I first began to record my impressions of life among the dog owners in my local park I had no idea that one day my journal might actually reach the point of print. *Strictly Come Barking*, published in 2007, altered this perception. The response to this volume, particularly from those whose stories it contained, encouraged me to persist in my observations and thus the sequels began, additional volumes in the "Life Among the Dog People of Paddington Rec" cycle. First there was *Have I Got Dogs For You!* (2010), then *DSI: Dog Scene Investigation* (2011), and now, in 2012, *A Doggy Day in London Town*.

My view of our local dogs is restricted, of course, to the hour or so I see them in the park—alone, at play, or in interaction with one another—and there is little I can say about the other hours of the day, when all the loyalty and love we associate with dog ownership holds sway. Indeed, I would not want to leave the impression that any of our Paddington Rec dogs is unworthy of such love.

I have continued to use only the first names of dog owners, except for celebrities, major and minor, though in every other way I have tried to make this chronicle a complete and accurate reflection of the times as we experienced them. I have also continued to use some British spelling and, for inconsistency's sake, American punctuation.

I need to thank many people for their generous participation in this project: the dog owners themselves and all those who supplied me with photographs—Janet and Dan and David especially. I also wish to thank Rob Taggart, who took the cover picture of me with my Fritz, for his work with the photographs. As well, I need to offer my enduring thanks to all those who have helped to make Paddington Rec the oasis that it has continued to be: the management, the gardeners, the café staff, the wise heads at city hall.

Enough by way of introduction. Let the tale begin again and the tails to wag once more.

Anthony Linick
London
August, 2012

June, 2007

Friday, June 1:

A lovely sunny Friday morning helps us to begin another year's adventures in Paddington Rec. I could have left my sweatshirt at home, it seems, and the only impediment to a smoother progress toward the park's central greensward comes with the ubiquitous sound of machinery—a tractor combs the artificial surface of the central pitch and a leaf blower is expelling roughage from this sacred spot onto the walkway beneath the cypress trees. Fritz, my four year-old Schnauzer, makes a fairly rapid progress along the paths here, stropping only to nibble a few blades of grass, and then streaking ahead, where, three minutes later, I can see his white bottom disappearing onto the green itself.

Back after several weeks in Cannes is Kate, our accountant and film financier, who is accompanied by her robust white Alsatian, Skye. I ask Kate if Skye enjoyed France and this seems to have been the case. I ask if she enjoyed the pool, and Kate says she did not, indeed the headstrong lass barked incessantly at anyone who used its waters. Kate, herself a cancer victim earlier in the year, asks me how my Dorothy is doing. I give the first of the day's medical reports, ones that I am required to offer to the many anxious friends who make up the canine confraternity of London W9. (In fact Dorothy received no chemotherapy for her lung cancer yesterday—as she is fighting a chest infection.) Kate says that when she was in France she lit a candle for Dorothy, "It's a Catholic thing."

At breakfast at the park's café we have a grand social gathering today. Yesterday I missed Georgie's birthday, but today there is a special feast in honor of the fourth birthday of Dan and Davide's Pug, Winnie. Gathered around our table we have Peter, with his Holly, Ellen, with Sandy and Jack, Dan with Winnie herself, Hanna with George (the original Hannibal Lecter of Paddington Rec), Ronnie with Rosie, Georgie with her Sparkie (and also Faz and Di's Jasmine), and Kate with Skye.

Dan has brought muffins and pastry for the humans and a plate of cooked chicken for the dogs. The latter also get their share of toast and even a plate full of sausages cooked by head chef Elian, one of the few café employees who actually enjoys dogs (his special favorite is the birthday girl). Dan has also laid on drinks for our table and I go inside to order my medium cappuccino. The English of the mostly Eastern European staff is improving. I used to get a simple, "I bring," but now I get a more expansive, "I bring for you over."

Kate gets lots of questions about her time in France. She says she met a lady from an English village who was *enchanted* to have encountered her first gay couple—"Wait till I tell the book club!" Dan says that perhaps he and Davide should offer themselves as exhibits in rural climes. Chiefly he is preoccupied with the arrival of Janet, who is supposed to be heading our way with her new Shih-Tzu puppy, Daisy-Mae. But a series of phone calls confirms that the pup is not ready for the company of other canines—as two more weeks must pass before she can enter the society of other dogs. Most of us begin a back passage walkround but not before Winnie has had a snarling food tussle with Jack. "It's my party; I can fight if I want to."

Saturday, June 2:

Frank the Chinese Crested Dog, Bianca the Boxer and Blake the Doberman are the first of the dogs we meet as Fritz and I approach the cypress trees on a warm and sunny Saturday morning, one that has enabled me to feel quite comfortable in nothing more than a short sleeved shirt. As these dogs pass by with their owners there is no sign of my own animal but we do hear his warning growl from a bush and so he must be nearby. I pass through the outdoor tables of the café—where Ellen and Ronnie are already in position—and continue on to the green, where there is a good deal of weekend activity.

Celine is trying to get Ziggy to do some running, but this is not a problem for our multi-tasking Kate, who is using the ball sling to keep Skye amused while dealing with a complex tax matter on her mobile phone. There is a small group of dog owners lying on a blanket at the head of the cricket crease: Dan, Davide, Liz, and Georgie. Fritz works the crowd in search of the odd cuddle or two and then takes off in pursuit of David. As usual there is a posse of owners trying to make appointments with our tall dog sitter. I have to tell him that the October dates, which we had discussed in connection with a planned excursion to New York, needn't be held in reserve for us now—given Dorothy's worsening health we have no travels plans at all, a most unusual circumstance in our lives. It is almost time to go in for coffee and I can see that, already making his way to this spot, is George, free-range for once, the park's oldest citizen waddling toward the spot where all those nice dog treats come from.

Hanna, of course, joins us at table, and we also have Peter (of Peter and Holly) and, before long, Janet—who is carrying the still embargoed Daisy-Mae in her arms. Much fuss is made again over this delightful fluffball. It is hard to see her eyes but her tail is wagging. Dan has brought with him a dog basket and into its capacious blue spaces the Shih-Tzu is lowered. Dan has also brought with him a bumper supply of first class air travel toiletries, ones that he has recently accumulated during a spate of holidays, and these are distributed to the rest of us as well. Liz says that she is hoping to add a wine bar to the Italian restaurant she owns in Kensington but this will require knocking down the wall and convincing the antique glass dealer, who owns the space in question, to part with her lease. (It's the glass that is antique here—not the owner.) Dan says that to help in the process of convincing the lady to do this we will all bring our dogs into the shop (he is eyeing Skye in particular) and then someone will launch a ball.

Sunday, June 3:

Another warm and sunny morning greets us as we enter the park; I am wearing only a t-shirt today. We catch up with Celine and Ziggy; they are stationed at a sunny bench where Nix is ensconced—with the giant Billy sitting beside her. I ask Celine, as we head for the green, how the delicately-stomached Ziggy's diet is coming along. She says that even the other day he threw up after eating an ordinary biscuit, but that she will see how he does on a Marks and Spencer variety today. On the green Fritz encounters Pepper and the two Schnauzers take turns claiming the attention of Linda by running into her at great speed. David is out here as well, today with the Greyhound/Lurcher veteran Lulu. Meanwhile there is a second center of canine interest at the foot of Mt. Bannister—where a number of the dog owners are sprawled on Dan's blanket. I whistle for Fritz, who is off in a distant corner, and, for once, he comes dashing back to me—just to impress all the others. Then we head over to see the others playing pass the parcel with Daisy-Mae—with Rob present now to take lots of pictures.

A decision is taken to try out another of the café's picnic tables, since there is a craving for some sunlight with coffee this morning and so, with the addition of three chairs, we squeeze our bodies around this uncomfortable wooden presence (even so, there isn't room for Pepper's family, as there certainly would have been with our old metal table). Dan points out that these massive structures keep us from actually seeing our dogs beneath our feet and that some of them are going to lose out on the treats that have been ordered for the canine contingent. Keeping Daisy-Mae in view is not a difficulty, however, since Janet places the puppy on the tabletop, where she drinks out of my cappuccino cup and then falls asleep on Hanna's hand. In other news Dan reports that he has had quarrels with the B&Q man, who didn't want to exchange his broken barbeque and with a chap at the bike shop—who wanted £30 to replace a lost nut. Hanna says that she has walked out of the Cochonnet in a huff after they wouldn't let her sit at an empty outdoor table for six. Ofra admits that she has absent-mindedly paid her neighbor's gas bill by mistake. Georgie says that she's not sitting at one of these tables again.

We begin a back passage walkround, threading our way through the joggers and the moms and dads on their way to supervise the toddlers' football matches in the five-a-side courts. One little striker is staring at the parade of dogs through the wire fencing—"Look dad, those two are twins." I have to turn around to see whom he is talking about, but of course he's right to so describe Saffy and Tinkerbelle, Albert's yoked Yorkies. Ronnie, who is lumbering along, says that he had trouble getting to his feet just now, "But then I remembered that I have MS, and it was okay." As we near the Essendine gate we encounter a new puppy, a miniature Sparkie named Jackson. Our adult version is not impressed, but the little fellow wants to give everyone a good sniff.

Monday, June 4:

Temperatures have cooled a bit and I am back in a sweatshirt as Fritz and I head for the park. There isn't much activity here today and we manage to make good progress on our way to the green. I head out to the dog owners group in the center and here I find Dan, Georgie, and

Ofra. Jess, the six month-old Labrador, is enjoying a romp with Simon the Cocker. The object of the game is not only to tackle the opponent but to flop down on top of him with your full weight. Jess's mom says, "I always forget just how much fun these morning sessions can be."

The others are heading in for coffee when Jean-Baptiste stops me for an update on Dorothy's condition. He has difficulty keeping track of his Hercules while doing this, and at one point he pulls out a squeaky bone in order to command the attention of the Cocker; I know immediately that he will have attracted another customer—my Fritz. Soon the Schnauzer is climbing the Frenchman's leg and, in order to retain this toy, Jean-Baptiste next produces a tennis ball. Fritz ends up with this object as well, but at least the bone is returned to Jean-Baptiste's pocket. At this point Hercules takes off like a rocket for the Grantully exit and his owner has to take off after him in hot pursuit. "He can keep the ball," is his parting gift to Fritz.

By the time I join the others (plus Ronnie, Kate, and Albert) at the café, the breakfast hour is well advanced and there is such a long queue that I forego any coffee today. Dan now tells us that he and Davide have decided *not* to go to the wedding of Helen, whose Pug Cleo was a fixture in this park until last summer, because it is just too difficult and expensive to get to the spot in Holland where the wedding will take place. He then adds that he is convinced that Ziggy—not Celine's dog but the only male contestant left on the current run of *Big Brother*, used to appear in this park with a Shar-Pei in tow. Kate, who takes several phone calls while at table, agrees. The last we see of Hercules' tennis ball comes when her Skye begins the trot home, the prize in *her* mouth.

Tuesday, June 5:

An instant replay in the weather department as Fritz and I penetrate Paddington Rec on a quiet Tuesday morning. Coming up behind us we have the Romanian rescue dog Gypsy and Sid the terrier, and both of these dogs manage to stick their noses into what should be a very private moment for my dog. Thereafter he trots along with these chaps as we head for the green, Sid hanging back occasionally because he somehow remembers that I am the source of treats.

To my surprise they have opened the café early today and there is already a queue at the counter. I play through with Fritz and we head for

7

the green, where Georgie is exercising Jasmine and Sparkie, but when she too heads for the café there is nothing for it, and we too have to join the others. An unexercised Fritz positions himself at the feet of Peter and Ellen—for he too has a long memory and no doubt recalls this pair as sources of the now forbidden sausages. I get in line, only to discover that Ronnie is treating everyone to drinks this morning. I prepare to take my seat outside but Dan says, "Did you know that Fritz has just headed for the kitchen?" The rascal, off lead, has indeed committed this breach of café etiquette, and he is placed under restraint again even before we reach the front door.

Our lot have moved one of the metal tables over to a sunny patch near the Carlton roadway and here we sit: Dan, Hanna, Georgie, Ronnie and Albert. Dan actually asks Elian if we couldn't have one of these tables out in the prow of the patio, now dominated by the dreaded picnic benches, and Elian agrees. "Unless it's raining," Dan adds. I tell Peter and Ellen as they pass by that as the earliest of the café's customers *they* have to hold such a table for the rest of us. Dan's phone goes off and he departs in short order for a rendezvous with his plumber—he has been without hot water since a week ago Sunday and showers regularly now at Janet's. As he leaves he and Georgie have a quick discussion on who gets which dog. Recently Dan has had the care of Sparkie, Jasmine and Winnie; he reports that the ladies are rivals for Sparkie's attention. Georgie is delighted—"My little Brad Pitt," she coos.

Wednesday, June 6:

We are still experiencing some chilly temperatures in the morning and I am glad I have worn my sweatshirt again as Fritz and I stroll along our usual pathways. Progress is impeded only by the presence of a pair of exercising kick boxers, the male retreating between the fences as the female advances with feet and fists—not what I would call the best possible space for such activities. On the grass of the green another mixed pair is practicing wrestling holds near one end of the cricket crease while a uniformed trio of school kids are kicking a football at one another aimlessly. Once I get to return an errant pass and this lot seems surprised that such an old geezer can get such force behind a ball. Fritz is off on his wanderings and I am well behind the other dog owners when it is time to go in for coffee.

At a metal table outside the doors of the café we have Dan, Ofra, Georgie, Ronnie and Kate. Dan announces that he finally has hot water and that he has phoned Helen to say that he will not be attending her wedding in Holland later this month (David the dog sitter is still going to be wedding photographer). Ofra admits she is still preoccupied by *Big Brother*, but Dan says the ladies on the show are becoming bitchy. The hungry owners are eating the toast that should have gone into the mouths of their dogs; for that matter Fritz is so reticent at such moments that he often misses a turn, yielding to more insistent diners, the ones who are climbing up the knees of those dispensing these tidbits. (Not mentioning any names, Winnie.)

Kate's Skye is usually not interested in food, far preferring to haunt the edges of the green in hopes of a play partner, but today she has cause to regret this preference as Maggie comes by with two dogs, neither of whom she owns. The first of these is the lively Miniature Pinscher Leila and the second is the black giant Hootch. Hootch has with him his famous and indestructible toy, the bane of all our ankles, the tough plastic thunderball. Today Skye decides that she would like to have a go with this object and, for her efforts, she gets bitten on the back by a furious Hootch. It is the end of Skye's innocence, for the stricken Alsatian, after a few barks of protest, staggers back into the precincts of the café and collapses in shock. Kate rushes to the side of her stricken pet, who vomits once as well. It takes a few minutes for the restoration of anything like her former good spirits and I think she brightens only when Saskia comes by with one of her favorite pals, the Golden Retriever Buddy. The rest of us set off after this excitement on a back passage walkround, one that ends when Fritz, on lead, decides to remove my left arm from its socket as he charges the docile black Taz, innocently sitting next to his mistress on a bench near the exit.

Thursday, June 7:

Mornings have remained on the cool side and today I decide that it would not be a mistake to wear my leather jacket again. Fritz is bewitched by two terriers who have followed us along our walkway. Their smoking mistress would really rather choose another route but with our dogs now engaged in an introductory sniff-a-thon she has to continue in our direction. "I hate it when these two both get interested in another dog," she concludes.

Out on the green there are lots of dogs at play and Fritz soon enters this scene, anxious to get a greeting out of any human on offer and eager to repel the conflicting claims of other dogs. When Sasha's guardian bends over to pet my dog he has to see off Sid and Chica, the Boxers, because they too would like a cuddle. Dan, Ofra, Georgie and Liz are on the green as well, though it takes me a while to notice that Liz is just here for the company—her Beagle, Roxy, having been left in the care of a dog sitter. About 9:40 we head for the café, each of us having to secure a dog against the dangers provided by a speeding park tractor. Dan also hands to me a present for Dorothy, a box of orchids that Davide has brought back from Singapore this morning. I place it next to a brick pillar outside the café. "I don't want any of you dogs to piss on this," I say.

Peter, Ellen and Ronnie are already at table. Summer travel sites are discussed and Dan expresses the wish that it *would* be nice to have enough money to visit them all. Ofra says that she and her Ricky have not spoken since a week ago Sunday—following a fight involving her ancient Mercedes, which is still in the garage. (Today she received a text from him saying that he was heading briefly to Switzerland.) Food and drink arrive. Ofra objects to the cheese in the croissant since it is cut too thickly for her taste. "Last week you objected to big coffee, now it's big cheese," I tease. Sure enough the buttered toast soon arrives and the slices are too thick as well. It is almost a relief to pass from these weighty problems to something that truly brightens Ofra's smile: Elizabeth Arden's Eight-Hour Day Cream.

Friday, June 8:

The little moisture that fell at dawn has lifted an hour or so before Fritz and I make our way into the park on a humid grey morning. I am wearing my leather jacket against the return of rain, but in the event the skies brighten and I could well have done without it. Fritz makes a lively approach to the green this morning and I see that my first task is to kick the tennis ball back to the portly white presence that is Chelsea the Chihuahua. Out near the cricket crease we have Celine with Ziggy, Dan with Winnie and Georgie with Sparkie and Jasmine. Fritz is soon bored and I have to follow him on a slow ascent of Mt. Bannister—as I have dubbed the park's only elevated space. When we descend on the other side the others are already at coffee and I am well behind in a queue that also includes park personnel making orders for the entire office staff.

Topics for conversation include Paris Hilton, *Big Brother* and Cliff Richard. There is universal outrage that the slutty hotel heiress has been sent home after serving only three days of a three-week sentence (already halved) after repeated driving offences in L.A. landed her in the pokey. There is a bit more sympathy for Emily, the unlucky *Big Brother* contestant who was expelled for using the "N" word in the presence of a black housemate. Though the word is often used casually by black rappers and comedians, the contestants *had* been warned not to allow even a hint of racism into a format that caused an international incident a few months ago. I tell Dan that a fairground operator in Dulwich has managed to scatter a gang of menacing hoodies by playing Cliff Richard songs from the loudspeakers of his dodgem deck—and that this might be a useful tactic if his own local gang returns to his front porch.

Davide arrives in high dudgeon after his latest battle with Westminster Council over the siting of his satellite dish, an apparatus he uses to summon a great variety of European channels, including two from his native Sardinia. The council has told him that he has violated the esthetic standards of a "conservation area"—this on a street on which neighbors store exhaust pipes and bikes behind their own dishes and drugs are hidden in the foliage of walled gardens. Davide's revenge is to take endless photos of satellite dishes that seem to prosper without council interference, including two on the façade of the building that we now pass on our walk to the Morshead gate, the park's clubhouse, a listed building.

Saturday, June 9:

It's a grey and humid morning as Fritz and I enter a park that is rapidly filling with football players, team after team, young and old, so many that they either have to use the five-a side-courts or stage several matches on the same pitch—with the players running from side to side rather than end to end. It takes us a while to weave our way trough this roiling mass of testosterone, though some players pause to pet the puzzled Fritz, but eventually we reach the green. Even here displaced youngsters are using cones to keep up their footy exercise and it is our knot of dog owners who seem out of place today at one end of the cricket crease.

The focus of much activity is the presence, off lead for the first time, of the twelve week-old Daisy-Mae. Everyone wants to pick up the fluffy bundle; for her part she is content to follow Fritz around the grass and when he pauses to scratch an ear she does the same. Faz and Dianah are back from their holiday, with Faz several shades darker and a factor 50-protected pregnant Di glowing from inside. "Were you pro-Crete or Concrete?" I ask. Faz says that he loved the food but with her vegetarian obsessions Di found little she could eat. Even in the short time that this conversation has taken my dog has disappeared. I spot him over near the bandstand but that turns out to be fellow Schnauzer, Oscar. Sabina says Fritz *was* here and spots him near the Grantully exit, heading for the tennis courts. I catch up with him here, just before he jumps up on a bench shared by Franca and Natasha and just as my dog is sticking his nose into the latter's purse. Frank is running around without costume today, Bianca has a green ball in her mouth, and Leila is delighted, as usual by Fritz, who seems to tolerate her company more easily than that of almost any other dog. I ask Natasha about the spelling of her dog's name. She confirms that the official spelling is Leila, but that she often spells it Layla as well. I tell her that she is the second female to be so named in this park since, when we first had our Bertie here, there was a little girl who was part of the dog group with this name (she must be in her thirties now).

We are eleven at table this morning, with Albert making it an even dozen, sitting as a satellite to our sun. It takes forever to get served—with all these people in the park—for the queue goes on and on. Dan and Davide are planning a back-yard barbeque for this afternoon and this topic dominates conversation. Daisy-Mae makes the round of laps here, but pretty soon she falls asleep on Faz's chest. The long-limbed Ziggy climbs into Celine's lap, something I haven't seen since the weather turned warmer. She says that she actually had a conversation once with the *Big Brother* star and that he was charmed to discover that her dog shared his name. When we begin a back passage walkround we have full participation for once, and so it is quite a parade inching its way through the football players and their families in the fenced defile. "Is this the dog-walking club?" one woman asks. She seems to think that this is a Saturday ritual for us, but we have to tell her that we are here *every* day. By the time we have reached the Essendine gate we are fourteen dog owners in number, having encountered Rowena with her rescue dogs,

Timmy and Toby, and Michaela with her recently hand-stripped Cairn, Skye. Much fuss is made over the latter, whose head now seems too large for his body, but Skye is still interested only in chasing his beloved tennis ball.

Sunday, June 10:

Again I have trouble getting Fritz to budge from the delicious grass shoots that he enjoys sampling on the hillside before we reach the cypress trees. Matters improve somewhat when Milly the black Staffy, now a year and a half old, bustles through and the dogs have to sniff one another. I haven't seen Milly since she was just a pup; now she has the burly authority of the adult—though she seems pleasant enough. We continue on to the green where the dog owners are lying down on the grass. Brave Daisy-Mae is also very busy checking everybody out; she does manage to pee on Faz's arm. Pepper and Fritz have one of their noisy recognition scenes and thereafter Fritz insists of kissing all the prone participants. Dan is a little the worse for wear after his barbeque last night and I hear many tales involving alcohol, games, and shrimp on the barbie itself. Then Janet and Georgie and their dogs make an early departure—they are going to Kenilworth to celebrate the birthday of Janet's mother.

We still have a crowded turnout at coffee time, especially since we are surrounding only a little metal table that we have pulled into the sun. Ronnie is here, as well as Kate, Dan, Rob, Linda, Liam, Celine, Hanna and Albert—who is here on one of his rare capless days. Indeed, it is warm and sunny and everyone seems to be enjoying the balmy weather. Faz announces that he has tickets to see Barbra Streisand. Linda says that she is going to Switzerland on Thursday. Hanna says that local cricketers have created a huge mess with their own barbeque here yesterday.

Just as we are about to make our departure a slender figure with sun-faded hair slips into an empty chair. It is the former king of the doggy scene of Paddington Rec—Michael! It has been months since we have seen the Scotsman in our midst and everyone is delighted. Michael tells us that he is not happy with the effects of his current medications; and he is certainly not comfortable answering questions about his Charlie, who was re-homed by Battersea almost a year and a half ago now—Michael, in fact, has no knowledge of how Fritz's former best friend is faring. Fritz remembers Michael, however, and is soon is his lap, licking his face in excitement. I have to tell Michael about Dorothy's illness as we sit, almost alone after the others have left, catching up after so long a time. That afternoon Michael calls to speak to Dorothy.

Monday, June 11:

It's a grey and overcast Monday morning as Fritz and I enter the park, a quiet place after the weekend's crowded schedule. Indeed, the staff have yet to come to grips with all the litter that a busy weekend can bring to the grassy surfaces of Paddington Rec. As usual these days, I have trouble getting Fritz to move much beyond the feeding grounds represented by the grassy slopes to the left of our walkway. Once we do get a move-on we encounter Kate, already on her way home because of an early business meeting today. School groups are beginning to make their noisy entrance along the Carlton roadway as we finally reach the green.

Even though the weather wouldn't seem to invite such a relaxed posture, dog owners are again lying on the grass near the cricket crease this morning. Daisy-Mae is making the rounds, earning a cuddle at every stop. This morning, however, she has a rival in the fifteen week-old Izzy, the Tibetan Terrier puppy. Champagne-colored, this delightful fluffball is also fussed over by the other owners while Fritz, assuming his role as enforcer, runs his cousin Oscar off when the latter gets too close to the pack.

There is a pretty good turnout at coffee this morning, with Ronnie, Davide, Dan, Hanna, Albert, Ofra, Georgie and Janet in situ. The latter also heads off for work, leaving Daisy-Mae in the lap of Auntie Georgie. This is very puzzling behavior from Sparkie's perspective—since *he* spends these breakfast sessions in Georgie's lap, and now he has to settle for a spot on Celine's. Charlie the toy poodle is brought into the café's forecourt (cries of protest from the canine regulars), accompanied this time by a Bailey lookalike, that is another tan and white King Charles, named Louie.

No one seems to be in the mood to linger for long this morning and soon we are off on a back passage walkround, during which Ofra passes the rabbi of her synagogue on Lauderdale Road. I ask her if she greeted this gentleman when we crossed paths and she says that, instead of this, she hid. This behavior can be explained perhaps by her less than synagogue-ready outfit today—for not only is she wearing her "Adored and Loved By Everyone" sweatpants but she has just endured, at coffee, an event which, though pronounced good luck by the others, may not be seen so by Ofra: a pigeon has just shat on her shoulder from a great height.

Tuesday, June 12:

There is little difference in temperature or atmosphere as Fritz and I again head for the park on a sultry grey morning. Out on the green there is a small collection of owners and their dogs, including Chica, Izzy, and Rufus—though Oksana gets no closer than Roof-Ooze when pronouncing the name of her Lab, whose long training lead continually wraps the rest of us up. Haring into the center of this pack comes the speedy Lurcher, Flea—though she is often confused with her slightly smaller cousin, the absent Ziggy. I have to follow Fritz all over hill and dale today as he carefully selects a spot worthy of his second poo. The other coffee drinkers have long ago headed for the café—but our eventual arrival there is not tardy.

The café is having difficulties coming to life today—someone seems to be having a lie-in and the rest of the staff is locked out until Vicky arrives breathlessly. It takes a while for the tables and chairs to come outside and food orders will also be slow to arrive this morning. While I am waiting to order my cappuccino Vicky speculates that perhaps she should give a set of keys to the doggy people, since we are always here first thing in the morning. "You don't want our lot behind this counter," I suggest. "You're right," Vicky responds, "just think of all the character checks we would have to make."

In fact we have only a small turnout this morning, with Ronnie, Kate, Georgie and Albert the only members present. Georgie has her hands (and lap full) as today she has her own Sparkie, plus Daisy-Mae *and* Winnie. The first two share the lap, though Sparkie has been bouncing the eager puppy off the turf for the last five minutes. A dog owner from Queens Park comes by with the seldom seen pair of Kiva, a Spaniel and Bubbles, a Yorkie. Ronnie announces that he is cold in his short-sleeved shirt and that he will not be joining us in our back passage walkround. In fact, most of us head directly for the Morshead gate, but this turns out to be a tortuous process as well.

15

First Daisy-Mae heads in the wrong direction and the only way I can get her turned around is to scoop her up in one hand. Georgie has the devil of a time harnessing Winnie and getting a barking Sparkie back on lead, especially when she tries to get a leash on Daisy-Mae as well. While we are bent over at this task Albert's yoked pair, Saffy and Tinkerbelle, get their leads tangled up in all this cordage as they try to kiss my bent-over face. I again pick up Daisy-Mae, as this seems the only way to make any progress, but a few minutes later it is Fritz who gets his lead tied up with Sparkie's. I suggest that Georgie might make better progress on her way home if we put Daisy-Mae in her blue plastic bag. The little Shih-Tzu slides in easily and I think this method *could* have worked well, but just as we near the gate Maggie and Natasha come in with Leila and they want to see the pup, so out she comes again.

Wednesday, June 13:

We have a lovely, warm and sunny Wednesday morning for our next outing in the park, but cries of protest rebound almost as soon as we enter. On the running track a Middle Eastern mom is slowly pushing a baby carriage around in circles—but the baby is not a happy passenger this morning and there is a good deal of shrieking going on. Also in high dudgeon is a park keeper, who has just discovered that a predecessor has failed to insert the black plastic liner into a poo poo bin and that the resulting untidy mess now has to be attended to. An oath-filled monologue accompanies Fritz and me as we make our way past the protestor and, without too many delays this morning, out onto the green.

Enjoying the balmy scene are some twenty dog owners, scattered in little groups all over the grassy space. Another baby carriage, this one with Tanya behind the wheel, is the first evidence we have for the arrival of baby Lucca, now thirteen days old. Tanya says that a worrying episode of jaundice seems to be over, and that older sister Isabella has welcomed the new arrival in good spirit. More out of sorts is Celine, who reports that she was in Regents Park yesterday and that the kiosk coffee wasn't a patch on Metty's—and that she was charged £1.50 for a bottle of still water. While we are standing near the cricket crease another staff member arrives to warn us of the imminent invasion of massed toddlers. These soon arrive in their white t-shirts and red shorts and before long the sounds of fascist chanting echo throughout the park. We are entering the school sports day season, a time of year that always leads to displacement for the dog owners. I tell Celine that with so many schools selling off their own playgrounds and using Paddington Rec instead, we are experiencing a "constructive change of use"—this park was never meant to be an extension of the schoolyard.

There is a large and untidy group of dog owners crowded around a metal table outside the café. Today we have Janet, Georgie, Dan, Ronnie, Hanna, Celine, and Michael the Pirate. The latter is into his favorite topic, symptomology, but Hanna has a lot of advice here too. Dan tells us that his watch and half his clocks are set fifteen minutes fast, something about his always arriving fifteen minutes late before he adopted this strategy. At my feet I have Ziggy, Fritz and Albert's pair, and before long Tinkerbelle has climbed into my lap for a cuddle. David is back from taking pictures at Helen's wedding in Holland. At another table Franca wants to know where are the pictures he took months ago of her baby, Valentina—"Is she going to be eighteen before I get to see them?"

Friday, June 15:

It would appear that I have missed a day in the park, but this is only partly true. Because Dorothy had a chemotherapy appointment at 9:30 yesterday, I had to bring Fritz to the park almost an hour earlier than usual. It is always interesting to observe how a shift in time like this introduces you to a whole new set of doggy characters, though even at 8:15 I met up with Hanna, helping Spadge along with the help of his harness as the ancient Schnauzer shuffled forward with yet another illness. Here also was Franca with Frank and Bianca, and I finished a complete circuit of the park, a grand circle as we used to call it, in the company of Jean-Baptiste and Hercules. Fritz seemed charmed to be part of this caravan; the naughty Cocker, when he was not barking, threw himself into a rain puddle and rolled over in joy.

Today, when the weather is much brighter and sunnier, we join a lively scene on the green, where little Daisy-Mae comes waddling at speed to greet each newcomer. Fritz visits each of the owners in turn and then he is off on his rambles, with me following slowly. First he explores the foot of Mt. Bannister, then he trots down the Randolph driveway, then he veers off to visit the back of the tennis courts, then it's over the hill and back onto the green. By this time the others are sloping off toward the café, but once again I cannot join them, for this morning Fritz has an appointment to have his annual jabs on Boundary Road.

I move a bit more slowly these days, still feeling the calf strain in my left leg, but I have left plenty of time for us to exit the Randolph Gate, walk up to Carlton Vale, turn right past St. George's (where a juice carton came sailing over the wall the last time we were here), and, crossing Maida Vale, to enter the upmarket enclave of St. John's Wood. Dr. Seddon now confirms that Fritz is doing just fine and we are soon on our way home, again a painfully slow progress—with my dog pausing to sniff every other inch and I too weary to pull him along.

Saturday, June 16:

There have been a number of brief showers this morning, but skies have brightened considerably by the time Fritz and I hit the streets. The walkway, as it approaches the first fenced field, is a busy junction today. First a very young King Charles pup named Princess dashes up to have a sniff, interrupting the old codger in his ruminations and earning a snarl or two in the process (these two dogs trot along happily together a minute later). Above the same spot I observe a wonderful scene: an almost fully grown magpie youngster is flapping its wings and opening its beak in anticipation of the delivery of some tasty snack—only to be rebuffed by the quite indifferent parent, whose attitude seems to be "You're old enough to fend for yourself, junior."

Out on the green Saskia is asking the other dog owners if it's all right for her to share some of Buddy's home-made vegetarian treats. Ziggy is an eager participant in this handout, but only Fritz knows to sit meekly at her feet. Meanwhile my dog has discovered that the Frenchwoman who accompanies Princess has a squeaky ball in her pocket and he actually tries to shinny up the poor woman's leg in pursuit of this prize. Daisy-Mae is following us around now and I pause to thank Janet for bringing the little package upstairs yesterday afternoon, since the presence of a puppy was just what Dorothy needed to cheer her up in her convalescence.

You can tell that Janet would like to sit at one of the picnic tables, hoping to absorb any sun going, but Ofra objects on the grounds that the benches are bound to be wet. So we sit at a table in front of the café doors, a spot clogged by dogs this morning—indeed we have to remove an anxious Holly, who is hovering at this spot, waiting for Peter to reach the end of the queue. Later Natasha also discovers Daisy-Mae wandering around inside. Davide is back from San Francisco and brings with him special orders that his friends have registered, including a yellow top for Ofra. Liz arrives with Roxy and tells us that, on the first morning in three weeks when she *could* have had a lie-in, she woke to discover that another incident had taken place on her doorstep. This time it was her own boys, celebrating the end of the term with a sleepover, one whose numbers had swollen from the advertised three to an unmanageable eleven. At three in the morning the lads had lined her balconies and pelted all the nearby houses with eggs, and it was the owner of one of these properties who was now knocking loudly on her door. Of course she apologized, said *her* boys would be over to apologize, and promised to the unforgiving chap ("This used to be a decent neighborhood till you lot moved in") that she would send someone with a high pressure hose to clean off all the eggs. "What more could I offer?" she asks now. "Bacon," is Janet's reply.

Sunday, June 17:

It is quite warm under sunny skies this morning and by the time I reach the green I am looking forward to taking my sweatshirt off. Faz, whom I have seen tooling up and down my street in a fancy black sports car, is lying in the grass—after already having had a run with Jasmine in Primrose Hill. He says that the two-seater is doomed and that the expectant parents are shopping for a family car today. While Buddy and Sasha are having a wrestling match (battle of the Golden Retrievers), with a circling Ziggy keeping score, Fritz is purloining a soft ball with plenty of chew from its rightful owner, Daisy-Mae. For some reason dogs are compared to menu items today. It starts when someone compares Daisy-Mae to a cappuccino, then Saskia says that Buddy is just a vanilla ice on a stick, And Dan, whose pet must now return to her diet, says that Winnie is a bit like a piece of pork scratching. Fritz doesn't remind me of any food; he is sitting in my shadow, still chewing on the purple ball, as I too slump down on the grass.

The dog owners are moving a metal table into the sun as Faz and I finally join the others. Ronnie and Janet have both recorded the first episode of *Jekyll* on BBC 1 last night. I tell them that James Nesbitt's wife is played by Gina Bellman, who has often occupied a table near the café window after having brought her Bulldog to the park. Dan says that he objects to a work colleague, in his thirties, who still sucks his thumb. He also objects to Paul McCartney's recent bouncy single—the conclusion: act your own age. As Liz is eating a portion of scrambled eggs I am reminded of yesterday's tale, adding that the egg incident in question, unfortunately, just feeds the anti-American stereotype that we often find hereabouts. The others (assuming their English personalities) now pretend to be offended by this generalization as well, and Liz retaliates by saying that at her barbeque next week she is no longer offering steaks to her friends, just hot dogs. "And pop coren," Ofra adds.

Ten of us head off on a back passage walkround, working our way in and out of the crowds of kiddy athletes and their parents. I notice that in the abandoned and fenced trackway that used to carry us between the old playground and the picnic area the untended red roses have blossomed marvelously this year. In this same abandoned defile there are even poppies growing. Just beyond this spot I also notice a flat cap in the walkway and I hurry forward to see if this once essential item of working class and countryside haberdashery doesn't belong to bareheaded Albert. Indeed the object has fallen from his pocket, so I turn Fritz over to Ronnie and rush back to the spot (tweaking my calf muscle in the process). Albert is very pleased to be reunited with this old favorite, and now, well behind the others, we can at last make our way from the park.

Monday, June 18:

I am wearing my rain jacket—against the return of the showers that have peppered our neighborhood in the last few hours, but in the event, skies remain bright enough while Fritz and I are in the park. The two unnamed Jack Russells who are usually given their morning walk by some East Asian nanny come up behind us, but today there is no scene and Fritz trots along happily with these chaps; indeed he pays no attention to Oscar or Scamp the Westie, coming in the opposite direction. Numbers on the green are reduced somewhat this morning but there is still activity worth checking out. Charlie the Cocker has stolen the purple ball that the already-departed Daisy-Mae lost to Fritz's teeth yesterday. Sasha has switched opponents to Chica the Boxer, but Ziggy is still here keeping score. This means that Fritz is not needed and he soon wanders off, followed by you know who.

At breakfast we have only a small turnout: Ronnie and Hanna, with Peter and Ellen arriving late, and Albert, his cap back in use, bringing up the rear. Peter is carrying an orchid which he has bought as a memorial for his late wife, whose birthday is tomorrow. He ends up with a cappuccino instead of his usual latte, but he diligently spoons out the foam. Hanna wants Vicky to give our lot a discount since we are the only customers this morning; Vicky, no slouch in such discussions, says that if we are her only customers then she probably needs to charge double. Our drinks are served by Bouzha, the stalwart barista of Metty's empire; we have not seen her in a while since she has been at his other café. Hanna picks up Spadge, the ancient Schnauzer whose carer and mommy she has been for years. Yesterday was his fifteenth birthday but there was no celebration, since Hanna, whose sleep is often interrupted by the urgent requirements of her charge, had a lie-in. Spadge is now recovering from an inner-ear infection and has been the grateful recipient of one of Hanna's patented Reiki treatments (Dorothy gets an extended version of this therapy later as well). Ronnie, in a good mood, says that he recently fell asleep during the Mahler at the Royal Festival Hall. This incident produces the giggles and for several minutes we can't understand *what* he is saying, since every word is choked with laughter. His Rosie evidently snores too, but he finds this a reassuring influence.

Fritz is meanwhile making a pest of himself, trying to get his head into Ellen's purse. There may be dog treats for Jack (the Jack Russell) and Sandy (the Corgi) in there, but my dog has his own biscuits available as well; nevertheless he prefers the sport of burying his nose in someone else's bag. When Hanna's own bag takes a nosedive off the table the subject of this essential female weaponry comes up and I tell her that I miss "the salmon," a capacious carryall that used to be her usual accompaniment. She says that if I miss it I can still see it in a photo on the Paddington Rec web site. We get up to begin a back passage walkround. Still a bit giddy, the ladies say that they have a new name for Jack: Kevin-on-four-legs. This title has to be explained to me. The Kevin in question turns out to be the *human* son of the elderly Aisne, whose dogs Ellen walks every morning. Many in Maida Vale will not know Jack but everyone has seen Kevin, a streetside fixture for years, laboring away with great care on the reconstruction and resurrection of yet another ancient Range Rover.

Tuesday, June 19:

I am still wearing a flannel shirt *and* a sweatshirt as Fritz and I head for the park under hazy skies—an hour later and I will be wearing a short-sleeved shirt instead. At the head of the track local scholars are tossing their aluminum batons into the air prior to a relay race (and then letting them hit the ground rather than risk catching these dangerous missiles). Fritz is fairly rapid in his progress through the usual obstacles and when we arrive at the green I am surprised to see another large mid-week turnout—fifteen owners and their dogs spread across the grass.

I have arrived just after a period of ill-natured snarling. Hercules is singled out as the culprit, since he perhaps senses that Chica is still in season and wants to contest his primacy with Buddy and some of the other big males. Dan is just removing Winnie from the line of fire, Janet is just handing over custodianship of Daisy-Mae to Georgie, and I notice that there is a new puppy in the mix. This is Monchhichi, so named for a Japanese plastic doll of the past—an eight month-old fellow who is part Jack Russell and part Shih-Tzu—a Jack Shit, so I am told. The other dogs spend some time asserting their authority over this handsome and self-confident fellow, even including Bailey, who two minutes later has resumed his more typical posture—lying on his back while an Alsatian licks his tummy. Fritz also has a turn bullying the newcomer and, in a feisty mood already, he next has to chase off Ziggy and Sid, who have just been part of a pack that has exploded with a second session of ill-temper from Hercules.

Monchi's owner, Johanna, joins us for coffee. She says she lives in Chelsea but wants to move to Maida Vale. Poor Peter, his Holly looking on concernedly, has to endure an extended play period featuring Sid and Monchi beneath his feet. Fritz manages to get his lead under Ronnie's feet so that he can launch another surprise attack on Ellen's purse. Before long he has his mischievous head buried in this object, a gesture that brings a laugh to all, even including Ellen herself, fortunately. Chelsea, the portly Chihuahua, now gets under the table and begins to sniff Bailey too. This is the signal for an early back passage walkround.

Wednesday, June 20:

A stormy night has been replaced by cloudy skies, with outbreaks of sun. Fritz and I make a spirited start to the day's activity, getting as far as the top of the running track, where two park keepers are attempting to refasten a portion of wire fencing that was separated from its moorings long ago. I applaud this gesture, for more than once Fritz has found this aperture and attempted a quick 220 down the middle lane. Today would not be a good day for such a gesture since there is a heavy police presence on the track, the start of a day of athletic activity sponsored by London's finest.

As we pass through the café I notice that Ronnie, Ofra and Georgie are already seated in front of the doors at 9:20 and that the café itself is already open. This would really be far too little exercise for my dog—were I to join them now—so we continue on to the center of the green where there is a lively doggy scene. Sasha's mom kneels to give Fritz a cuddle and the groans of pleasure/protest that issue from my dog keep everyone amused—everyone but Sasha, who gets growled at by my dog when she approaches her own mistress too closely. Fritz then decides that it has been quite a while since he checked out the doggy area adjacent to the Grantully gate, and so we head for this spot, empty this morning. A lot of sniffing goes on (Hanna has recently observed two fox kits playing nearby) and then I put Fritz on lead so that we can join the others at coffee.

Georgie says that her sister Jean is due soon for a visit and that Sparkie will soon be playing host to his Scottish cousins, Mozart and Billy. Winnie is patrolling the cobbles, looking for something to eat: once again she is on a diet. Ofra complains that Bailey's nose is not as wet as Sparkie's. Albert says that he is taking Saffy and Tinkerbelle for their check-ups and that he is sure to get scolded because they have put on some weight. He and Ronnie accompany me on a back passage walkround, an adventure punctuated by the sounds from the public address system through which the assembled adolescents, in their bleachers, are being brought up to date about the special guests (QPR footballers, minor British track stars) who will help them during their sports day. One might complain about this unnecessary noise, but as it is being made by a policeman, I think this not likely to be productive.

Friday, June 22:

Dorothy's schedule at the London Oncology Clinic has again caused me to miss my usual hour in the park yesterday, though I did manage to visit its walkways just an hour earlier than usual. It was again interesting to note that this subtle shift in time produced encounters with a number of dogs not seen in some time: Suki the Vizsla, Jonesie (short for Bridget Jones) the Lhasa Apso, Tia the athletic sheep dog and Cosmo the Tibetan Terrier.

Today we have just missed a morning shower and the skies are still cloudy, though bright. Fritz overtakes a jogger as he speeds toward the green, where I can see a very lively scene indeed. Daisy-Mae has finally found someone her own size in the tiniest Yorkie, Jack, and these two are having a magnificent tussle. Chica and Sid are ganging up on the Golden Retrievers and, romping around as through they had never migrated to Glasgow, we have two former denizens of the park, Jean's sheep dog, Billy, and Mozart—the rescued long-haired Jack Russell. Fritz investigates these groupings and then heads off to the enclosed doggy playpen near the Grantully gate. He has the place to himself and I get him moving only when I spot some bread left for the birds. This is *not* the place to scatter bird treats—for dogs will gobble up such tidbits too, after they have peed on them first.

At breakfast Janet says that she is trying to unload two tickets to the Concert for Diana, which she bought by mistake, and Dan gets on his mobile phone to see if he can help out. Winnie hits her head on the table as she jumps into his lap again. Jack the Yorkie and Daisy-Mae resume their wrestling, scattered every now and then by the huge paws of the red bandana-clad Rhodesian Ridgeback, Tara. I ask the others if anyone else turned off their lights between 9:00 and 10:00 last night—as London attempted to see how much energy could be saved by switching off for an hour at twilight on the longest day of the year. Most of those at our table, however, hadn't even heard about the campaign. We begin a back passage walkround, with Daisy-Mae attempting to keep up with Sparkie, Mozart and Billy in their manic sprints. I can see that it will not be a restful day in Georgie's house today.

Saturday, June 23:

We have double entry park keeping today, as Fritz is whining near the front door at 7:45 and so I have to act on this urgency and head for the Rec an hour and a half early. This proves to be totally unnecessary, as Fritz shows no compulsion to pee or poo with any greater necessity than usual. Now, at 9:15, we try it again, reaching the walkway near the kiddies' playground a second time, though on this occasion we are surrounded by a number of miniature Drogbas and even one retro Best as the Saturday morning football camp is now in full play.

Out on the green Kate is wrestling not only with Skye's addiction to ball chasing but with Buddy's rambunctiousness as well. Buddy, indeed, insists on treating his own lead as a pull toy. I hope that Kate has life jackets for all parties because she is planning on taking these dogs onto a boat at Brighton later today. Celine, meanwhile, has lost track of Ziggy, but fortunately I can tell her I have just seen him streaking for the café, where Ronnie is distributing dog treats. Fritz is making the rounds of the other dog owners, receiving one cuddle after another, a series of encounters in which he squeals and growls in delight—turning nasty only when the actual dog belonging to Dan or Janet makes an appearance.

At breakfast Dan reminds the rest of the crew that Liz will have her housewarming party tonight, but that it will not be an outdoor affair, since Liz has failed to secure a gas canister for her barbeque. Faz says that he has failed to secure a new car since options are limited; Dianah has to be able to drive it, so it must be small, automatic and four-door. Janet says that Kilburn High Road is closed due to a double knife attack. Faz says he had to attend a shooting yesterday. Dan says that Winnie needs an operation on one of her eyelids and that he has to buy a present for his nephew, whose first birthday party he and Davide will attend today. "All right," I conclude, "just try to stay out of the ball pit this time."

Sunday, June 24:

The wet weather continues as we slide into the park on a grey Sunday morning. It is still spitting a bit and I have the hood of my rain jacket up, but it is not cold and one advantage of the inclemency is that the walkways are largely empty. This means that there is an appropriate silence, which I enjoy tremendously after days of noisy competitions on the fields of Paddington Rec. Things liven up only a bit when we reach the green, where a stalwart company of dog owners are braving the light rain.

Fritz soon finds plenty to occupy his attentions, beginning with his pal, David the dog sitter—here today with Campbell, the Westie. Sasha and Buddy are again duking it out, with Ziggy circling this pair and barking out the score. To their credit, the owners remain rooted to the spot for a full fifteen minutes after the café has opened its doors. When we do at last shuffle in, our usual table is occupied by a lone mom, who folds her newspaper the moment we arrive—"This is your table, isn't it?"—and moves to another spot outside the doors. Kate announces that today is Skye's second birthday and that the refreshments are on her. She did not take Buddy and Skye to Brighton yesterday, which is just as well.

Today we have Jean, Georgie, Dan, Kate, Ofra, Hanna, and Janet. Much of the conversation is devoted to a post-mortem on Liz's housewarming party, which seems to have been a big success, even though, as Dan says, "We forgot to bring the eggs." Dan is about to take off for a week in Sardinia with Davide. I ask him if I can trust him to deliver the five pounds I owe to Davide and he says I can (while shaking his head in the negative at the same time). Ofra announces that she is getting a personal trainer—just as well since she complains every morning about having to walk all the way to the park from West Hampstead. She now joins us in a back passage walkround, hoping that Dan will give her a ride home at the end. On the narrow walkways a disgruntled gentlemen, eyeing all the dogs he must wade through, says, "Fuck me!" Janet replies, "I'd rather not." On the pavement, as Fritz and I leave the park, I can see a small rat scuttling away.

Monday, June 25:

No one would be surprised if more rain, which was a constant yesterday, returned in the next few hours, but at least we have dry conditions underfoot this morning—just as well since I have forgotten to put on my scruffy park shoes. When we reach the green I can see a small knot of dog owners near the bandstand: much of our greensward has been ruled off for games, as though we didn't have lanes on our running track, and preparations are being made for another juvenile onslaught.

Fritz makes his own circle around the perimeter but at last I succeed in tempting him onto the grass with the promise that his Uncle David (here with Skye) is present today.

At coffee we have Georgie, Jean, Hanna, Ronnie, Albert and Liz. The others are still reminiscing about Liz's Saturday night party, though a few of them don't remember how they got home. Liz tells us that she now has Irish citizenship and that she needs to get the relevant passport before beginning her summer travels soon. Ronnie wants to know if he would be entitled to a Polish or Russian passport on the grounds of national ancestry. A lot of toast is distributed to the dogs; one of Albert's Yorkies nips Hanna's fingers in her eagerness, and it takes a long time to shove toast through the slots on Billy's muzzle.

We are joined by Timmy and Toby as we begin our back passage walkround but Rowena stays behind to chat with someone and it takes us a while to figure out that Toby, who is wearing a heavy coat today, has decided to keep *us* company. Daisy-Mae also distinguishes herself by limboing under the picnic ground fence. I have to go back in order to use the gate into this spot, where I can retrieve the little madam. As we near the top of the track she tries this trick a second time but someone spots her and her low level entry into this place is prevented. As we near our first exit a children's crusade of young people streams in on the way to another sports day.

Tuesday, June 26:

There is a brisk breeze driving clouds in a bright blue sky this morning, and I might have hoped that Fritz would have responded with a lively march toward the green as well. Instead, however, he settles in to sample the tips of some long leaves of grass and not even the bouncy presence of a manic black dog (Poodle or Puli, I can't tell) can get him to put on some speed. Eventually he runs ahead and joins a sizeable pack of dogs on the grass.

At one point I count eighteen animals busy at their exercise and spread out the full width of the green. Carly the Labrador is waddling around and another Sid, this one a Cairn Terrier, is mixing it up with all the regulars in a manic pile at the east end of the scene. Fritz goes from owner to owner, insisting on a welcoming cuddle, and keeping everyone amused with his variety of noises, growls of delight and squeals of protest whenever another dog seems likely to interrupt the moment. Surprisingly, my dog then undertakes an extended period of exercise, chasing after a spare orange tennis ball lofted either by me or by David the dog sitter. And even more surprisingly, Fritz remembers to bring the ball back after retrieving it—almost unheard of.

At breakfast we have Peter, Ellen, Hanna, Ronnie, Jean, and Georgie. Sour milk and *Schadenfreude* are the chief diet, with Tony Blair completing his last full day as prime minister and nothing but pessimism awaiting his successor, Gordon Brown. The weather, which has lead to flooding in many parts of England, also provides plenty of opportunity to bewail the effects of global warming. Hanna wants someone to tow icebergs to the desert, rather than let them melt and raise ocean levels. (Ronnie wants to place some unwanted immigrants on the icebergs before the towing begins.) The mood brightens a bit when Mozart and Sparkie begin to bark at the presence of certain strangers in our midst. These include Jasper, the Patterdale Terrier, and his cousin, a portly Yorkie named Toby. Mozart also objects to men in caps, Sparkie dislikes anyone in uniform (and a blackbird hopping along a fence) and Billy dislikes the scent of alcohol on anyone's breath. Mozart and Billy, as rescue dogs, are obviously experiencing the memories of an unhappy youth, but Sparkie must be reacting to a previous life, one in which, perhaps, he was issued far too many parking tickets.

Thursday, June 28:

Again it would appear that I have missed a day in the park, but this is also only partly true. Yesterday I was here an hour early because I needed to get ready to take Dorothy to Harley Street for a routine blood test. I had quite a long session in the park yesterday afternoon, indeed completing a back passage walkround in reverse with Hanna and Rowena. Such encounters, and much of my park time these days, turn into an extended health questionnaire. As we neared the kiddie's play area we did make a local celebrity sighting, as ITV's *London Tonight* reporter Ben Scotchbrook, often seen on our streets, was playing here with his toddler on the swings.

Today it is cloudy and bright in the park and the nice weather has again summoned a large contingent to the green. Celine reports that Ziggy, he of the delicate stomach, is again showing signs of digestive discomfort—though she agrees that he can have one of Fritz's Shapes (whereupon he stalks me for much of the rest of the session). Pepper is present today and he and Fritz have their usual mock scrap. A woman is having great difficulty getting her young Lab, Honey, to answer her call—because there is just so much fun to be had among the other dogs. Daisy-Mae remains the apple of every dog owner's eye; she is so brave and so busy and has to check out what everyone else is doing. Twice she attacks Fritz, bouncing off of him without even getting a flicker of response. His attitude reminds me of the pasha in *Beat The Devil*, "In my country a woman's lips may move, but her words are not heard."

At coffee we have Georgie, Jean, Hanna, Albert, Ofra, Kate, Ronnie, and Liz. Ronnie has to buy a birthday card for Susie, and keeps asking us to remind him to do it on the way home. Liz announces that she is going to the States for a week or so tomorrow, and that she will not have to spend any time in a Heathrow holding cell on her return this time because she will get her Irish passport today. That's the good news; the bad news is that she has just discovered that son Jack's U.S. passport has expired. A beautiful long-haired Weimaraner, named Molly, prances over to participate in the toast eating. Sparkie barks at everybody and quite frightens one of the park personnel, who is innocently on her way into the cafe. In a previous life not only did Sparkie get lots of parking tickets but he must also have been one of those women no one would listen to.

Friday, June 29:

There is rain at dawn today and the moisture persists for several hours. I am worried that we will have to march in rain ourselves this morning, and, indeed, I am wearing my rain jacket when Fritz and I enter the park. By this time, however, things have brightened considerably. We squeeze past Ellen, who is waiting patiently for Jack and Sandy, who appear to be intent on a foraging expedition in the bushes near the entrance gate. Then we pass the midsized black Rebel and the all-white Arran, who is an exotic Coton de Tulier and whom, I note, is the seventieth canine whose presence in our park I have recorded this month. With the sun beating down I am beginning to regret wearing my rain jacket; the plus side is that I have discovered two lost poo poo bags and fifteen quid in the pockets of this garment.

My heart sinks when we reach the green, for preparations are well under way here for another dreaded sports day. Tables and chairs have been set up on the cricket crease and someone even delivers a bouquet of flowers—it's all the evidence we need to conclude that some posh academy has reserved the village green for its own purposes and that the villagers have been driven off the common yet again. Fritz actually charges through a mass of kiddies—marching in lock step toward the start of the sack races—not because he wishes to participate in this event but because Janet is manipulating a squeaky toy at the far end of the green. A security guard asks me to remove all dogs from the green because of the children.

Just as I am heading in for coffee with the rest of the dog owners Celine stops me to inquire if I know of any short-term rentals in the area—since she and Christopher need a place of refuge while builders are at work in their flat. Matters are further delayed by the appearance of Hanna, who has brought in a special can of dog food for the delicate stomach of Ziggy. The only problem with interruptions of this type is that by the time I can reach our table the others will have penetrated the café and made their orders and there is no one to whom I can hand my £1.80 for a medium cappuccino. The remedy is twofold: someone could remember to ask me what I wanted (since I always want something and always pay for my own drink) or I could pass Fritz off to Ronnie and join the queue myself. This is what happens most days, but on a sports day there are always lots of extra adults milling about and the queue can go on forever. So it is today, and so it is that, already cross over the pitch invasion, I have to sit without refreshment while the others sip and munch away.

Saturday, June 30:

The rainy weather persists and I am back in my rain jacket as I take my dog into the park on a grey Saturday morning. The moisture is not very bothersome at this point and I feel no need to take cover, but it is frustrating to stand around like a dummy while Fritz has a sniff and an occasional bite as he samples every leaf of grass. (This is the second time we have been out today, as the rascal has again managed an earlier foray by whining at the front door). Eventually I have to put him on lead, just so we can make some progress along the margins of the football pitches, where the little lads are doing their star jumps as they warm up for the big game. In the narrow fenced passage I see an unusual sight—a pair of gloved hands has reached through the links and is clutching an escaped ball which, for obvious reasons, cannot be wrestled over the fence and returned to the field of play. I am asked, very politely, if I can lend a hand, and I do so—throwing the ball back over the fence.

The green is empty when we reach its edges, not surprisingly—since the rain is beginning to pelt down. I join Ronnie, Peter and Ellen at the table in front of the café doors and we are soon joined by Janet, Jean and Georgie. Kate, who has been slinging the ball to Skye, stops by, her uncovered head dripping, but she isn't stopping today. "I suppose if we got you a hat, you wouldn't wear it," I tell her. Jean also has a wet head, but Georgie has a fur-lined hoody. "Did you happen to see that program on the Inuits?" Peter is reminded to ask her. Meanwhile we have a collection of sodden dogs and the trick is to get through the session without letting any of them jump into our laps. This is particularly disconcerting for that momma's boy, Sparkie, who has just had the hair cut from his shaggy forehead. Ronnie says that it will stop raining at 10:00, so we settle in for a leisurely breakfast session, in order to see if he is right.

I notice that both of the Scottish sisters are smoking again. Jean says that her arthritis got worse during the four months she was off the weed and Georgie says that she is only smoking because Jean is. Today is the last day for smoking in enclosed public places in England and there is even some question over whether Ronnie will be allowed to puff at his cigars during our morning session. We are not enclosed here, so the consensus is that he will not be bothered. Jean has been trying to outdo her sister in folding Ronnie's plastic sacks for him, and she has two goes at this art today; Georgie says that her rival still has a long way to go. As predicted, the rain stops at 10:00—but starts again at 10:05. During a relatively quiet spell we begin a back passage walkround, almost forgetting Daisy-Mae, who lies calmly on the pavement watching us as we stroll off. (Perhaps she senses what is about to happen: when we reach the grass near the Essendine exit the other dogs bounce her off the turf like a flattened football.)

July, 2007

Sunday, July 1:

I have not been able to abandon my raincoat yet, for the showery weather that has, in a more intensified form, brought floods to much of central England, persists. Fritz is no laggard in making his way toward the green this morning; here, under cloudy but bright skies, there are a lot of dogs at exercise. I have brought with me the orange tennis ball that we found the other day, and Fritz has a go at chasing this down—that is when the other dogs will let it lie there on the grass without undue interference.

One of those with a special interest in this toy is Rufus, and I throw it to him during moments when Fritz is off policing the green and checking out everyone's membership status. Another contestant is a lively Labradorlike black dog named Brea. This dog is accompanied by a charming long-haired standard Dachshund named Ali. The latter seems to me to be much larger than the usual Dachshunds we have hereabouts, and his deep baying voice certainly re-enforces his membership in the hound fraternity. Also back for a return visit in Monchhichi. Johanna says that in Chelsea there will be a dog show in which a prize will be offered to the dog most resembling his or her owner. Celine nominates Ziggy and her husband Christopher.

It seems as though some of our lot are heading toward one of the wooden picnic tables, but there is still a strong hint of rain so we settle instead for our usual spot under the eaves. Today we have Faz, Ofra, Hanna (dogless today), Janet, Ronnie, Jean, Georgie, and Albert. Because we have a policeman present the conversation naturally focuses on the spate of (foiled) terrorist attacks in London and Glasgow this weekend. Ofra gets a text message from Dan and Davide, who will return from Sardinia tomorrow night. Faz gets a phone call from his dad, who has accidentally activated the mobile phone around his neck while innocently eating his breakfast. A squall brings flecks of moisture to those of us who are seated too close to the forecourt. When it stops we complete our back passage walkround while discussing The Concert For Diana. It is pointed out that Diana, who was seen as a real liability by the royal family while she was alive, is, now that she is safely dead, Its greatest asset. Next year: Boat Race for Diana, then London Marathon for Diana, then Bingo for Diana, then Big Brother for Diana—the list is endless.

Monday, July 2:

I have a devil of a time getting Fritz to make any decent progress toward the green this morning. He reaches the cypress trees speedily enough, but I can't see where he is once he penetrates their shelter and on three occasions I find myself waiting for him to emerge—only to discover that he has advanced far beyond my spot. Then he seems to take root in the grassy field at the corner and none of my patented tricks work—he agrees to take a biscuit from me, but then he spits it out. Finally I send his orange tennis ball down the defile and he has to chase *this*. I find the ball, abandoned, on the Carlton walkway. Fritz is already out on the green.

We have one newcomer today and this is a Jack Russell-Chihuahua cross named Bonito. Little Bonito, who sports a David Beckham Mohawk, is entranced by Chica and chases her everywhere. Fritz agrees to pursue his tennis ball a few times, then he makes his way from dog to dog, checking everyone out. I am just on my way into coffee with Faz when Linda arrives with Pepper. Naturally he and Fritz have to spar a bit and then I have a conference with Linda, who is going to undertake some clothes shopping for my wife, who is now too thin for all her clothes. I am certain that the usual will have happened, that the others will all have ordered their coffee and I will be at the end of a long queue, but this time Faz, bless his heart, has a cappuccino waiting for me when I finally reach the café.

Today we have Ronnie, Faz, Albert, Hanna, Peter, Ellen, Linda, Georgie and Jean, and together we spend a very pleasant session, interrupted only by the annoying intrusion of a loudhailer that accompanies the foregathering of another school group in front of the clubhouse (more adults than kiddies, as far as I can tell). Faz has ordered sausage and toast for the dogs and so there is a feeding frenzy once the sausages have cooled down. Mozart chases several men and gets muzzled in punishment. Billy gets this treatment as well—and so does Sparkie when we begin our back passage walkround. Jean will be taking her dogs back to Glasgow this afternoon, and so it is farewell for a while when we at last reach the Essendine gate. Georgie has managed to take £31 off her sister in card games during this visit.

Tuesday, July 3:

The heart sinks at the stentorian voice of the gamesmaster as the park again faces a day of screaming kids in sports kit celebrating an annual ritual in the presence of their proud moms and dads. The younger the kids the more high-pitched the screaming; their older siblings are here as well but they scream less and swear more. I put Fritz on lead in order to make some orderly progress this morning. We pass through the café and, anticipating the queues to come, I give Ronnie my coffee money ten minutes before the doors open.

Out on the green (which fortunately does not seem to be under siege this morning) I can see that Dan and Davide have returned after a week in Sardinia and that they have retrieved Winnie from Dan's folks in Essex. Bonito is also back and has attracted the attentions of Sparkie. Kate is here with Skye and a friend in shorts named Bob. Fritz chases his orange tennis ball and works the crowd happily. I tell Dan that on Saturday I saw the desperate chap, whose presence here always enrages Winnie, sitting outside the cash machine of the Nat West in Maida Vale Parade—with a dog of his own. We have never seen this dog in the park but the chap was putting on a show of cradling the animal in a piteous heap, one that might attract the loose change of bank users.

The others head in for coffee, Fritz following them, and I have to follow Fritz. For a second day in a row my cappuccino is waiting for me. I sit down next to Ellen, which means that my dog soon has his nose in her purse—though matters are not improved when it is revealed that she not only has snacks in there but also a squeaky ball. A toddler named Ilona appears to cuddle all the dogs, especially delighting in the soft brindled coat of Gypsy. Jack, the tiniest Yorkie, shows up to check out his playmate, Daisy-Mae, but the latter has gone to work with Janet this morning. Her auntie, Georgie, says, "I told her if she was going to spend all her days at my house she needed to get a part-time job." Jack has to content himself with jumping from lap to lap, wriggling in pleasure when he gets his share of snacks. Georgie has worn her wellies today, which means that we actually have sun to accompany us on our back passage walkround.

Wednesday, July 4:

I am hoping that the resumption of our morning routine will help restore the good spirits of my dog today, because they were certainly at a low ebb last night. The difficulties began in the late afternoon, when a series of fierce thunderstorms lashed our part of London from the west. To make matters worse, Dorothy and I, attending another medical appointment, were out when this heavenly blast was overhead, and poor Fritz had to endure his fright alone. When we got home he was nowhere to be seen—I discovered him at last cowering under our bed, a sanctuary where he remained for the next few hours, though the skies were bright enough by now. At one point I slipped some Rescue Remedy into his mouth and he eventually emerged from his hidey hole, first appearing in the bathroom, then the TV room. He did not eat a bite at dinnertime and he was a most reluctant participant in the evening's walk.

Today he seems a bit brighter, his breathing restored to its normal rhythms, and he trots along toward our entry gate in a lively enough fashion. Here we encounter an enthusiastic Staffordshire female named Casey, his old friend Leila, and a dark-toned Yorkie puppy named Alfie. Alfie (or more properly Alfie Doodle) is also present on the green a few minutes later. Dan is discussing collars with Alfie's mom, who wants to dress her pup in pink—Dan says that Alfie will never live this down and suggests a camouflage collar in order to let the little fellow keep in touch with his masculine side. There is a good turnout this morning, though once again Daisy-Mae is the star. Two little kids are toddling over to take turns stroking the docile pet and chortling in delight.

I have again left coffee money with Ronnie since I fear café queues on a day when we are again being invaded by legions of school kids in an an extravaganza so large that there are some eighteen open-sided tents set up on the pitch as we get ready for a day-long track meet—incomplete without the intrusive broadcasting of "Year Seven Shot Put, Please Report." I ask Georgie if she knows how Daisy-Mae got on in the workplace yesterday and she tells me that the little Shih-Tzu slept most of the time, bestirring herself only when it was time to get up and pee

35

under the boss's desk. I ask Ellen and Peter if they can tell which item I have forgotten this morning, since hardly a day goes by, in my present preoccupied state, without my forgetting something. Ellen has no trouble with this question—"Your hat." Meanwhile Ofra is fretting over another item of apparel, a dress suitable for Guy's bar mitzvah in a few weeks. When we begin a back passage walkround we see a spirit of running times past. We used to call her the "Mad Mum," for she used to mow us down with her baby carriage—which was being propelled at great speed on our narrow walkways. By now the baby must be taking his GCSE's, but mom seems as preternaturally thin and driven as ever.

Thursday, July 5:

I have had my hands full with Fritz again, for last night, believe it or not, we actually had the sounds of distant fireworks on the Fourth of July. I would say that celebrating American Independence Day in the country from which you won your independence might be counted as bad taste; the outcome was a frightened dog who had to be hauled along for a block or so before he could relax enough to complete his late night walk. Earlier we had spent some time with Dorothy's oncologist, who, seeing the weakened state of my wife, had decided to suspend chemotherapy in favor of some other strategies. This is why I am in the park at all on this, a Thursday morning, a grey day with more rain threatening.

St. George scholars in their yellow shirts are arriving for their sports day and the broadcasting system is already being tested as we complete our passage to the green. Here Winnie is in an irascible mood, her rubber conch with the treats inside having already yielded up all its contents. Fritz chases his orange tennis ball and then stations himself at my feet, hoping for a biscuit. This means that when I take out the bag I can count on Ziggy's nose gently brushing my hand in supplication. Ziggy then returns to his job of refereeing the bout between Rufus and Sid the Boxer, while the toddlers from yesterday return to stroke some more dogs. This time they have brought a little Westie named Luna, a perfect match for our Daisy-Mae.

There are delays in getting the café opened today and when we go in we find Peter and Ellen on a bench inside the forecourt—Fritz attempting to winkle out a squeaky toy from Ellen's purse. When chairs and tables are in place we sit down in our usual spot, with Georgie, Linda, Liam,

Ofra, and Dan present, and Albert and Hanna soon arriving as well. Georgie says that her hubby arrived home so late and so drunk last night that she had to put him to bed without his supper. Hanna says that she has had such an interrupted sleep pattern, because of Spadge getting her up all night long, that this morning she put him in her back garden, went back to bed, fell asleep, and only three hours later remembered he was still out there. She and I are alone as we complete a back passage walkround. She tells me that her neighbor, who works at home, has made a formal complaint following yesterday's all-day park noise. I tell her that none of my P.E. teachers would have required a loud hailer to address the tidy group we see sitting in the bleachers as we near the track.

Friday, July 6:

It has been some time since I had to wear gloves on a morning expedition in the park, but today is the day. There *is* a chill wind blowing on a day dominated by grey skies (ah, July in London) but, in fact, the donning of my garden mittens has nothing to do with the weather. What it does have to do with is the administration of a dose of anti-flea elixir between my dog's shoulder blades, a somewhat messy operation that I conclude as soon as we have reached the park. Last night Fritz also had his worming tablet so, now protected against all nasty beasts, internal and external, we can make our way to the green.

Janet counts fourteen dog owners standing about in a lively scene in the center of the greensward. I try to get Fritz interested in his orange ball, but there are too many other contestants for this prize, including Charlie the Cocker. Showing a great interest in Fritz himself is Beano, the Tibetan Terrier who has had a special affection for my dog since they were both youngsters. Buddy and Rufus are again knocking one another over, though I notice that this time Ziggy is able to abandon his role as referee to participate in this scramble himself. The next time I look up Fritz is following Janet, Georgie and Ronnie into the café.

When I catch up I see that Fritz has once again got his nose buried in Ellen's purse, with her Jack fretting over the fact that his precious ball might go missing. I offer a biscuit as a distraction and we take seats at our own table, just four of us today. Behind us dozens of kiddies are marching toward their fate on the playing fields and a car is being driven down the Carlton roadway at considerable speed by a chap with a mobile phone in one hand. Ronnie, who has brought a large supply of biscuits and carrot slices, is very natty in his twenty year-old Harris tweed jacket. He says he is hoping for warmer weather tomorrow, when he will host a party for the Tories in his back yard. The dogs consume a mountain of food and then we start off on a back passage walkround, slowed by the dilatory habits of Winnie and Daisy-Mae. Indeed Fritz is soon far out in front and even overtakes Peter and Ellen as well. When we exit the park he is rewarded for this speed by the discovery of an abandoned mini-football in the gutter.

Saturday, July 7:

Some brighter weather has reached us at last and, when the sun shines down, there is some real warmth to be experienced at last. The small fry, perhaps scattered by the end of the school term, are not present in great numbers on the football pitches this morning and their adult counterparts are also slow to arrive. As Fritz and I make our usual entry I notice that the wire fence at the top of the track is bent out of shape again—any dog wishing to do a few laps would have free entry this morning. Fortunately my dog is oblivious to this temptation and he makes a speedy enough work of his morning duties, so that we have soon reached the green.

Roland seems to have assembled some pupils for a training session; some of these chaps are soon tied to the little metal gazebo at the foot of Mt. Bannister and we have a chorus of frustrated barkers as a consequence. Ziggy rushes out to greet me as we march onto the green; this is cupboard love, since he knows that I have biscuits in my pocket. Celine says that she and Christopher have at last succeeded in obtaining a local rental—since they expect to be out of their own flat for at least half a year while a major conversion project gets underway. Fritz chases his orange ball a few times and then he begins to wander, visiting the canine school kids first, and then heading for the Randolph exit. By the time I get him to turn around the others are heading in for coffee.

I find Fritz camped at the feet of Peter and Ellen. He has already tried to get his nose into her bag; later I have to release him so that he can participate in the distribution of a rare but welcome plate of chopped sausage. At our own table we have Hanna, Dan, Ronnie, Janet, Georgie and Dan's friend Cleoni, who is making her first visit to our world. Ofra has very kindly brought with her a jar of home-made chicken soup for Dorothy. She joins the others in a discussion of the latest doings on *Big Brother* and then the topic switches to Wimbledon. In the café they have discovered that they have no gas, so Dan has to switch from a fried sandwich to a toasted one. John arrives with his Alsatian Ché; our hippie jack-of-all-trades has discovered Winnie's lost telephone tag and, fortunately, he is wearing the pants in which he has secreted this object days ago. Lots of little kids are inching their way past the dogs and into the café; three little boys outdo one another is claiming, "I'm not scared."

Sunday, July 8:

We have almost balmy weather on this lovely Sunday morning and Fritz responds by making a lively progress along the walkways. When we reach the green I can see our friends standing in the center of this open space and, following his lofted orange ball, Fritz soon sprints toward them. The scene, with its high sky and puffy white clouds, would be idyllic if it were not for the intrusion of a car radio blasting away from a van parked on the roadway between the loos and the metal gazebo at the foot of Mt. Bannister. This noise is needed as an accompaniment to the erection of a fancy tent (with glazed windows), one that is being raised as part of some fete. I don't know which group is responsible for hijacking yet another corner of our public space but Hanna says that it is the "Mongolians." I try to get as far away as I can from the noise; Dan is complaining that he has lost his keys, perhaps during the blackout that brought darkness to the Phoenix Theatre (No *Blood Brothers* on Friday night) after a junction box blew up on Oxford Street.

There is again a call for a place in the sun at coffee time and so we occupy a picnic table in the prow of the forecourt ship, though a tree branch means that there is as much shade as sun, and we have to add chairs for Hanna and Albert. Even here there is not enough room for a second grouping, which includes both of Ziggy's parents, Celine and Christopher. Dan now reports that he has a whole tribe of sparrows in his backyard and that the hanging basket prepared by Hanna is burgeoning. She tells him that he needs to add tomato food. He says that gardening is Davide's province. She tells him to tell Davide to add tomato food. I tell her that Dan already has so many things he needs to nag Davide about that he can't be adding tomato food to the list. Dan agrees, turning to me with, "You know us *so* well." Jo Lynn comes by with Tilly and stops for a chat and then John arrives with Ché.

The last stages of our conclave do not go well. Ofra is having bladder problems, but the loo is padlocked. Ché manages to poo in the bushes and we have to wait for John so that we can remind him of his clean-up duties. Winnie's rubber conch, the one that leaks food pellets, goes missing, and we can't find it anywhere. We make another visit to the green, assuming that some other dog has made off with it, but it is nowhere to be seen. Wheezing Winnie is obsessed enough by her food problems—she doesn't need this. At last we get turned around and begin a back passage walkround. Daisy-Mae manages to squeeze through the fencing and into the kiddies' playground but she comes back quickly enough. As we near the Essendine exit she and Sparkie (who now barks at anything and everything) are having a mock fight. Heading toward us in a wheelchair is a stroke victim, beaming with pleasure over the hi-jinks of the dogs, even clapping his hands in delight. I can't help wishing that the invalid in my house could take such pleasure in anything these days.

Saturday, July 14:

Almost a week now passes before I can return to the park, for on Monday morning, my wife, who had been staring off into space for two days, asked to return to the hospital. Linda then took over the care and feeding of Fritz, though he often came home to be with me at night. My days were spent at Dorothy's bedside at the London Clinic. Her condition weakened rapidly as she bravely refused all forms of treatment—interventions that, from her perspective, could only prolong the agony. At 6:20 in the morning on Thursday I was called by the Oncology Ward with the news that her condition had deteriorated considerably, and that she was asking for me. Linda drove me to the hospital an hour later. Here Dorothy could recognize me and twice she was able to squeeze my fingers. The worse day in my life came to an end in the late afternoon, when I saw her breathe her last.

Or, rather, Dorothy's day came to an end—mine was prolonged in misery and tears. I made many phone calls, for Dorothy was loved and admired by so many, and used an email to reach others: "Dorothy died this afternoon at 5:15. The courage she displayed in her battle with lung cancer and her bravery at the end were exemplary. For over forty-three years we have been a part of one another's lives and I will miss her more than words can express. Indeed, her wit and style and good heart have brightened the lives of many of us and she leaves dozens of stricken friends and relatives who can't believe that she has gone—and so quickly—from our midst. No sentimentalist, Dorothy wanted neither funeral nor memorial service. Her ashes will be scattered on Hampstead Heath."

Her sister Naomi arrived the next morning from Philadelphia and we went together to obtain a death certificate and to arrange, at a funeral home in Kensington, for cremation. Phone messages and emails came flooding in. Fritz returned from a night at the Taggarts and we tried to make our schedule somehow correspond to his routine as much as possible. On his late night walk we met Jean-Baptise and Hercules and I had yet another opportunity, tears choking my voice, to pass on the fateful news. I had not slept well in days and Friday night would not be very restful either—with a raucous party in the flat below us, hurtful backbeats and screaming and singing in the halls until 2:00 in the morning. At one point this brought so much distress to the dog that he began to bark hysterically. I don't know how Naomi got any sleep.

This morning at 9:00 she and I pick our way through the crushed plastic glasses and the sodden cigarette butts on our front stoop as we make our way into the park. Fritz seems mercifully unaware of his changed circumstance as we again encounter Jean-Baptiste and Hercules and then make our way onto the green, where I steel myself to accept the condolences of the dog people, the tears welling up with each embrace: Janet, Georgie, Celine, Dan, Hanna. Peter comes out with his Holly; he had lost his June only eight months ago and so he is acquainted with grief. The dogs play blissfully at our feet—when they were not seeking biscuits from my goody bag.

When we arrive at breakfast Bouzha informs us that Metty has ordered that all our treats will be on the house this morning—as a mark of respect for me. We sit down for one of our regular sessions and for most of the time I can hear the usual laughter. I know that to be part of such a society will be a great comfort to me at such a dire moment in my life. Just before we get up for a back passage walkround, Ronnie calls to speak to me on Hanna's cell phone. We had carried home from the hospital a bouquet that he and Susie had sent; it was still wrapped in its cellophane.

41

Monday, July 16:

It's not that we weren't in the park yesterday, for we were: me, Naomi, my brother-in-law Adrian and Fritz, of course—it's just that most of what happened is lost in a mist of tears and condolences—as each new friend came forward to give me a hug. (Much later I learned that yesterday many of the dog people used yesterday afternoon for an impromptu memorial service on Primrose Hill.) I remember that there was a five month-old Westie puppy named Pickle, a perfect match for the roughhousing Daisy-Mae, and that, at breakfast, no one could rouse Dan on any of his phones. Today we learn that our man-about-town hadn't gotten home until 7:30 am.

There is a lively turnout today, an active roiling mass writhing at our feet as Ziggy has one of his last adventures for some time; Christopher and Celine will shortly move away for half a year (and not to a local sublet, as they had wished) while their flat undergoes a major modernization. Kate has brought with her a hard rubber ball and Fritz is just able to get a squeak out of it, so he is satisfied, and Skye doesn't seem to mind. A veteran brown dog named Foxie also joins the group; Buddy and Rufus have their usual wrestling match, though Buddy is recovering from an encounter with a fragrant Staffie, who did not appreciate his nose up her bum.

Fritz carries Skye's ball in with him when it is time for us to have our coffee; he heads straight for Georgie's blue purse and, in his investigations here, manages to deposit this toy in *her* purse. Today we have Peter, Ellen, Ronnie, Kate, Georgie, Liz and a resurrected Dan. The early comers have staked out a table under the eaves and this turns out to be just as well for, after we have been sitting for half an hour, the heavens open and we are lashed by an insistent shower, one that requires us to inch our table toward the café's doors—twice. At last skies brighten a bit and we are able to conclude our back passage walkround without further incident.

Tuesday, July 17:

Each of us has an umbrella at the ready as we make our way into the park on a breezy and bright Tuesday morning. Hercules and Ziggy are doing a grand circle and we soon meet up with Buddy near the cypress trees. Fritz is not in the mood to linger and before long we have reached the green, where more dogs are milling about. I tell Dan that I have received, among the dozens of messages that have arrived by post and email, a nice letter from Joanna Pettet, who was once a stalwart of this scene, with her dog Jake. Dan, who has an early day of work, soon makes his way from the park with Winnie, and the rest of us turn our attention to the café, whose doors are just about to open.

Today, in addition to our trio, we have Ronnie, Georgie, and Hanna—though Kate comes by to complain that she has to go home and get dressed for a formal day at the office. Hanna says that she has not seen the cavalry horses, the ones whose trotting so disturbs our Schnauzers, in some time—and I agree that our local streets have been remarkably free of horse manure for some time. Adrian has to explain the intricacies of his toy soldier collection, after a fruitless search for more good specimens in the specialty shops of London yesterday. Ronnie notes that his espresso is especially thick today, and I suggest that it should have been served with a knife: this sets him off on a choking fit ignited by his own cigar smoke. When he recovers I congratulate the Tories in coming up with a viable (and amusing) mayoral candidate in Boris Johnson. Bouzha arrives for work, ten minutes late, but nobody dares to tease her about this.

The dogs are active beneath our feet in sharing out the tidbits that come their way, though Spadge is allowed to rumble about in the fenced forecourt, where Daisy-Mae spends the entire session wrestling with yet another young Westie. The pup is so tired out by this session that Georgie has to carry her home; she has Sparkie and Bailey in tow as well. The chalked-in lane lines that have just been renewed out on the green have all been washed away, after another night of rain, but today's school group is using the actual track as we begin another day of running and chanting.

Wednesday, July 18:

Anything could happen—weatherwise—as the three of us accompany Fritz into the park on a cloudy bright day with sun and dark clouds fighting it out in the July skies. We have to squeeze into the Carlton walkway between a food delivery truck and a car unloading mountains of equipment for yet another sports day. I note, with approval, that this lot seem to have a *bell* to start races with; soon thereafter an endless parade of kids is marched into the park. They are followed by Tanya the animal warden, but she seems to be on an official visit and doesn't stay long enough for us to garner any poo poo bags.

Out on the green Fritz chases his green tennis ball a bit and then takes off on his rambles, with me in pursuit. Roxy, another animal who is made uncomfortable in the presence of men in uniforms, takes exception to the chap who is re-inking the boundaries of the cricket field. Fortunately this guy treats the dressing down he now receives as a kind of joke, and that certainly helps to lighten the tone of these proceedings. Absent today is Daisy-Mae; when I ask about this, the others tell me that *she* is at a sports day—an annual works outing that Janet has taken her to. Meanwhile Georgie reports that her husband, the beleaguered James, has had a choking fit after ingesting a piece of steak and, in his efforts to dislodge the offending morsel, has accidentally flushed his own false teeth down the loo.

We have a large turnout at breakfast this morning: Dan, Hanna, Liz, Kate, Ronnie, Georgie, Celine, and our trio, of course, though Peter and Ellen, as usual, yield their seats to latecomers half way through the session. Liz is reporting that her youngest son has been complaining of homesickness at his summer camp and this somehow reminds Dan of his own doleful experience at a summer-long Army Cadets camp. "Army cadets?" Kate says, "I'll bet you joined just for the uniform." Dan then describes the many humiliations visited on him by the stern sergeant major in charge of this enterprise, a series of bitter memories made palatable only years later when he ran into this chap in a gay club. It takes a while for us to get home today since Adrian and Naomi are spending their last day in the park and need to say goodbye, departing as they will tomorrow morning for Philadelphia, at 8:00. In the meantime we have a cremation to get through this afternoon.

Thursday, July 19:

Just Fritz and me this morning—as Naomi and Adrian have headed for the airport an hour earlier, and leaving a very empty house. It is again cloudy bright but there is just enough warmth in the muggy air to make me wish I hadn't worn a sweatshirt. Ronnie is already sitting with Peter in front of the café as we play through. On the edges of the green we encounter Jean-Baptiste and Hercules. I try to keep Fritz amused with his tennis ball but in a moment's conversational inattention I lose track of this green presence and it disappears forever.

Sitting out on the cricket crease are Dan and Janet. I ask Janet about Daisy-Mae's sports day, but by doing so I have opened a very explosive can of worms. It seems that a co-worker has denounced Daisy-Mae to the health and safety folks and Janet's bosses have had to remind her that only guide dogs are allowed in the workplace. Furious, Janet says that she then refused to participate in the works outing and that she is gunning for whoever denounced her. Usually so mild-mannered, Janet is the picture of outraged motherhood today: love me, love my dog.

At coffee there is a near miss as Roxy almost manages to snag Hanna's bacon sandwich while the latter is unleashing Spadge in his morning picnic pen. Georgie reports that her husband's workmates have started referring to their toothless pal as "Gnasher." I am digesting this information as I walk Fritz toward the Morshead gate, on my own and a bit earlier than usual, as I have a doctor's appointment at 10:30. I have just had time to note that the clubhouse clock has again come to a grinding halt, while out on the green, Kate is pacing back and forth with a mobile phone in one hand and Skye's ball sling in the other. Then I am stopped by the police, who ask if I would be willing to help them with a survey about local policing and community crime. This goes on for some time and I have to dash to make my medical appointment.

Wednesday, July 25:

Again I have missed several episodes in the park, though again I can say that, at least physically, I was often actually here—for instance I was here, briefly, on a dark Friday morning, July 20th. I had a blood test scheduled for 10:10 at the Randolph surgery that day, and was expecting to bring Fritz back home before starting out on this medical errand, but during the night I began to experience a serious ache in my gut, a pattern of front and aft pain that I have always associated with the dreaded kidney stone. So my mission to the park changed and I knew that, if the hospital beckoned, I would have to hand Fritz off to a new carer (Linda and her family having headed for Devon). Fortunately I found Hanna and walked her home with my lad. So this is how it is going to be from now on, I reasoned: endless worry about my dog and no one around to worry about me. No wonder I started to weep when Hanna said that Dorothy spoke to her from a new star in the firmaments yesterday.

I had to wait out the whole of the morning surgery before getting a chance to see my doc. She took a test, which confirmed that there was some blood in my urine, and we decided that, with the aid of painkillers, I would try to wash the offending matter out with lots of liquid before we tried anything more profound. It didn't help that London was now undergoing a period of torrential showers (one that did in the lower floor of Kate's new house) and I was soaked by the time I got home from the chemists. I dozed for much of the rest of the day in a very lonely house but there was some temporary relief in the morning, and so I was able to return to the park and reclaim my dog. The weekend dragged on and my visits to the park with Fritz were often brief (I was drinking water only at the café) and my mind was far removed from the antics of the dogs.

On Sunday Fritz fell ill as well, with projectile diarroeha lashing many a local tree. This meant that my first stop on Monday was the Hamilton Vet Clinic, where the poor fellow, who registered a temperature, received a shot, antibiotic pills, and some gloop to spray on his intestinal formula food. At least I wasn't quite as poorly; the stone had shifted and it came out at five in the morning on Tuesday and was duly presented to my own surgery, where I had to go to repeat a blood test. Fritz, too seem to respond well to his new diet and to a bath that I had to give him later that afternoon—since he had been scratching himself incessantly.

So this morning, a Wednesday, was almost a normal one for us: the snarleyboodle park keeper yelling at a dog owner for letting his pet pee on a crate of rolled turves, Daisy-Mae again strung by a bee, Sparkie again hysterical because Hercules had stolen his toy, Metty's cappuccino again the consistency of melted marshmallow. But, also following a new pattern, I had to drink and run, facing another long day of endless errands and meetings that are just part of the aftermath of losing a loved one.

Friday, July 27:

I've lost another day and the memories of Thursday's session are fading fast. In dog terms, the morning was dominated by Fritz's check-up visit to the vets, where Sarah Saddiqui, having determined that my dog's poo had only progressed from watery gruel to chocolate mousse, ordered

A Doggy Day in London Town

a continuation of his antibiotic regime, with the next check-up scheduled for Tuesday.

Today Fritz joins a walkround with Leila, Jonesie, Winnie, Frank and Bianca. He seems to enjoy such pilgrimages and manages to stay quite close as we use the back passage, in reverse. For some reason Natasha and Dan are holding hands—this fools no one. As soon as we reach the green Dan spots Davide and reminds Winnie that "Daddy" is waiting for her (Dan is "Daddy" too). Fritz finds some fascination in a small rubber ball—which manages to retain some squeak even though Bailey chewed a hole in it long ago. Daisy-Mae, who had earlier hurt herself just jumping about, is much better and has renewed her assault on Sparkie (Janet has a long holiday weekend in *Poland*—how times have changed).

At coffee we see, for the first time in many months, Suzanne, accompanied by the backgammon-playing Ray. These are people who have known Dorothy for years (in Suzanne's case almost a quarter century) and the reunion is particularly poignant. Ronnie announces that the medicos want to operate on his sinuses. Davide reports that he had Liz as a passenger on his recent flight to Boston, and that she slept most of the way. I suggest that we need a new rule: people who leave us in order to pursue their holidays need to pay for the coffee of those left behind. Hanna thinks this is a splendid suggestion and so does Georgie who, after all, usually ends up dog minding the canines left behind.

Saturday, July 28:

We have a bright and sunny Saturday for our next visit to the park. I bring with me a green plastic ball that we found in the gutter last night, and we begin our reverse back passage. Here we encounter Suzanne with her Sunny, the Springer Spaniel who has been in Horsham during her three-month sojourn in the States. When we get to the green I can see the usual Saturday division, our lot at one end and, occupying center stage today, Roland's obedience class. I meet up with Suzanne again (Sunny is barking at shadows) but when I ask an owner (and not for the first time) what is the name of her junior Bailey, she tells me it's Maddy and that we *have* met—but that she has never met my *wife* before. I head back for the cricket crease, letting Suzanne straighten that one out.

Georgie and Dan have actually taken seats on the felt and from this position Dan keeps Fritz occupied in chasing the formerly squeaky rubber ball. Even though he may not be as fast as Sparkie, Fritz usually manages to obtain possession of this prize by out-growling the other contestants at the end of the process. Dan and Faz have an argument over which of their dogs, Winnie or Jasmine, is actually faster, and Dan tries to get Winnie moving on her little stumpy legs. Bailey is content with munching on the rubber ball and when Georgie takes this away from him, he settles for biting a hole in Fritz's new green toy. Fritz doesn't care; he has infiltrated the training class and is successful is leading some of these dogs away from their perch. This may include the delightful long-haired Dachshund, Snoopy. Someone points out that a year ago the grass had already turned brown; with all the rain we have been having it is a lush green today.

We join Peter, Ellen, Davide, Ronnie and Hanna at breakfast. There are more complaints that the only comfortable table is far removed from the day's sunshine. Faz is dissatisfied with his hot chocolate and says that the café at Primrose Hill does a better job. For that matter, the coffees are doled out one at a time this morning and we are long at table. Faz announces that he doesn't seem to be able to sell his BMW sports car and that his microwave has exploded but that he will *not* be taking Dianah with him on the next shopping expedition since she asks too many questions; the recent memory of five and a half hours in the curtain department of John Lewis—at the end of which no purchase was actually made—obviously rankles still. As we are leaving a Middle Eastern mom grabs the shoulder of a clearly delighted little boy, and pulls him away from the seduction of the dogs on parade. Later I see a better indoctrinated little boy, cricket bat in hand, hide behind a tree in order to escape the depredations of Daisy-Mae.

Sunday, July 29:

It has rained much of the night but things have brightened some as Fritz and I enter a strangely empty park. No classes, no ball games, just the odd eager jogger pounding along the pathways or around the track. Fritz makes a fairly rapid progress toward the green, where I spot Georgie and her trio near the bandstand. Nearby, Faz is chatting with Suzanne, while Sunny is barking hysterically at shadows again; at least this means that we now have some sun. Fritz chases Sparkie's tennis ball for a while and then I have to follow him over hill and dale just to see that he is not up to any mischief.

When we go in for coffee we have Dan, Faz, Peter, Ellen, Hanna, Georgie, and Ronnie for company. It turns out that Faz *did* take Dianah on his shopping expedition yesterday. This was a necessity because, in addition to the space-age microwave (one that Faz has installed, even though he hasn't figured out how to use it yet), the couple were also shopping for a baby carriage. Faz complains of the egregious price he was forced to pay for this vehicle and I suggest that he should have traded in his BMW. The staff have donated two packets of sugar wafers—Faz can't get one of these open either, but where a London cop has failed an MS victim succeeds. Ronnie has been interested in the fact that Dianah is due to deliver during the first week of October. He wants her to hold her legs together until she has reached *his* birthday. "Mind you," he mumbles in a *sotto voce* that I hope Faz can't hear, "if she had held her legs together in the first place we wouldn't be shopping for baby buggies."

Breakfast is a frustrating time these days for Fritz, since the vet wants him to eschew all snacks until his next check-up. We begin a back passage walkround, which means that we all get drenched by a misplaced sprinkler near the kiddies playground, one that is causing its own flood, especially because we have had all this rain recently. Today, instead of heading for home immediately, I accompany Georgie on her homeward journey so that I can pick up a paper at the Nosh store. By this time she has Bailey, Sparkie and Daisy-Mae each on a separate lead, though Daisy-Mae, whose new upper teeth are just coming in, chooses the crossing of Elgin Avenue to gum Sparkie's ear. Georgie doesn't have enough dogs so I hand her Fritz's lead as well in order to complete my transaction.

Monday, July 30:

Skies are sunny and blue, with fast-moving clouds hovering above, as Fritz and I make our way into the park on a quiet Monday morning. There is not much activity on the green; at one end we have Flash the Border Terrier and Sasha; on the opposite side I can see Georgie and her threesome. She has had to follow them into the wet grass and this is cause for complaint as she is wearing only sandals. I have brought with me a yellow rubber ball with Santa embossed thereon, part of a Christmas package bought in happier times at Sainsbury, and I try to keep Fritz amused with this. He does chase it down, but he is more interested in his incessant wanderings and I have to follow him on his peregrinations again today.

When it is coffee time it is clear that the holidays have decimated the ranks: today we have only Peter, Ellen, Ronnie and Georgie, though Jasmina, Sasha's mistress, sits down with us as well. Ronnie has been trying to send to me a photo he took on his mobile phone of Dorothy at the dance program we went to at Covent Garden last fall—and there is a long palaver on how best to do this. Ellen has just taken delivery on a new flat-screened TV and there is universal consternation that there is nothing to watch on it (thank god for sports, I say). Ronnie, Jasmina and Georgie light up their cigarettes and there is some discussion of the recent ban on smoking in public spaces.

When we get up to begin a back passage walkround we are preceded by a sports group made up of little kids, some sort of summertime playgroup I would guess. As our dogs near them there is earnest discussion on which one of these tots is afraid of dogs. Many think our procession is cute but one little kid says, "Look, that one is wearing a bucket." This is a reference to Sparkie's anti-barking muzzle. Sparkie is full of woe since Daisy-Mae keeps up an extended assault on his person, biting his snout and his ears as though he were just a fancy fluffy toy. No wonder, when we encounter the Shih-Tzu Thomas, that the frustrated Yorkie takes out his hurt feelings by mounting the stranger and pumping away vigorously.

Tuesday, July 31:

It's a bit warmer than many of us have anticipated this morning and I suppose you could say it's about time—as this is the last day of July. I follow Fritz onto the green and here we are reunited with Janet, back from her visit to Poland. She tells us that Daisy-Mae was delighted to be reunited with her mommy, but there then followed a series of spite wee-wees and spite doo-doos in the house: don't leave me alone again. I try to keep Fritz occupied with his yellow rubber ball but I am even less successful with this attempt than yesterday. My dog much prefers to wander to the margins of the green, first to visit Hanna (who has poor Spadge in hospital again) and then to cross to the Randolph walkway, where he is soon bathed in a shower of dirt, courtesy of the ubiquitous leaf-blower.

At coffee we have Peter, Ellen, Kate, Ronnie, Georgie, Janet and Dan. Janet tells us that her visit to Krakow was first to attend a wedding and then to get a quotation on some dental work. Kate says that someone is coming soon to cart away all the sodden furniture from her bottom floor, and that she will be without an office for three months—while the dehumidifier does its work. Fritz, still forbidden the odd snack, has another frustrating time of it and takes his displeasure out on any strange dog who happens to wander near our table.

At 10:00 we leave the park, following our usual route toward Boundary Road, where Fritz has what turns out to be his final check-up with Dr. Sarah. Then he accompanies me as I complete a number of neighborhood errands. First we walk down to the Barclay's Bank on Elgin Avenue, where he sits patiently while I use the cash machine. Then we head for Lauderdale Parade where I need to speak to Sylvia, Dorothy's faithful hairdresser, about a haircutting appointment for myself later this afternoon. Finally we get home and I am able to give Fritz something that he has been missing in this unhappy period of tummy trouble and grief: a biscuit.

August, 2007

Wednesday, August 1:

I have declared today the official opening moment of the summer season, and I have done so by wearing only a colored t-shirt into the park. Not that it is actually very sunny: Suzanne's Sunny passes by without being bedeviled by any shadows for instance. But it is warm enough as we reach the green and begin our usual ritual of play and evasion. The yellow ball comes out of my pocket but soon Fritz is exploring the margins and I have my own exercise in pursuit. Out on the cricket crease there is a suspicious pile of poo and there is some speculation on the nature of this specimen; it is dark enough to have been deposited by our friends, the foxes. When Hanna arrives, however, she has a look, pronounces the mess dog after all and, being Hanna, cleans it up. I have to pick up Daisy-Mae, who is eating something nasty; fortunately she is still only a handful.

At breakfast we have Peter, Ellen, Ronnie, Dan, and Kate. Fritz, having received the all-clear from his vet yesterday, is once again able to enjoy the canine bounty, but what really excites him is a squeaky yellow ball which he finds under our table. Unfortunately this toy belongs to Franca's Boxer, Bianca, and there is an urgent request for its restoration. I manage to pry the object from my dog's jaws, but as I do so, Bianca, enraged by the loss of this object, attacks the now innocent Fritz, growling furiously and quite upsetting the little fellow until Franca can extract her animal. Thereafter my dog seems more shaken than hurt and many rush forward to comfort him. Dan says that, believe it or not, Winnie can sometimes behave this nastily—but everyone pretends that there is no way we can believe this.

The recent contretemps has lead to the spillage of Franca's white coffee and pretty soon Hanna is warning us, from an adjacent table which she has taken because Jack and George don't get along, that Daisy-Mae and the others are lapping the coffee up. Poor Georgie—she can now look forward to a house full of wired dogs. Hanna and I have spotted the animal warden's van parked in front of the clubhouse and so, since this is a rare visit these days, we head over here in order to pick up some poo poo bags. Here we meet the new warden, Heather, who says that she will be in the park a bit more consistently from now on.

Friday, August 3:

I have missed another day. Yes, I was in the park, but—as so often happens on such mornings—my thoughts were miles away and I couldn't remember a thing when I sat down to write, later in the day. I do recall one unusual moment. I had gone to Paddington Station to renew my senior rail pass, repeating a ritual that I often completed with Harold. Now it was Tosh who met me here, finalizing arrangements that would lead to the resumption of our day walk schedule, now sadly interrupted. When we went looking for a café in which to have a cup of coffee Tosh chose a spot called The Cauldron on Norfolk Place, but as we entered I was surprised to see one of the park stalwarts in command. This was Barbara, owner of the late lamented Hendrix and participant in the Paddington Rec's Saturday morning exercise class. I had always known that she had a café near Paddington Station (and well remember her objections to a Starbucks moving into Maida Vale), but I had no idea that it was here.

I am wearing my red t-shirt as Fritz and I enter the park this morning. The park is undergoing its summer siesta and it's pretty quiet now. We pass Ronnie, already at his place in front of the café doors, and head out to the green, where Dan and Georgie are sitting on the cricket crease. Dan is complaining about the slugs who are infesting his garden and he does a whole routine in which he invents a dialogue among these creatures, one in which they decide to ingest these lovely blue pellets, and then explode. Fritz is soon bored and wanders off, this time admitting himself to the doggy play area on the Grantully side. Here he conducts a detailed sniff inventory and then it is time to cross the green and get some coffee.

In addition to Ronnie we have at our table Dan, Georgie, Kate, Peter, Ellen, and Hanna—with Albert sitting as an outrider. Dan is organizing a gift and card in honor of Bouzha's forthcoming birthday and we all sign the card. Hanna has bought a chair as a housewarming present for Dan and Davide and when Dan says he finds it really comfortable she insists on buying him a second one *now*. Dan is not very comfortable with this second act of generosity and tries to abort the mission, which Hanna wants to undertake immediately—so it will be interesting to see which one them succeeds. We begin a back passage walkround, where we discover that Skye is mesmerized by Daisy-Mae, and tries to follow her everywhere. "Perhaps she is getting broody," we suggest to Kate.

Saturday, August 4:

It is again a warm and sunny morning and for the third day in a row I am able to enter the park wearing only a t-shirt (in this fashion I have now worn all three t-shirts in the Hawkshead package that Dorothy ordered for me some months ago). Given the balmy nature of the day it may be a cause of some wonderment that I am also wearing my black garden gloves. This mystery is explained when I also note that I am carrying a pipette of Front-Line flea killer since, with Fritz scratching and licking with some intensity, it is time for his next treatment. This requires me to rub the liquid into the back of his neck, and then to repair to the men's room, where I can wash (but not dry) my hands.

I can see that Janet has joined Dan and Georgie in a seated posture on the cricket crease and here Fritz and I head. Fritz insists on the obligatory cuddle, though I have to warn Dan that he might now have to wash *his* hands. The woman who has been bringing Flash to the park now produces a squeaky blue ball. I warn her that Fritz will have it if she is not careful but, ignoring this advice, she tosses the ball to my dog. Five minutes later, time to go in for coffee, and the ball cannot be extracted from my dog's jaws. We agree to make an exchange later, since Flash is now playing with a large plastic ball belonging to Winnie.

At breakfast there is a large turnout with Ronnie, Janet, Georgie, Hanna, Dan, Peter, Ellen, Linda, and Nicholas. Bouzha is brought to the doorway (she won't come any further as she is still afraid of dogs) so that we can sing happy birthday. Nicholas tells a lengthy and boring story—one that leaves all of us glassy-eyed—about an entrepreneur who has invested in a factory that burns tires to produce energy. Albert, who is again riding shotgun, gets up for a minute and Tinkerbelle and Saffy, who are attached to his chair, follow in hot pursuit, scaring themselves because the chair is now pursuing them. Hanna provides the obligatory lecture, "Albert, never attach dogs to table or chair," but the laconic vet replies, "Well, at least you know where to find them." We begin a back passage walkround, one that concludes with an impromptu visit to our house from Linda and Pepper.

Sunday, August 5:

Temperatures are again up a notch as Fritz and I enter the park on a warm Sunday morning. I can see that sun worshippers are already staking out places on the grass, and that there is a large contingent of dog owners sprawled on the cricket crease. As I dislike such direct encounters with the sun I am just as happy to follow Fritz into the shadows on the Grantully side, where he makes slow, sniffing progress in the direction of the bandstand—which today is surrounded by a new addition to park furniture, a dozen or so deck chairs. It is time to go in for coffee but my friends are still basking in the sun and so I head toward the café on my own.

Our usual table is usurped by a gang of Kosovans, including some of the counter staff, so I sit down in a corner with Peter and Ellen. When the others arrive we have to choose a picnic table: Dan, Janet, Georgie, Hanna, Davide, Faz, and even old Albert, who takes a seat at the table for the first time. Unfortunately, the subject of Dan's second chair comes up again. Dan has snuck out and bought the chair himself and Hanna wants to know why he didn't go with *her*—since she wanted one too. Dan says that he was feeling a bit bullied and Hanna says that no one can bully *him*. I try to lighten the mood by suggesting that we now have two nominees in the category of most boring conversation topic: Nicholas' story of burning tires as the world's next great energy source and Dan's latest chair.

A great parade begins a back passage walkround, but there is a pause at the empty five-a-side courts—where some of our animals are invited to try out the artificial surface in pursuit of an empty water bottle. I can see that Daisy-Mae has had a bit of a trim—we can see her merry, mischievous eyes now, and that Sparkie has been scalped. (Georgie says he now resembles Johnny Depp more than Brad Pitt). I follow her, Sparkie and Bailey as they head for home, stopping long enough outside the Nosh store so that I can hand off Fritz while I dash inside for a *Sunday Times*.

Monday, August 6:

In spite of a little early morning rain and an obvious reduction in temperatures I decide to wear only my red t-shirt as Fritz and I head for the park on a quiet Monday morning. Unusually we do not pass another soul, human or canine, as we reach the kiddies playground, where Fritz hives off to see if there is any action at the café. There isn't, though I do see Peter and Ellen already seated on their bench and café workers waiting to be admitted to their place of employment.

Out on the grass I can see Hanna, with both dogs, Georgie with three, David the dogsitter with both Skyes, Dan entering stage right with Winnie, and two Golden Retrievers, Buddy and Sasha. Or should I say three members of this breed, for today we have a third contestant in the endless wrestling match undertaken by these large dogs. This is a recent arrival from the States, a honey brown specimen named Auro—I tell his Indian owner that he even has gold is his name. Hanna leaves George with David while she takes the slow-moving Spadge home. I kick the ball to Skye the Cairn while I ask David if he doesn't want some of Dorothy's specialty film books. Fritz makes a circuit of the other owners; I notice that he particulary seems to crave cuddles from women—understandably so.

We have a very small turnout at coffee this morning—just Georgie and Dan, initially, though Jasmina and Hanna soon arrive as well. Dan insists that, with her new hairdo, Daisy-Mae looks like a little old man. Bailey gives a yelp and there is some concern that he may have been the lastest victim of wasp bite. Dan adds that there is a nest of these creatures at the top of his building and that they are so abundant in his kitchen that he has had to hoover them up. There follows some discussion on what to do with the live vacuum cleaner bag, though no one can suggest which mail slot to drop it into. Bailey, for his part, seems to be okay; he jumps into my lap and spends enough time there that I have to put my trousers in the wash when I get home.

Tuesday, August 7:

Another lovely t-shirt day. I follow Fritz as he checks out the early action at the café. In fact only Ronnie has assumed his usual seat in front of the still-closed doors, but I do want a private word with him—since his Susie lost her mother, at age 88, only two days ago. An MS sufferer, like Ronnie himself, Susie's mom had lived much longer than anyone could have anticipated, but this will not ease the pain of the moment. Having received so many condolence cards myself recently I am now in the position of presenting one, and this I do, passing on a card for Susie to Ronnie.

Dog owners are widely scattered this morning but I head for the center of the green, passing a spot where the chalk-spreading gardener is actually preparing the outlines of an impromptu softball pitch. I end up kicking the tennis ball to Skye the Cairn again, though this time I have learned, via a question on *Mastermind*, that the breed actually originated on the Isle of Skye. After a while I notice that I don't seem to have a dog anymore—as Fritz has done another one of his vanishing acts. I attempt my recall whistle several times and, from some far corner of the park, he comes dashing forward, doing me proud and quite impressing Aunt Hanna. The latter has just claimed a large feather from one of the trash gatherers—since she uses such objects and white sage in one of her ceremonials. "Don't think me mad now," she tells us. "But we think of you as mad all the time," is my response.

Ronnie has placed coffee money behind the counter for all of us today and we have a jolly enough time, joined just as we get up to begin a back passage walkround by Linda and Liam. Often, these days, Bailey, Sparkie and Daisy-Mae are admitted to the empty five-a-side court during this peregrination: they love chasing one another at great speed over this artificial surface, especially if there is a net that also has to be dodged during this pursuit. Linda and Dan now make arrangements for a matinee visit to *Blood Brothers* this week. Linda is only one of a number of dog owners who have drawn my attention to the state of my dog's bottom. As yesterday I had to attend to my trousers as soon as I got home, so today it is one befouled Schnauzer bottom that requires immediate attention.

Wednesday, August 8:

A storm has brought moisture to Maida Vale overnight. In our house I could tell there would be something unusual in the atmospheric pressure when Fritz, disdaining his usual spot on the bed, chose to remain in the bathroom, one of his places of retreat when there are thunder and lightning about. Later I could hear him pawing at the little rug in the bathroom and before long rain began to fall quite steadily. Fritz now joined me, pressing his warm furry body against mine, but I could tell that my little canine barometer was satisfied with the weather prospects when he moved away to his own place on the bed. In the event there was no thunder.

It seems a bit chilly in the breeze (I am still wearing only a t-shirt) but it is pleasant enough in the sun as we make our way into the park. Suzanne is heading our way with her own Sunny, with Suki the Vizsla and with little Nicole, who has grown quite a bit since I last heard her do her famous impression of a growling Fritz. On the green Dan is just departing, having left Winnie in the care of Georgie—who now has four dogs to take home with her. Fritz heads for the Grantully side of things and I follow him around the perimeter until it is time to go in for coffee. It's time for *me* to go in for coffee; it's time for Fritz to do a second poo.

At coffee we have Ronnie, Suzanne, Nicole, Hanna, Peter, Ellen, Georgie, Linda and Liam. Georgie reports that she has at last heard from Ofra (who, however, forget to ask how her Bailey was doing). Not surprisingly our absent-minded one has been up to her old tricks in Israel, taking the bus to Jerusalem, discovering in a shop that her wallet was missing, leaving her cases with the shopkeeper, returning unsuccessfully to the bus station, giving the shopkeeper an anxiety attack over these mysterious cases, and then discovering her wallet on his counter. Sunny is hooked to the wall that separates us from the forecourt and she protests in an upsetting high-pitched squeal. She is evidently just coming out of season and Franka protests that her Bianca is confined to the doggy pen during such episodes. We head straight for the Morshead gate when coffee hour is over for Fritz and Pepper have a joint booking at the puppy hairdressers in St. John's Wood.

Friday, August 10:

I have missed a day in the park as I have had a long country walk with Tosh, finishing up the London Outer Orbital Path. Fritz has had a lively day with Pepper and I can tell this because he has a long sleep-in prior to our visit to the park. He is just tired, but I am tired and footsore, after fourteen warm miles, and I have no reason for wanting Fritz to hurry toward the green. It is a lovely warm sunny morning and there is already a group of dog owners sprawled on the cricket crease.

Fritz works the crowd and then heads for the Grantully side of the park where, after a second poo, we enter the doggy area and I have a chance to sit down on one of the two surviving benches—there are only two left in the Morshead dog pen as well and this may show us how serious the park authorities are about wanting dog owners to make greater use of these spaces. There is no one else about and I am just as happy to be alone with my thoughts.

When 9:30 rolls around we cross the green and head in for coffee; as I enter the café I am able to pass Fritz off to Liam, but they forget about my medium cappuccino order and have to start all over again some fifteen minutes later. Today we have Peter, Ellen, Ronnie, Davide, Linda, Liam, Hanna and Georgie. Liam makes himself master of ceremonies and distributes quite a few slices of toast to the assembled pooches. They don't believe him when he tells them that all the food is gone because they can see that he still hasn't finished *his* chocolate muffin. Hanna and I discuss an expedition which we shall shortly undertake to Homebase—as I need to fill in some window box holes occasioned by the demise of the spring pansies.

Saturday, August 11:

Still weary from my efforts on Thursday, I take Fritz into the park on another sunny Saturday morning. I am shuffling along on my sore feet and my dog does a really good job of outstripping my efforts. I find him again after I have passed the usual Saturday morning footie crowd—as they try to figure out who gets to wear the orange vests today on the five-a-side courts.

I can see Fritz touching noses with his pals, human and canine, as I reach the green at last. There is a lot of activity out here but I don't get any chance to participate since my dog is soon off on his rambles and I have to keep in touch. After a brief foray along the Randolph walkway he begins a leisurely trot around the perimeter of the green and when we have completed the circle I decide to head in for coffee, as the café is now open. Behind me I can see that the dog people are being ejected from the cricket crease (and everywhere else on the green), their places taken by, of all things, cricketers. We don't usually see this breed here this early in the morning.

I take a seat at the bench that is the second home for Peter and Ellen, planning to join Dan, Georgie, and Janet when they arrive (they have John with them this morning as well), but the sun worshippers select a picnic table and I decide to stay where I am and drink my cappuccino in the shade. Albert comes to chat with us, standing with Tinka and Saffie, as there are no chairs in here. Janet hunts up John because, wonder of wonders, Ché has taken another one of his patented patio poops. When Peter and Ellen get up I decide to follow them. This means that neither on the green nor at coffee have I been able to exchange more than a nod with my usual group. Indeed, Fritz soon races ahead of Holly, Jack and Sandy and I complete the back passage walkround on my own as well. Maybe it's just as well, in my exhausted state, that I have been essentially on my own today.

Sunday, August 12:

Temperatures have cooled considerably, though there is still some sun about, and I have resumed the use of a sweatshirt as Fritz and I make our way to the park on a quiet Sunday morning. Fritz is full of beans and I am very glad to see it, for he has been most lethargic at home, and last night he disdained his puppy supper. I know he senses that a great energy has gone out of our house; he hardly plays at all. Dorothy died a month ago today.

Out on the green I find David the dog sitter bemoaning the sad start that Spurs have yesterday made to the new football season. He is with Skye the Cairn (a sore foot preventing the usual ball chasing) and Buddy, but he has time to give Fritz a nice tummy rub. Janet has arrived with yet another Peter, this one a friend of Lyndon's. Lyndon is having tests in the hospital and Peter is caring for Lulu, the French Bulldog, whom we have not seen in some time. She has grown into a delightful dog and she soon has her paws full fending off the attacks of the relentless Daisy-Mae. With Winnie and Lulu there is never a moment without spirited wheezing.

Peter of Peter and Ellen is not about this morning so we decide to add chairs to his usual table in the corner of the forecourt at the spot where benches against the wall already provide some seating. Today we have Janet, Georgie, the visiting Peter, Dan, Davide, Ronnie and Albert. Dan reports that the wasps have again begun to make night-time raids on his flat, attracted by the light. He now has to wait a long time for his cooked breakfast and the dogs grow restless beneath the table. Fritz jumps up on the bench and sits next to me. Eventually we are free to begin a back passage walkround but once again the littlest dogs are admitted, against all the rules, to the empty five-a-side court, where the speedy Sparkie leads them on a merry chase in great swooping circles. He is once again being zapped with a form of remote-controlled spray (attached to his collar) whenever he starts one of his barking jags, but so far this seems to be working.

Monday, August 13:

There is a lot of cloud about this morning but it is still bright and still comfortable enough for me to wear just a t-shirt. As we near the kiddies play area Pepper, having somehow sensed our presence, comes tearing around the corner to greet us. He had been our houseguest for seven hours only yesterday. When we reach the green Linda and I turn Fritz over so we can see what he has been obsessively licking between his legs. There is, indeed, a sore spot that he has worried at all night, and this may require some salve.

At coffee we return to our usual table; Linda goes off to get Liam out of bed but Dan, Georgie, Ronnie, Ellen and Albert remain. It is unusual to see Ellen without Peter, but he is vacationing at Leigh-on-Sea, a site that our Essex boy, Dan, knows well. (Ronnie says that he once had a lawyer named Leon Fish.) Big Blake comes around the corner and is chased away by Tara the Ridgeback amid some deep barking. Georgie says that her new remote control anti-barking device is working well on Sparkie. It has three settings, some beeps meaning good dog, and two levels of spray depending on the severity of the offence. In fact the little Yorkie is afraid of the beeps so she hardly ever needs the spray. Sparkie barks only once and Dan grabs the gadget, explaining, teasingly, "I think that was a three . . ."

On our return walkround there is some payback for the naughtiness of admitting the smaller dogs to the empty five-a-side court. Only two footie playing boys are here but Sparkie, spotting an opening in the gate, rushes in, soon pursued by Bailey, Daisy-Mae and Winnie. It is impossible to get them to stop their circling antics (Fritz is on lead for these return journeys) and it takes some time before we can get started again. Some of the blackberrries are ripening on the bushes at the corner of the running track but they are so high that only the birds will benefit.

Tuesday, August 14:

Sometime near dawn a light rain begins, and it is still falling when it is time for us to go to the park. I am wearing my rain jacket, hood up, and this is quite sufficient to protect me from the wet. The dogs, on the other hand, soon show various signs of dampness—though, truth to tell, there aren't many of them about. On our back passage entry Fritz and I encounter only Terry, the American chap who owns the Alsatian Cristal. He is on the telephone and at one point he beckons his dog over to hear a few words spoken by his interlocutor. She listens intently, but makes no comment in reply.

I find Dan and Georgie huddled against the elements in the vestibule of the clubhouse, where some of the park personnel soon take shelter as well. Dan is off to a meeting at work and so Winnie is left in the care of the generous Georgie. (What is going to happen to all these dogs when she takes Sparkie off to Scotland for five days starting on Friday?) "I see you are down to four dogs," I remark, as she and I head for the café. Bailey is one of these and Daisy-Mae, looking like a floor mop with big eyes, brings up the rear.

It is just the two of us at coffee today and so there is plenty of room at our usual table beneath the overhang. Georgie tells me that we have not seen Hanna recently since George is poorly—he has a growth on his liver and a decision will soon have to made on whether to end his suffering. This news does nothing to brighten the day, which is depressing enough weatherwise (I also have major email problems as home); at least I don't face another day like yesterday when, just to deal with the aftermath of my wife's death, I had to write eight letters, send off eight emails and make five phone calls. Not surprisingly we do not linger for long at table today and, the rain lifting momentarily, make our way along the back passage one more time.

Wednesday, August 15:

There are still lots of clouds about and I don't trust the weather and so I am wearing my rain jacket again as Fritz and I begin our morning visit to the park. Almost immediately we encounter Suzanne, who has a question I can't answer about social security. On the green I can see that Georgie is down to three dogs but the fourth member of this elastic band soon arrives in the form of Winnie, who comes in with Dan. The sun now comes out and both Suzanne and I have to take our jackets off. Sunny, of course, begins to bark at shadows almost immediately and a number of us recommend that Suzanne consider investing in the device that seems to be working so well with Sparkie. Dan phones Hanna, who is still keeping a vigil at George's bedside.

Nicholas arrives with Monty and Suzanne reminds him that she wants the drawings he did of her kitchen—sounds like Liz and her curtains all over again. The kitchen magnate buys me a cappuccino but it turns out that he has not heard yet that Dorothy has died. The turnout at coffee is a little bit better than yesterday, for today we have Georgie, Ellen, Nicholas, Dan, Albert, and Rhian, who comes in with the little Bichon Frise, Otw. Rhian is still trying to sell her flat, mostly because of the noise generated by a nearby ethnic center, and she has to harm her own chances by declaring that she has had noise problems at her address. This is equivalent to Kate, who now sits down as well, not being able to sell her flat if she claims on the insurance for flood damage.

We begin a back passage walkround, though Daisy-Mae is so deeply disappointed by the closed gate at the five-a-side pitch that she pees on the step. I tell Fritz that, once again, we will have Pepper as our guest today and, sure enough, he arrives at 1:00, just in time for a group nap on the bed. His arrival also means that there will be a second visit to the park in the afternoon, though I usually find it easiest just to take the lads into the Morshead Road play area, where I can keep an eye on both of them.

Wednesday, August 16:

It is lovely and bright this morning but a little fresher than yesterday and I am quite comfortable in my blue sweatshirt. Again we encounter Suzanne and Sunny as we enter; they turn around and follow us out to the green. There is a lively scene out here, with one newcomer, a brown poodle named Hendrix—just like Barbara's late dog. Dan says that Hanna says that George seems free from pain, but that he is not eating—and that can't be a good sign. An American dad comes onto the green with a kite and a toddler in a pink fairy dress. Sparkie distinguishes himself by barking at the little girl and then pissing on her kite. You can't take him anywhere.

At coffee we have Ellen, Janet, Georgie, Dan, Albert, Suzanne and both Ronnie and Susie—who yesterday attended the cremation of Susie's mother. Sparkie soon jumps into Ronnie's lap. With his spray box strapped to his neck one is tempted to tell him, "Beam me up, Sparkie." Buster the latchkey dog plays through and Fritz sets up a cry of protest, which Winnie erroneously concludes is directed at her. She therefore attacks Daisy-Mae, who is in the next lap. Meanwhile Sunny, who has already scarfed down three chicken breasts for breakfast, becomes so agitated by the presence of foodstuffs on the table, that she too begins to bark, hysterically and piercingly.

Before we begin our back passage walkround we are visited by the elderly Australian lady who often comes over to fuss about the dogs and to claim that she is, in fact, a healer of dogs and cats (she wears a large piece of cat jewelry dangling from her neck). She has evidently also claimed that she was one of Australia's greatest country and western stars—a claim that seems to be a contradiction in terms. She is actually quite sweet but, curiously, our dogs don't seem to have warmed to her and today, much to our surprise, the usually docile Rosie actually snaps at the visitor.

Thursday, August 17:

Truth to tell, I've a bit of a gut ache again and my trip to the park this morning is more duty than pleasure. The park continues to be much quieter than usual, with only a week or so to go before the resumption of the next school term. Fritz makes his usual inspection of the café premises, but, finding only Ronnie, he plays through and rejoins me on the green. Here we have a very small turnout—and getting smaller as Dan bids farewell and heads off for work. Linda soon takes Pepper off as well; he and Fritz had a wonderful time together at Pepper's house last night. This means that only Davide is present when it is time to go in for coffee. He is a bit overfaced by all the dogs in his care since, to his own Winnie, they have added Daisy-Mae and Bailey. This must mean that Georgie has departed for a short visit to Glasgow with Sparkie.

At our table we have only Davide, Ronnie, and Ellen, with Albert soon arriving to take up a seat just outside the circle. While we are having coffee we meet for the first time a darling eleven week-old puppy, a cross between a French Bulldog and a Boston Terrier. His name is Vito, for his jawline resembles that of the famous *Godfather* Don, and he is handed around like a prize parcel—with Natasha declaring undying love and Leila showing no signs of jealousy. The same cannot be said of Winnie, who is evidently perturbed by her new roommates; she kicked Bailey off the bed last night.

The back passage walkround has only Davide with his three dogs, Albert with his two, and me, with my one. This gives me time to quiz Davide about the state of his long-running battle over the placement of a satellite dish. I tell him, as we near the Essendine exit, that on this street I have noticed a unique solution to the same problem. One householder, forbidden to deface the front elevation of his flat, has mounted the dish in his sitting room, where it can look out the front window all day, even if the flatmates can't.

Saturday, August 18:

Under grey skies (my mood is a little better than grey, though I still have tummy pains) Fritz and I hit the park. Fritz makes slow work of this stage of the adventure, sniffing his way along in minor stages as we at last reach the cypress trees. I lose track of him as we reach the café, finding him only after looking into the middle of the Saturday morning obedience class, where he is checking out the new pupils. He then makes a pass at the trio of Janet, Faz, and Dan and continues on down the Morshead roadway, where he eventually finds Albert sitting on a bench with Saffy and Tinkerbelle. The girls are delighted by his presence but my dog is soon bored and, passing the famous trio again, now heads for the Grantully gate, where I have to follow him—at last getting his attention with the biscuit bag.

There are quite a few customers for the café today and our drinks are slow in coming. In addition to those already mentioned we have Ronnie and Ellen at our table—which even has a nice ashtray for Ronnie's cigar. There is a good deal of talk about missing parties: nobody has seen Hanna in days; Kate is missing also but there is a strong rumor that she has acquired a Puli puppy; Georgie is in Scotland and I suggest that the next time she appears we should surprise her up with an envelope full of poo poo bags that need refolding for Ronnie. Winnie, who continues to bully her houseguest, Bailey, is haunting the threshold while Dan is at the counter of the café, and this means that some people have to step around her or over her. This is clearly unsettling for one of the black Vista security guards, who opens the other half of the door rather than do this, and her presence is also clearly unacceptable to a black mod who is wearing his jeans as high as his knees, his underwear in our faces. (At least we have one black dog owner on the green, for a young chap has brought in his Staffie for some instruction from Roland.)

On the back passage walkround there is an incident. First a misplaced kick sails from the central field into the five-a-side court and I go in pursuit of the lost yellow object—unfortunately the naughty dogs squeeze in after me and it takes some time to get them out. On the other side of the walkway they have left the gate wide open during a kiddie footie tournament and Winnie seizes this opportunity to wander down the touchline and take a crap. Dan is right behind her to clean up the mess but not before a mother, sitting with her back to the fence, takes time off to offer a gratuitous lecture on the gravity of this offense. Dan is furious and he and Janet both get into an angry exchange with this woman, who doesn't understand that the reason for shutting the gate is to prevent such incidents in the first place. Pre-empting the enemy, Dan and Janet then conclude a back-passage walkround by returning to the clubhouse to report to park management on this contretemps themselves.

Sunday, August 19:

Having escaped a drenching during a wet Saturday night, our luck runs out as Fritz and I face a rainy morning in the park. I remember, at the last minute, to strap on Fritz's raincoat—he hates the ripping sound that the Velcro makes and he acts as though he can neither pee nor poo in this straight jacket—but of course he can do both with no difficulty. Given the inclemency it is surprising that there is a really good turnout on the green, though I find Dan huddling under the little metal gazebo with Winnie and Bailey. Linda also arrives with Pepper so I venture forth myself and spend a few minutes in the light drizzle.

I can see Dan and Janet heading for the café after a few minutes so we follow them. At our table we have Dan, Janet, Suzanne, and Ellen. Dogs keep jumping into our laps with their wet feet—only to be repeatedly rejected by most of the owners, the only exception to this pattern being Janet, who has brought a towel for Daisy-Mae to sit on. The weather often worsens and it becomes very dark, with showers lashing away at the trees; then the moisture dissipates and calm returns for a few minutes.

After a while Hanna arrives under her big maroon umbrella and tells us, quite calmly, that George has died on Friday. She sings the praises of the Beaumont Animal Hospital in Camden, where the Hannibal Lecter of Paddington Rec was put to sleep, and tells us that he was cremated in a box containing an Indian shawl and a red rose from the back garden. It is the end of an era, for George was the oldest of the park dogs, at nineteen and a half, and had lead such a very interesting life, including a stint in Malibu. Hanna says that she cried on Saturday but that she is coping now. Later I see her on the pavement with that other ancient patient, Spadge.

Monday, August 20:

It is a depressing, grey day and my mood is not much better for I have just learned that one of Dorothy's friends, Vicky, is undergoing chemotherapy for lymphatic cancer. Preoccupied with this news I am overtaken by Laura Brown, pushing a pram with a toddler whose blond curls rise in tangled abundance from the top of her head. Laura, once a middle school colleague, stops to offer me her condolences. I am never far from reminders of Dorothy's passing these days. Then I have to catch up with Fritz, who seems to have a bit of string hanging from his bum.

Out on the green there is not much activity, indeed the whole park has a deserted feeling to it today. A lovely King Charles named Sam does rush over to greet me on my arrival. I follow Davide, who has Bailey as well as Daisy-Mae and Winnie, and Hanna, who is making slow progress with Spadge, into coffee. Hanna wants to sit at the corner table inside the forecourt because only then can she let her one surviving dog off lead. This is the table usually occupied by Peter and Ellen but today the latter chooses a little table under the eaves; indeed, it does look as though it might start raining again at any moment. Suzanne comes by and I give her two of the eight or so floppy disks, most containing earlier drafts of Dorothy's writing, that I can no longer open on any of our machines; she will see if she has any better luck at ASL.

Davide is full of complaints over Bailey, who is so ill-disciplined that he is impossible on lead (and he insists on jumping onto every surface at home). Evidently last night he attempted to mount one of the kitchen work surfaces and succeeded in knocking over the ketchup—which Davide's sister is still trying to clean up. Hanna says that she is going to the dentist (in Chorleywood) and that she and her flatmate take turns sitting with Spadge in the car while they trade places in the dentist's chair. She adds that Spadge misses George; he can't figure out why he doesn't collide with the white dog as he shuffles down the hall. Spadge is on a strict diet; he has had the runs and he twice pissed his own bed last night. As we begin a painfully slow march along the back passage it is not hard to imagine that he, too, may not be too long for this park.

Tuesday, August 21:

The chill wind that we could feel on our exit from the park yesterday is back in force today, another grey morning, and there is just a hint of mist in the breeze as well. Once again the park is almost empty and we don't encounter any other dogs before reaching the green. Here we find David with Skye (he confirms that Kate has a new Puli puppy), Saskia with Buddy, Suzanne with Sunny, Dan with Winnie, Daisy-Mae and Bailey, and a young woman with another Shih-tzu, Humphrey. Humphrey tries to mount Sunny, but his advances are rejected with some spirit. The incident doesn't seem to have dulled Sunny's appetite for hysterical barking and Suzanne's use of a bitter apple spray doesn't seem to be working at all at such moments.

Dan and I are alone when it is time to go in for coffee but we are soon joined by Albert and Suzanne. Dan's dogs are again poised on the threshold and every now and then one of us reminds them that they are *not* supposed to enter the café itself. Unfortunately, Elian, behind the counter, encourages Winnie, his favorite, to ignore this command, and so there is great confusion. Fritz insists on his freedom—not to enter the café, but to reach Ellen's table at toast time. When food arrives at our table Sunny again becomes hysterical. I try to appease her with a biscuit and she snatches it and two of my fingers in her eagerness for this treat.

Next to arrive is Jeremy, the retired GP, who is here on a rare visit with her Cressida. This pair used to be seen often in our park (and heard when not seen, for Jeremy has a stentorian voice when calling her pet) but they now live much of the year in North Yorkshire or on a long boat in Wolverhampton. Jeremy eats a muffin and a toasted sandwich but refuses to share any of this bounty with our dogs, who are quite puzzled by this selfishness. As we leave Dan passes on to the arriving Hanna a present from Janet, a beautifully framed photo of poor George.

Wednesday, August 22:

A stormy morning shows no signs of lessening its ferocity and so Fritz has to be hunted down and made to don his raincoat again. A light rain, intensified by the strong winds raking the park, keeps up a steady tattoo as we complete the back forty and head out to the green. A few stalwart dog owners are braving the elements here but Suzanne has no headgear and no raincoat and soon departs for the comforts of her flat. As the rain intensifies, Dan leads his trio off the grass and into the sheltering embrace of the little metal gazebo at the foot of Mt. Bannister.

I head here too but Fritz soon begins to wander and I have to follow him along the Randolph roadway. He gets far too close to the gate on this side before I can catch up with him. Bribed by a biscuit, I can attach his lead and begin the long walk back to the café. Dan, who soon falls into step beside me, is chafing under the responsibility of all these dogs, particularly the undisciplined Bailey. There is a consensus that leaving Georgie with Bailey for almost two months is a bit of a liberty—especially because Georgie has refused Ofra's offer of payment and because Ricky has been at home for much of this time. Dan and I agree that Ofra just has to insist on rewarding Georgie next time.

At coffee we have Ellen, Peter (returned from his holiday), Ronnie and Dan. The wind and rain continue to lash down as dark mutterings are heard about the absence of a real summer this year. The wet dogs keep trying to jump into our laps and such attempts are resisted successfully—but finally Dan takes pity on Daisy-Mae and settles the wet rag-mop down in his lap, even dressing her in Winnie's raincoat for warmth. There is no talk of a back-passage walkround today and we soon attempt a direct assault on the Morshead gate, where Dan has his car—Ronnie also having been offered a ride home. Unfortunately, as we leave, we encounter lots of poor little kids being lead into the park for some sodden sporting activity.

Thursday, August 23:

It isn't actually raining this morning, though I am still wearing my rain jacket against a chill wind. We haven't seen any sun here in days. Out on the green we encounter Linda, who has just trodden in something nasty, David with Skye, the ever-cheerful Saskia with Buddy, and Georgie, returned from Glasgow, and saddled once again with four dogs. Liam is on his way to jiu-jitsu class and he is wearing white—a big mistake for he is soon covered in brown paw prints. He helps me extract Fritz from the Grantully area where my dog has undertaken a private junket. Then he goes off to his lesson and I follow the others into the café.

When I arrive, some five minutes after the opening hour, I am struck by a most unusual sight. There are no lights on in the establishment, no chairs or tables have been taken out, and all the dog owners are sitting disconsolately on the picnic benches, staring into space. Eventually Elian and the pretty red-cheeked barista manage to get the place going but the till ribbon hasn't been changed and it takes another ten minutes for the doors to open definitively. This is enough time for Blake to lick leftovers from the table surfaces and to go foraging in the nearby bins. "Blake," someone says, "you've got yoghurt on your nose!"

Eventually we are able to sit down at our table in front of the café doors: Peter, Ellen (who treats everyone to coffee this morning), Ronnie, Hanna, Georgie, Albert and even Linda, who has returned from dropping Liam off. There is a huge queue inside and it takes forever for everyone to get served. Discussion turns to the epidemic of murderous activity among Britain's teens today. No one has much confidence in the response of government (Ronnie just wants to shoot some kids). Georgie reminds us that, in some matters, Scotland is leading the way in attacking public order offenses: all alcohol in public places (even at picnics in the park) confiscated, fines for improperly disposing of cigarette butts. I point out that Calvinist Scotland must be euphoric; if only they could bring back the Scarlet Letter.

Saturday, August 25:

I have missed a day of park duties as Tosh and I completed a seventh stage on the Chiltern Way and Linda kept an eye on Fritz. The sunny weather that we encountered in Oxfordshire yesterday afternoon has arrived in Paddington Rec as well—what a relief after so many grey and rainy days! Fritz and I make fairly speedy progress toward the green, where there is a large turnout, with the regular crowd sharing space with Roland's Saturday morning pupils. One of these is an eager Staffordshire who is dragging his master, a young black man, in his eagerness to join the class.

Dan is trying to escape the attentions of Bailey, who has just thrown up on the cricket crease. Daisy-Mae is behaving thuggishly to all the other little dogs, but she is always indulged in this behavior because of her junior status. Sparkie is stealing the balls belonging to other dogs and Fritz is staying reasonably close for once. As we reach the café we are joined by Suzanne and Sunny and, back after several weeks on Cape Cod, Liz with Roxy. The Beagle seems sleek and trim under the tutelage of the housesitter, but perhaps it is just that she has had a bath.

At coffee we have Georgie, Janet, Dan, Liz, Ellen, Peter, Suzanne and Ronnie. Liz is telling us that it was a hoot watching Davide at work on her flight to Boston and that, in an attempt to distract him from his very correct and professional demeanor, she tried to flirt with him whenever possible. A dominant topic of conversation is the Notting Hill Carnival, which gets under way this weekend. Because of its proximity to Maida Vale the event has a way of affecting our lives and our hearing and there are mixed reviews on the whole enterprise. Liz says she is taking her kids to see it tomorrow, Dan says he dislikes the event, and Hanna says that she plans to head over to Meanwhile Gardens and pick up some rice and peas, some curried goat and some jerk chicken. We begin a back passage walkround, which means we have to make way for the bumbling presence of Alfie the Briard.

Sunday, August 26:

It is a sunny morning (although clouds are heading our way) and I am happy with a short-sleeved shirt today. I keep a close eye of my dog's poo—since he wouldn't eat his tea last night (perhaps because I wasn't eating just then either) and there were a lot of tummy noises issuing from the pillow next to mine last night. Were these the signs of distress, or just an empty stomach contracting? His poo seems alright when I scoop it up just before we head out to the middle of the green. Here there is a lively weekend scene and the weather is so inviting that a movement toward the café comes some ten minutes after opening time.

Today we have Liz, Dan and Davide, Georgie, Hanna, Faz, Albert, Ronnie, Suzanne, Peter, Ellen and Janet. Just off in the distance you can hear the first wave of broadcast sound as the Notting Hill Carnival gets under way. Liz is wavering in her decision to take her boys to the event; few would want to accompany her but the consensus is that everyone should go at least once. There is some discussion of an article in the *Evening Standard* detailing the distribution of London's gangs. Peter suggests that we form our own gang and I say we already have one, The Dog People of Paddington Rec—no one messes with us. Elian sends out a gratis treat, two chopped up fried sausages. These are distributed when they cool down, at first by Faz and then by Dan and Janet. Faz, meanwhile, says that he is considering studying for a law degree; now that he is it be a father he wants a profession a little less dangerous than that of policeman.

Dan then reports that he spotted Michael and Frances yesterday and no sooner is this said then Michael himself makes a guest appearance. Fritz goes crazy in his delight over this reunion with his old pal, protesting loudly when any other dog wants some attention. Michael looks well enough but I notice that he has a tremor and that he has some difficulty rising from the crouching position after kneeling to greet the dogs. He tells us that he can no longer manage his garden and that, to preclude the inevitable disappointment, he keeps the shade down on that side of his flat permanently. In fact Michael is fighting his way through the housing bureaucracy in search of some form of sheltered accommodation. He seems in good enough spirits, however, and everyone enjoys his visit, which comes to an end when we attempt our back passage walkround.

Monday, August 27:

I could have used a bit more sleep this morning but for some reason, at about 5:00 am, a helicopter started hovering over West Kilburn, waking me and also, I soon learn, Janet. She and I complain to Faz, whom we meet on the green, about this typical Carnival-time intrusion, and he says he will try to discover, from internal records, just what his police colleagues were up to at such an early hour. ("Because we want compensation," I add.) It turns out that quite a few of the dog people did attend events yesterday (I was invited) and that the evening ended at Dan's house, where the host lost two pounds in a card game and then accidentally set fire to the paper on which scores were kept. He thinks that this is the end of the matter, since there is no longer written evidence of his debt, but Faz assures him that with all these witnesses a verbal commitment is enforceable.

Fritz is charmed by a rubber ball belonging to Sparkie and gets in some athletic jumps in snatching this toy off the turf on the bounce. It is pleasant on the green but again I could have used more clothing than my orange short-sleeved shirt. Three members of the ground crew are also wearing such shirts and I feel I should be chalking foul lines myself as they pass by—urged on by the houndlike baying of Roxy, whose cries of protest are greeted with good humor by the lads. It is about this time that I learn of another piece of mischief undertaken by my friends last night. For some reason they have bought a domain name off the Internet for £5.88—Fucktheplanet.co.uk. Today they are trying to figure out how they can exploit such a purchase, with a number of ideas for a tongue-in-cheek treatment of environmental issues.

We sit down for coffee: Faz, Dan, Georgie, Janet, Liz, Peter (no Ellen today), Albert, and Bailey—well the latter often takes a chair for himself before being displaced by one of the humans. Faz is discussing all the special purchases he has made for the expected arrival but Liz says he won't use any of it. ("That's all right," I say, "Jasmine can sleep in the Moses basket.") Near the end of our chatter the Australian lady arrives and takes a chair next to Albert. "I have healed more dogs and cats than any other human," she begins again. She gets up to circle the table and greet all the dogs, with Rosie again snapping at her. She says that she is 78, that she entertained troops in Viet Nam, that she wants to return to Australia but she has to wait for some money—which may be coming later this year as she has written something. While this monologue is going on, incidentally, Albert is signaling to me that I need to write all this down and Dan has had to excuse himself because he has gotten the giggles and left the table. Our visitor can't seem to finish a thought, "I've healed over 100 dogs, anyway . . ." On our back passage walkround Janet and I begin to speculate that perhaps it is all true and that we had better look her up on the Internet. Unfortunately no one seems to know her name. "I've asked her a couple of times," Albert adds, "but such information is always withheld."

Wednesday, August 29:

I have missed a day in the park because the glaziers arrived to repair a broken window, but now, under sunny skies, Fritz and I head for the park on a lively Wednesday morning. Fritz pauses to sample the grass shoots at the head of the track and then we make steady progress toward the green, where the other dog owners are already foregathered. David is here with Skye the Alsatian and he is deep in conversation with Liz, while Roxy rolls around in the grass, raising the oft-asked question, what is she rolling *in*? At the east end of the green we also have the three blonde bombshells: Sasha, Rufus, and Buddy. I approach the cricket crease where there is a strange apparition.

I am referring, of course, to the sight of a man in pin-striped trousers, white long-sleeved shirt, and necktie, in short a dress far more formal than would seem appropriate for this spot (where I am likely to wear the same schlock clothes for a week). The chap is the owner of the delightful puppy, Vito, who is having the time of his life wrestling with an equally excited Daisy-Mae. From the Morshead walkway I can see Linda arriving with Pepper. There is a recognition scene as Fritz squats down to face Pepper's charge, evading his advancing cousin only at the last minute. Thereafter the two Schnauzers pal around in the far corners of the park, but when I see Fritz heading for the Randolph exit while Pepper is heading for the café, I know it is time to follow the former. One more poo poo later we follow the others to our local eatery, where a party of interlopers has taken our usual table!

A smaller version is selected nearby and we sit down: today we have Suzanne, Hanna, Georgie, Ronnie and Susie, Linda, Liz and Albert. Much of the morning's conversation is devoted to horses, since Susie's daughter has just bought a miniature Shetland pony, Linda used to instruct the disabled in horsemanship, and Georgie's daughter Lynn is taking up the sport. The dogs, after snacking on toast, sausage, carrots and biscuits, begin to misbehave. Sunny is barking hysterically at shadows, Roxy has to be apprehended after frightening a child at another table in her relentless search for chips, and Daisy-Mae has camped at the feet of a table full of community policemen. We are also beginning to see faces that have been absent for a while. Peter, for instance, arrives with Gypsy and two spaniels and, on our back passage walkround, we encounter a well-tanned Denise, walking with Rizzo.

Thursday, August 30:

Gray skies have returned, though the temperatures are still mild enough, as Fritz and I make our way into the park. Progress is quite rapid and after a brief penetration of the precincts of the café, where Ronnie is already seated, we head for the center of the green. As yesterday Fritz crouched down to withstand the charge of Pepper so today it is Pepper's turn to hide in plain sight as Fritz attacks. Thereafter my dog disappears—I find him doing a poo in the foliage behind the bandstand. On the cricket crease the owners are engrossed in their conversation; somebody tells me that two dogs (with Pepper batting leadoff) have peed on Daisy-Mae. Hanna says that Fritz has a beard that smells of fox pee.

Out onto the green comes another in the recent line of rovers returned. This time it is Ofra, who has been away so long that this is the first time she had seen me since Dorothy died—and that was seven weeks ago today. At coffee she tells us about Guy's bar mitzvah in Israel. Not surprisingly, the dress that she chose for the occasion was mistakenly locked up at the shuttered dry cleaners, which had to be opened especially for her only half an hour before the ceremony. Bailey seems delighted to be reunited with his mistress but Georgie now blames Bailey's food foraging for the loss of James' teeth in the toilet. Dan tells Ofra that her dog, though sweet, is awful on lead and—he doesn't know how to put this—dumb. For her part Ofra responds, "I hear you have been throwing ketchup all over my dog."

Also joining us at breakfast are Liz, Hanna, Ronnie, Linda and Albert. Fritz jumps into Linda's lap—he hasn't jumped into mine in months but then he craves female attention especially now. Liz has brought with her series 5 and 6 of *The Sopranos*—which Dorothy had so much looked forward to seeing. Lots of little kids are herded into the forecourt and, as they begin to focus on our lot, there are suspicious growls from Winnie. "She doesn't like children, does she?" Albert says. "Oh I don't know," Dan responds, "she can get through at least two, maybe two and a half on a good day."

Friday, August 31:

Shortly before 9:00 Pepper arrives for a day-long visit, and five minutes later I head for the park with two Schnauzers on lead. This lasts only as far as the entrance gate, where I let Fritz go—I am not confident enough in Pepper's behavior off-lead to duplicate this gesture. Before we have travelled far the first of the morning's poo poos has to be cleaned up (Pepper wins this sweepstakes today, 3-2). A pigeon is hanging upside down sampling the elderberries as we continue beyond the cypress trees and make our way out to the green. I lose track of Fritz here; he turns up in the middle of the pack, where Peter (of Peter and Holly) is trying to take individual portraits of the dogs with his camera.

At 9:30 we head in for coffee and, handing both dogs over to Ronnie while I go inside, I order my cappuccino and some toast for the dogs. At breakfast we have Ronnie, Dan, Peter, Ellen, Faz, Suzanne, Georgie, Hanna and Albert. Ellen has been missing for several days with a stomach complaint and Suzanne is getting a cold. Her Sunny becomes hysterical over the presence of food and begins a round of piercing barking, with Suzanne explaining that dogs who look appealing but don't bark get much more food than the barkers. Faz is tired after a late night antenatal class but Dan is bubbling over with plans for a weekend in Sardinia. I keep Pepper anchored to my chair and, for once, he adds little to the barkathon.

Just as we are winding up proceedings a BT van comes racing down the Carlton roadway, hurtling over the speed bumps as though they were just so many launching pads. There is universal condemnation among the dog owners, who recognize the danger such speed presents to their animals and to the toddlers arriving for play in the adjacent playground. Five minutes later the driver begins a reverse lap and this time the usually mild-mannered Dan jumps from his seat, a coffee cup in one hand, Winnie under the other arm, and dashes out to the roadway to intercept the miscreant. We can hear raised voices and Faz rushes over to the spot as backup, flashing his warrant card in the process. We can hear the driver agreeing that he has taken Dan's point and the incident comes to an end. I allow Fritz to remain off-lead on the back passage walkround, not caring to play cat's cradle with the leads until we round the final corner, where Fritz accepts his usual restraint. As soon as we reach home the two begin a day of furious wrestling and recuperative naps.

September, 2007

Saturday, September 1:

It's bright enough as Fritz and I begin another day in the park, and I am even wearing my sunglasses—but after only a few minutes I realize that these specs are completely redundant; it is soon overcast, cloudy and grey, and there is even a hint of moisture in the air. I am expecting Fritz to make a slow start of it, tired from a day of wrestling with Pepper, but he makes his move toward the green in a lively enough fashion. At a picnic table in the forecourt of the café I can see two early-comers, Faz and Suzanne, bending intently over a backgammon board.

Out on the green we have the usual Saturday grouping; one of Roland's assistants has a small class of canine scholars including Polo, the straining Staffie, and Sabina's Oscar, who is here for a little help with recall. Fritz acts as the control group, visiting all the pupils in an effort to distract them from their studies. On the cricket crease Georgie with Sparkie, Janet with Daisy-Mae and Winnie, and Rhian with Otw, are sprawled comfortably. Several non-dog owners have arrived with little kids—just to see the doggies—one toddler begins to cry when her toy (a small plush dog, ironically) is pinched by Daisy-Mae; another wants to hand out my biscuits to the dogs and he even follows me as I begin to dog Fritz's footsteps, demanding more biscuits for the remaining pooches— "I need more because they're waiting!"

Numbers are somewhat diminished at breakfast—Peter and Ellen have their own table, so do the backgammoners, Liz is attending a bar mitzvah in Jerusalem, and Dan and Davide are at a wedding in Wales, so we just have Georgie, Janet, Hanna, and Ronnie. Janet says that Daisy-Mae is relentless in her pursuit of the harried Winnie and Georgie decides to take the Pug home in order to give her some peace. (Janet also reports that Daisy-Mae was discovered chewing on a snail that she had brought in from the garden.) Ronnie announces that Susie is away at the Burley Horse Trials ("I say they're all guilty," he adds).

Things are winding down when we have another visit from our Australian octogenarian (well, she is several years younger today), who joins us with her cappuccino—after again exciting the protests of the usually docile Rosie. Our guest launches into another biographical monologue and this time Janet says, "What's your name—so we can look you up on the Internet." Kathleen McCormack, for that is the name supplied, now tells us she has written seven books on clairvoyance and asks each of us where we live and how old we are. Then she wants to know who's coming over to visit her today. There are no takers—but then she should have known that. When I get home I look her up; yes, there are titles on Tarot reading by the lady.

Sunday, September 2:

It's a sunny day (i.e., a day on which Suzanne's Sunny is bedeviled by shadows and the rest of us by her hysterical barking). It's cool enough to make the wearing of a sweatshirt a comfortable choice. The park itself seems quite empty and, indeed, the only sign of life as we near the green is the lively presence of Beano. As usual the Tibetan Terrier is delighted to see a pal of his youth, but Fritz is his customary intemperate self. "A full body wag," his mom says to Beano, "and all you get is growls."

Only Georgie and Janet are present on the green; under any circumstances I don't linger long in this spot as Fritz is off on his rambles and I have to follow him. We stroll along the Randolph walkway then turn right at the tennis courts, then return to the green—where I can see a much larger turnout now. Dan has arrived, Ofra is heading toward the group and Suzanne is being urged to purchase the same anti-barking device that seems to have been effective in reducing Sparkie's bad habits.

Ofra is a bit wistful when we forego the pleasures of a picnic table in the sun but, in any event, we could not all sit comfortably at one of the wooden colossi, since we have more than eight: Janet, Georgie, Suzanne, Dan, Davide, Ronnie, Peter, Ellen, Ofra, and Albert. Georgie begins the session by telling us that her James has been cautioned for smoking in a forbidden part of his local pub. Ronnie circulates a letter from a friend who traps squirrels and then drowns them. Ronnie finds this amusing; the rest of us are appalled. Simon, Maddy, and Princess each have a go at penetrating the darkness beneath our knees and each time Fritz reacts to this intrusion by non-pack members with his customary growls. The others seem rooted to their seats this morning and I can't stand it any longer—so for once I depart first, heading directly for the exit gate.

Monday, September 3:

It is a cool grey morning as we begin another week in Paddington Rec. On the walkway between the fences we encounter Storm, the Alsatian puppy. It is the first time I have seen him off lead. He is delighted to see Fritz and bounces up and down on his huge paws. Fritz pays little attention and we have soon reached the green, where, hiding under Kate's feet, we have the first appearance of her new nine week-old Puli puppy, Isla. (This little bundle of black fur will be a long time in developing her Rasta dreadlock curls, evidently.) Fritz heads over to the bandstand to greet Hanna, here with Spadge; here he also does a poo, and then it is time to go in for coffee.

This morning we have Janet, Georgie, Albert, Ronnie, Jasmina, Kate, Hanna, and Davide—whom we send to join the long queue with our orders. Janet passes around some pictures showing our dogs misbehaving with plates of food. I have to remind her that the other day I saw Daisy-Mae (no longer the youngest kid on the block) with a cigarette in her mouth. Kate has just returned from a long holiday in France but I think she drank too much wine because she says she twice went canoeing on the Loire and when I asked her what part of this river she utilized her answer was that it was somewhere between Nimes and Avignon.

Once again I feel the need to make a move before the rest of them get underway and so, when Kate leaves, I get up as well. It's just as well that Isla has touched the turf (after spending coffee hour in her new mommy's lap) because a runny doo doo—which Kate has to cover with loose earth—follows almost immediately. Kate, like so many other friends, spends the next few minutes quizzing me on how well I am functioning on my own. (I am functioning.) We pass Peter sitting on a bench with Holly, Sandy and Jack, obviously pulling triple duty today. At the exit gate I ask Kate if Isla is to go on lead. The answer is that Skye (who seems quite comfortable with her new sister) goes on lead; Isla doesn't even have a collar with a belt loop; she has to be tucked under Kate's free arm for the journey home.

Tuesday, September 4:

At 9:00 Linda arrives with Pepper, fearing that the tube strike and the consequent traffic chaos will make it difficult for her to get back to her dog after an appointment near St. Paul's. (For that matter we decide to reschedule an appointment with my lawyer that we had made for tomorrow morning.) So I have Pepper again but by now he is very used to our routine. After a few minutes of roaring face fighting I put leads on both of the boys and we make our way over to the park, where I let Fritz go. We also encounter Jean-Baptiste and he reverses direction with his Hercules so he can accompany us back to the green and fill me in on his holiday in Turkish Cyprus.

On the green I can see dog owners in several groupings and I head for the one nearest the cricket crease. Vito is present this morning and he and Daisy-Mae have resumed their ecstatic wrestling match. The little Shih-Tzu also manages to distinguish herself by eating some of the chalk that one of the park attendants is laying down nearby; she ends up with paint on her nose, but then Winnie also has paint on her whiskers. At one point Rufus wanders over from the other doggy group and Fritz, uncertain if Rufus has a paid-up membership, chases the Labrador away. When we go in to coffee we do pass the other grouping; here we find Chica the Boxer, whom we have not seen in some time, and little Jack, the tiniest Yorkie.

At breakfast, where there are lots of complaints that the coffee is cold, we have Peter, Ellen, Ronnie, Georgie, Dan, Ofra, and Liz. The latter has just returned from a bar mitzvah in Jerusalem and we get a full report on her adventure. Ellen has bought a bacon sandwich for the dogs and Liz orders some sausages for them as well. I anchor Pepper to one chair leg and Fritz to another; this leaves my arms free to clutch my chest, for although it is sunny today and I have a sweatshirt on, I am still chilly. When we begin a back passage walkround I rush ahead with my lads so that I can retrieve and then return a Tupperware bowl that Ofra had sent over with chicken soup some two months ago. As I return to the park with this piece of plastic I encounter the American mom who has the two cockers, Jake and Domino. Jake has been missing for some time.

Wednesday, September 5:

The skies are grey but it is warm enough as Fritz and I make our way into the park on a quiet Wednesday morning. Out on the green there is a lively scene—at one point I count a dozen owners, all known to me except for the chap who has brought Humphrey the Shih-tzu this morning. Out of my pocket comes the little blue ball that has been residing for many months in one of the freezer drawers of the refrigerator. It has made its home there because, if allowed to play with this toy *within* the house, Fritz manages to knock it under sofas and other low-lying pieces of furniture and I am always on my knees trying to winkle it out while my dog moans in distress. My object this morning, as Cathy defrosts at home, is to *lose* the ball—as we have lost so many others—but after chasing it down several times Fritz manages to retain possession of the accursed object.

At coffee we have Dan, Georgie, Hanna, Ronnie, Linda, Ofra, Natasha and Liz. I say we have them but it is clear that the latter two ladies are more interested in their texts and their phone calls and so we *don't* have them; indeed if the mobile phone is supposed to facilitate communication it also has to be said that its presence can eliminate it altogether. Behind us Albert comes to sit down with Saffy and Tinkerbelle. I remind him that the new Keira Knightley film, *Atonement*, is about Dunkirk. "That sure separated the men from the boys," he adds, "never seen so many runners in all my life."

The dogs enjoy a bounty of biscuits, toast, sausage and scrambled eggs. When the feeding frenzy is concluded Winnie, perched on Dan's lap, decides to leap on Bailey from a great height: no more Miss Nice Gal today. Behind us a group of young pupils, having completed their laps around the green, enter the forecourt for refreshments and they soon make a spectator sport of our gathering, perching themselves atop the wall in order to comment on each of the pooches in our group, eventually coming forward to embrace Daisy-Mae and Bailey. Just as we are about to begin our back passage walkround, Michaela arrives with Skye the Cairn; we have seen neither recently; their return is another sign that summer is coming to an end.

Wednesday, September 6:

I am able to wear a short-sleeved shirt again as Fritz and I head for the park on a sunny and warm Wednesday morning. Once again I have forgotten something, in this case my necessary supply of poo poo bags. Improvising, I empty all of Fritz's biscuits into my pocket and tear the biscuit bag in half. This strategy pays off when, a few minutes later, Fritz backs up to a tree and deposits his second installment directly at the feet of a lime-vested Vista security guard.

Out on the green there is a lively scene. Bekki is chasing her Chica, and Vito is making off with Natasha's sweater, having noticed this intriguing sleeve lying on the turf. Skye the Cairn resumes his usual obsession, dropping his tennis ball repeatedly at my feet. And Fritz is not very interested in any of this, beginning a ramble around the periphery at the Grantully gate. I follow slowly and in this fashion miss a visitation by the head of the Orangemen, who marches out to address the other owners on some matter of urgency. It takes me a while to make contact with someone who has heard the word: some owners have been allowing their dogs to run loose in the flower garden and this is clearly not on! Are you listening, Bailey?

When I go in to coffee (the red-cheeked barista taking my order and my money while delivering an outside order) we have only Ronnie, Peter and Ellen. The others arrive in dribs and drabs, first Liz, then Ofra, then Hanna, then Georgie. The latter arrives with Bailey's lead, which Ofra has forgotten on the green. The café is a hub of activity this morning, with yesterday's school group returned and lots of moms, having deposited older kids at school, enjoying a few moments with the toddlers. Many of these little kids want to pet the dogs and this leads to a great confusion, with kids on roller skates, moms, prams, baristas, and dogs in a disorganized mess. Liz reports that last night Roxy ate a whole pint of Haagen Dazs Belgian Chocolate ice cream. There is an enduring supposition that chocolate is bad for dogs but Roxy seems fine—in fact she seems better than fine, she seems hungry.

Friday, September 7:

The weather continues on the warm side as Fritz and I head for the park, a goodly supply of poo poo bags in my pocket this time. On the green I am surprised to see just how many dog owners have brought their pets out on a weekday; indeed I have counted up to fifteen by the time we reach the cricket crease. Soon after I arrive a woman appears with a shopping bag and begins to distribute copies of a new magazine, *London Dogtails*, which is edited by her son, Ryan Gottsche. She has picked the right people to interest in this project; indeed, Dan reminds us that Winnie has actually attended the Pug party in Green Park—which is covered in one of the features of this publication.

Fritz has Pepper to play with while other pairings include Vito and Daisy-Mae. The grass is wet after a little overnight rain and the latter is soon a sordid mess, half her usual size. I notice that a number of the dogs are wilting a bit in the sun. Otw has run out of steam, Fritz is lying in Dan's shadow and Sunny is barking at the shadows. When we at last head for coffee, loath to abandon the sunshine, the first port of call is the water trough outside the loos.

At breakfast we have Liz, Georgie, Janet, Dan, Faz, Ronnie, and Suzanne, with Albert as outrider and Hanna and Rowena at a small table of their own. For some reason three sausages are ordered and the dogs get to share out this rare treat. Faz, who has the job of tearing these tidbits into little pieces, looks really tired, but he is beginning a four-day rest period. The dogs give their owners no rest—as one after another they wander off on their own missions, each time necessitating an anxious query, "Where's Sparkie, Daisy-Mae, Roxy, etc?" This is how Fritz used to behave as well, but then for the last couple of years he has been firmly anchored to his lead while I finish my cappuccino.

Saturday, September 8:

We have grey, overcast weather this morning and I am back in my sweatshirt as Fritz and I make our entry today. Very soon we encounter Michaela with Skye and Linda with Pepper. Fritz insists on a mega-greeting from Linda and this means commanding her undivided attention, especially when her own dog tries to get into the act. When we reach the green Sparkie is playing keep-away with a small leather ball belonging to Maddy, the King Charles. The other dogs do try to chase the speedy Yorkie but he is much faster than any of them and the only time they have a chance is when he lies down in the grass to recover. Fritz, of course, has nothing to do with these hijinks and I am soon following him over hill and dale on his own secret mission.

When it is time to head in for coffee I notice that my dog disdains our own table in favor of the bench in the forecourt where he can sit next to Ellen and bury his nose in her purse. Eventually he returns and scarfs down a series of biscuits while we wait (a long time, this morning) for something more substantial. Today we have Ronnie, Janet, Faz, Georgie, Ofra and Davide. Faz has a new mobile phone and so he and the others have to exchange numbers. He complains that Di has thrown away his favorite jacket and he is consequently freezing. Janet is taking portrait shots of the dogs with her camera—always a difficult task since these animals are in perpetual motion. Jasmine throws up. Just as we are about to leave Ofra asks Janet if her trousers actually look like pajama bottoms and Janet says that they do.

We begin a back passage walkround. Sparkie finds an empty plastic bottle and begins a game of keep-away with Daisy-Mae and Jasmine. Five-a-side football players are laboring on our right and as we near the top of the track we encounter the Saturday morning exercise class, circling the playing field and throwing down their heavy poles in a pile at our last corner. Here Ofra, who has been carrying a DKNY shopping bag, produces another container of chicken soup for me. "Wait," she adds as I head for my exit, "you forgot the croutons!"

Sunday, September 9:

It is still somewhat overcast when Fritz and I reach the park this morning, with temperatures mild enough, and the sun attempting to break through. On the green things are pretty quiet for a Sunday morning, just Saskia with Buddy, Georgie with Sparkie, Janet with Daisy-Mae, Ofra with Bailey, and Faz with Jasmine. One of these dogs throws up on the cricket crease. In sporting news Saskia reports that her husband has returned from France—where he went to watch England play in the rugby world cup—in a surprisingly sober state. Asked for an explanation, he evidently blamed the poor quality of French beer. Ofra, meanwhile, has accompanied her family to the new Wembley, where she watched England trounce Israel 3-0. I ask her if she is greatly disappointed and she says that after the first goal she put on her red England shirt.

When it is time to go in for coffee I have some difficulty getting organized. Ofra has, for the second day in a row, brought me my lunch, chicken and rice today, and I put my shopping bag down on our table and go in to place my order at the counter. But when I return Fritz has gone walkabout and I have to follow him as he strolls down the Morshead walkway, turning around only when I offer the bribe of a biscuit. By the time I get back to the table my medium cappuccino has been delivered but the foam is frosting over.

Today we have a large turnout of Peter, Ellen, Faz, Janet, Ofra, Georgie, Ronnie, Liz, and Davide, with Hanna at her own table, Albert sitting behind us, and Linda and Liam taking the places of the early-departing Peter and Ellen. Faz is more warmly dressed today but the subject of disappearing clothing returns. Ronnie says that his ex-wife once gave away his favorite green jacket; he arrived home one day to discover that the window washer was wearing it. Ofra reports that she has another bar mitzvah to go to and that, once again, all the dresses she might wear today are locked up at the dry cleaners. There are still ten of us in the untidy procession that next undertakes the back passage walkround. Near the end we encounter Rowena, who has been wrestling with the undergrowth where her Timmy has lost his ball. At our exit we are joined by Rob and Pepper; the latter then returns to the house with Fritz to begin another play date.

Monday, September 10:

It is still overcast, though not at all chilly, as Fritz and I make our way into the park at the beginning of another week. I can hear a roar of disapproval as Fritz is greeted by Cosmo, here making his way along the walkway with Lancer the Lab—but soon thereafter we have reached the Carlton walkway where it is Oscar who wants to say hello. I am baffled a bit by Fritz's next move—paying no attention to Oscar or Scamp, my dog races up the road purposefully because he has spotted an abandoned yellow tennis ball just asking for a new owner.

We take the ball with us to the green and here Fritz has a good time chasing it down after I have thrown it or (in some cases) kicked it for him. I notice that, for the first time, little Isla has actually been allowed to run free; she seems to be afraid of the really big dogs (except for her big sister, Skye) but she seems content to stay pretty close to Kate's feet.

Vito is also here and he and Daisy-Mae have a prolonged tussle near the cricket crease. Jo arrives with Tilly, the Border Terrier, from one corner and Faz arrives with Jasmine from another, but it's past 9:30 and time for me to head in for coffee.

At breakfast this morning we have Ronnie, Suzanne, Ofra, Georgie, Hanna, Davide and even Jeremy. I have to let Fritz go so that he can check out the toast dispersal at Peter and Ellen's table. Meanwhile Rosie takes exception first to Fritz and then to Cressida—and Ronnie fears that he might have to take her home. I have to head for home early today, an appointment in the offing, and so Fritz and I begin a slow stroll toward the Morshead gate.

Tuesday, September 11:

I am wearing just a short-sleeved shirt again, though I wouldn't describe the temperature as warm; at least there is plenty of sun as Fritz and I head for the green. There are about ten dog owners milling about and Fritz checks out a number of them in search of a welcoming cuddle. He then begins his wandering; I can see him staring down at the rest of us from the hillside leading to the Grantully gate. He is certainly the most independent of all these dogs, but he rarely abuses this privilege.

At my feet are the blonde trio of Buddy, Rufus, and Sasha. Buddy is lying on his back with an orange ball belonging to Chica in his mouth. Saskia is a bit distressed by this behavior and tries to extract the ball without success until I produce the bribe of a Shape biscuit, whereupon Buddy rights himself and yields the prize. Now Saskia explains that last February Buddy did the same thing, bit the ball in half, then swallowed everything. Nothing emerged from the other end and his stomach showed signs of swelling so he had to go under the surgeon's knife. No wonder Saskia was worried.

At breakfast we have Georgie, Davide, Suzanne, Ronnie, Ofra and Kate. (Hanna seems happier with her own little table in the background these days.) Fritz actually jumps into my lap, a real rarity these days, joining the other elevated dogs like Sparkie, Isla, Winnie, and Bailey. Georgie says that Daisy-Mae sneezed twice this morning on the way to the park and that both times Sparkie jumped, thinking that his anti-barking collar had been activated. Ronnie tells us a joke. An Arab is crawling through the desert, dying of thirst. Eventually he spots an Israeli who has a roadside stall. His attempt at obtaining a drink is foiled, however, because the stallholder explains that he sells neckties only. "But half a mile over this hill there is a really nice restaurant; you can get a drink there." So the Arab crawls on and an hour later he is back, still on his knees. "What happened?" the Israeli asks. (Here Ronnie, begins to splutter in merriment as he gets to the end of the story and we have to get him to repeat the punchline.) "They wouldn't let me into the restaurant," the Arab says, "without a necktie." The surprising thing about this joke, I add, is that it defies all our expectations—having nothing whatever to do with the Arab-Israeli conflict.

Tuesday, September 12:

It is another pleasant morning in the park, but it is also two months to the day since Dorothy died, and my heart is heavy. We make two entrances today—since at 7:00 Fritz shows obvious signs that he would just as soon go out *now*. I take him into the doggy area next to the Morshead gate and here my ill-advised decision to give my dog some superfluous Chinese food last night results in a bit of an explosion. Hopefully a few more sequels will have cleared the tummy—but I decide not to give Fritz any more food today.

At 9:15 we are back on the green, with Fritz heading for a small contingent near the cricket crease. Dan has returned from his long weekend in Sardinia and he kneels to give Fritz a cuddle. He is talking to a pretty young blonde woman in a tracksuit; she has brought with her an adorable three month-old Dachshund puppy named Roxy. Roxy, who is sporting a leopard-skin halter, bustles about on her little legs and soon attracts the attention of Isla, who pursues the newcomer in delighted circles. After a while I move on to a grouping of larger dogs including Sasha, Buddy and Chica but while I am talking to Saskia she asks me where Dan is going. I turn around and see the returned rover heading for work via the Grantully gate—with Fritz is tow. "More importantly," I add, "where do you suppose Fritz is going?" My dog soon returns to the center of the green, just as Davide comes in to take charge of Winnie, whereupon Fritz heads for the Randolph walkway and I have to follow him. I discover an abandoned soccer ball on the flanks of Mt. Bannister and this keeps some of the dogs occupied until it is time to go in for coffee.

This morning we have Ronnie, Georgie, Davide, Peter, Ellen, Suzanne, and Ofra. I have to tell the others not to give Fritz any food and they comply, though Ellen does a wonderful job of comforting the invalid, whom I have attached to the leg of my chair. Vito rushes in to wrestle with Daisy-Mae—it has been some time since we have had so many puppies in our midst. Things are winding down when Liz arrives with the original Roxy and grabs our attention by telling us that she has another family saga to relate. It seems that on Sunday her tenth grader, having knocked a ping-pong ball into the backyard of the surgery next door, attempted to retrieve it by climbing onto an overhanging awning. Unfortunately he fell twenty feet, and broke his arm in two places. There was no one home but Liz soon arrived to hear the lad's screams for help. It took her a while to find where he was located and to call the emergency services. The surgery, of course, was closed and ambulance crews (two of these) and firemen (two trucks worth), sixteen emergency workers in all, wrestled with stretchers and cranes for two and a half hours before the doctor showed up and unlocked the surgery. An operation at St. Mary's left the injured youngster with two pins in his arm and an excuse not to write for six weeks—or so he quoted his doctor. Liz soon discovered that this was a lie, part of a pattern of misbehavior that has manifested itself in the shadow of a marital breakdown. At home the local barber now approached Liz to tell her that her boys, their friends and girl friends, had been climbing to the top of five-story houses, leaping between them and holding nighttime parties in the skies. I tell Liz that this is all her fault; if she had bought her son a *second* ping-pong ball none of this would have happened. She agrees—after noting, in mitigation, that Roxy had eaten all the other balls. Things happen to Liz.

Friday, September 14:

My visit to the park yesterday was a very brief one—as Fritz is again ailing. The problem was perhaps occasioned by that mistaken gesture on my part—as I was concluding my evening meal on Tuesday night I let the ever-attentive Fritz finish off some of the ready-meal Chinese food that I had been eating myself. I was a bit surprised to see him do two poo poos on the street that night but by the time he had twice vomited in the TV room the next afternoon and had produced increasingly runny poos (culminating in a bloody stool Thursday morning) I knew it was time to phone the vets.

I got an appointment almost immediately and, a vial containing some of the aforementioned specimen in my pocket, we made our way through the park a second time and by 10:15 had reported to Dr. Sarah. She was not quite convinced that Chinese food was the culprit in the present incident, but she decided to have my sample tested, gave Fritz a shot, and issued pills, intestinal formula food, and colonic paste—"You're getting to be an old hand at squeezing this on his food, aren't you?" she said of the latter. Fritz twice squatted on the way home, issuing a horrible bloody mess, but he likes his convalescent food and he seemed to settle down comfortably enough.

This morning he produces a quite satisfactory poo as we are walking through the park on the way to *my* doctor's surgery where I have to drop off a prescription renewal request. Thereafter we join a small grouping at a table outside the café doors (Georgie, Ronnie, and Liz), though I have to remind the others not to give Fritz any food. Liz says that ASL has cancelled athletic competitions in Surrey after another outbreak of foot and mouth disease. "I don't think there is any chance of our students catching it," I add unkindly.

Saturday, September 15:

I have a keen interest in my dog's poo this morning, but I am gratified by color and consistency when he squats in a sunny weed patch. I am glad *I* am making such an effort to restore Fritz to good health. His contribution to this convalescence last night was to snatch a chicken bone off the pavement and carry it for six blocks in his mouth before it was disgorged at home. We have to work our way through the Saturday morning obedience class on our way to the cricket crease. Fritz makes his usual attempt to disrupt matters (Polo the Staffie is back for more tuition) but today the opposite is also true; two small dogs, Zimba and Paddy, play hooky and so does a Sunny look-alike named Mungo.

There are some anomalies in the ownership line-up this morning. First, Ofra arrives with her rarely seen husband, Ricky (Bailey is beside himself with pride over the presence of his daddy here). And Ronnie arrives with no dog at all, since Rosie is having her hair cut. "I didn't want to miss a day," he says. "Quite right," I reply, "no unexcused absences for you." When we go in for coffee the group settles around a picnic table in the sun. I choose Albert's chair. Almost immediately Sparkie jumps into my lap (Ofra has noted astutuely I must be going somewhere directly from the park because I am wearing my tan chinos). I quickly brush the cheeky Yorkie off; unfortunately he lands on Fritz and there are words. I do know why has Sparkie selected *my* lap—it is hard to find lap space when owners are bellied up to the unwelcoming picnic tables. Peter comes in with Gypsy and the two fluffy spaniels often seen in his company these days, Flo and Daisy.

I have not settled in because after only five minutes Fritz and I have to make our way to Boundary Road, where at 10:00 Dr. Rachel gives him the all-clear. Our group has scattered by the time we return to the park, though I suspect that may be them *far* ahead of us as we begin a lonely back passage walkround. The Saturday morning exercise class is stretching those lazy muscles as we reach the last corner and head for home.

Sunday, September 16:

We have a sunny morning in the park but it is no longer very warm and I am wearing a sweatshirt comfortably. Fritz gets some distance ahead of me, which is not altogether advisable—since these days I want to check his poo. Out on the green Janet tells us that her neighbor has spoken to her to the effect that Albert's wife is ailing with cancer and that she hopes Janet will look after the old fellow and the two little dogs if anything happens. Albert, it is assumed, is in complete denial. At coffee he joins our conversation about the Post Office Tower—which he had helped to wire when it first went up.

This morning we have Faz, Georgie, Janet, Ofra, Dan and Ronnie. For some reason the conversation is devoted to the subject of flying. Georgie and Albert hate flying and Dan loves it. Ronnie says that he isn't afraid of flying, it's just crashing he doesn't like. I describe the balloon ride that Dorothy and I took at Luxor in February, the one that ended with our slicing into a sugar cane field—where the local urchins grabbed the ropes and put their hands out looking for a contribution. "And so they finally discovered what de-nile really means," Ronnie adds.

Doggy activities are not over for the day, however, because in the afternoon we have the annual doggy-park picnic (or D.P.P., as it is written on the chocolate cake that Dan brings to the gathering shortly after 2:00). We are foregathered this time on the hillside overlooking the tennis courts adjacent to the bowling green. There is a groaning board, with all sorts of goodies including a lasagna that my friend Morag has baked for me. I am complemented on it repeatedly. "Great defrosting," someone says. "It took me hours," I reply truthfully. Fritz is attached to a leg of Ronnie's chair and he is soon frustrated by this and by my refusal to let him have too much people food. Most of the other dogs are free to roam, but only Sparkie abuses this privilege. There is a constant danger that the dogs will help themselves to food, especially when Roxy arrives. I am sitting on the grass and while I am distracted Fritz pulls a humus and tara soaked pitta onto my trousers as he helps *himself* from my plate. Vito arrives (with parents and two of their friends) and he and Sparkie take turns mugging Daisy-Mae. Kate is here with her friend Bob and her two dogs. Isla takes a hunk of fur out of Skye's tail and runs around with it in her mouth. Angie arrives with Trouble and tells us that Michael won't be coming this year. Hanna arrives late, just as I am leaving, with her Spadge hopping along. She has missed the group photo, which included eighteen humans and about the same number of dogs.

Monday, September 17:

It is overcast this morning, though it is again a mild enough temperature as we make our way forward at the start of another week in the park. A woman who has been stopping at the workout apparatus is followed by a big black and white dog, who, trailing well behind her, squats to do an undetected poo near the parallel poles. Making his way toward us is a chap being dragged by two huffing Staffies. "Would you mind putting your dog on lead?" he shouts. I do this, though I *do* wonder what the point is of keeping dogs that are so unreliable that the rest of us have to adjust to their menace.

On the green there is a gathering of dog owners near the cricket crease. Unfortunately Fritz is not interested in any of this and begins a long period of wandering, with me in slow pursuit. I say unfortunately because I feel rather light-headed today and so it's not easy bending over to pick up my dog's deposits. We pass behind the tennis courts and revisit the site of yesterday's picnic. Someone has done a good job of clean-up; you can't tell that anyone was here yesterday. By the time we have returned to the green we have Pepper making an appearance and Linda accompanies us into coffee soon thereafter.

Much of this morning's conversation involves further news and analysis of yesterday's doggy picnic. The event continued until darkness had drawn in, but not before there had been a contretemps, with security guards intervening, when Dan asked some tennis players, who had been on the same court for hours, if Ofra and Liz's boys could have a turn—a request denied. A number of the owners were a bit the worse for wear after drinking wine all afternoon (and can't remember how they got home). Meanwhile Sparkie and Bailey had begun to mount Isla and Daisy-Mae. I object to this episode of under-age sex but I am assured that a zap on Sparkie's remote control collar could get him to jump off. Kate, listening to this tale, wonders if there is a human version of this collar—"only this one would make the man jump on."

Tuesday, September 18:

There is a cool tang in the air this morning, though the sun is shining brightly—a reminder that autumn will soon be here. The park has yet to come to life, with no one on the track or on any of the playing fields. Fritz is interested in a Bichon Frise, whom he passes as we enter our gate, and thereafter he charges ahead briskly; he runs right by a flattened mouse, which lies outside the five-a-side courts. A hose is stretched across the walkway as we near the playground; watering is necessary because, after a period in which we had devastating floods, we have had no real rain in weeks.

Out on the green Vito is wrestling with Daisy-Mae while Sparkie, trying to referee, gets a collar zap every now and then, when he slips back into barking mode. Chica has a wonderful toy, a large rubber hammer; it has lost its squeak but the other dogs like it anyway and Sparkie makes off with it. He decides that he needs to roll in the grass, however, and this means that Fritz gets his turn with the toy, proudly trotting all over the place with me in pursuit (well, Chica follows warily as well). I try to get the toy back with the offer of a biscuit but Fritz is too clever to fall for this ruse. Meanwhile Reina and Christian, Vito's parents, go off on an errand, leaving their puppy (still obsessed with Daisy-Mae) in Dan's care. I have at last succeeded in returning the rubber hammer to Bekki.

There is no objection to occupying seats around a picnic table in the sun—with Ofra complaining about the chilly air. Her Bailey has a bad paw and everyone who has a look at it advises her to take him to the vet. Bailey feels that insult has been added to injury—since his mommy is cuddling Vito and he is mad with jealousy. Daisy-Mae jumps onto the tabletop (it is easy for our dogs to do this since they often sit on the benches first) and tries to help herself to my biscuits. Winnie, who has been sitting next to me, does the same, but I think *she* feels that there are scrambled eggs up here.

Carrying Spadge, Hanna arrives. Kate says she is still recovering from Sunday's party and Georgie says that she thinks her heart is still pumping red wine. It is time for us to begin our back passage walkround but Vito's parents are still missing so Dan has to take the pup with him, using Winnie's lead to secure the little fellow at the end. By this time Hanna has removed the dead mouse with the use of a paper napkin.

Thursday, September 19:

It seems quite chilly outside this morning; there has been a dusting of moisture on the pavements and skies are still quite overcast. As soon as we have entered the park we find Dan heading our way with Winnie. He reverses his direction to accompany us back past the cypress trees and between the sports pitches. He has noticed that some irresponsible dog owner has left an unattended poo outside the gate to the five-a-side pitch and some kid has stepped in it before reaching the new rug.

On the green Davide is just entering and there is an immediate spat as Dan has to go to work and the cleaner has arrived at home and Davide doesn't have any cash. Kate is here with both of her dogs and Isla is still chasing her big sister and taking bites out of Skye's tail. In just a week the timid Puli has decided that being a puppy in Paddington Rec has its upside. She no longer dogs Kate's footsteps but runs around in search of play; today she has Daisy-Mae pinned to the wet grass. I see that Fritz is sitting at attention at Sabina's feet—with Oscar and Scamp. As he usually has nothing to do with these dogs I realize that Sabina must have food with her—and so she does. With the promise of more treats to come, Fritz and I then head for the café.

Ronnie is just leaving (something about a delivery man) but we have Peter, Ellen, Faz, Georgie, Suzanne and Kate this morning. Faz is besieged these days with questions about the imminent birth—now expected in slightly less than two weeks. Georgie has been salivating over a toasted sausage sandwich with mustard and now is the time for her to realize her fantasy. A sodden Daisy-Mae is in her lap so Sparkie spends some time in everyone else's. Isla is perched on Kate's lap and when she gets up there is a large wet patch left behind. Important topics include how to make a chip butty and whether chips with gravy is a suitable combination. Kate says she could go for some chips with curry sauce.

Friday, September 21:

I have missed a day in the park with a medical appointment, but Fritz has been active with his Auntie Linda, who took him to Regents Park, where, I understand, he distinguished himself with non-stop and speedy dashes hither and yon. Just as we are about to leave for the park today Ronnie calls to tell me that, wouldn't you know it, in my absence yesterday the lady from *DogTails* has come looking for me, and that she has promised to return today. So we start out under grey skies and head for a rendezvous with Brenda.

Out on the green I meet Christian who, having talked to the lady in question, repeats the same message. Linda comes in with Pepper and he and Fritz spar a bit while Isla tears another strip out of Skye's tail and runs around with it in triumph. Vito's parents have forgotten his lead and so they have to carry their puppy away when it is time to go. Fritz is off on his rambles and I have to follow him since he looks like he's in second poo mode. By the time we have finished this business the others have started in for coffee and so we follow them.

Dan now approaches me with further information about the *DogTails* lady. She wants a story about the Paddington pack and is particularly intrigued by the recent picnic. So Dan, who has photos of the event, wants me to write an article for the magazine. Brenda is sitting at our table with Peter, Ellen, and Georgie. I discuss details of the needed text and then Brenda, a Canadian who has spent many years in Australia and who is also an actress, fills us in on a number of aspects of her biography. She tells us she couldn't stand living in a suburb of Sydney—I ask her if she had ever met Dame Edna. Now she lives near the ferry in Sydney Harbor—Ronnie says he doesn't believe in fairies. I ask her if she has ever heard of Kathleen McCormack but she hasn't—even though our clairvoyant has cured more dogs and cats than anyone else in history.

Saturday, September 22:

The sun is trying to come out on a mild weekend day, the first of autumn. Fritz makes a lively and orderly progress toward the green, where some of the dog owners are gathered near the cricket crease and another set is milling about, waiting for Roland to arrive for Saturday morning training classes. Among the latter is Sabina, whose Oscar has been making some progress in returning when he is called. I notice that Scamp the Westie is missing but Sabina says that he is so possessive over his brother's attention that it is better to leave him at home when it is class time.

Two little kids have chosen an awkward moment for an unscheduled game of cricket. They are using a real cricket bat and ball on the crease and I can tell that this is going to lead to trouble. At one point I see that Brea, the portly Lab, is running around with a flattened football skin in his mouth, his mistress in hot pursuit. "I'm sure he can have that," I say, but the response is, "He's got the cricket ball *too*." The next time Brea plays through I grab him by the harness and the ball is extracted, though not before there is some ill-tempered growling, since the Lab is convinced that some of the other little dogs want his red ball. I throw it back to the lads and head in for coffee, though I stop only long enough to anchor Fritz's lead to Ronnie's chair before dashing off to Maida Vale parade for some errands.

When I return it is to a crowded table at which Peter, Ellen, Dan, Davide, Hanna, and Georgie are seated. Hanna says that Fritz was a real pain while I was gone (separation anxiety) and Ellen says he was a very good boy. Go figure. Janet arrives with Daisy-Mae. The latter is wearing a plastic collar after having undergone a neutering surgery at only six months. Hanna says that she has ordered some doggy diapers for Spadge, who is seated in her lap, hoping that she will be able to get a good night's sleep at last. Dan knocks over a full cup of milky white coffee but fortunately none of the dogs is beneath our table at just this moment. He goes inside to pick up a second cup from the assistant I call Lurch. I have had a devil of a time explaining to this fellow that when I say I like American football I am not talking about David Beckham and the LA Galaxy. "You mean you watch rugby?" he says.

Sunday, September 23:

It is cloudy bright outside and I am wearing my sunglasses from the outset. Fritz gets well ahead of me on the out-lap and I don't catch up with him until I find him depositing his poo in the bushes opposite the café fence. Thereafter he has a brief look at the action on the green and heads for the Grantully gate. I decide I had better follow and when I reach the danger spot there is no sign of the rascal. He doesn't answer my whistle or my call and I step out into the street with some anxiety. No sign. Then I notice that the door to the doggy area is open and so I have a look inside. This doesn't seem very promising because there are dozens of pigeons picking over the grass and any dog worth his kibble would long before this have launched them skyward. But, also nosing around, I find Fritz—intent on his sniffing. A black man with a Mastiff is walking down the pavement on Grantully and, when I put my dog on lead, he asks if I am leaving. If I wasn't before, I am now.

Fritz and I cross the green, dodging a slow parade of joggers who, for some reason, are clinging to the chalked cricket pitch boundary line. Georgie is in conversation with Rhiann, who is complaining that the boxing gym that she goes to on the Harrow Road (located in an abandoned church that I pass every time I walk to Sainbury's) may be sold off for development by Westminster Council. A young couple have brought a delightful puppy with them today. Her name is Coops and she is a Pugalier, that is part Pug and part Cavalier. She is very curious about the other dogs and bravely chases a few. For this she is rewarded by the speedy Sparkie, who cannot resist giving her a tumble in the grass.

The turnout is quite poor for a Sunday, though Janet eventually arrives with the plastic-wrapped Daisy-Mae and a sleepy Dan arrives with Winnie. At a picnic table in the sun we are joined by Ofra as well. Daisy-Mae is bothered by her incision, which she would dearly like to scratch. Bailey is sitting on a bench, his paws on the table expectantly. Winnie, however, manages to get her bottom onto every one of the four benches that surround our table and, when no one is watching, she goes and sits at the table where Sweep's parents are having breakfast as well. It is hard to tell whether Winnie is more preoccupied with cadging toast and scrambled eggs for herself or in making sure that none of the other dogs get any. Twice she jumps off a bench in a furious rage, managing both times to catch her forehead on the lip of the table. By this time Ofra and Dan are discussing finger injuries in such graphic detail that Georgie is turning green. It is time to begin a back passage walkround.

Monday, September 24:

Fritz is such a good barometer. His little body just seems to know when a storm in heading our way and, always fearful that it might bring the dreaded thunder and lightning, he begins to take evasive action. Last night at bedtime I found him lying on the bathroom rug and later he positioned himself on the floor between the bed and the wall. Of course I knew from these clues what to do—I got up and closed the kitchen window. Shortly after dawn a violent downpour covered this glass with sheets of rain.

When it is time for us to head for the park it is still raining, though very little now. (Nevertheless I have put the raincoat on Fritz, who offered less of a protest than usual.) We make rapid progress toward the green, where there is a Schnauzer explosion, with Spadge, Pepper, Oscar, and even Monty in evidence. Monty's mom says that she is about to go on a trip and that Monty, not wanting to be left behind, has been sitting in her suitcase.

Christian and Vito follow us around as Fritz undertakes a pilgrimage to the Randolph Avenue side of things. Christian says that he spent the weekend in Wales playing war with other boys who never grew up. He also says that his wife, Reina, works for Endemol, the company that has brought us all those reality TV shows—including *Big Brother.*

I am dying to pass this information on to Janet, but neither she nor Daisy-Mae is present today. For that matter Georgie doesn't make it in either, another victim of today's inclemency. The rain has died out now and we have a knot of dog owners in the center of the green, jawing away until 10:00 or so. Fritz grows bored and demands biscuits and I have to offer these to Chica, Vito, Winnie, and Pepper as well. Indeed I have so exhausted my supply of these treats that we have to order some toast for the dogs when we at last go in for coffee. Today it is Christian's treat and the Danish businessman even accompanies us on our back passage walkround.

Tuesday, September 25:

It is a lovely sunny Tuesday morning as Fritz and I head for the park today. When we reach the café we find Ronnie and Suzanne already at table. Ronnie has to get home early for the damp-course man and is soon seen leaving the scene. Taking advantage of the pleasant weather, we have a huge turnout on the green; in scattered groups all over the place I can count over twenty owners exercising their pets. We even have Hootch and his thunderball, though today Guy has also brought two huge Weimaraners.

Christian and Reina are trying to make their getaway, which is not easy since Isla will not let go of Vito, even when the chap is on lead. Georgie has to carry the Conehead, Daisy-Mae, since the latter is having an uncomfortable time trying to play with the impediment of her Elizabethan collar. Dan also passes Winnie's lead off to Georgie, as he heads off for work. Fritz noses around among the other dogs and plants himself at my feet, hoping for a steady supply of biscuits. For this he is teased by his Aunt Hanna, who has left Spadge sleeping at home. At about 9:35 we begin to make a move toward the café, but it takes me some time to get Fritz moving in the right direction.

I sit down opposite Ronnie's abandoned espresso cup, joining a group that includes Peter, Ellen, Faz, Georgie, Hanna, and Ofra. We are joined by two rovers returned. First we have Nicholas, arrived with American Cocker Monty; it is the first time we have seen him since his recent marriage and his honeymoon in the Maldives. We get a very detailed account of the accommodations offered in the latter site; it is almost but not quite as boring as the story of the burning tires. Then Tanya pulls up with Pasha, *her* Weimaraner, and Isabella and Lucca, her babies. Isabella has a lonely tear on her right cheek and Lucca, soon dandled by Ofra, has one on his left cheek. I give Pasha a biscuit and one of Guy's Weimaraners attempts the theft of Hanna's cheese-stuffed croissant—foiled by his own muzzle. Pretty soon Nicholas is discussing mortgages with Faz and Tanya is discussing babies with Ofra and my head is sinking further into my chest. "Isn't it about time for a walkround?" I suggest. As usual these days Fritz, who often brings up the rear at the outset of these expeditions, sprints so far ahead that by the time *we* are ready to exit the park the others have yet to emerge from the cypress trees behind us.

Wednesday, September 26:

Although I have been warned that it is really nippy outside I am surprised how chilly it really is as Fritz and I head for our morning session in the park. There is a chill wind raking the open spaces and nullifying any effect that a watery sunlight might provide. I notice that we now have kids from the resurrected and rebuilt Paddington Academy on the track this morning—the park as extension to the schoolyard continues apace.

Fritz reaches the green well ahead of me as he heads for the cricket crease, reaches it, ignores all the other dogs, and keeps on trucking. I have to follow him toward the Grantully exit where he does turn around, distracted by the offer of a biscuit. Then he heads for the Randolph walkway and I have to follow him here too. I get him to turn right at the walkway that runs behind the tennis courts. I don't think I've ever seem him explore the territory near the bowling green and behind the Grantully doggy area but, his curiosity satisfied at last, we can head in for coffee. Georgie is still carrying Daisy-Mae at this point; for some reason the Shih-Tzu has a plastic spoon in her teeth. "I think she wants feeding," Georgie concludes.

A very chilly assemblage hunkers down around our metal table outside the café doors. Today we have Ellen, Peter (always the first to get his gloves out), Georgie, Christian, Dan, Hanna, Kate, and Faz. The subject of exercise comes up—the general consensus being that it is bad for you. "My body is in perfect shape," Kate insists, "it's never been used." Every owner who can do so has nestled a warming dog in his or her lap, but the cold wind continues to whistle and soon there is a collective desire to get moving. I walk with Christian and Faz, but Fritz, on lead, is not happy with the hectoring charges of little Vito, who wants my dog to play. He's picked the wrong candidate.

Thursday, September 27:

I am back in my park leather jacket (I have a second, almost similar model, one that Dorothy bought me for more formal occasions) and I am wearing my scarf as well for we have another brisk morning in Paddington Rec. I would have considered using my gloves but in the interim I have lost one of these. There is sun and bright skies, but nothing resembling warmth; Fritz nevertheless finds the smells fascinating today and he makes slow progress toward the green. I can see our group milling about near the cricket crease, the tall figure of Christian, the bobble-headed Faz, Georgie still carrying Daisy-Mae, Ronnie slightly hunched over. Linda is here too, as I soon discover, but Pepper and Fritz don't have much to say to one another and my dog is soon off on the margins, nosing about. He does return to run around a bit with his pal, Leila, but I have a devil of a time coaxing him to join the rest of us for coffee.

Today we are a hardy half-dozen as I sit down with Ofra, Dan, Ronnie, Faz, and Georgie. Faz varies his usual morning order to experiment with the vegetable soup; pretty soon everyone is sampling this fare and enjoying Elian's culinary efforts. The latter has delivered the dish with only one proviso, "Save some for the Winnie." His favorite is off chasing a blackbird, but her eating habits become one of our topics of conversation. At home she has taken to sitting next to Davide because he gives her more food than Dan—so Dan has had to compensate in order to compete for the affections of his own dog. At dinner she evidently sits at the head of the table, issuing peremptory moans as a reminder that there is a third mouth to feed here. Things are pretty quiet in the park this morning, though we can again see Max and Barley, the two Weimaraners, dashing around outside and playing with Pasha. Tanya passes through with her babies in their carriage; she looks radiant and Ronnie tells her so—we can all remember when she had to endure so many disappointments before motherhood finally dawned.

When it is time to make a move we begin a back passage walkround, encountering Albert and his dogs almost immediately. He is late into the park this morning and knows he won't have many companions when he gets to the café. Georgie has to crash through the cypress trees in pursuit of Sparkie's ball. Then we meet a six month-old Coton de Tulier named Lulu. Her owner explains that Lulu likes people—but doesn't have much experience with other dogs. We again hear the story of the breed having been developed at the behest of the royal family of Madagascar, but both Faz and I can't imagine that Madagascar ever had a royal family—it evidently did. A conversation worthy of Abbott and Costello ensues. Dan asks for the name of the animal for which this island is famous. "Is it lemmings?" he asks. "Lemurs," I reply. "You mean like in Peru?" Faz continues. "Only if you mean Lima, Peru," I respond, "I think you're thinking of llamas." They congratulate me on being so patient with their ignorance. "You must have been a terrific teacher," Faz concludes.

Friday, September 28:

It's a grey day outside but the scene is lively enough as Fritz and I prepare to descend to the street for our usual morning ramble. Today we have the *unusual*—as ITV is out front filming an episode of Linda La Plante's *Trial and Retribution*. I have had a little advance notice but I am surprised to discover a chap in a lime green vest at the bottom of my stairs; he asks me if I can wait 30 seconds before exiting the building. The street is crowded with members of the film crew, milling about, directing traffic and snapping their clapper loaders. No one offers to make Fritz a star.

Inside the park we meet up with Lizzie and Yoyo, the black Schnauzer. I ask about the new premises for the wallpaper showroom on Nugent Terrace and Lizzie says the move is complete and that I should come by for tea and biscuits. Fritz has no time for this idle chitchat and continues on toward the café, where I find Ronnie with his nose pressed up against the glass door, encouraging the staff to get a move on. On the green Fritz runs about a good deal and even manages to complete two circus catches of a tennis ball sent his way by Georgie. Thereafter he heads for the Morshead gate and it takes me quite a while to get him turned around and headed back to the café. By the time I have done so the others are seated around our table in front of the doors.

This morning we have Peter, Ellen, Faz (now off work for a month as he anticipates the birth of his baby), Davide, Georgie, and Nicholas. Pushing a biscuit into Daisy-Mae's upturned plastic collar is like using a garbage disposal. For that matter she has a real offensive weapon there—War Shih-Tzu. Jasmine, meanwhile, also arrives to accept a treat; Faz says that he is going to bring some of the baby's clothes home from the hospital so that his pet can get used to the smell. "Don't bring any of them here," Ronnie says. Some of us begin to make a move but Hanna, recently arrived, begs Georgie and Davide to stay behind so that she can have some company while she eats her breakfast. I walk home alone, checking with the film crew that it is all right to cross the street. Victoria Smurfit is standing on my front steps, running a hairbrush through her long blonde hair. Soon she can be seen springing out of a black cab and crossing our street with a look of injured incredulity.

Saturday, September 29:

I have a companion with me as Fritz and I head for the park, a few minutes behind our usual starting time, for Janet has arrived from Michigan for a week's visit. This is the first time she has experienced the Essendine entry to the park and I can satisfy her curiosity about what exactly a five-a-side pitch looks like—for the gentlemen are foregathering here for their usual Saturday morning contests. Our group is already settling down in front of the café when we near this oasis and I leave Janet here as I continue out to the green with Fritz for another few minutes of exercise. One of the reasons for this early arrival at the café is that the cricket pitch is actually occupied by cricketers—very unusual at this time in the morning. The season is essentially over in this country so one wonders why this latter-day enthusiasm for the sport.

At the other end of the green Roland is presiding over his training class; Fritz has a go at disrupting proceedings, as usual, and then he follows me back to our crowded table.

Today we have Ronnie, Liz, two Janets, Georgie, Hanna, Ofra, Dan and Faz. Liz has been taking an intensive interior design course at the Chelsea Design Institute, but she is planning already on playing hooky. She has recently run into a bollard in the park's parking lot. Ofra says that Ricky is afraid to risk his new car by driving it. Dan reports that he now has to answer an angry letter from a disappointed customer—who wants to know why the Phoenix Theatre doesn't protect itself against further power cuts by installing its own generator. The dogs keep jumping into our laps and in other ways attempting to get their heads onto the tabletop. Winnie chases away a giant poodle—there's no food for you here, mate.

Janet and I disdain the back passage walkround and head out the Randolph walkway so that she can visit a cash point in Maida Vale Parade. On the way we meet Nemo, the Lab, and a wonderful Australian Shepherd named Summer, a recent arrival from California; the latter is suffering from a sun complaint on her white nose. I tell her owner that she will soon recover in this country and it *is* chilly and grey today, by way of illustration. We also walk through the park on our way home; the waiting batsmen are slumped down in the bandstand. I tell Janet that in the old days they would be on the balcony of the clubhouse, though perhaps they wouldn't be allowed to open their cans of Fosters up there.

Sunday, September 30:

We have a lovely, crisp sunny morning to bring the month of September to an end. Janet again accompanies us as we complete our usual entry ritual; this brings us by the café, where Suzanne and Ray are just setting out the backgammon board on a sunny picnic table. Out on the green Daisy-Mae and Sparkie have already arrived, with Winnie, Jasmine, and Bailey joining them soon thereafter. Fritz manages to stay within touch; in this regard I suppose it helps that he is hungry, having refused to eat his dinner last night, and knowing he can wheedle a biscuit or two out of me even before we head in for coffee.

There is no change whatsoever in the round-the-table line-up today, the same ten club members as yesterday. Michigan Janet switches to a toasted cheese, ham and tomato sandwich, which Dan was eating yesterday. Faz denounces the luxurious life style afforded the British prisoner these days (PlayStation, TV, duvets in the cells) and this sets Dan off on a masochistic fantasy in which Faz throws him into a cell and is mean to him. John arrives with Ché and it is interesting to see that grown men are afraid to exit the café with the Alsatian lying peacefully at the entrance. For his part, Fritz lets out a roar of disapproval whenever the big dog sticks his nose into our magic circle.

When we get up we do not head for home—since Janet and I have errands to complete across Elgin Avenue. Sister-in-law Naomi and her Elizabeth and Matthew are expected later in the day and we have decided to offer them scrambled eggs and bagels with lox and cream cheese—so we head first for Bon Appetit. The latter *has* only six bagels—this happens all the time, since they can never get their planning right—but Janet buys some croissants as well. Then she goes into the Nosh store to buy other comestibles and the *Sunday Times*. Tiny Roxy the Dachshund comes by and she and Fritz touch noses. When all the purchases have been completed we head for home. Today, to explain this occasion more fully, we will be heading up to Hampstead Heath, where Dorothy's ashes will be scattered this afternoon.

October, 2007

Monday, October 1:

A light ran begins sometime around dawn today, and I have to get up to see if all the windows are closed. When I go back to sleep I remain at my rest until long past my usual hour of rising; there isn't much use in getting up early since Janet is in my study these days. That lady failed to set her alarm correctly and was just rising as Fritz and I, alone today, head for the park on a damp grey morning. At least it isn't raining. Almost as soon as we enter Fritz does his first poo, turning right instead of the usual left, and taking the fastest way to the green.

Here we find a very small group of stalwarts: Peter and Ellen, Ronnie, Michaela and Linda. Fritz is reunited with Pepper, with whom he spent several hours in riotous play only yesterday—while Linda and I and eleven others, including Hanna, were scattering Dorothy's ashes on Parliament Hill. The two dogs do spar a bit, but I think both are still a bit tired, and soon I am pursuing my animal all over the place. He would really like to enter the doggy area on Grantully Road but I spot a Rottweiler in here and decide it is time to put my dog back on lead and cross the green one last time in pursuit of coffee. Faz is just leaving and we may not see him for a while; tomorrow is delivery day.

At our table we are also joined by Nicholas—whose sausage sandwich proves its popularity among the canines at our feet. We have a nice relaxing time of it—if you discount the intrusion of the leaf blower and the snide remarks of passing teenagers. These are nothing compared with the park's latest designs on our peace—for some of us have received planning permission notices for an extension of the floodlights until 10:15 at night, with all the consequent noise, parking problems, and disruption to residential lives of no consequence whatsoever to the culture of the jocks.

I take Fritz along the back passage with Nicholas and Linda and prepare myself for another day of letter writing. Soon we have an all-day rain.

Tuesday, October 2:

Under gray skies we get ready to depart for pastures green. I have a special interest in monitoring Fritz's poo—since my dog has managed to throw up on my Double Crostics book just a few minutes earlier. In the event his poo seems fine and I continue along the back passage, where I encounter Sabina and Denise. I see that Oscar has had a spiffy new haircut but Sabina thinks that the shorter style reveals that her Schnauzer is a bit overweight. I don't, but we have a long discussion on diet while the lads from Paddington Academy are getting a lecture on footy and Fritz is racing ahead to the green. Janet, who has left the house only a little bit behind us, is entering from another side and her calls to Fritz are answered not only by the latter but by Daisy-Mae, still in her War Shih-Tzu collar. When she lands on Fritz's back there is an indignant protest.

Out on the green this morning is Saskia, whom we have not seen of late. She says that she has been in France with Buddy, who evidently specialized in lurking beneath the white starched tablecloths of adjacent tables and poking his naughty nose between the knees of startled diners. I notice that Saskia is wearing high-top designer trainers without any laces. "You say you have been in France but you have obviously been in a cell," I tell her. She explains that her usual park shoes are no more. "I put them outside our tent in Africa and a jackal made off with them."

At breakfast this morning we have Peter, Ellen, our Janet, Hanna, Ronnie, Georgie and Dan. Dan is growing a goatee but Davide evidently thinks it adds *years*. I notice that Scamp has followed Sabina into the café—Oscar has responded to his beauty treatment by rolling in something nasty and emergency napkins are needed. Janet says she doesn't like her sandwich as much this morning as they have merely toasted the *bread*, rather than nuking the entire assemblage. She also gets caught up in Fritz's lead as we complete a back passage walkround prior to our trip to the British Museum and a visit with the Terracotta Warriors. A few blocks from the tube stop we encounter Natasha and Tanya. Natasha is actually pushing Tanya's baby buggy but Isabella is holding Leila's lead—so it looks like the whole outfit is being pulled forward by a Miniature Pinscher.

Later in the afternoon Fritz has a second session in the park when I take him into the doggy area on Morshead Road as a fine drizzle descends.

Over the fence I see Daisy-Mae's Janet, Georgie, Linda and Hanna. They want to know what I thought of the Terracotta Warriors. "Fine," I say, "now I want to see a line-up of Nigella, Gary Rhodes, Jamie Oliver and Gordon Ramsay—the Pannacotta Warriors." Linda and Hanna come in to the doggy area and Fritz gets a damp play period with Pepper as Linda keeps a tennis ball in play with her rainy-day leather boots. There is another unexpected dividend to this day as well: we learn via text that Faz and Dianah have had a baby girl.

Wednesday, October 3:

It is still a bit damp this morning but skies are brightening and it is mild enough as Janet and I accompany Fritz to the park. His tummy still seems to be okay, though he does pause to sample a few grass shoots before racing along the back passage. Peter, Ellen, Ronnie and Georgie are already at table; the café seems to be opening a bit earlier than the 9:30 time advertized on the door and these dog people are happy to get their orders in now.

Out on the green we find Hanna (dogless) and Dan, but there are also some figures seen less often—including Humphrey, the one-eyed Shih-Tzu, and a Bichon Frise named Charlie. Ofra arrives to complain that she has finally dressed smartly (she is wearing blue jeans and a grey sweater set) and now it's too hot. "It is not too hot," I protest, "and you don't look that smart anyway." Fritz can soon be seen heading for the margins, in this case the Randolph walkway, and I rumble after him. At the foot of Mt. Bannister I meet a lady named Sue with a new dog from Battersea, a Cavalier named Sidney. They are walking with Suzanne and Sunny and I have a parley with the former on the topic of local protests against the plans to extend park hours—with Suzanne taking charge of one division of campaigners. Fritz is waiting for me and, after cleaning up a second poo, he agrees to rejoin us for coffee and treats at the café. Not that the treats are much to write home about these days; even toast has become thin on the ground.

In addition to the aforementioned we also have Nicholas, Ofra, and Suzanne this morning. Bailey welcomes his new cousin Sidney by humping the newcomer, which sends his new owner into a tizzy. Ofra is inside the caff and doesn't even know what is happening behind her back, but eventually the two dogs are separated. I tell Ronnie and Suzanne that I have sent a copy of my protest letter to Jan Prendergast and each of them now has a suggestion on how I *should* have accomplished this task. "You can tell I'm among Jews here," I protest, "I tell you about something as simple as sending a letter to Westminster Council and each of you wants to tell me how I could have done it better." Bailey is trying to jump into people's laps but he is too fidgety and is usually rejected. Winnie refuses a biscuit as she eyes Janet's croissant. Soon I can see a disaster brewing. A little boy at the next table is innocently holding a snack while the Pug circles ominously. As we get up to begin our back passage walkround I say, "That's what you call loitering with intent."

Thursday, October 4:

Skies are beginning to clear as Fritz and I head for the park; we are without Janet's company—our guest, suffering from a bad cold, is again well behind us in her preparations. Fritz makes only the slowest progress toward the green but when we at last reach this sacred spot I have to rub my eyes—for I have reached Schnauzer Heaven. Today we have four specimens of the breed, three minis (Fritz, Pepper and Oscar) and a new Standard, Alfie. This foursome makes up its own pack for a while, dashing about and investigating all the action.

I follow Fritz over to the Randolph walkway. Here I discover for the first time that Chica the Boxer is going to live in Spain. This information comes to me from David the dog sitter, who is today looking after Stella, a black Staffie in a pink halter. *Our* Janet has not yet appeared but Daisy-Mae's owner can be seen moving across the green on the way to coffee. Her presence mid-week can be explained by the fact that this morning the pup has had her stitches removed—a War Shih-Tzu no more.

We have quite a crowd at breakfast and food and drink are slow in coming. Hanna has to wait quite a while, for instance, for her scrambled eggs on toast, and in the meantime a saltcellar is turned over and the leaf blower starts up outside the café fence—bathing everyone's breakfast in fumes. The chief topic of conversation today is another fight involving Hercules. The incident took place several days ago, but this is the first time I have heard about it. Linda says that the testosterone-fuelled Cocker got into it with a Staffie and that a small child was almost drawn into the bloody melee. This is one of those issues where the dog owners are united in their views: Hercules needs the snip. Many of the diners have already left before our Janet makes an appearance. She decides that she'd just as soon have coffee at home and so, soon, we are catching up with the other owners in their back passage walkround.

Friday, October 5:

Sunny skies are dominant on a crisp, pleasant autumn morning as Janet, for the last time on this trip, accompanies Fritz and me as we make our way into the park. First we have an obligatory snarling match as my dog and Chelsea, the portly Jack Russell, reach the entry gate at the same time. A minute later, both off lead now, they pay no attention to one another. Phoenix passes us as he emerges from the cypress trees and then we are able to head directly for the green without further interruption. Here, however, is an unusual sight. A teacher has brought his class of youngsters to the grass in front of the clubhouse for some practice in rocketry! Each kid has made his or her own device and, after pumping the device up, lift-off takes place amid shouts of surprise and approval.

Here we find a small body of dog owners, soon on their way into the café, where we join them. Suzanne reacts with distaste because Sparkie is licking the croissant that is also going into Georgie's mouth at the same time. Dan gets tired of doling out Winnie's health kibble a nugget at a time and dumps the whole tray on the ground, with these treats hoovered up by our dogs as though the latter were so many Trafalgar Square pigeons. Tinka and Saffy are trying to excite Chica, who holds down these mischief-makers with one insouciant paw. Michigan's Film Commissioner eats a portion of toast and then says her goodbyes to the remaining owners.

She and I are unaccompanied as we begin a back passage walkround. There is a jam-up in the narrow defile between playing fields as Paddington Academy kids are heading for home. Mixed up in this lot is a Rottweiler with a large stick in his mouth; it catches Janet on the leg and causes quite a scratch. An hour after she has left for the airport I witness a potentially frightening park scene from my window. Vito has been chasing a young Cavalier and the two dogs, still being puppies, manage to squeeze through the bars of the park fence and out onto the sidewalk—whizzing cars only a few feet away. The owner of the Cavalier actually climbs over the fence in his anxiety, but he manages to get hold only of his own dog—while Reina is having kittens trying to get Vito to squeeze back through the bars. Eventually he does so—no harm done after all.

Saturday, October 6:

The sun is still having its way with the clouds as Fritz and I enter the park on a mild weekend morning, but this is a battle that will be lost with some frequency later in the day. The park is full of little boys, some having instruction ("Touch your nose, touch your knees," etc.) while their older mates are already in competition—with moms and dads (and even dogs) crowding the sideline. Add the Saturday morning exercise crowd and some adult hockeyettes and the place is buzzing.

Even on the green we have an alien presence, the army in camouflage fatigues—well yesterday we had rocketry here. These chaps are on a recruiting mission (I wonder if the M.O.D. is getting a bill for this use of the village green) and Georgie is agitating for an early café sortie, on the grounds that the queue will soon be crowded with soldiers. This makes some sense ("Very wise decision—for a Scot" is her reward for this prescience). Indeed our group just manages to get in line before the army joins in as well. "Yes," I say, "But do they have to march in place?"

We have a large turnout this morning, with Peter, Ellen, Dan, Kate and her friend Bob, Georgie, Janet, Liz, Hanna, Ronnie, and Ofra. Kate has a furry black scarf that can easily be confused with Isla in her lap. Dan says that he is taking Winnie to a Pug party in Green Park later today; he is also organizing a wine-tasting party for the evening. Hanna is a bit under the weather, with swollen glands obvious beneath her chin. Liz now gives us a full report on her interior design class while, at the same time, doling out her scrambled eggs and toast to a large assortment of dogs at her feet. The crush inside the café finally comes to an end. "Now's your chance," I tell Georgie, "get in there with tomorrow's orders."

Sunday, October 7:

The day begins with one more dog than usual, as I have had Pepper, on a sleepover, since yesterday at about 1:00—the Taggarts having suddenly been offered tickets to the World Cup Rugby Championships in Cardiff. Fortunately Pepper does not need to go out any earlier than Fritz; I found both of them asleep on my bed when I arose this morning. Unfortunately Linda arrives to reclaim her dog while I am still in the shower and she has to wait out front before we all emerge and the reunion can take place. She seems to be in a happy enough mood—something which can not be said for the men in her family, who are still suffering from New Zealand's defeat at the hands of the French.

We all head into the park together but Linda leaves when we reach the green and Fritz and I continue on to the cricket crease, where our gang is foregathering. Jo Lynn is here with Tilly; she has been minding Jasmine for the week as well but all members of Faz's family are at home now (and the in-laws are still hovering), though no one seems to know what the baby is called yet. Fritz admits himself to the doggy area on Grantully and then emerges in time to investigate a number of canine newcomers, who are just now crossing the park, and to piss on Winnie's head. Dan is describing last night's wine-tasting fiasco. The wines were indifferent, they weren't properly identified and Ofra got in several more glasses than everybody else—by neglecting to surrender her tickets.

When we go in for coffee our table is already occupied by a number of people, including Ronnie and Suzanne, but, with a large number to follow, there is no way we can all squeeze ourselves around this site and so a picnic table has to be selected as well. Here ten of us make our temporary home; two chairs have to be added to the corners to make even this arrangement a possibility. Skye the Alsatian is in disgrace after running across the street to growl at a little dog. Daisy-Mae *is* a disgrace, sopping wet again after a roll in the grass; Dan says that touching her is like putting your hands in seaweed. She and Isla are on the tabletop—disgraceful behavior, while Winnie coyly tries to make a place for herself on one of the benches. The chief topic of conversation is the electricity bill and several members of the troupe have quite naughty tales to tell on the subject of fiddling the meter. Jo Lynn is the first to leave—mocking herself with the parting shot, "Well, I have to go chant for fucking peace!" No one else seems about to budge so I get up soon thereafter and make my solitary way with Fritz to the Morshead gate.

Monday, October 8:

Weather remains on the overcast side (though mild enough) as Fritz and I penetrate the precincts of the park at the start of a new week. Jean-Baptiste is heading our way with Hercules and the Cocker is riveted by the sight of Fritz squatting to poo on the grass at the top of the running track. Not only does Hercules pee on this pile but he manages to step in it as well—sending his owner, who now turns around to accompany us toward the green—into a tizzy.

When we reach the green itself there seems to be a lot of activity for a grey Monday morning. Balls are flying willy-nilly and the puppies, like Isla and Daisy-Mae, are turning each over in spirited play. This does not sit too well with Sparkie, who runs around in agitated circles, barking out the score. "I think that's a two," I suggest to Georgie, hoping that she will do something to silence her pet. The problem is that the scamp jumped into the water on a visit to Regents Park recently and she has to wait for his collar device to dry out before any zapping will be effective. She does begin an early agitation for coffee and so we head in. Crossing our paths is the latchkey dog, Buster.

There is a very large turnout at breakfast and we have difficulty getting enough chairs around one table. Nicholas is complaining that his new wife has bought a lurid pink collar for Monty. Dan tells us that yesterday a number of the dogs were left in Liz's basement in St. Johns Wood and that when the dog owners themselves returned to the house they were astonished to see Sparkie staring out the front window at them. It seems that the rascal managed to break down the kiddy gate at the top of the basement stairs and liberate all his pals, who then had the run of the house for hours. Much of the morning conversation is devoted to dog poo. Linda has been handing out bags to absent-minded or reluctant owners, claiming that the park is full of uncollected specimens. She and I begin a back passage walkround and I am afraid she is right.

Tuesday, October 9:

A light rain is falling as I prepare for Tuesday morning in the park. I have donned my own rain jacket but Fritz is somewhat reluctant to wear his own: I think he dislikes the ripping sound of the Velcro fasteners. Temperatures are mild enough as we enter the park but I do feel sorry for the youngsters from Paddington Academy who are taking instruction in sodden platoons on the playing fields. Fritz growls at a large, bouncy dog who is heading our way on the paths but he makes no objection when we pass Rizzo, Oscar and Scamp. Near the cypress trees we pass one of the veteran dog walkers. She is hurrying along with two dogs on lead and one trailing far behind. This is the one, true to yesterday's theme, who squats and poos next to a cyclone fence—an act that his carer isn't even aware of.

When we reach the café I see a small group, made up of Nicholas, Dan, Peter and Ellen, seated outside the window of the eatery, waiting for the doors to open. I suggest that, at least, they ought to occupy our usual table under the overhang—since Peter, in his exposed position, is getting rained on. They get up to move but I continue on to the green, hoping for a little more exercise. It is one of those rare mornings when there is not a single soul about and Fritz and I have the whole place to ourselves. We cross the wet surface several times as Fritz selects a useful spot for his own poo. Then, after chasing off Oscar one last time, he agrees to follow me into the protection of the café. The red-cheeked barista has seen me coming and has my cappuccino ready almost as soon as I place my order.

Georgie and Hanna join the aforementioned group—which is full of self-congratulation on surviving this weather and getting in some exercise for their dogs at the same time. Hanna, of course, is dogless—Spadge having already had a foray in the garden at 6:00 this morning. Inquiries are made on the subject of the doggy nappies that were supposed to obviate such early rising, but Hanna now says that Spadge doesn't like to use them. We discuss rocketing Maida Vale property prices and Hanna's hunt for new pajamas at Primark. When we begin a back passage walkround we can see that the persistent rain is bringing with it a shower of leaves from the chestnuts and the plane trees.

Wednesday, October 10:

The falling leaves may have caused the cold-like symptoms I have been suffering with for the last few days; I do seem to have allergies at this time of year and in the spring as well. Handkerchief in pocket (that of my leather jacket these days) I lead Fritz into the park. Once again we cross paths with the bouncy Bruce, a Labradoodle I have been told—but this time the presence of this white cloud does not even elicit a growl. Slowly we make progress toward the green, Fritz checking out the early action at the café on his way.

There are a number of dogs at play on the green this morning and Fritz briefly visits with each grouping. Then I notice that he is heading for the Randolph walkway and this means that I have to follow suit. By the time I have neared the footpath I can just see my dog's bum disappearing in its progress toward the Randolph gate and, as this is dangerous and forbidden territory, I pick up my speed in pursuit. There is no sign of the rascal as I continue forward and I can't believe that he could actually move fast enough to exit the park without my catching at least a glimpse of his disappearing tail. I walk out to Randolph Avenue in some anxiety but as there is still no sign of the chap I turn around and head back to the green. Naturally I spot my dog nosing around among the other canines in the center of this vast space. Eventually he spots me heading for the café and rushes over enthusiastically, as if to say, "Where have *you* been?"

When I reach the café I don't even bother putting Fritz on lead, feeling he has already achieved the worst he can do in the disappearing act department—I don't bother to secure his presence until I sit down with my cappuccino a few minutes later. Today we have Nicholas, Dan, Ronnie, Peter, Ellen, Georgie, Ofra and Hanna. There is considerable outrage among those assembled when someone mentions that Mayor Ken wants to supply ethnic minorities with free scooters so that they can gain a step-up in their pursuit of black cab knowledge. This leads naturally to a front page article in the *Sunday Times* in which it was stated recently that medical school Muslims with objections to treating sexually transmitted diseases are seeking leave to avoid lectures on such topics, and that Sainsbury's has (1) excused similarly inclined chemists from dispensing medicines for conditions that are offensive to them and (2) checkers from wringing up alcohol purchases on their tills. There is a feeling of displacement among the dog people this morning—as one detail after another seems to encroach on their own sense of society. A shower adds to the dour mood but when it lifts we begin a stolid back passage walkround.

Thursday, October 11:

A thick fog obscures all distant views and Fritz and I have a chilly Thursday morning in which to make our progress toward the cypress trees. Up behind us come Cristal and Hercules but they have soon passed us by as Fritz inches forward, sniffing with great concentration. The foul weather has driven a large party of dog owners off the green and into the precincts of the café, where I can see them pressing their noses up against the glass of this still solidly shuttered oasis.

One of these disappointed customers is Nicholas and he determines to complete another walkround in the interim. Fritz and I join Monty and his master and we return to our entry point, but at this point Hercules, on a second circuit himself, decides he just has to mount Oscar the Schnauzer and he is oblivious to the importunate commands of Jean-Baptiste. Oscar is heading toward the green, that is in the opposite direction, and Nicholas very generously reverses his steps, pursues the randy Cocker, attaches Monty's lead to the rascal, and delivers him to his frustrated owner. Dan now agrees to join Nicholas in that interrupted half circle but I head with Fritz directly back to the café, now open.

Suzanne has just preceded me at the counter and has confounded the staff with her request for toast with Marmite. "You mean marmalade?" Suzanne is assured that the café doesn't carry the sought-after comestible but five minutes later Elian delivers a jar of the savory sauce to her table. At our table Dan is delivering a report on the reconstruction of his new bathroom, where a cracked pipe has caused major damage. He is interrupted in this recital by the arrival of an American woman, Cheryl, who has just appeared in our midst with two Pugs, seven year-old Lola and thirteen year-old Ginger. Cheryl joins us for coffee, wheeling in a covered cage on four trolley wheels, Ginger's mode of transport when her ancient legs are a bit too tired for further progress. Winnie is essentially indifferent to these American cousins, whose wonderful craggy faces are soon being stroked by everybody. Linda has agreed to give Ofra a ride at the end of today's proceedings, but Dan says that *he* has to give Ofra a ride today because he needs to ask her a favor—"Can I have a shower at your house?"

Friday, October 12:

It's again misty this morning and there is real moisture soon evident on my leather jacket as I head into the park with Fritz. Far ahead of us I can see Alfie the Standard Schnauzer heading for the cypress trees, but there is no chance we will catch up because today is one of those mornings when our progress is painfully slow—as Fritz has to sample all the foliage on the margins of our walkway. On our right rugby players are practicing their moves—the field is scorched by the frequent occurrence of the "F" word. Out on the green the dog owners are in two separate groups. Isla ventures over to test her luck against Vito, but the latter can't play today because he is wearing a plastic collar after having had surgery on his tear ducts. Suzanne and I are the last to leave the wet greensward; the others have taken an early refuge from the wet in the embrace of the café.

Heading in with us are the two new Pugs, each in a raincoat, and Cheryl again joins us at coffee. London Janet has been on a junket to Bruges and has brought back a lovely box of chocolate truffles. These are shared out before the others tuck into their cheese croissants. The cheese is very generously sliced this morning and the dogs are the beneficiaries of this largesse. Ellen is particularly handsome in her handouts—she has to be reminded to eat some of her own snack. Two people stop by to get a light from Hanna; these days I am almost smoked out of my seat by all these cigarettes and Ronnie's cigar.

We begin a back passage walkround but Daisy-Mae, looking like a rag mop again, soon squeezes through the fence into the kiddies' playground where she quickly deposits a poo. Poor Janet has to retreat, therefore, enter this forbidden zone, clean up the mess, and retrace her steps. Daisy-Mae has by this time been through the fence several times but, reunited with her mistress at last, she is still not finished with her naughtiness. Someone has left the door to the five-a-side field open and the little Shih-Tzu is in like a shot, pursuing a bottle cap and resisting all attempts to get her to rejoin the rest of the party. In spite of these delays a loitering Fritz has soon rejoined the group and then passed even the front runners as we seek dryer climes.

Anthony Linick

Saturday, October 13:

It looks like there might even be some sunshine today as Fritz and I head for the park on a busy Saturday morning. Progress toward the green is a little swifter than yesterday and soon Fritz is checking out the café scene (not a soul about) and having a sniff at all the scholars in Roland's obedience class. I head directly for Saskia, who is standing on the cricket crease with Buddy, for I know she is a scholar also—of gardening in this case—and I want to ask her for some advice on the care and feeding of some house plants. She promises to return with answers tomorrow and so I next turn my attention to the rambling of my dog, whom I have to pursue at great length until it is time to go in for coffee.

We have our usual packed weekend turnout crowded around our table, which is again decorated with Janet's superfluous Belgian truffles. Kate is sulking over the prospect of a Saturday morning expedition to Sainbury's, necessary because yesterday morning there was extensive flooding on Maida Vale itself, due to a burst water main, and many of the shops (including Clifton Road's Tesco) are still closed. Dan is reminded to tell us that yesterday he had a run-in, quite literally, with a fellow shopper at Sainsbury's, whom he accidentally nudged with his cart—only to be attacked quite viciously by the lady in question with her own vehicle. Security had to be called and the lady, still not over her trolley rage, escorted off the premises. Things also happen to Dan (who is having an "adults" only visit to Alton Towers on Monday).

Our back passage walkround begins with a bout of furious barking from Skye the Alsatian, who no longer seems charmed by the bouncy antics of Bruce the Labradoodle. Hundreds of little kids are participating in Saturday morning footie on our left and, with parents manning the sidelines, it is easy to spot at least three of their dogs who have been invited to enjoy the proceedings. Our dog owners are always outraged at such a liberty. They know that if one of *our* animals entered into a fenced playing field disapproval would follow immediately. But, perhaps because money has changed hands for the use of the field in question, no park official arrives to expel the illegal canines today.

Sunday, October 14:

It's a grey but mild morning as Fritz and I make our way into Paddington Rec on a fairly quiet Sunday morning; there are no sounds of church bells to intrude on our solitude as we make our way slowly toward the green, eager to see what activities are going down this morning. The answer is not much. Isla and Daisy-Mae are wrestling and Sparkie, whose anti-barking collar seems to be gummed up, is barking manically as he dances around this pair. Soon he is off on a few of his speedy circles, the fastest dog in the park. Then he shows that he can perform at this speed with a biscuit in his mouth as well. Fritz cadges a few of these treats himself and then has to chase off a new and nameless Schnauzer, who is circling the green with his mistress. A thirteen week-old Staffie puppy, with a half brown and half white head and an all-white body (if you don't count the mud) comes over to make friends by rolling on her back in submission. The pup's name is also Roxy and Fritz gets to growl a lot in welcoming her to the scene.

When we go in for coffee they are blasting us with golden oldies in the café, where Dan very kindly takes my place in line and then himself delivers our coffees a few minutes later. Dan has to do a shift at his theatre today as the Phoenix plays host to a comedian who will do his entire act in Russian. (A Russian comedian sounds like a contradiction in terms these days.) Several of the dog owners have seen *Strictly Come Dancing* last night and most of them think Bruce Forsythe should call it a day. On the other hand they seem to regret the fact that Michael Parkinson, whose show was also on last night, is retiring soon. There is universal agreement that England beating France last night to advance to rugby's World Cup final is a good thing. The dogs haunt Hanna as she tries to eat her scrambled eggs and the brazen Daisy-Mae even takes a biscuit out of Fritz's mouth. In the background this morning we have the gentle giant Ruby, who is half Rottweiler and half French Mastiff.

Linda arrives with Pepper and, this being a lazy Sunday morning, several of the coffee drinkers decide to have a second cup. The conversation turns to the encounters our dogs have had with other animals. Dan says that when Winnie visits rural Essex she risks life and limb by barking at the horses in their own paddock—while these beasts try to stamp her out. He also recalls that when he and a school friend were walking his dad's dog that angry cows chased all three into a river. I am reminded of the time we were walking along the Severn and a large tribe of cows followed us (and our Toby) for a mile. Dan tries to describe what it is like to be licked by a cow. Ronnie, a faraway look in his eye, says that when he was a kid his dad took him to the London Zoo, where a giraffe leaned over its fence and licked him on the face.

Monday, October 15:

Fritz lingers for a long time among the leaves near our entrance gate and in this fashion we are overtaken by the one-eyed Humphrey. Coming in the opposite direction is Artemis, the Border Terrier—today accompanied by a small black dog with a grizzled chin named Jeffrey. Fritz falls in step with Humphrey and two trot on to the café, where the leaf-blowing groundsman is trying to outblast the chap who is spraying the westernmost pitch, assisted by the insistent motor on the back of a truck. The leaf-blower's motor is on his own back.

Out on the green we encounter Christian, Georgie, Ronnie and Davide, the latter having just returned from a long junket to Bangkok and Sidney. At one point I count eleven little dogs at play, none more lively than Daisy-Mae and the lampshade wearing Vito. I can see Fritz at the west end of the green, where he has found a family who are kneeling down to give him a good cuddle. As I approach I can see that the mother is, in fact, Linda, but the two kids are much younger than Liam, and I have not seen them before. They are the siblings of a boy much closer to Liam's age, part of a family Rob and Linda have known since their Singapore days. Linda feels she needs to tell me why she has the care of this lot today and her explanation is a shock: the father of the family, a 47 year-old lawyer, has dropped dead in his kitchen at 6:00 this morning.

Somewhat stunned by this instant lesson in mortality I lead Fritz over to the café, where we join a group that includes Ronnie, Peter, Ellen, Georgie, Cheryl, Davide and Ofra. Cheryl's Pugs keep trying to run into the café, from which they are immediately withdrawn, but the same cannot be said of the sheep dog Flossy, who is so spooked by the other dogs that she cannot be left outside and has to wait out the queue on lead. Davide is telling us that he had to change his Sydney hotel because the entire town was infested by moths. Saskia drops by to give me some information on orchids and this gives everyone else a chance to bark at

Buddy. Ronnie announces that he has too many appointments and won't be here tomorrow. He has just discovered that Peter has forgotten his leather gloves on the table but that gentleman is on his way back to recover these, and the rest of us get up for a back passage walkround—Cheryl pushing Ginger's empty covered wagon all the way.

Tuesday, October 16:

I have to break the bad news to Fritz: it is raining outside and this means it's raincoat time. There is an ineffective protest over this imposition and then we are off, crossing the street and entering our gate just in time for Fritz to have a welcome growl at Oscar. Next we meet Saskia and walk with her and Buddy toward the café. Some of the Paddington Academy kids are barking at us, but they can't replicate Buddy's deep voice. He is using it to encourage his mistress to kick him the indoor football she is carrying.

I can see Georgie, Cheryl, Peter and Ellen already sheltering from the wet weather in front of the café doors, but Fritz seems prepared for additional activity out on the green, rain or no. Somehow he has picked up a leaf, which is plastered to the back of his raincoat, and no matter how often he shakes himself or trots around it can't be budged. He ventures out to the middle of the sodden green where, to their eternal credit, five dog owners are busily slinging balls to their wet pets. I am getting really damp, in spite of wearing my own rain jacket, so this time I corral Fritz and head for the caff. You would think that in weather of this type we might be spared the sound of the leaf blower but, no, one chap is working his way down Mt. Bannister with the loathsome object on his back and we soon have it blasting away outside the café fence.

After a few minutes the aforementioned grouping is augmented by the presence of Dan, Davide and Hanna. In the "things happen to Dan department" we now learn that on Sunday night he was rear-ended when he pulled up at an intersection to avoid a collision with an unmarked police van. Now his neck is sore but that may also be due to all those rides at Alton Towers. Pugs dominate the breakfast scene—with Cheryl cuddling Winnie and Dan picking up first Lola, then Ginger. We learn that Winnie can fart and bark at the same time. "Now that's what I call multi-tasking," I say. We wait for a break in the weather and begin a back passage walkround. Dan surprises me by asking, "Isn't today Dorothy's birthday?" She would have been sixty-seven today.

119

Wednesday, October 17:

The rainy weather has at last come to an end and we have bright sunshine for our entry into Paddington Rec today. It is still on the chilly side and I am glad I am wearing my leather jacket. I should have brought my sunglasses. Phoenix and Freddy the Dachshund pass us by somewhere near the cypress trees and we find Ronnie outside the café, holding his solitary vigil as he waits for the doors to open. Out on the green I am soon in conference with Saskia over what to do with the tendrils of my Stephanotis plant. At my feet Fritz is bossing Roxy the Staffie puppy around and fending off the attacks of Pepper.

I meet Ofra in the coffee queue. She has forgotten to fill in section 10 on her passport application and needs the signature of a witness. I can't do it because I don't have a British passport, but Dan says, "Anyone can sign this; I can sign it, Georgie can sign it, Ronnie can sign it." I say, "This forms requires the signature of someone with 'standing in the community'—*none of you* can sign it." Lola and Ginger continue their raids on the interior of the café and someone is always getting up to expel them; they keep pretending that, as newcomers, they can't be expected to know the rules. It's a lap-jumping day. Ofra has Fritz, I have Bailey and Winnie, and Dan has both of the new Pugs. Bailey manages to put his tail in Dan's coffee. Near the end of the session there is an incident that brings cheer to the heart. A leaf-blowing gardener is raising clouds of debris inside the café forecourt and wafting petrol fumes over the food of the alfresco diners. But the captain of this orange-clad troupe marches in, taps the chap on the shoulder, silences the machine and, a few minutes later, replaces him with another gardener who attacks the same space with a seldom-seen weapon of choice—a rake.

I don't accompany the others on their back passage walkround since Fritz and I have an errand to run at the doctors' surgery on Randolph Avenue. We do return through the park and I have to let my dog off lead again so that he can defend himself against the antics of Leila and Roxy the Dachshund puppy. Soon we have intercepted the others, just completing their walkround. Cheryl, pushing Ginger's covered wagon, is making arrangements to see *Blood Brothers* next Friday.

Friday, October 19:

I have missed a day in the park, walking with Tosh on the Chiltern Way in Oxfordshire and Buckinghamshire. The effects of this eleven and a half mile ordeal (14 ascents) can still be felt as I shuffle forward into the park, my tired legs ready to betray me at any moment. It is, like yesterday, a wonderful autumnal morning, with bright sun, chill temperatures and a crispness in the air. The fuzzy Fritz, also tired from a romp with Linda, Rob, and Liam in Regents Park, is never bothered much by the weather and skips along contentedly toward the green.

A small group of owners is standing on one end of the cricket crease but Dan, handing Winnie's lead over to Georgie, soon departs for work—leaving only Peter, Ellen, Ronnie, and Georgie of course, still standing. Sparkie's "cough suppressor," as Peter calls it, doesn't seem to be in play and the little Yorkie is importunate; he wants someone to chase him and there isn't a volunteer. Fritz heads off for the Randolph corner and I follow him around for a while. Cheryl is just entering, pushing Ginger in her blue Conestoga. "Wagons west!" I remark. When I turn around, the green, which is so inviting on a radiant morning like this, is deserted. It's time to head in for coffee.

Someone remarks on the poor turnout but our chairs soon have to be squeezed closer together as latecomers make an appearance: Hanna, Linda, and Nicholas. Peter is teased by Ronnie for fretting about global warming and Cheryl (who claims both Oklahoma and Texas as homes) says she thinks global warming is just a natural phenomenon—Houston, you are the problem. Sparkie jumps into Georgie's lap and accidentally sits on the cough zapper, thereby dosing himself. The two new Pugs are oddly dressed: Lola in a red and white striped sweater that looks like it belongs in an ancient seaside postcard, and Ginger is a black outfit with "Bling, Bling" stenciled in sequins. Both of these dogs are still innocently making forays *into* the café. Our group gets widely separated during the back passage walkround and by the time we reach the Essendine gate it's just me and Linda.

Saturday, October 20:

The beautiful autumn weather persists and the lovely fall scene is made even more perfect by the total absence of sound: not a single machine can be heard droning in the background. Fritz, who expelled his evening meal last night—again my fault, after having given him some overly hot chips—seems to be suffering no ill effects from the incident and makes good progress toward the café—where he gets a greeting from a solitary Ronnie. Then he reports to the wet green.

There are a lot of dogs out here, including a number of Saturday visitors I do not recognize. David the dog sitter is here with Campbell the Westie but Fritz seems less manic than usual in his greeting to his old pal. It has been so long since David has actually had a stint as Fritz's sitter that perhaps the old bond is weakening. I follow my dog as he heads for the east side of the green. Sparkie is just disappearing into the foliage here and Fritz has to see what the Yorkie is up to. Thereafter Fritz spends a lot of time in the deep bushes, emerging at last when it is time to head in for coffee.

We have a very large turnout at our usual table this morning, with Peter and Ellen giving way to Hanna and Liz and the total number of those present at any one time never dipping below eleven and a half. The half is represented in this case by baby Valentina, whom all the dogs want to sniff; she is a delightful character who can walk now, supported by tables and chairs, giggling and gyrating in the sunshine. Liz reports that she is falling behind in her design course homework. Dan says that he has had another episode of road rage, chasing a driver down St. John's Wood High Street in order to castigate him for throwing litter out of his car window. Cheryl announces that she will be watching Oklahoma play in college football today while many of the other coffee drinkers are planning to watch England in the World Cup rugby final against South Africa tonight. A car races into the park along the Carlton roadway but half a dozen community policemen on bikes are interested only in their coffee and fail to intervene. We start a back passage walkround and Fritz soon outraces all the others. As we leave the park we pass a beaming Andrew the Akita, sitting on a bench in the sun.

Sunday, October 21:

Another crisp sunny October morning. Fritz makes rapid progress toward the green and here we meet a number of the regulars and also Lyndon, his pal Peter, and the visiting French Bulldog Lulu. Fritz doesn't hang around for long, however, and soon I am following him over the foothills of Mt. Bannister. I succeed in coaxing him into a rapid descent with my biscuit bag and we then make contact with a second doggy group out on the green. Buddy sits at my feet so calmly and beseechingly that he gets a biscuit as well. I learn from Saskia that he and his family are moving temporarily into a flat—which mine overlooks—while major renovations are undertaken at home.

We are a very large group at breakfast and a second little table is squeezed up against our usual round one in order to accommodate everybody. Hanna is embittered by England's loss to South Africa in last night's rugby World Cup final; now she has her hopes set on Lewis Hamilton winning the Formula One championship at this afternoon's Brazilian Grand Prix. The subject of tattoos comes up and Lyndon is urged to put his own on display. Up comes his jumper (revealing a pierced nipple) and a well-decorated shoulder, but the girls all get up to see the art work on his back. He has recorded here the names of all his beloved dogs: Chester, Koko (who ended her days with Janet) and Lulu. (The tattooist, given this list, evidently said, "You date boys *and* girls?") Ronnie, it is obvious, doesn't approve of tattoos ("it's not a very Jewish thing to do, is it?") and suggests to Lyndon that he might as well go ahead and add the name of Ronnie's dog to his back as well—"Antidisestablishmentarianism."

The breakfasters are in a jolly mood and there seems to be no sign of movement, so Ronnie gets up to begin a solo back passage walkround and I follow him with Fritz. I notice that five young trees have been chopped down in the picnic area on our right. Ronnie wants to know if I have always kept Fritz on lead during this part of the morning ritual. I remind him that just outside the central field Fritz, on the loose, used to celebrate his freedom by hiding in the bushes in order to tease his pal Charlie. "Of course," I add, "in those days we *had* bushes. Now all we have is green iron."

Monday, October 22:

After first a rosy and then a golden dawn grey skies predominate as Fritz and I, after performing a brief local errand, enter the park on a quiet Monday morning. It is especially quiet (give or take two leaf blowers over by Mt. Bannister) because the half term holiday means that there are no organized school groups: the kids who are at play now are here because they really want to be.

There is a small group of dog owners out on the green and we join them briefly. Ronnie is trying to get them to move toward the café, even though this institution won't open its doors for another ten minutes. I follow along because I want to hook Fritz to Ronnie's chair—as I have a second errand to run on Maida Vale Parade. When I return I see a dire prediction on a sign at the counter. Because of all the building work needed to shift offices from the clubhouse to this building (while a new wing is added to the latter), there might be no electricity on Wednesday and hence no café. I tell Nicholas this news when he enters; he says we will all have to go to Porridge on Lauderdale Parade for our coffee.

We have only a small group at coffee this morning—just the aforementioned souls plus Georgie, Peter and Ellen. There is a brief memorial service held over the second blow to British sporting hopes—with Lewis Hamilton's failure to capture the Formula One championship yesterday. Earlier than usual we begin our back passage walkround. I am surprised by the two unattached leads hanging from the hooks on the forecourt wall ("ghost dogs") but these turn out to belong to Lola and Ginger. The latter is soon aboard her covered wagon anyway. Georgie is making today's farewell procession with Winnie and Daisy-Mae as well as her own Sparkie. The latter is raising a ruckus because he wants his ball but when he gets it (if he gets it) he loses it in the bushes. I tell Georgie that when Sparkie first appeared as a puppy we all thought he was *so* sweet. "We got that one wrong," she says.

Tuesday, October 23:

A lovely autumnal morning, sunny and not too chilly, provides the setting for our slow entry this morning—with Fritz pausing to sample selected grass shoots on the way to the cypress trees. Out on the green there is a lively scene; lots of dogs and their owners and even the head groundsman in conversation with Saskia. He is supervising, from a distance, the trimming of trees near the café as lower branches are lopped off in a process called "lifting." Buddy stations himself at my feet and is soon rewarded with a biscuit. Fritz manages to stay pretty close today and I don't have to go too far to snag him when it is time to go in for coffee. Joining us for the first time in many a morning is the proud dad, Faz, who comes in with Jasmine but without baby Scarlett.

As soon as we have entered the precincts of the café we realize that we have made a mistake. Fallen limbs make for a very hazardous entry and I have to unhook Fritz so that he can fight his way through the foliage while I step over it. At least the tree trimmers have turned off their mulching machine and their chainsaws in order to have some coffee. No one objects to their presence or the necessity of the task at hand but someone does have the wit to suggest that perhaps *tomorrow* would have been a better day for this activity—since the café is supposed to be closed then anyway.

We gather around a large table outside the doors, though behind us Franca is presiding over a second table in the forecourt (one from which Blake escapes a number of times). Eventually baby Valentina is wheeled between Dan's chair and mine. She is in her usual jolly mood and Dan, who seems to have many nieces and nephews and godchildren, is always wonderful with babies; today he tickles Valentina, replaces her fallen shoe, and keeps up a non-stop babytalk patter. Daisy-Mae gets into the act as well, chewing on Valentina's little fingers but this only raises *one* of Boxer Bianca's eyebrows; the baby is cool with it.

Michael the Pirate wheels in his bike as Hanna is asking if Franca has remembered a consignment of red tail feathers from her parrot's bottom (I don't know why Hanna wants them) and Nicholas has to get up to take two phone calls. Janet distributes CDs with pictures and videos from the September doggy picnic (144 items!) and, the chainsaw massacre having started up again, I make a solo dash for home.

Wednesday, October 24:

I am trying to decide if it is going to rain today but then the heavens are having the same quandary. Under any circumstances it is quite dark this morning and still rather quiet. Far ahead of me I can just see Janet, who has a bad cold, making a rare midweek visit with Georgie, who has just finished a cold of her own. They are heading for the cypress trees, not their usual entrance at all, and somehow my dog picks up their scent (or that of their dogs) and speeds off in pursuit.

I can't tell when or where or even *if* he has done a poo by the time I catch up with these ladies near the café. They are having a grand walkround and soon we are inching up Mt. Bannister from the Carlton walkway. The quiet, by this time, has been shattered by the leaf blowers.

Janet says that autumn used to be a time when drifts of leaves made an agreeable crunch beneath your feet but in our park they aren't allowed a moment's peace on the turf before someone arrives to hoover them up.

Out on the green there is a small circle of dog owners and we join them. Christian notes that his Vito and Janet's Daisy-Mae are so besotted that when they catch sight of one another they freeze first, then advance in slow motion like some movie out of the '70s. Their wrestling now is very upsetting to Sparkie, who feels excluded. When it is time for Vito to go on lead he walks backward toward the exit, staring mournfully at his receding girlfriend.

A rumor surfaces that if there is still some electricity the café might be able to make us some coffee today. A slow migration begins but the place is locked up tight and the decision is made to move toward Porridge on Lauderdale Parade. I follow the others only as far as the Morshead gate, however, and head for home. It still hasn't rained.

Thursday, October 25:

It is a grey, chilly day in Maida Vale and there is a hint of mist as well. They are still pulling electricity cables on the walkway outside the café but I step gingerly over these and make my way out to the other dog owners in the middle of the green. Christian is about to drive Reina to work and Dan agrees to keep an eye on Vito while his daddy is gone. From the other side of the green we can see Ginger, in her covered wagon, making slow progress over the grass. Fritz, of course, has little interest in this group activity so I am soon in slow pursuit as he meanders down the Randolph walkway. When I get him turned around we head for the back of the tennis courts, where Saskia is exercising Buddy with a mid-sized yellow ball. A chap is knocking *his* ball off the wall of the bowling green building and, as I see Fritz heading in that direction too, I know what's coming next—my dog soon has this ball in his mouth and is trying to make off with the prize. I succeed in distracting him with a biscuit long enough to retrieve the purloined object. Then it is time to cross the now-deserted green and head for the re-opened café.

We have a lively group this morning, with Peter, Ellen, Georgie, a croaking Janet, Ronnie, Cheryl, and Ofra. The dogs seem in perpetual motion this morning. Vito, who is evidently very strong for a lightweight, is wriggling in Janet's lap, Sparkie is dragging Daisy-Mae around by her fur, Bailey, on a restricted diet, is hopping from lap to lap hunting for a handout, and Fritz has stationed himself in front of Ellen, hoping that she will produce something useful from her purse. Lola is also being passed from lap to lap (Winnie is not pleased) and Daisy-Mae, freed at last from Sparkie's teeth, is ingratiating herself to a chap at a picnic bench who is trying to talk on his mobile phone—when the Shih-Tzu is not playing with a piece of dried poo.

Peter and Ellen are always the first to depart and today their places are taken by Davide, back from his holiday in Brazil, and Hanna. Davide is fuming because Dan has taken his car keys (and his car) this morning. Hanna tells us that poor Toby, Rowena's thirteen year-old Tibetan Terrier, has died this morning. The news casts a pall over proceedings as everyone remembers the hairless invalid, a rescue dog with a purple sweater, whom we will see no more.

A back passage walkround begins. As we near the final field we can see that naughty Charlie the Cocker has taken his ball onto the running track and his owner can't figure how to get him off this forbidden, fenced surface. We show her where the wire fence can be pulled back and several minutes of unanswered importuning follow—how much power does the dog suddenly possess when he can clearly withhold obedience from a frustrated owner, who can do nothing to reverse this pecking order? Near the Essendine gate Dan is kicking leaves while Winnie dances forth and back in the exploding foliage.

Friday, October 26:

Another grey day, though the temperatures are mild enough. We enter the park with Saskia and Buddy; these two have now become my neighbors, temporarily, while their own flat undergoes conversion. Saskia says that last night the first rocket of the fireworks season was launched against the café wall but when she asked the security guards to do something about this incursion they just shrugged. Buddy was evidently traumatized.

On the green we have a busy scene with Izzy the Tibetan Terrier, much matured since she was last here, drawing a great deal of attention. Vito and Daisy-Mae resume their courtship and Michaela, who is usually earlier than the rest of us, arrives with Skye the Cairn. Linda brings Pepper as well and tells us that yesterday Liam and his musical pals were visited during their half term rock and roll workshop at the Roundhouse by Sir Paul McCartney—who joined them in a chorus of "Yesterday." Linda has brought a hard yellow ball with her and Fritz gets some real exercise chasing it down.

At coffee the Pugs, Winnie and Lola, are staring at one another from opposite sides of Hanna's scrambled eggs, and get into a barking match on the subject of who gets the leftovers. The Shi-Tzus Tilly and Boo make an appearance and this unsettles the rest of our pets temporarily. Michael the Pirate is reading a copy of the *Times* and talking on his mobile phone at a little table behind us while Ronnie, pulling out *his* phone, talks to his plumber at the same time. We begin a back passage walkround but our farewell to Pepper at the exit gate is only temporary—since he returns for a play date with Fritz an hour later.

Saturday, October 27:

It's a mostly grey morning as Fritz and I enter the park today. Progress is very slow indeed, with a lot of stopping to sniff and sample shoots of grass. The five-a-side pitches are filling up with youngsters and a lorry is parked at the end of our walkway, impeding everyone else's progress, in order to offload more footie equipment. I finally coax the reluctant Fritz onto the grass.

There doesn't seem to be any instruction taking place this morning—perhaps it's half term for dogs too. Fritz finally notices David the dog sitter, here with Campbell, and rushes forward for a greeting. A blonde woman brings in a small Rhodesian Ridgeback (the smallness attributed to a persistent liver complaint). I ask for the dog's name and she says it's "Prune, French for plum." The other dog owners start to call this timid animal Plum and Winnie takes an instant dislike to the visitor, growling, barking and circling Prune until the Ridgeback dives for safety under the legs of her owner. The Pug is lead off in disgrace and the rest of us head in for coffee.

Michael the Pirate is sitting at our usual table and we move on to the picnic area, where we choose a table in the forecourt. Today we have Dan, Georgie, Janet, Cheryl, Liz and Nicholas. Dan is much the worse for wear after three mojitos at the Idylwild, the new posh bar that has replaced the Truscott Arms on Shirland Road. Cheryl presents him with a box of chocolates in recognition of his arranging for tickets for last night's performance of *Blood Brothers*. Winnie would like one of these but she has to content herself with the usual snacks; she is hyperventilating with excitement and she jumps from one bench to the next.

Cheryl's Ginger is feeling poorly this morning and remains in her covered wagon throughout our session. Janet is also poorly; she can barely talk by now. Liz arrives in good health but her ear receives a persistent bashing from Nicholas, who wants to impart every iota of his wisdom on the subject of interior decorating. As we near the exit, fifteen minutes later, I can see that he is still at it. Oh yes, I passed another kidney stone yesterday.

Sunday, October 28:

We have left summer time behind and I have been going from room to room turning the clocks back—though on many of these I can't figure out how to do it: this was Dorothy's job. Fritz does a good job of waiting until 10:00 (body time) before our 9:00 departure (clock time). As we near the green I am very impressed that the clubhouse clocks have made the proper adjustment—but they shine down on no one, for the green is strangely empty. From the right I can see Dan entering with Winnie. I am just about to remind him that this is the day on which, traditionally, we used to have either Jo Pettet or Ofra arrive absentmindedly an hour earlier than the rest of us, when he says, "Ofra's been wandering around the park for an hour."

There is a very substantial turnout on the green this morning. Roxy the Staffie puppy is again the center of attention and almost knocks me over as she dives between my legs. Pepper is here and, indeed, Rob arrives with his camera and in soon snapping away—though the lowering grey skies provide only a poor light. Fritz wanders everywhere. He spends some time by himself in the Grantully dog pen and then I see him up on Mt. Bannister. When I call to tell him that Pepper is here he begins a very rapid headlong charge down the hill and out to the rest of us, his ears bouncing up and down in his thrilling run. Buddy arrives with his daddy for once and soon the Golden Retriever is sitting at my feet, cadging a biscuit. Considering the fact that yesterday at this time it would have been 10:30, no one objects when there is a move toward the café when its doors open at last.

Today coffee and dog treats are on Liz, who is celebrating her Roxy's birthday—but whether the Beagle is four or five or, indeed, whether her birthday is today or several weeks ago, has been a matter of debate between Liz and her boys. She tells us that her youngest lad has been invited to a bar mitzvah by a classmate, one in which all of the guests will be spirited away to New York on a private jet, all expenses paid. Our most frequent flyer, Davide, announces that he has a flight in two hours and he hasn't shaved or ironed his shirt yet.

When we get up to begin a back passage walkround Dan discovers that Winnie is missing. She has started to follow her other daddy home and has come to a puzzled halt on the green. We get her turned around in the right direction and make our way past dozens of bussed-in footie lads, undertaking instruction on the first two fields. A solitary jogger is pawing the turf behind us, trying to excuse herself as she inches past us.

Monday, October 29:

After a night of light rain we now have clearing skies and the reappearance of sunlight. It is still a bit chilly and this will explain why Leila is in costume, though I have to say that the outfit in question is the epitome of cognitive dissonance: camouflage with a fur-lined hood. Fritz seems to be limping slightly, but I can't figure out which paw he is favoring during our attempt to reach the café at last. Here Vicky is interviewing the tree trimmers on their immediate intentions—as she would like to open the café without the hazard of falling limbs. Ronnie, whom we have not seen in a few days, is already seated at our table and I tell him that I will be back soon.

Around the corner I see a once-familiar sight: Lee the animal warden has brought his van into the park and this gives the dog owners the opportunity of replenishing their supply of green poo poo bags. A few minutes later Saskia wants to borrow a tissue in order to remove some saliva from Buddy's snout but I have only plastic to offer. She reports that Buddy was pleased as punch to have the company of his daddy in the park yesterday and that her husband came home to report that Buddy seemed to know everyone at our table. Peter (of Peter and Gypsy) is here with three dogs and a mobile phone on which he is having a loud conversation on the subject of the Crown Prosecution Service.

At breakfast we have Hanna, Liz, Cheryl, Georgie, Ronnie and Rowena. Georgie is quite shaken after a park incident yesterday afternoon. While she was having a walkround with Dan and Janet an intemperate jogger tried to kick Sparkie during one lap and did so, with a blow to the ribs, on a second. The poor Yorkie was in this case completely innocent and not even on the footpath at the time of the assault. A cry of protest rose in Georgie's throat and the jogger departed. Janet now arrives, sent home from work, and we hear the story all over again. The ladies are planning to report the incident to the office and to see if the villain shows up on any of the CCTV cameras. This is my signal to start for home alone, strolling with Fritz along the Morshead roadway. This turns out to be a protracted process—as my dog needs to sniff every leaf, and there are a lot of them.

Tuesday, October 30:

I follow Fritz into the park on a sunny autumnal Tuesday, happy to see that there is no sign of yesterday's slight limp. Almost immediately we encounter Stella the Staffie and Tilly the Border Terrier. Jo Lynn suggests that perhaps Fritz is having a few too many treats these days, for he does appear heavier when his coat gets woolly. Sabina, whom we soon meet with Scamp and Oscar, also notes that it is almost haircut time—but as a Schnauzer owner she is in a better position to understand that my dog is *not* putting on weight.

Out on the green we have Bailey, Vito, Daisy-Mae, Winnie, Sparkie, Lola and Ginger. Vito, who is shortly to undergo the neutering procedure, has his nose buried in Fritz's belly and Christian says that Fritz must like this because his leg is trembling. "His leg always trembles," I reply, "when he is about to piss on another dog's head." The ladies in our group are agitating for an early departure for the café (Janet is still suffering and now Dan has a cold as well) and so we head off in the right direction. There are still five minutes to go before opening time but Vicky takes pity on us and opens the door.

Fritz has not been himself of late—a combination of firework season and noisy scaffolders at the front elevation—and he expresses his need for extra comfort by jumping first into Janet's lap, then on to Dan's and finally on to Cheryl's. While he is so situated a lady brings in an alien presence, a Cairn named Mack, and Fritz goes crazy, undertaking a high

131

pitched scolding aimed at the intruder. Winnie, so Dan says, always seems to fill up with such rage and, periodically, some object has to be chosen on which to vent this anger. Today she leaps off Dan's lap and attacks a flock of pigeons. We are at table for almost forty-five minutes and in this time Ronnie has been able to accommodate the recent time change on Dorothy's watch, which I wear now; he is eminently qualified since he used to have shops in every railway station that performed similar services. No one else seems poised to move—as the sun is actually providing a little warmth—and so I begin a solitary ramble toward the exit gate.

Wednesday, October 31:

Grey skies predominate as Fritz and I reach the park today. My dog seems to have spent a more restful night, eating all of his tea, joining me in watching TV and sharing the bed, disdaining his usual hidey holes, and bouncing along bravely on our night-time walk. (During the latter we met the elderly gentleman from Ashworth Mansions who nightly crosses the road to throw food through the park railing for the foxes.) The scaffolders are still around but the key to an improved disposition in Fritz is that there were no mortar attacks last night.

When we reach the green this morning Christian and Reina are just leaving with Vito—"I sure know how to clear a green," I say. It turns out that Vito has just been a participant in an ugly confrontation between two un-neutered Cockers, Monty and Hercules. Dan, trying to extricate Monty from this fray, has ended up with a jacket covered in mud. Ofra is by herself at the end of the cricket crease, talking into her mobile phone as if it were a microphone—and at a volume that would obviate the need for any instrument at all, it would seem. As we head in for coffee she receives a rapturous greeting from a youngster she knows, here with a school group of joggers. I ask Ofra what school this girl goes to and she says that it is an international school in Hampstead. Of course you would bring such kids to the green in Paddington Rec—instead of trying out the pathways of Hampstead Heath.

Peter (of Peter and Ellen) is missing this morning, having gone for another session in Leigh-on-Sea. We do have Dan, Davide, Georgie, Janet, Ronnie, Ofra and Albert. Ronnie reports that Dr. Bruce Fogle says that Rosie has a problem with her trachea and she has been given some anti-inflammatory medicine. Georgie reports that the water has been turned off on her street—the water people never seem to bring their work to a conclusion hereabouts. While we are sipping our coffee the sun makes an appearance and we have a lovely fall morning for our back passage walkround. Fritz exits the park and almost immediately he turns tail and re-enters. When he does this a second time I realize that there is a problem: he can sense the intrusive presence of the scaffolders at work across the street.

November, 2007

Thursday, November 1:

We begin a new month in the park under grey skies again, but our progress toward the park is made more interesting by the presence of a series of dogs who are making their way against our flow. First we have Cristal the Alsatian, then Oscar and Scamp, then Leila and Jonesie—with the former wearing her skull and crossbones coat today. Leila always rushes forward to greet Fritz, who is one of her favorite pals. This furry gentleman seems willing to accept the honor, although he has again had a very bad night, even sleeping under the bed after Halloween fireworks.

When I reach the green my heart sinks at the sight of a pitch invasion by Paddington Academy; as predicted the park has become the schoolyard for yet another educational institution. Michaela with Skye and Linda with Pepper are heading our way and there are some noisy greetings. I can now see that the displaced dog people have migrated to the foot of Mt. Bannister. Here a randy Vito is terrorizing the other dogs. Ginger is heading off in the wrong direction and Hanna is trying to herd her back to the group. A few minutes later, when we are sitting down to coffee, Nicholas carries in a still bewildred Ginger, whom he has found wandering around on the green. Cheryl reports that she had a good round of golf yesterday.

We say goodbye to our red-cheeked barista, Mariana, who will soon be returning to her native Colombia. I have Sparkie on my lap on several occasions today while his mommy, Georgie, says that she has accidentally stabbed herself with a kitchen knife. Once again the skies begin to clear while we are having our coffee, and the back passage walkround takes place in much happier climes. Sparkie is at his noisiest during such peregrinations. "Rowena," Georgie now adds, "says that Sparkie has Canine Tourettes."

Saturday, November 3:

I was in the park briefly yesterday morning, but I had a 10:15 appointment with my urologist and so I could not stay for coffee and gossip. My impression is that there were a lot of dogs in the park, including Zara and Dash, the rarely seen Cavaliers belonging to the teen-aged Lisa—whom I had not seen in some time either. Lisa is wearing braces now.

Poor Fritz has had another troubled night, terrorized again by the nightly bombardment we get at this time of year. He did manage to eat his tea but by the time we went out for his late walk he would barely budge on the pavement and I had to take him home almost immediately. At 4:00 in the morning I could hear him scrabbling away at the carpet behind the bathroom door, one of his favorite hiding places.

The morning is bright and warm for November. I have forgotten my cap but I don't really need it. Not surprisingly, Fritz deposits a lot of stored-up poo as we make our way along the back passage. In the forecourt of the café we have the army again, but they seem poised to play some footie today, rather than undertake any recruiting. They would have one volunteer in Fritz, who accepts the cuddles of one of the camouflage-wearing troopers before passing on to the green.

Roland seems to have only a handful of students today but out on the cricket crease our lot have arrived in numbers: Janet, Dan, Georgie, Ofra, Michaela, Suzanne, Rhiann, and David the dog sitter. David, here with Campbell, is reluctant to let Fritz put paw marks on his clean jeans. The same can be said of Rob, who soon arrives from the Grantully gate with Pepper. Rob is wearing dog-phobic trousers since he and Linda are on their way to a country wedding and I will have the care of Pepper on a sleepover. Fritz toys with following Rob out of the park and Pepper, on lead, sets up a howling objection to his abandonment. Ofra is again all by herself on the margins, talking into her mobile as if it were a microphone. "She looks like a reporter," Dan says, "or a madwoman." "I know which one I'm voting for," I reply.

We take up our seats around our usual table; I have Fritz anchored to one leg of my chair and Pepper to another. Suzanne is discussing a forthcoming expedition to Peru but Dan says that Davide is too ill to fly to Delhi today. The subject of the lottery comes up and I am reminded that I dreamed last night that I had won a million pounds. This is a stimulus for a number of us to fork up a pound each so that Janet can buy eight lucky dips for tonight's draw—which offers a top prize of £18 million. Kathleen McCormack comes in with John (clairvoyant and shaman) and Ché. Kathleen's hair is redder than we remember it. She stops to greet Rosie, who again snaps at the elderly healer. When we get up to begin our back passage walkround I notice that Fritz's lead has not been anchored to a chair leg after all, and that he has been free to wander about—were it not for the seductive appeal of all those tabletop biscuits.

We begin a back passage walkround but opposite the cypress trees there is an ominous moment: Pepper squats to produce a very sloppy poo. When we get home he spits up as well, but he seems well enough to eat his evening meal at 6:00. By this time Fritz, already growing restless under the strain of the first fusillade in a nightlong bombardment, is refusing to eat. At about 8:15 Pepper shows signs of wanting to go out. I prepare to take him, but at the last minute Fritz, who has been hiding under the bed, rushes out the front door as well, and I have to hook him when I get downstairs. The two Schnauzers get as far as the bottom of the stairs, realize that Maida Vale is under attack, and scrabble back up to the front door again.

Now we begin a night that will live in infamy. Fritz is pawing the carpet behind the bathroom door or climbing under the bed. Pepper, when he is not trying to hide behind my head on the TV room sofa, is vomiting and defecating, horrible runny stuff that manages to stain the carpet in the sitting room, the hallway and the bedroom.

Once or twice he manages to indicate that he wants to go out and we have a repeat of our earlier expedition about 11:30. This time I manage to get the dogs a little farther away from our front door but Pepper resists further progress with such vehemence that he manages to slip his halter and rush back to our steps unhooked.

I try to turn out the lights after midnight but Fritz is pawing the carpet under the bed and at one point I have to slide a drawer out so that I can be sure that he is not trapped beneath. I have been spraying carpet cleaner like mad and I am soon out of paper towels. Once, at 1:15 and again at 4:30, Pepper wakes me up and I have to take him out so that he can produce all-liquid poos on the pavements. Only later do I learn that Rob and Linda have returned from their out-of-town wedding at 11:00—an hour they thought would be much too late to rouse me from my rest!

Sunday, November 4:

My house looks like a slum as I prepare to take the dogs outside on a sunny Sunday morning. I let Fritz run free when we get inside the park, keeping Pepper on lead and witnessing a horrible pink poo on the pavement, a sure sign of the bloody stool we associate with gastroenteritis.

(Perhaps Fritz has tolerated his dose of Rescue Remedy better than Pepper—my dog's poo is, in fact, more solid than usual).

Out on the green I learn that none of us is an instant millionaire, as our lucky dip numbers were far from prize-winning. I am scanning the horizon, eagerly looking for Rob or Linda, but they haven't arrived when it is time for us to go in for coffee. I announce, as we near the café, "Nothing for Pepper today, please." This statement takes on a special significance when, a few minutes after Rob and Linda have at last materialized, Ofra pops a treat into Pepper's mouth. Hanna addresses the dreamy one in tones of stern recrimination and Dan, sitting opposite me at our sunny picnic table, upbraids Hanna for her tone. Hanna and Dan have a serious contretemps at this point—to the embarrassment of the rest of us, today including Janet, Georgie, Ronnie, and John, who arrives with Ché. Not surprisingly, the latter does a poo in the forecourt bushes.

Linda is now heading for the vet on Boundary Road with her pet and Rob follows me home so that he can survey the carnage. A few minutes later he returns with round one of a major carpet cleaning operation, one that spills over to the pavement outside our front door, where one of Pepper's worst poos has been deposited. For that matter, Fritz also has a poo-encrusted bottom.

Monday, November 5:

We have endured another difficult night when it is at last time to exit the house. Indeed, I have not seen my dog in almost twelve hours, that is ever since he abandoned my lap for the security of the tunnel beneath the bed as a second night of bombardment gathered strength. In the middle of all this Linda had called to inform me that the convalescent Pepper seemed to be soothed by listening to music and so I placed a radio at the tunnel entrance for Fritz. I don't know if Classic FM worked or not but I think there were fewer instances of carpet pawing.

Temperatures have dropped a bit, I discover, as I follow my dog's still befouled backside into the park. Heading our way are Stella and Cosmo, the latter half his size after a serious clipping. Out on the green there is very little activity (we are about ten minutes early) so, passing Cleo's mom, who is searching for a missing Charlie (I don't know which one), I just follow Fritz as he undertakes a serious sniffathon, first along the Randolph walkway, then behind the tennis courts, and so on to the bowling green—where we find Albert with the recently shorn Tinkerbelle and Saffy. Fritz next disappears into the bushes outside the Grantully doggy area and when he doesn't emerge I poke my nose into the foliage and discover the missing Charlie, who turns out to be one naughty Cocker Spaniel. Fritz soon exits as well and then admits himself to the aforementioned doggy area.

By this time we can join Ronnie, Georgie, Ellen, Janet, Cheryl, Suzanne, Davide, and Hanna at coffee. I have to provide a health update on Pepper while Daisy-Mae jumps into every empty seat when she is not face-fighting with Vito, whom Janet is minding while Christian is taking Reina to work. She keeps complaining that the little fellow is very strong, a point proved tellingly when, his lead pulling against a table leg, he manages to move the table itself several inches. After we have been seated for fifteen minutes or so Faz arrives—pushing baby Scarlett's buggy! It is the first time that most of us have been able to see the little bundle. She is hard to see, under her blankets, but everyone has a peek. When she begins to cry, daddy takes her off for her next feed.

Tuesday, November 6:

I have to put my head into the mouth of Fritz's tunnel again this morning for, once again, Bonfire Night (Part III) has sent him scurrying for cover. In this case he disappeared at nightfall, that is shortly after 5:00, when the first explosion went off—and I did not see him emerge for almost 16 hours! I had dosed him with Rescue Remedy and put the radio on the floor as well, and this formula seems to be the best strategy that can be expected from a period like this: it's just not convenient to leave the country—though that is what I feel like doing. Meanwhile poor Pepper is back in hospital and my carpets and Fritz's mucky bottom have both received some attention.

Now I can see a nice white tail bobbing down the bunny trail as we enter the park on a chilly but sunny morning. Just before we reach the cypress trees I see Fritz madly scraping away at his left rear leg. Thinking he has a twig stuck here I try to brush the offending object off myself and, to my surprise, I manage to dislodge a huge dozy bumblebee. I don't think Fritz has been stung—he never cries out—but this seems a close escape for both of us. Just at this minute Michaela comes by with Skye and we reverse direction to reach the green from the Morshead roadway. For once Fritz does not wander too far from home base. Since he ate nothing last night he is quite peckish and I have to keep up a steady biscuit service.

When we go in to coffee we have Georgie, Dan, Ellen, Hanna, Suzanne, Ofra and Ronnie. The latter announces that Dr. Bruce Fogle has discovered that Rosie has an enlarged heart and that this is interfering with her breathing—more tests are scheduled for Friday. Cheryl arrives with her dogs and says that she went to the most recent Pug convention in Green Park and that Ginger was easily the most senior and most photographed pet and that American tourists considered her covered wagon to be a quintessential sign of *British* eccentricity! She also reports that the buses were so crowded at the end of the session that no driver would take on the pushcart, and she had to walk all the way home. Sunny is running in manic circles, barking at shadows, and Suzanne says that, as a consequence, she is not to have any television tonight. Faz arrives with baby Scarlett again, but I have errands to run, so I excuse myself and head for home.

Wednesday, November 7:

Fritz has spent another night under the bed as fireworks season never seems to come to an end. This morning, however, he surfaces a full hour before it is time to go to the park and runs into my study so that he can sit in my lap and look out the window. It is a mostly grey morning, chilly and windy, as we make our way past Rebel, Chelsea and Lancer and reach the café—where Ellen and Ronnie are already staking out their positions.

Vito and Daisy-Mae are locked in combat as usual, though Christian recognizes that his dog is becoming a problem with his aggressive behavior and that the snip is needed soon. Fritz is quite hungry, as he has missed his evening meal again, and when I offer him a series of biscuits every other dog in the pack gathers at my feet. I make them all sit down before receiving their treats, though this is a concept that Vito does not seem to understand. One of my customers is Buddy. Saskia reports that Rescue Remedy worked wonders on the Golden Retriever during the recent bombardment but he is disturbed by the hijinks of the little dogs and begins to bark hysterically. His mistress, intent on an incoming phone call, grabs him by the collar, which comes off in her hand. I replace it.

At coffee we have a large turnout for such an uncomfortable morning: Georgie, Janet (off work again after an unsuccessful return yesterday), Suzanne, Ronnie, Ofra, Dan, Christian, Ellen, Hanna and Faz (with baby Scarlett). Suzanne climbs onto the wall in order to take a group photo while Dan is announcing the date for his Christmas party. Hanna wants Georgie to use the BA flight simulator in order to get over her fear of flying. I notice that Georgie is stacking all of our cups and dishes when it is time to begin our walkround. "I think she misses her pub job," I conclude. She denies this.

Thursday, November 8:

Fritz has spent a fifth night in a row beneath the bed, reacting like a ninny to a night of only mild bombardment, but this morning he emerges early on, eats his breakfast (that is, last night's untasted dinner) and then settles down on my sofa to growl at the odd workman marching along the scaffolding boards and scraping away at our windows.

In the park we have a relatively mild day under grey skies. When we reach the green I discover a group of Paddington Academy kids at play in the area between the cricket crease and the bandstand—this at a time when both of the football pitches are unused. There is a large group of dog owners on the other side of the crease and I can see some new faces among them. First we have a young Labrador pup named Fenway. I ask his owner if her dog is from Boston and she says, "No, but I am." Next we have Alfie (or Alfie Doodle as he is sometimes called); he is a young Yorkie who is dressed identically to Leila today—that is in camouflage and fur-lined hoody. Then we have an eleven week-old half Staffie-half Yorkie named Gracie; she is interested in all the other dogs and also afraid of them. Finally we have a six month-old Bailey look-alike named

Tarquin. Puppies rule! Fritz has little interest in all these small fry but he does take a fancy to Buddy's yellow ball and I have to bribe him with a biscuit in order to get him to release this prize.

At coffee we have Cheryl, Dan, Janet, Georgie, Ronnie, Suzanne, Ellen, Ofra and daddy Faz. Janet is still suffering from her chest infection and so is Davide, who is not here today. Dan says that his partner will not be still, even when he is poorly, and that last night he was cleaning the kitchen rather than resting (Felix Unger lives). A lot of the dogs are barking in their excitement over the food distribution, none more so than Sparkie. Last week we had a diagnosis of Canine Tourettes for Sparkie; today someone suggests that he is suffering from pawtism. A few minutes later Suzanne notices that now that the feeding frenzy is over silence and good order have replaced the noisy disorder of the earlier period. Peace at last.

Friday, November 9:

Fritz seems to have spent a far more comfortable night, disdaining his tunnel at bedtime and even finishing his tea at midnight. This morning he seems raring to go, perhaps too eager for me because in order to accommodate him I head off without my sweatshirt. Although it is sunny outside there is a chill wind and not only do I regret the absence of my sweatshirt I also wish I had my wool hat and my gloves as well.

When we reach the green Christian and Dan are discussing whether it is permissible for men to wear red shoes. Daisy-Mae is wrestling with Vito and the little fellow is gallant enough to allow her to pin him to the grass on a number of occasions; he could easily overpower her if he wanted to. I distribute biscuits to the dogs and it is interesting to see that no one is more protective of her prize than Daisy-Mae, who will even contest a scrap with Fritz. Winnie always takes a biscuit but often spits it out, hoping for something much more interesting instead.

When we go in for coffee we move our usual table into the sunlight. Our group today includes Dan, Georgie, Janet, Suzanne, Hanna, Faz (with baby Scarlett), and Cheryl—wearing scarlet shoes. Fritz joins the company of lap dogs this morning; I am just as happy to have him here because he provides some warmth on a morning that is tolerable when the wind is absent, but icy when it is present. The sun provides plenty of shadows for Sunny, however, and the session is flavored by her hysterical barking. The discussion turns to knife crime. Cheryl says that they wouldn't pull a knife on you if they knew you had a gun—and she means it.

Saturday, November 10:

Fritz has had another uncomfortable night as Diwali has caught up with Bonfire Night as the proximate cause for hours of unending noise. Fritz, to his credit, managed to stay above ground during the bombardment, cuddling up to me on the sofa in the TV room, where I kept him covered up with my puffer vest until it was time to carry him to bed. Today he begins activities with breakfast, and then we are ready to hit the park.

It is grey again, though not too chilly; I am wearing my wool cap anyway. The park is full of tiny football players and I have plenty of time to study their form as Fritz makes only the slowest progress toward the green. Here there is surprisingly little activity, though Skye the Alsatian has just throttled poor Sparkie and a shaken Georgie has made an early departure for coffeeland. Fritz soon heads for the Grantully gate and, to my horror, leaves the park for the traffic of the nearby street! Fortunately he doesn't wander too far and he soon returns to the siren call of the biscuit bag, enduring quite a scolding first.

We have a large turnout at breakfast, though Ronnie, who is having his sinus operation at St. Mary's today, is absent. Several incidents in the annals of incivility are discussed. Kate says that last night she was awakened by a fusillade at 3:30 in the morning. Her friend Bob says that some of our seasonal celebrants have thrown fireworks into the local telephone exchange and that his phone service has been inconsistent ever since. Dan says that, with fire having restricted the number of open pumps at the Tesco petrol station on Sutherland, a long queue formed behind a workable pump. The driver of the car at the head of the queue filled his tank and went in to pay as Dan and others were now lining up in the street behind him—and then he decided to spend the next ten minutes completing his grocery shopping as well! After quite a while we begin a back passage walkround, Georgie and Sparkie following me home so that I can pass on to her some of Dorothy's shoes.

Sunday, November 11:

Fritz has been agitating for some time when we at last head for the park on a grey and cool Sunday morning. I suspect he might have a poo or two in him because he did nothing in this category during our late night walk—squatting only once but then thinking better of it when a distant explosion disturbed his concentration. I suppose we should have been thankful that he agreed on a walk at all, for once again we endured festive bombardment for hours. This morning we have no noise, just a fine mist falling on our heads.

As we near the cypress trees I can see Janet, Georgie, and Dan heading toward me with their dogs. This is because Georgie has spotted Kate's Skye on the green—and she is still uncertain about an encounter with the occasionally violent Alsatian. Daisy-Mae has had a haircut and it is possible to see her merry eyes as she skips along and has a drink from a forbidden muddy puddle. At any rate, she is soon going to lose her well-groomed appearance as Fritz and I reverse directions and accompany the others in a counter-clockwise mini-circle into a real rain. We pass Albert, sitting on a park bench with Saffy and Tinkerbelle, and approach the café. Here I meet Kate and Bob; the former is hosting a party this afternoon (many of the dog people are invited) and has to get home to complete her preparations.

Peter, Ellen and I move our table out of the rain and wait for the doors to open. Curiously, there are two customers inside the café already, thought the door is bolted. I say this is a mystery worthy of Edgar Allan Poe; our conclusion: they must have spent the night inside. Dan is trying to tempt Winnie into ingesting some of her diet pellets by dipping the latter into the cheese of his panini. This strategy fails utterly when the Pug spits each pellet out in disgust. We have better luck letting Fritz lick the cappuccino foam from our coffee cups. Janet says that his poor body must be whipsawed between caffeine and Rescue Remedy. We discuss Ronnie's recent operation. "I love anesthetic," Ofra says. "Yes, but it's not good for you on an everyday basis," I conclude.

Monday, November 12:

We have had a reasonably quiet night but Fritz seems reluctant to part with his gift on our final rambles recently, and the result is that he is both anxious to get the day's expedition started and quick to squat once we reach the park. Today it is quite chilly (I'm back in my ear-covering black wool cap) though sunny enough, and I've put my dark glasses on by the time I reach the green. Over in the maintenance area you can now see half a dozen or so medium-sized palm trees in tubs. Global warming here we come.

The park seems very quiet this morning and there is only a small turnout on the green. Even here, Vito soon departs with Christian and Reina and Winnie with Dan—or does she? While her master heads off for work, expecting to be followed out by his pet, that little madam is thunderstruck by the effrontery: no visit to the café *at all* today? He is almost off the green before she makes any move in answer to his call, and the move is in the opposite direction—toward the café. Eventually she gets turned around and departs and then the rest of us make our own journey to this oasis. Fritz is first in and by the time we arrive he is sitting on a bench with Ellen, waiting for croissant crumbs.

We have only a small group at our table: Janet, Georgie, Hanna, and Cheryl. The latter suffered a pinched nerve playing golf yesterday and is moving very gingerly. Janet has a wonderful tale to tell: a postscript to Kate's party, which most of us have attended yesterday. It seems that when it was time for her to depart, that is about 9:30, Bob, Kate's partner, decided to walk her home—taking Isla and Skye for their late night walkies at the same time. Five minutes later he had delivered Janet and headed back home but when he got there he couldn't rouse the sleepy hostess and he had no key. So he found his way back to Janet's street (the dogs lead him up to the right house) and threw himself on her mercy. Phone calls failing to rouse Kate, Janet made him comfortable in her spare bedroom and went to bed. She was awakened at 3:30 in the morning by the loud sounds of the television in her sitting room. "How rude," she thought, but when she went to investigate she discovered that Bob was not the culprit. Isla and Daisy-Mae, who had been having an all-night wrestling match, had accidentally sat on the remote control and were now, somewhat guiltily, pretending to watch the screen. When she checked at 8:30 Bob was still sleeping, Skye on the duvet at the foot of the bed.

Tuesday, November 13:

It's a grey and chilly morning as Fritz and I make our way into a quiet park. On the green a randy Vito is just being detached from a series of love objects. Someone points out that his little face is pink with embarrassment. Georgie has found a large green football and Sparkie is barking at everybody to give it a kick. I have to follow Fritz down the Randolph walkway, getting him turned around just in time to meet Dan, Janet, Hanna, and Georgie, who have decided—the café closed today because of building works—to head for Starbucks on Randolph Avenue.

Dan goes inside to get some paper napkins so that the chairs in front of the coffeteria can be dried off. (I recall that Starbucks didn't have *any* outside tables when it was first opened but Dorothy and I were among those urging the management to add same.) Nicholas joins us as well, though both Janet and the kitchen impresario spend much of their time on business calls. Winnie is having trouble with her right eye and Dan calls his vet to get an appointment as well. The Pug is, as usual, obsessed with food and she seems to be suffering an irate meltdown when the stump of a muffin lies just outside her reach. The others seem satisfied with their drinks but I complain that my cappuccino foam somehow tastes of onions.

Georgie, Janet and I begin a walk back to the park, using the pavements on Elgin Avenue initially. Fritz is his usual annoying self on lead, either falling behind or sprinting ahead as we reach the Grantully entrance. Inside we meet a chap with a thirteen week-old Labrador puppy. When Janet pauses to pet the fellow his owner presses his card on her: "The Dog Man, Training and Correction." "In that case," I conclude, "you better pass that card on to Georgie."

Wednesday, November 14:

Wednesday mornings require just a small variation in our usual departure routine, as we must welcome Cathy, who now bears most of the responsibility for keeping the house in order. Fritz is always thrilled to see her and no more so than today, when she begins her tasks by emptying the refrigerator prior to defrosting. Fritz knows that this process sometimes disgorges a sequestered ball, which I have hidden in the freezer compartment after losing patience with its charms. There is only one small blue ball still secreted here, one that is not serving out its sentence because of excessive squeaking but because it is so small that Fritz continually knocks it under the furniture and then whines piteously for its return. Now he rushes up and down the hallway, not knowing whether it is better to see what Cathy is up to or better to get today's stroll in the park underway.

It is again a chilly and sunny morning and we make reasonable progress toward the green—though Fritz does make a pit stop at the café to see what Peter and Ellen might have for him. Although there does not seem to be any competition for possession of the green today, the dog people have nevertheless migrated to the foothills of Mt. Bannister. Here we can see four gigantic portaloos, objects that have been deposited behind the café in preparation for a major redevelopment of the clubhouse site. Saskia says that on Friday poor Buddy was savaged by an intemperate mostly Boxer bitch, an attack that originated when her own mistress was having an innocent tug of war with the Golden Retriever. A number of the owners run their fingers over the sore spot on Buddy's neck. The latter seems happily recovered from his ordeal and trots over to sit at my feet in anticipation of a handout. Joining our group for the first time is a white curly-haired five month-old Bichon Frise named Jack. A number of us note that he is much too clean to be a proper member of *our* lot.

At coffee we have Dan, Georgie, Janet, Hanna, Cheryl and Georgie. The latter has the custody of Bailey for a week—as Ofra has gone to Israel for a wedding. We discuss Ramsay's *Kitchen Nightmares* and *I'm A Celebrity, Get Me Out of Here!*, both on at 9:00 last night and each inspiring lots of conversation and side-taking. Hanna says that she has spoken to Ronnie, home recuperating from his recent nasal polyp surgery, and she says that he is much easier to understand as a consequence of this retreat from adenoidal misery. "I hate to drink and run," I say, "but I have to meet some people in the West End in an hour, so I have to get started."

Thursday, November 15:

The weather in unchanged: sunny and cold. Because of the bright light I have to wear my dark glasses with my wool cap, an unusual combination. When we reach the café Peter and Ellen are in the process of choosing a table in the sun of the forecourt, and Fritz has to see if there is any food going. (He even manages to jump up on the brick wall behind Ellen's head.) It's much too early for food but I do notice that a portion of the picket fence that usually surrounds this spot, that bordering on the Carlton roadway, is missing. Also missing are most of the dog people; the green is almost deserted and there is also a very small turnout at coffee a few minutes later.

Only Georgie, Davide, Nicholas and Hanna are present. Georgie reports that next Monday morning, when Daisy-Mae is dropped off by Janet, she will have five dogs in her flat—including Sparkie, Bailey and two Scottish visitors, Billy and Mozart. Nicholas decides that he has to develop a new furniture sideline: dog beds upholstered in the same fabric as your sitting room sofa. This proposition is discussed at length. Georgie says she'd just as soon pay for a conventional dog bed. I say that I have a dog bed for Fritz—my bed. The general conclusion is that Nicholas is on to something here—as there are a lot of people with more money than sense.

I have to break away early in order to drop off a prescription renewal form at my doctor's surgery. It's never easy undertaking such an expedition with Fritz on lead, since he continues to stop and sniff at every tree and it is impossible, since he is covering home territory, to get him into the "heel" rhythm. Nevertheless we manage to complete this errand and return to our icy flat—where the painters still have the windows wide open.

Friday, November 16:

If anything, it is even colder this morning than yesterday and I am once again driven to wearing wool cap and sunglasses. There is a small group of dog owners in the middle of the green and I join them briefly—Dan is already passing out invitations to his Christmas party on December 23rd. I can see Fritz disappearing down the Randolph walkway and I begin my pursuit. When I catch up I am surprised to see that he has discovered a loose hockey ball (I hope no one was has been using this to play tennis with) and he proudly trots back toward the green with this prize, only abandoning it (just as well) in the bushes near the café.

Today we have Dan, Georgie, Peter, Ellen, Hanna, Nicholas and a rare visit from David the dog sitter, who even agrees to imbibe a healthful pear nectar as the rest of us sip our coffee. When we are settled down (Fritz in my lap again) I pass on to them a tale of woe told by Rowena in the Morshead doggy area yesterday afternoon. She says that she has heard from a park employee that this popular area, the most frequently used of three similar sites, is to become a lorry park and marshaling yard for the construction workers who are shortly to undertake the rest of the "improvements" in the park. Furthermore, so Rowena has stated, this will become a permanent maintenance site and the dog owners will lose the spot permanently as, according to her source, "there are too many of these already." What such an attack on one of our precious spaces might presage (let alone the effects on flat dwellers who thought they were buying living spaces across the street from a lovely grove of mature trees) casts a pall over our breakfast conversation.

As we get up to begin a back passage walkround Georgie says that yesterday afternoon, as she and Janet undertook a similar peregrination, they were pursued by Hugo the Collie, whose owner (described as "Chinese") was relaxing inside the café. There were several difficulties in this pursuit; first Hugo would not cease his lustful attacks on poor Bailey (so that Georgie had to carry the Cavalier) and, second, the unattended Collie deposited two poos in the process. When the ladies returned to the café with Hugo, his indifferent owner allowed him his freedom a second time and the same thing happened. Fortunately there is no Hugo around as we conclude this morning's sequel successfully.

Saturday, November 17:

It's still very chilly (I am wearing my thermals for the first time this season) but sunglasses are no longer needed. Unusually, Georgie is walking my way with Bailey and Sparkie and we soon encounter Janet with Daisy-Mae as well. So we have a foursome undertaking a back passage walkround in reverse as the Saturday crowd of football players, from tots to jocks, are getting down to their labors. Out on the green I can see Bob with Isla and Skye and Dan with Winnie. Skye seems to be behaving in a hostile manner again and Georgie, fearing for Sparkie's safety, heads for the café ten minutes before the rest of us.

Fritz begins his wanderings, first near the bandstand, then down the Randolph walkway. This gesture seems particularly irksome to me because I will soon be undertaking an expedition along this route myself.

First I have to pass the lead of my dog on to a seated Georgie, then I have to give my coffee money to Liz, then I have to take off for the Vineyard pharmacy—where I have some prescriptions waiting for me. In the old days I would have tied Fritz to a post outside this establishment, but those gentler, safer days are long gone.

At coffee, to which I soon return, we have all of the aforementioned plus Hanna. Dan is in a particularly mischievous mood. At one point he says that sitting around this table reminds him of a scene out of *One Flew Over The Cuckoo's Nest*. I ask him, innocently, who gets to play Big Nurse, and he proposes Hanna. But the latter is not at all amused by this nomination. Then, when Liz spends ten minutes on her mobile phone, he tells her that in her absence Roxy has eaten a croissant off the plate on an adjacent table. The problem with this tale is that it is believable—and it takes us some time to convince Liz that he is just having her on. It's time to get back into the warmth of our own homes.

Sunday, November 18:

There has been some moisture overnight but the front has done nothing to ameliorate the severity of the temperature. A wind, trying to strip the last of the leaves from the trees, is at work on the backs of our necks as we inch into a relatively quiet park on a grey Sunday morning. I can see Georgie, with Sparkie and Bailey, coming up behind me, and Janet heading my way with Daisy-Mae. Fritz does not seem interested in any socializing and we are soon on our own on the almost empty green; only Kate and Bob, both bundled up, are here with Isla and Skye.

I follow Fritz around for a while and in so doing I encounter the Yorkie-like Fonzi, whom I have not seen in some time. His Slavic-accented mistress says that she usually takes him to the parking lot doggy area because he is unpredictable and often barks at children. Fritz heads for the foxes' lair near the bowling green but emerges quickly enough when it is time to head in for coffee and treats. Dan has arrived with Winnie by this time and so has Liz with Roxy. Liz hasn't put on enough clothes and looks miserable. Sparkie has a mid-sized rubber ball and I kick this to the dogs a few times. Fritz takes a momentary interest in the object and Sparkie becomes hysterical with the loss, barking away in his usual manic fashion: "mine, mine, mine, mine!"

No one wants to linger over coffee for long. I tell the others that Rowena, whom I passed on the street on Friday and who has since talked to Westminster officials, now says that everything she heard about the doggy area on Morshead Road is wrong!

At coffee Kate says she is picking up a Mercedes sports car today. Bailey hops from lap to lap and uses my chest as a launching pad to climb onto the table—amid outraged protests from the other owners. Liz says that her son Jack is visiting a film set where Kiera Knightley is filming today. I suggest he ask her to visit us in the park, though why anyone would want to be here today is hard to grasp. "I can't stand it anymore," I say—having had enough of my own attempts to drink a cup of coffee with my gloves on—"I'm getting out of here." This precipitates an early departure by all concerned.

Monday, November 19:

A steady downpour peppers the street as I pull on my rain jacket. This is a bit of a struggle, since I am also wearing my leather jacket. I have forgotten to put his rain jacket on Fritz, but the latter doesn't seem to be too bothered by the moisture as we brave the elements and enter a sodden park. Save for a few brave joggers, the Rec seems to have been deserted this morning; none of the school groups has arrived, for instance. Fortunately there is little wind and I am able to wear my Michigan Film Commission baseball cap facing forward—in a steady breeze I need to wear it backwards.

We approach the café, where Metty and Vicky seem to have taken pity on the few early customers and opened the doors at 9:20. Nicholas and Hanna are already here (Hanna has to loan Nicholas his coffee money) but Fritz passes them by and heads for the green. It is still raining steadily, though there are some brighter patches in the sky, and the green is, not surprisingly, empty. Fritz trots about a bit, and then, after several efforts, I manage to coax him back with the offer of coffee and biscuits.

Nicholas soon leaves but his place is taken by three Scottish ladies, Georgie (with Sparkie, Bailey and Daisy-Mae), her sister Jean (with Billy and Mozart) and Jean's friend Andrea. The latter two have driven down from Glasgow only the night before. "If you've brought this weather with you," I tell Jean, "you can turn around and go back." I notice that Sparkie is also wearing a camouflage hoody, the kind of outfit you need if you want to sneak up on the GAP. Jean asks Hanna if Num-num, her bird, still has his flying suit. "Yes," Hanna says, "but it doesn't fit properly, he looks like he's wearing a condom, and he squawks whenever I put it on." Jean then says that Mozart has a t-shirt that he wears when he is patrolling the garden: it bears the simple legend "Security." Daisy-Mae is shivering in her coat and she keeps trying to climb into dry laps.

Hanna calls Dan and reminds him that there is a rule that anyone who fails to make a park appearance because of bad weather has to buy all the coffee and food the next day. "Have you got that rule in writing?" Dan evidently asks. "Yes," Hanna says, "it's in the book"—meaning the one you are reading now. I see a break in the weather and Fritz and I begin a solo march home.

Tuesday, November 20:

It is very dark this morning, prefiguring another damp day. It hasn't started to rain just yet, though we have been enduring wave after wave of showers for well over a day—Fritz has spent a lot of time under his orange towel. Today we are followed into the park by Elvis the Westie; Jeff complains bitterly over the noise of the distant ear-shattering leaf-blower and, indeed, you often get the feeling that for park personnel this place is just a place—nothing but surfaces that need to be tidied and polished—a space that has no human element in it at all.

We continue forward and Fritz gets to greet his old dog-sitter, David, who today accompanies the gentle, long-legged Lulu. (Peter later says that Jack the Jack Russell has been chasing this senior citizen.) Out on the green the focus of all attention is David (the 1-1-8 man) who has brought not only Jasper but his infant daughter Edie, a beautiful black-headed baby in her stroller. I have a chat on the cricket crease with Jo Lynn, who has been watching Lynn Franks, for whom she used to work, on *I'm A Celebrity, Get Me Out Of Here!* We agree that Lynn is game and characterful (which is why she may be resented by the others, who, like the leaf-blower, are interested in surfaces only), though, unfortunately, she keeps rubbing her agenda in the faces of her fellow contestants. By the time we have concluded our conversation I have lost track of Fritz—but he emerges from the Randolph walkway in time for a trip to the café.

This morning we have Dan, Georgie, Jean, and Ofra. The dogs are in a pissy mood. Winnie is enraged at the local pigeons and often jumps off Dan's lap to chase them. Billy is muzzled because he is unreliable around kids and Mozart, who hates men, is muzzled when he takes exception to the passing ankles of a workman. (Sparkie is already muzzled in an anti-barking gesture.) Most of these dogs accept their restraint in good measure, though Billy tries to knock his muzzle off by burying it between my knees. A lot of time has passed since we sent Ofra inside to order our coffee and it slowly dawns on me that the coffee has been ready for some time—it's just that Ofra can't stop jawing with Metty. Dan (who has been fretting over the sighting of a lone magpie) gets up and reminds the lady that our drinks are getting cold. Faz arrives with a sleepy baby Scarlett asleep on his chest. He complains of the weight and a mom, standing next to the door of the café, says, "Yeah, well try carrying one of those inside you for nine months." Ofra's phone, which she has left on the coffee tray, begins to ring and she has to get up to answer it. This means that she is well behind the rest of us in her tea-drinking and so I get up to begin a solo walk home. It has started to rain again but at least we have four magpies in the tree above us.

Wednesday, November 21:

My dog day begins at 6:15—when Linda drops Pepper off for the day while she and Rob are attending a memorial service in Rochdale. Any more sleep is impossible as the Schnauzers choose my bed as their playground and I have to get up and get dressed. Pepper is very suspicious of Cathy, who arrives for her usual cleaning assignment at 9:00, but we are ready to depart for the park soon thereafter. I keep the visitor on lead throughout the proceedings, marching into a bright sun as we head for the green. Here we encounter Vito, who has had the snip six days ago, though he seems well recovered. It is hard keeping track of Fritz while I am chatting with the others and he is nowhere to be seen when it is time to go in for coffee. My whistle, however, fetches the scamp from the distant confines of the Randolph walkway and we join a large group at our usual table.

Today we have the return of Ronnie, who has been convalescing from his nasal surgery—he seems to be in good spirits. He is chatting with Rhian, Otw at her feet; she says that she will be doing dog portraits in her photo studio a week from Sunday and many of the coffee drinkers are interested. We also have Hanna, Georgie, Dan, Jean, Ofra and, for the first time in many a moon, Dianah—with Jasmine and baby Scarlett. Cheryl also arrives with her Pugs. It is a reasonably mild day but Cheryl is wearing only her Oklahoma Sooners t-shirt and the rest of us are agog. At one point I count a dozen dogs milling about at our feet; a feeding frenzy is on and when they are not scrapping over sausage and toast they are barking at passersby and at one another. Pepper's bark is piercing and relentless and Lola is a very bossy Pug who climbs into her own chair and barks at Billy. Winnie, in the next lap, is scandalized by such behavior.

Most of these animals take their place in a back passage walkround. It is hard to get us all moving at the same time, especially because a jogger comes by with an Irish Setter on lead and first Fritz and then Winnie have to chase this dog in the direction of the green. Then we have to work our way around Andrew the Akita, who is kicking leaves in our faces. We can see the mothers lining their kids up against the fence of the playground so they can see the doggies on parade—"We're just a floor show to these moms," I tell Jean. Heading our way is Jeff with Elvis. "You look like an L.A. street gang," he says. "That's right," I respond, "don't mess with us!"

Thursday, November 22:

Rain and sun are still fighting it out in skies that have been dumping on Maida Vale for hours. Fritz and I have timed our last walk of the night just right—between two of these showers—and now we head for the park to begin another busy day amid changeable conditions. I am dressed in a semi-respectable outfit because I have errands to run at the conclusion of the morning's activity. I'm still in brown cords (though these don't have holes in the pockets) and leather jacket, though only Linda, who soon arrives with Pepper, knows that this one is a newer version that Dorothy bought me when the original became too shabby for polite society.

The green is a sodden mess, muddy everywhere and in the center both the cricket crease and surrounding areas are actually under water. This would be a problem when Dan kicks Sparkie's ball into this lake, though fortunately Billy wades in and pulls it out. Buddy, Sasha and Skye the Alsatian are tumbling in the morass as well and Fritz seems to be having a wonderful time chasing a little yellow ball that Sparkie found out here earlier. Indeed all the dogs seem to delight in paddling through the standing water in their play. It's just as well that I don't have to take my sodden dog home (though Linda does apply a towel from her boot) because both of our dogs now have a car ride and an appointment at the beauty parlor on Allitsen Road.

It is to this spot that I make my way at 1:00, after a series of tedious errands in the West End. I pause for a stop at a gents' in Regents Park and when I try to leave I encounter a squirrel, who is trying to enter. "Out!" I say, pointing to the door as though I were addressing a naughty dog who had just penetrated the interior of the café. The squirrel considers this request and dances around on the threshold but I notice that as soon as I depart he rushes in to replace me. In short, I could have used Fritz to restore some order on this occasion, but it is still a few more minutes before my reunion with the beautiful boy in St. John's Wood.

Friday, November 23:

Fritz has spent a restless night, exhausted by all his activity yesterday (including dinner with Linda, Rob, Liam and Pepper) and feeling the cold now that he has been shorn—indeed he seems to have spent a good deal of the night *under* the duvet. This morning we have sunny skies but it is very cold outside. Entering the park we meet the oddly-matched pair of Tay, the shaggy Jack Russell with the half black, half white face, and his younger brother, the portly Monty, a chocolate Lab. Once launched on our walkround we also meet Jo Lynn, with Tilly. She says that her dog has a Border Terrier playdate later today with Artemis. She makes a big fuss over the handsome and sporty Fritz, who looks half his former size with all the wool removed.

Out on the green the sun is shining so intently that, even with dark glasses on, I can't see who is out here. We have come a bit earlier than usual and have the place pretty much to ourselves. I join up with Suzanne and Sunny and we soon encounter a woman who has two senior Jack Russells in coats; one has to be carried because he is intemperate. Near the loos there is a white Westminster van and I soon discover that it is the animal warden's vehicle, Westminster having recently decided to add its own logo to the van, which heretofore has borne only the name of the private contractor. The warden today is Lee, who spots Billy out on the green and accompanies me to a spot where he can have a reunion with the Glaswegian dog. Fritz chases a tennis ball that I have brought with me but pretty soon it is time for us to head in for coffee.

Today we have the three Scottish ladies, Cheryl, Nicholas and Dan. Nicholas stretches the lateral thinking of the kitchen staff by inventing his own sandwich, sausage and cheese in a croissant. Having learned that Cheryl uses her Pugs' kennels as coffee tables, I propose that Nicholas add this item of furniture to his new line of dog-decorated living room suites. Although there is a little warmth in the sun there are many complaints about the extremely cold temperatures and the dogs, lead by Lola, insist in getting off the cold flagstones and onto the warmer laps of their owners. Fritz is among this lot; his nose is soon deep into my cup as he hoovers out the cappuccino foam. He is just as happy to get moving again and we are both looking forward to returning to some nice indoor warmth.

Saturday, November 24:

It is still bitter cold outside and today we do not even have the promise of warmth in the presence of sunlight: it is a grey overcast morning. We encounter Ofra and Bailey as we reach the Carlton walkway; she is delighted by Fritz's haircut, though she seems to feel that it is an exceptional act of cruelty to have reduced my dog's coverage in such chilly conditions. Dan and Janet are standing on the Randolph walkway and Ofra now insists on a walkround, since she is too cold to remain in a stationary position. We catch up with this group a few minutes later, Fritz having taken off on his own adventures. He is full of beans this morning, running all over the place to greet man and dog, even jumping up on a bench when the group stops to greet the Scottish ladies and their dogs.

Liz also arrives now with Roxy. In the "things happen to Liz" department we now have the story of Liz's failed Thanksgiving. A few weeks ago she had invited a number of the dog people (Fritz was invited too) to this traditional American feast, though the date was shifted to last night, which is not traditional. However the smell of gas in her kitchen, which she has been complaining about for some time, reached such an alarming intensity that she had to call for assistance and the kitchen was disassembled yesterday—hence no meal. To make matters worse her kids are now calling her an idiot for referring to her mobile phone as a Minolta (when it is a Motorola) and the gas experts can find no leak after all!

At icy coffee this morning we have the Scottish ladies, Ronnie, Liz, Dan and Davide, Ofra, and Janet. Davide has had such a bad cough that his ribs are sore. Dan has his scarf wrapped around the southern half of his face—he's so cold and I am trying to drink my coffee with my gloves on. At this point John sits down; he is appropriately wearing a baseball cap with the legend "Chill." Fritz, indeed, is so chilly that he is shivering and I decide I had better head for home. Over in a distant corner Ché is having a poo behind a planter.

Sunday, November 25:

We overtake Lulu the Lurcher as we make our way toward the green; the senior citizen on her spindly legs no longer looks like the speedster she must have been in her youth. I lose track of Fritz (for the first time) as we approach the café and by the time I have reached the green he is already nosing about among his pals near the cricket crease—which has once again emerged from its watery grave. The usual crew is here (save Dan, who arrives much later) and we even have Lynn, Georgie's daughter and a Winnie-like Pug named Monty. When the other dogs come over for a sniff Monty sticks out one of his back legs at a ninety degree angle to accommodate them; he looks like he is about to undertake some strenuous ballet exercise.

Passing among us is the chap who usually accompanies the Beagles Baija and Charlie. Today he is passing out cards announcing the opening of his new pet store, Grand Union Pets on the Harrow Road, opposite the Queen's Park Library. I pass this establishment on my way to Sainsbury's Ladbroke Grove and, indeed, I have already received a verbal introduction to this new emporium from this chap's partner in the Morshead doggy area. There is a picture of a Beagle on the card, which advertises "Holistic grooming by *Dogs Delight*." In fact the chap complements me on Fritz's grooming while Liz goes into a rant on the subject of her own Beagle, Roxy, whose motto seems to be, "I pee in the house when I want to, especially when it's too cold to go outside." Hanna suggests that Roxy needs to spend some time in the country with other Beagles so that she can be properly socialized. Liz says, "I'm not going down that route."

The group begins to meander in the direction of the café and Fritz, who has been chasing down muddy footballs, seems to follow suit, but by the time I have put my lead and the dog biscuits down on our table and sent my coffee money into the café with Liz, I notice that the rascal has veered off and is now nowhere to be seen. I go out onto the green and try my whistle but there is no response from any corner. Now I am getting really worried and I am ranging around the café to widen my views of the scene. Finally I begin a brisk walk along the Randolph walkway, since I have seen my dog show an interest in this forbidden corner earlier in the session, and just as I reach the tennis courts here he comes, missing for the last five minutes, heading my way from the Randolph gateway. I am too relieved to give him the scolding he deserves. I have left his lead on our table so I have to count on his good behavior now and, just before we reach the café, he goes missing yet again and I have to march out to the green and put him on the now recovered lead.

My cappuccino is getting cold as I take my seat at our table, which now has the seated figures of Georgie, Lynn, Jean, Ofra, Dan, Faz, Hanna, and Janet. Other owners are hovering in the backround: Rhiann, Albert, John, and the guy who has the cute little Pugalier, Coops. It's musical laps this morning. Sparkie twice jumps into mine—and so does Daisy-Mae. Fritz jumps into Dan's lap and makes his presence known; he is still there when Winnie joins him. It looks like a formula for disaster but he jumps off in order to lick the foam from my cup and some of Liz's coffee from hers. "He's not mischievous enough today," I say, "now he's *wired* as well."

Monday, November 26:

Temperatures have moderated just a bit as Fritz and I head for the park on a reasonably sunny Monday. I have noticed that if he hasn't done a poo during our late night walk that Fritz is very likely to squat at an early moment in the morning, and so it is today. He then turns his attention to a little close order grazing, plucking shoots from the leaf litter like a deer searching for foliage buried in the snow. Finally he puts on some speed, racing past some lads from the Paddington Academy, one of whom recoils in fright at this apparition.

The chain saw is attacking tree stumps on our left and a tractor is racing around the green itself as Fritz and I reach the grass. David the dog sitter is here with Vito today. He says he prefers looking after Vito to an assignment with Daisy-Mae, who is covered in mud. Buddy comes over to sit at my feet, waiting patiently for his biscuit and starting a stampede of similarly-minded pooches (Vito cannot be made to sit). I put Fritz on lead well before it is time for us to go in for coffee—remembering yesterday's disappearing act—but when I get to the café I pass him on to Faz, whom I now call Kindergarten Cop, so that I can return to the green and make a quiet phone call.

It has taken me a day to figure out that I need to dial 001 before using the cell phone numbers of my friends the Platts, who are visiting London this week, but this time I *am* successful in reaching DeWitt (who says he spent eight hours yesterday rolling around on the floor trying to figure out how to use his U.S. cell *here*). Arrangements made for a luncheon rendezvous at the British Museum, I can now return to my cappuccino—whose foam crown has suffered considerable deflation in my absence.

Today we have Dan, Faz, Georgie, Andrea, Jean, Ofra, Cheryl and Hanna. Lola and Billy clearly don't like one another and there is a lot of ill-tempered barking. Daisy-Mae is scouting for food at a nearby table and at one point I begin to fear for the toes of a baby who is eating a banana there. When the little Shih-Tzu jumps into an empty chair Georgie has to get up and remove her. Meanwhile I am conducting a quiz, since Michigan Janet has sent me a list of the most popular dog names and I want to see if we have any park parallels. Max, Jake, Buddy and Bailey top her list of male names (Janet has expressed surprise at the inclusion of Bailey—"it's just a drink to me") while Maggie, Molly, Lady and Sadie top the list for females.

We get up to begin our back passage walkround. At the cypress trees Corky's mom Wendy expresses concern over the presence of muzzles on both Billy and Mozart. "It's just because they're barkers," Dan explains. "You should have said, it's just because they're Scottish," I reply. "It's just because they're barking mad," Georgie concludes.

Tuesday, November 27:

Mist obscures the more distant corners of the park as Fritz and I make our entry into a grey, chilly Tuesday morning scene. It isn't raining, but no one would be surprised if rain were to come at any moment. They seem to be extending the fence of the five-a-side courts to include the little meadow at the corner by the cypress trees; this means that two green areas off this walkway, one at either end, will have been lost forever to our dogs.

Out on the green Vito is messing it up with a cute three month-old black Staffy puppy named Cain and the former is lead off the scene in disgrace by David the dog sitter. I keep a close eye on Fritz, who keeps returning for more biscuits from my jacket pocket. When my dog begins to head for the Randolph exit I have to follow him. By the time we have returned from these ramblings it is time to go in for coffee.

This morning we have Hanna, Rowena, Cheryl, Ofra, Davide and three Scottish ladies. I note, at one point, that Rowena is the only English person present—and even she was born abroad. Two of the Scottish ladies are returning to Glasgow today, but not before one of the park keepers calls Jean's attention to one of Bill's poos out on the grass. Cheryl is accompanied by Lola only today; Ginger evidently sensed the damp as the front door was opened and has put the brakes on. Peter comes by with Holly, Jack and Sandy; Ellen, who has been poorly for some time now, has evidently suffered heart problems that have required surgery.

The others get up to begin a walkround but Fritz and I have to head in another direction as he has an appointment on Boundary Road for a kennel cough booster. Here also I pick up some worming and flea medicine and a new lead (just to have a spare ready) and also my holiday cards at the printers across the street. Fritz seems to enjoy this outing and on the way home he tries to dance away with the lead in his mouth, but when I depart soon thereafter for a trip to Sainsbury's he responds with howls of betrayal over the abandonment.

Wednesday, November 28:

Grey continues to be the dominant color as Fritz and I penetrate the precincts of Paddington Rec on a chilly Wednesday morning. Slow progress is made as Fritz samples the grass shoots again but eventually we encounter Nicholas with Monty; they reverse directions in order to accompany us to the green. Here David is just leaving with Vito but Buddy is joined by his old pal Rufus and Winnie is surrounded by a number of small dogs as she attempts to winkle treats out of her rubber conch. The presence of other animals is taken, however, as a sign of competition by the willful Pug, and there are words, especially when it looks like the conch might end up in an alien mouth. Winnie chases Crissy the Alsatian away from the scene and then has to head-butt Rufus for good measure.

Fritz rushes off to greet other canine parties, first Cheryl, who arrives with Lola and, back in her covered wagon, the fragile Ginger. Then my dog makes himself part of Peter's party near the clubhouse. Today this includes not only his own Holly but Jack and Sandy, who are usually walked by the ailing Ellen, and even Corky, whose mistress, Wendy, is having trouble with her feet. It is unusual to see Corky in tow like this (he is even wearing a blue coat) since he usually prefers rustling about in the underbrush. I do learn a new fact, however; he is called Corky because he's an Irish dog—from Cork.

At coffee we have Nicholas, Ronnie, Georgie, Cheryl, Dan, Ofra and Hanna. Nicholas has a tantrum when someone takes his seat; soon he is trying to wrap Bailey around the shoulders of Ofra, but the lady has a bad back and objects. Daisy-Mae is relentless in her attempt to claim every empty chair and there is almost a dreadful accident when Ronnie comes close to sitting on her. The group tries to organize some sort of get well gift for the stricken Ellen as Michael the Pirate comes by and reports that he is actually feeling better—"I decided I would not be heading for my coffin just yet." We begin a back passage walkround but Bailey, Sparkie and Daisy-Mae admit themselves to the empty five-a-side pitch and we have a devil of a time getting them out of there. As we near the exit gate we encounter the giant slobbering Mastiff Max—we have not seen him in some time but, ironically, we were just talking about him yesterday—when Max turned up as the most popular dog name on the list we were studying at breakfast.

Thursday, November 29:

Skies are clearing a bit as we near the park fence this morning. Inside I can hear Georgie exhorting Sparkie to pick up his ball. Fritz is interested in this conversation and puts his nose through the fence, but when he extracts it he is followed by Daisy-Mae, who is still small enough to slip between the bars and now wants to say hello to her grey furry chum. Georgie is a bit anxious about all this but Daisy-Mae soon slips back through the bars and all is well.

Out on the green Saskia is pretending to throw a tennis ball to Buddy: though the ball itself has gone missing, Buddy still takes off dutifully. He is covered in mud—only the tip of his nose is clean, and it is soon poking into my pocket in search of treats. Fritz too makes a place for himself at my feet. It is interesting to note that my dog seems far more popular with the other dog owners now that he has had his spiffy haircut. They all want a cuddle; only a week ago no one was interested in the raggedy woolly bear called Fritz.

We head for the café but Fritz decides to take out a guest membership in Courtney's gym, that is instead of turning half left as we near the café he heads directly into the open hallway of the temporary headquarters of the fitness emporium—with me in pursuit. He passes beneath the reception counter, turns right to pass one of the receptionists, who is chatting out of her back door with Lurch, himself leaning out of a café door. Then my dog toys with the idea of entering the exercise area and ends up behind this room in a little courtyard where he can be seen by several hard-charging girls on their conveyor belts.

Hooked at last we return to our table, where today we have Dan, Georgie, Ronnie, Ofra and Cheryl. I tell Dan that I have spoken to Natasha (during last night's late walk) and she has a Snoopy suit for him to wear at the opening of the new doggy boutique at Village Vets on Saturday. You can tell that Dan is beginning to regret his decision to volunteer for this assignment and the job is offered (by Hanna) to everyone else at our table and to the ideal candidate, Nicholas, who is absent.

Friday, November 30:

It is damp outside (though not actually raining) as Fritz, just awakened at last from his night's sleep, hits the ground running. We are approached by Lulu the Lurcher, but she is unable to get a rise out of my dog, who also snarls at the trio of Rizzo, Scamp and Oscar. When he squats to poo I realize that I too am sleepy, having forgotten my supply of bags and having to decant the biscuits from their usual pouch now. The only thing that seems to get a rise out of Fritz is the sight of Humphrey, the one-eyed Shih-Tzu being carried (I don't know why) by his mistress.

Out on the green there seems to be a reduced number of participants, though I detect that the Boxer with Bekkie is not Chica (who has moved to Spain) but her sister's dog, the burly Bounce. Fritz wanders off and I have to pursue him on a sore right knee but he has rejoined the group when it is time to head for coffee. That is, he seems to be heading here as well—but at the last minute he veers off and I have to wait another minute for him to reappear. Indeed all the dogs seem restless this morning. Lola keeps jumping into my lap or onto empty chairs, so does Daisy-Mae, and Sparkie disappears altogether. Georgie gets up to begin a search, whereupon the scamp returns. Peter then goes in search of Georgie but by the time he returns Sparkie is inside the café. All these dogs end up on lead.

There is a very small turnout at table this morning, just Georgie, Cheryl and Nicholas. The kitchen magnate is holding his head in his hands after a bust-up with his new missus, a contretemps ascribed by that lady to hubby's ogling the cleavage of a third party at Le Cochonnet last night. Marital relations are the topic of conversation this morning and the wisest advice we can offer the newlywed is that his alleged crime is just a pretext for a hidden agenda that has yet to surface. Nicholas pushes Ginger's wagon as we begin a back passage walkround. "I wonder if we could get all the dogs into this," he speculates. Yesterday, as I neared my exit gate, Sparkie followed me out; today it is Daisy-Mae who again decides to join Fritz and me as she squeezes through the fence and runs across the street. Georgie is wailing in distress but this causes me to turn around and scoop up the naughty madam, re-crossing the street and stuffing her between the bars as we bring to an end another eventful month in Paddington Rec.

Daisy-Mae joins the party

Skye, the ball-obsessed Cairn

Roxy, the food-obsessed Beagle

Billy makes a return visit

Mozart returns as well

Pepper (l) and Fritz, the Schnauzers

Cheryl leads her Pugs into the Rec on a foggy day in London Town

On a field trip to Southwold. From left: Bailey, Winnie, Sparkie, Daisy-Mae

Young Vito applies for membership

December, 2007

Saturday, December 1:

We begin another month in the park on a sunny but chilly Saturday morning. Fritz ambles along slowly as we pass the lads and lassies at their footie, eventually reaching a second set of pupils, in this case the canines belonging to Roland's obedience class. I recognize some of the class members, including Oscar the Schnauzer, but our group has avoided the green (whose cricket crease has a covering of rainwater and floating leaves again) in favor of a perch at the foot of Mt. Bannister. Fritz ascends the peak itself and disappears down the other side, but my whistle fetches him back from the tennis courts and I hook him so we can go in for coffee.

We have a large turnout this morning and this makes it hard to hear and be heard during our coffee chatter. Kate and Bob sit on one side (with a grey-haired woman, who remains unidentified). They are joined by Faz, who stands for the entire session, hovering lovingly over baby Scarlett, who now weighs 13 pounds. Then we have Liz (who has spent the week hunting for her lost mobile phone), Georgie, Dan, Ronnie, and Janet—with Hanna and Cheryl at a little table by themselves, Albert in his outrider pose as well, and Peter hovering in the background as Ellen's get well card, made by Janet, is signed by each of us. Dan also takes up a collection for a present, with many unsuitable suggestions on what to buy for a heart bypass patient (chocolates, cheese, cigarettes).

From what I can hear in this crossfire of chatter the following bits of news are confirmed. Liz, who announces that she is *not* going into the hairdressing business in St. John's Wood, is still having trouble with her oven and Dan with his shower. That gentleman, not having heard from Natasha, is not planning to put on a dog suit down at Village Vets today. Bob has been locked out a second time at Kate's house. I suggest, echoing our recent advice to Nicholas, that this is no accident and there

172

may be a hidden agenda in such an occurrence. Bob agrees but Kate says, "It's not *so* hidden."

Sunday, December 2:

Somewhat groggily (all-night party in a nearby flat) Fritz and I head for the park under grey, blustery skies. The park is appropriately deserted—just the isolated, unorganized football configuration or solitary jogger. When we reach the café no one is about but the odd old chap with the trenchcoat, the flat cap, the plastic glasses, the bushy moustache and the cotton-stuffed ears. He often talks to the dogs (and to himself) but usually he takes no refreshment here; today he just seems to be hiding from the occasional drop.

I lose track of my dog as I round the corner, but Brea's mom tells me he went thataway. This means that he is patrolling the lower elevations of Mt. Bannister, where I see only Georgie standing, with Sparkie in attendance. Janet is also here with Daisy-Mae but that naughty Shih-Tzu, rushing up to greet Rosie and Ronnie, has managed to trip that gentleman in her eagerness. Ronnie makes several attempts to rise from the pavement but he is unsuccessful until I arrive and hoist him to his feet. Fritz has headed down the Randolph walkway and I have to follow, but I lose track of him and double back to the green, where Nicholas is just arriving with *two* American Cockers. "Where's Fritz?" he asks; fortunately my dog emerges just as this moment from the bushes so I am able to point him out without answering, "I haven't a clue." Accompanying Monty this morning is the tan cutie Winston, who belongs to Nicholas' brother-in-law and is, in fact, Monty's half-brother. It begins to rain in earnest so we head for cover. I am trying to convince Nicholas that, no, come Christmastime we will not be playing Secret Santa among the dog owners. "Why not?" he whines petulantly. "Because some of us are Jewish!" I reply.

At the counter of the café Nicholas is trying to get Lurch to reveal how he spent last night. "That would be a private matter," Lurch says, "but next weekend we will call you so *you* can pay for the drinks." Outside we have to move the table twice (one more move and no one could open the front door) because the rain is horizontal today and half of us are getting soaked. Indeed there are a lot of seating problems today. Peter is hovering in a spot that could really offer space for a dry chair and Ronnie keeps trying to get him to sit down. Ofra thinks she has a seat reserved for *her* but she immediately abandons it to take another phone call in Hebrew and someone else claims the chair. The last of the arrangements is made for Ellen's card and present and there is some discussion on the photo session that Rhian is conducting this afternoon for the park dogs. Liz announces that another thing has happened to her; she has gone to her home printer to run off some photos, only to discover that not only are all the cartridges missing but so also is the housing for these objects as well—and no one can explain this mystery. The rain is relentless and I am getting really wet so, considerably earlier than usual, I announce my departure. Nicholas accompanies me; Winston has a crush on Fritz but before his attentions can get really nasty we reach the exit gate.

Monday, December 3:

Bright sunlight has returned to Paddington Rec as Fritz and I make our Monday entry. Fritz is anxious to compare notes with a number of the other dogs (Ginger, Lola, Winnie, Spadge, and Rosie among them) for yesterday these animals sat for their portraits in the ground floor studio of photographer Rhian, located in a mews house about a ten minute walk from the park. David the dog sitter served as her assistant—it was his job, for instance, to remove all the blonde hairs deposited by the Pugs on the black velvet sofa that served as the setting for this shoot.

Fritz, of course, had trouble remaining in a stationary position but this same energy now carries him with some speed between the twin menaces of jackhammer and leaf blower and out to the green, where seagulls are surrounding the lake that has formed over the cricket crease—Lake Botham I like to call it. The happy news this morning is that Ellen is not only out of hospital but (even before our flowers have reached her) she has resumed her position at the end of the leads attached to Jack and Sandy. Evidently there will be a bypass operation in the future.

At breakfast today we have her and Peter, Ofra, Georgie, Dan, Hanna, Ronnie and Cheryl. Cheryl not only backed her car into her security gate yesterday but managed to crash her computer; she seems remarkably cheerful in the event. Sparkie, after a session of annoying barking, settles into Dan's lap and pretends to be innocent of any wrongdoing. Dan has picked up a copy of the magazine put out by Roland's sponsors—also confusingly called *Wag (Mag)*. In it we learn that our Slovakian trainer has missed a number of park sessions because he has been spending so much time appearing in shows with his own dog. None of our dogs has spent any time in his Saturday sessions—perhaps this would make a nice Christmas present for Sparkie.

Tuesday, December 4:

Grey skies have returned as Fritz and I reach our park entrance. Almost immediately we are overtaken by Tay and Monty; Tay seems to want to make friends with Fritz today and follows him along all the way to the cypress trees. As we are rounding the corner we also encounter Lulu and, walking with David the dog sitter, Frank and Bianca. Frank, the Chinese Crested Dog, seems to be dressed in a blue boiler suit; it's a pity that we don't have Michael to ask, "Frank, what *can* your mommy have been thinking of?"

Fritz now races ahead and by the time I have rounded the café I have again lost track of him. I find him with Georgie, all by herself at the foot of Mt. Bannister—with Sparkie and Daisy-Mae. Ofra is just arriving with Bailey. He too is dressed today but he is wearing a smart brown outfit with buttons. I have to keep an eye on Fritz (who is naked) as he heads eastward along the Randolph walkway. Who knows how far he would have gone had I not been right behind him, reminding the stubborn Schnauzer that we don't go that way and that, indeed, if he would just reverse his direction, there's a biscuit waiting for him now (a bribe that doesn't seem to have its usual charm today) and even more treats at coffee time. At last I get him to sit and, on lead, we make our return journey.

We have a large turnout at breakfast, especially as this is a weekday and also because it is beginning to rain just a bit. Around the table we manage to squeeze a dozen bodies including Nicholas, Hanna, Georgie, Peter, Ellen, Dan, Ofra, Cheryl, Ronnie, Faz and Suzanne. Ellen's husband has sent in coffee money for all of us—as a thank you for our card and gift—which has yet to arrive. The Pugs are very much in evidence this morning. Winnie manages to follow Dan into the café, where her presence is sniffily noted by a young woman in a Courtney's coat. Then she and Lola spend a lot of time on laps; it's as if each acts as a red flag to the other and when they are both on the ground there is unpleasantness. This is all very amusing for the rest of us (and Dan enjoys winding them up)—and why not enjoy a lighter moment on a day that is getting greyer and wetter?

Wednesday, December 5:

A light rain is falling as I stare out the window at the sodden park on a grey Wednesday morning and there is no question but Fritz *must* wear his raincoat today. He makes little fuss this time and we are soon out in the wet; at least temperatures are quite mild. We meet Sabina with Oscar and Scamp and she asks for details on Fritz's smart coat, since she is thinking of getting a similar one for her Schnauzer. We meet this trio a second time as we near the green and, after we have done some wandering over near the tennis courts, we return to the Grantully entrance and meet them a third time. There is a small group of dogs over here including the two mud-wrestling champs, Buddy and Sasha, and this pair line up immediately for a biscuit handout. Fritz and I continue around the green and enter the forecourt of the café—which seems to have lost its westernmost fencing permanently. This makes for a more welcoming entryway but the old comfort of putting your dog or your small child in what was once a secure space is now gone. As the opening fronts the Carlton roadway (down which the mail van is speeding again) this is worrying.

Dan, who has had an early morning coffee, has taken off for work, leaving Winnie with Georgie. Inside the café Elian is trying to explain Winnie to a new barista. I return to our table with my latte and retrieve Fritz from David the dog sitter. Only Hanna joins us on a very small turnout day indeed. Soon she receives a sausage sandwich from Elian, who has now donned his chef's hat, a traditional white affair bearing the legend "I love cooking and Arsenal."

Hanna is preoccupied with the prospects of Christmas dinner—or the lack thereof. She has been trying to find out who is entertaining on the holiday night itself (though she rather dislikes Christmas) but almost all the dog people plan to be away, either abroad or off with other relatives. David expects to be heading for home, but his mother (who would much prefer Campbell or Fritz) has banned Isla and Skye—"I'm not having that big white dog here again." Today our dog sitter has arrived with Bianca and Frank, though the latter has taken objection to the rain and returned to the car. David says that Bianca is as thick as two planks and that Frank enjoys stealing her ball and relaxing with it in his mouth while the Boxer moans. We have been hoping for some change in the weather but it is still pelting down when we begin our back passage walkround.

At least there is a glimmer of brightness in the western sky—the sun will soon reappear.

Thursday, December 6:

The raincoats have to go on again as wet weather dominates yet another morning in the park. If anything, the rain is coming down even harder today than yesterday and the park is appropriately empty—though we pass Jean-Baptiste (bare-headed) and Saskia as we make our way toward the café. It is very quiet—none of the school groups have ventured forth this morning—and I consider the irony that the only time we are ever likely to get this kind of peace in our park is in a downpour.

Dan is just turning Winnie over to Georgie as I reach the safety of the café overhang. He reports that the flowers that Janet ordered for Ellen have, in fact, ended up at Janet's house, and that the same thing happened when flowers were ordered for Ronnie. This seems highly suspicious and our absent friend clearly has some 'splainin' to do. I decide not to continue the morning's exercise and so I sit down with Georgie. Peter and Ellen soon arrive and so does Hanna. The latter has quite a tale to tell.

It seems that yesterday at noontime she was walking with Farrah along the fenced passageway between the playing fields. A school group was heading for the five-a-side pitch and so she picked up the geriatric Spadge. Most of the kids passed by without incident but one pipsqueak went out of his way to shove a shoulder into her and the dog she had pressed to her chest. She let out a howl of protest at this, followed the miscreant (identified as a Moslem—I don't know how) onto the playing field and denounced him to his teacher. The chap was now trying to hide behind his friends, but he was summoned forth and Hanna demanded and eventually received a face-to-face apology. A few hours later, she can now tell us with a chuckle, she was preparing to go out when she realized that an evil odor was rising from her purse. This object had been hanging from her neck during the incident and the frightened dog, it was now clear, had, in his distress, deposited a sausage-shaped turd *in* her bag.

Peter is wondering when the rain might stop so he can make a break for home. Ellen suggests that it should be brighter tomorrow and Peter says, "Oh well, I'll wait 'til then." They do get up, however, and their places are taken by three late arrivals, Cheryl, Nicholas and Jo Lynn. Cheryl has walked all the way in the rain (with Lola only) in a tracksuit (again without head covering) and is now complaining about Seasonal Affective Disorder and another bad back. Nicholas begins pumping Jo for public relations advice for his every-burgeoning furnishing empire and this is the signal for the rest of us, bored to tears, to get up and head for home.

Friday, December 7:

A night of howling winds has given way to a much calmer morning, crisp, cold, but also radiantly sunny. I follow Fritz through his usual morning peregrinations as we meet all the counter-clockwise dogs while remaining steadfastly loyal to the clockwise. I have followed him along the Randolph walkway and edged him toward the back of the tennis courts at the critical turnoff—only to see him disappear into the foliage at the north end of the Grantully doggy pen. He does come when I whistle but no sooner has he approached for a reward biscuit then he is off again, rubbing noses with a mid-size hound who is accompanied by a woman carrying a seasonal cup of Starbucks coffee. This, I soon see, is Mary McCartney, photographer daughter of the famous Paul, and her Paddy. Once notorious for antisocial behavior, this Irish rescue dog is a reformed character these days and I have heard the doggy people say on a number of occasions that Mary has done a wonderful job on the fellow.

She is staring down at the ripples on the surface of Lake Botham but, complaining of the cold, she is soon off and Fritz and I complete a circuit of the empty greensward and go in to coffee, where we join Ronnie, Georgie, Dan, Faz, and Peter. Georgie says that Ellen's flower mishap will be rectified tomorrow. Dan tells us that he will undertake a holiday in Cuba in January and Ronnie defends Boris Johnson as a serious mayoral candidate. Peter wants to know if it is possible to extend the number of rings before his cell phone goes to voice mail and Faz, who says he needs a bigger car, wants to know when Rhian is photographing dogs again—though he plans to sneak in the sleeping Scarlett while Jasmine is posing for her photograph.

There is such a long queue at the café counter that I miss my chance for a cuppa altogether this morning. I have to get home anyway, since Linda has offered me a ride to Sainsburys, in part so that I will be back in time to begin a babysitting assignment with Pepper, who reports for duty at about 12:20. The boys have a lively time together and both manage to run out the front door at least once while the Polish work crew are here adjusting my recently painted windows. Later Pepper eats a cardboard tube and throws up twice in my hallway.

Saturday, December 8:

Just as we set forth for our Saturday session in the park a light rain begins to fall. Soon I am all zipped up, but it is still rather unpleasant (Fritz doesn't seem to mind). Lulu the Lurcher is coming up behind us but she is spooked not by the rain but by the noisy boys who are undertaking footy instruction in the pitch on our right. When we reach the green I can see Dan, Liz, and Janet in front of the clubhouse, so we turn right instead of our usual left. Had we continued in our normal direction we would have encountered the early stages of the Christmas party, partly sheltered under the little metal gazebo, of Roland's obedience school. I can see that in the center of the green Lake Botham has been walled off with a mesh fence in blue and orange. The seagulls have taken possession of the lake itself and are wading about happily.

There is little incentive to linger for long in the wet and so there is an early migration to the confines of the café. Dan is trying to figure out if the staff has been on the razzle last night, "You all look the worse for wear." "They look like that all the time," I add. Bouzha and Lurch are attempting to instruct the tiny new barista in her duties here. Bob says, "I don't think she can speak or understand English." "Or any other language, I fear," is the unkind addition.

There is a large turnout this morning at table: Dan, Georgie, Bob, Kate, Janet, Liz and Ronnie, with later arrivals in Ricky (Ofra is still in bed) and Nicholas, who briefly introduces us to his new bride, the blonde Edwina. Hanna arrives as well, though seeing the crowd at our table she takes a little one for herself next to the café's front door. There is much discussion of holiday travel and Dan even organizes a kind of pub outing for the dog owners, many of whom are soon to scatter. I realize that my distribution of holiday cards, something I would normally not do for another ten days or so, had better not wait much longer. The others get up to have a look at Roland's Christmas party around the corner but, the steady rain still falling, I decide to head for home with Fritz.

Sunday, December 9:

The sun is trying to make a breakthrough as Fritz and I head for the park. My dog is attempting to assert his independence today for, after we have reached the Carlton walkway, he is determined to turn left instead of the usual right and, ignoring my calls, he next begins an ascent of Mt. Bannister. I have to follow him on my gimpy right knee, but once we reach the top I can see him heading down a side path toward the tennis courts. This time, at least, he answers my call and returns to the summit in order for us to begin our descent to the green. The other dog owners are milling about on the grass opposite the café entrance and I join them, not forgetting to put Fritz on lead as a precaution.

At coffee we have a robust turnout including Dan, Georgie, Janet, Ellen, Ronnie, Bob, Kate, Hanna and Liz. Georgie has to tell Janet that a second orchid has failed to show up at Ellen's, even though Janet received a dispatch conformation yesterday. Faz arrives with baby Scarlett but he is soon rushing out from the café's interior, having noticed that Skye's head has just disappeared inside the baby buggy. No one is eaten. Elian arrives with a bag of doggy treats (Santa Gnaws) obtained at yesterday's doggy fete. These are shared out among the pooches (following biscuits, toast, scrambled eggs, and carrots). Kate is holding one of the new goodies in her hand and Bob asks her if she is going to eat it herself. "Any more of that," she says, "and you'll find it well disguised in your lunch." Then she gets up and returns some change to Liz. "I didn't really need that," Liz says. "Well," Kate replies, "we've all seen how you dress."

I distribute my holiday cards to all assembled, including Albert, who is arriving with Saffy and Tinkerbelle just as the rest of us are getting up to begin a back passage walkround. "Do you think we'll beat the rain?" he asks. Indeed there are already drops and it is easy to answer the question as a real rain begins to fall again. On the journey home both Sparkie and Daisy-Mae throw up, the consequences of too rich a diet at breakfast it appears. We are all getting drenched so there is no dawdling on the way home.

Monday, December 10:

It has been raining much of the morning (we also had rain during our outing yesterday afternoon) so I have decided to dress Fritz in his raincoat. Just as well—for shortly after we enter the park there is a brief shower. Then the moisture lessens to the occasional droplet and we are able to continue without too much discomfort. Fritz manages to stay closer to his master today, though he is tempted to visit some of his pals over at the clubhouse—where some of the other owners have taken shelter in the vestibule. This means that he has to catch up with me a few minutes later for I have begun a desperate plod across the green in an attempt to head off Sabina and Saskia, for whom I have holiday greeting cards. Fritz has time to chase Oscar off with a peremptory growl.

A few minutes later I deliver cards to Metty and to Peter as well. Those who opened theirs yesterday seem to be very happy with the photo of Dorothy and me in Paris and with the lengthy message that I have had printed this year. At breakfast today we have, in addition to the aforementioned Peter, Davide, Ellen, Georgie, Ronnie and Hanna. Hanna is upset that Davide has succeeded where she has failed, that is in getting the kitchen staff to prepare an open-faced cheese toasty—though she disdains the local cheddar as too mild. A post-mortem is held on the surfeit of treats that caused upset to several doggy stomachs yesterday. I mention that Fritz was a bit gassy as well and for some reason Peter, who has never heard this euphemism before, is sent into gales of laughter. The usual palaver continues of the subject of the delivery of the get-well orchid to Ellen; it still hasn't arrived. "One day you'll get three," I propose.

Albert arrives with Saffy and Tinkerbelle. He pulls up his usual chair behind me, but the wind is so chilling that he has to move it behind a pillar a few minutes later. Sparkie then goes missing, as he often does, and Albert gets up to help in the search. We tell him to relax but he says he's worried. Soon Sparkie shows up—just as well because Albert has left his two dogs tied only to a chair and this is a formula for disaster. The old fellow can relax now—the ubiquitous bead of snot resting on the tip of his nose. We get up to begin our back passage walkround; Albert can't see that his mischievous little madams, trailing behind on their leads, are able to squat and poo without breaking their stride.

Tuesday, December 11:

I can see Albert, already perched on a park bench, as Fritz and I reach the park on a sunny by cold Tuesday morning. There is not much activity in the Rec today; even out on the green we find only Sparkie and Humphrey. Dan soon enters with Winnie and I can hear a roar from Fritz as Dan's own dog gets too close to her master while my dog is getting a cuddle. The ever-expanding Lake Botham is frozen in parts today. As I walk in my new hiking boots over the marshy surface of the green it feels like I am back in the Pennines, struggling through a series of peat hags.

The others are settling down to coffee as Fritz and I report to the café, which is just in the process of posting the dreaded news: the annual Christmas closure is coming. Dan ends up paying for my black coffee, having added my order to his and then not having change for a ten pound note. At breakfast this morning we have Dan, Georgie, Ronnie, daddy Faz (at a little table behind us), Cheryl, Peter and Ellen. Dan is making phone calls to other dog owners since he has organized a pub night for the bunch tonight. Even Albert, who now pulls up with his dogs, is invited.

We learn that the famous missing orchid has at last made it to Ellen's house, that Cheryl is planning a return trip to the States soon and that Dan is spending a weekend in New York on Saturday. David comes by with Yoyo and I am able to distribute more holiday cards; Yoyo's parents are in China. I am sitting in my sunglasses and gloves, staring into the sun, but this fiery orb provides no warmth today and I am just as happy when an early march for the exits begins.

Wednesday, December 12:

The morning after the night before. We arise today after a dozen of the dog people have spent the night together at the Idlewild gastro pub on Shirland Road. Our numbers included Dan (the organizer of this outing), Davide, Janet, Georgie, Hanna, David the dog sitter, Kate, Bob, Cheryl, Linda and Liz. There were no dogs. I walked over to the pub with Hanna and Cheryl; Dan picked this date because a holiday time scattering was about to take place—indeed Cheryl would be on a plane to the States a few hours after our outing. The upstairs room in this recently converted institution received high marks for comfort and ambience; many will remember the place as the old Truscott Arms, a pub well known for its variety of interesting beers of tap; Georgie spent nine and a half years behind the bar in those day and was offered the manager's position on three occasions. I must say that no one disgraced him or herself on this occasion, in spite of those three mojitos, Hanna.

Anxious to see if there were any sore heads, I enter the park at my usual hour today, soon passing Ellen with Jack and Sandy. It is extremely cold, with frost everywhere and Lake Botham frozen over. Nevertheless Ellen is only the first of the dog people to suggest that this is a beautiful morning (the sun *is* out). Hanna seems to revel in these cold temperatures as well, particularly if there is no wind, but then she is from Finland.

At breakfast this morning we have Janet, Georgie, Peter, Ellen, Davide, Hanna, and Nicholas. Janet continues the distribution of the coming year's "Dogs of Paddington Rec" calendar. Each year she manages to outdo herself as her Photoshop skills improve. She has managed to get 37 dogs onto the cover and she has also presented many of us with Christmas cards featuring our own dogs and a fridge magnet with a likeness of our pet as well. Nicholas notes that he has missed the deadline for submitting photos and he knows that Monty will *not* be represented in the collection. The Schnauzers have a month of their own—Fritz is pictured sniffing Pepper's bum. I notice that Janet has managed to sneak a picture of Daisy-Mae onto many of the pages as well.

The Pugs have a page of their own too, but Winnie is the only Pug in our village for a while. She is in a pissy mood, however, and tries to intercept Davide's food as it travels the short distance between plate and mouth. (At home she evidently sits on her own chair at the dining table while the lads eat.) We are just about to leave when Vito is discovered under our table. He begins his usual mugging of Daisy-Mae and it takes us some time to find Christian, on the other side of the green, so that he can be presented with his own pup and we can begin a back passage walkround.

Thursday, December 13:

My day begins far earlier than usual as Fritz jumps from the bed, in which I have spent a restless night anyway, and begins to whine at the front door. I know what is coming next (having witnessed a rather runny poo on our late night walk six or so hours earlier) and I am not surprised with several runny doo-doos and two bouts of vomiting. It is incredibly cold outside, with frost covering the parked cars and sparkling everywhere in the streetlights.

Temperatures are not much better at 9:15 when we enter the park, though the sun is again in place. Fritz continues with a series of runny squirts and pauses to hunt for grass shoots, also covered in rime—a sure sign of stomach distress. We are overtaken by Skye and Isla (who seems to get bigger with every day) and by Kate and Bob on the eve of their holiday in Kerala. Fritz seems to skip along happily enough with the other dogs, but I put him back on lead at the café, letting the other dog people know that we will not be joining them for coffee and dog treats this morning. Fritz manages two more squirts before we reach home, where my first duty is a call to the vet.

At 4:15 we report to Dr. Seddon, who administers two injections, listens to some violent tummy rumbling, and predicts there is still more to come from the rear end. In fact, the rate of rumbling soon dies down and neither on the walk home nor on our late night ramble is there any further explosion. I am able to get a good night's sleep.

Friday, December 14:

We are able to emerge at our normal time this morning but I keep Fritz on lead throughout, wanting to keep him close at hand in order to monitor any fecal activity. There is none. On the green there is a lively scene, with Vito up to his usual mischief and a dozy Chocolate Lab named Wisley lying on her back for tummy rubs. When the others go in for coffee I leave Fritz with Hanna so that I can dash over to the chemists and pick up a prescription (for me). On the way I pass the seldom seen Alsatian, Pumbaa.

When I retrieve my dog we head for home and I leave Fritz, amid howls of protest, for some more local errands. Shortly after my return he begins whining near the front door and so I have to take him out again, though there seems to be no urgency and again he does only a few wee-wees. When we return he begins whining all over again—then it hits me. He is just letting me know that I have forgotten to give him his welcome home biscuit (twice). I have *not* forgotten.

At 3:50 we set out for a return visit to the vets, but we get no further than the café when we encounter Linda with Pepper; she volunteers to give us a ride to Boundary Road. Here Dr. Seddon is gratified by the lack of noise in Fritz's intestines. Tablets and intestinal formula food are issued and one more shot administered, but he may not have to return. Linda, bless her heart, is still waiting for us and she comes up to the flat with us at the end, Pepper and Fritz having a fine impromptu tussle.

Saturday, December 15:

Pepper returns at 6:45 in the morning, since I will be dog sitting the noisiest Schnauzer while his owners are in Oxford for the day. The dogs keep whining to go to the park and I delay this as long as possible—finally reaching a frigid Rec at about 9:10. It is gray and the wind is not helping matters. I keep Pepper on lead throughout the proceedings but Fritz runs free. At one point he dashes ahead to catch up with a slow-moving circling party made up of Georgie, with Sparkie and Winnie, and Janet with Daisy-Mae. On top of Mt. Bannister he does a much-better looking poo. At the foot of this precipice the Saturday morning obedience class is foregathering and Roland is a bit frustrated because some of the owners have arrived without any reward treats for their willful pets.

I make an early stop at the café, where we are soon joined by Janet, Georgie, Ronnie, Peter, Ellen, Liz and Ofra. Fritz is not allowed any food and this proves to be a considerable problem, since the little fellow is ravenous and the other owners' hearts are broken when they have to deny him so much as a crumb. Pepper is allowed the occasional mouthful but he keeps up his high-pitched squawks throughout the session and once he even manages to frighten an elderly tennis player. Liz says that her youngest is back from his trip to New York, where he attended the bar mitzvah of a schoolmate, the occasion for lavish spending, including a private 20-seater jet to take the group to the Big Apple. One of the highlights was the presence of a ping-pong phenom who entertained the lads by offering anyone who could beat him a $1000. None could, even though he used a variety of household objects instead of a paddle, including his mobile phone (with which he conducted a conversation with his mother during the match). We begin a back passage walkround. It is so cold that my hands sting when I have to take my gloves off to hook a galloping Fritz.

Pepper manages to spend a whole day in the house without throwing up, but dog stories are not finished for the day for at 8:00 I pay a visit to Michaela and her family. Skye the Cairn is supposed to remain upstairs

but he manages to escape on a number of occasions and likes to greet
guests when he hears the doorbell ring. At one point he settles down
between Faz and myself on the sofa, though Faz is a bit wary, considering
the fellow to be unpredictable. A few minutes later Skye returns with his
beloved tennis ball and we bounce it for him a few times—but tragedy
strikes when it bounces through the legs of a number of party-goers and
right into the fireplace, which is well-lit. The dog has the sense not to
rush in after his ball but he is clearly anxious and one chap sticks his
foot into the fireplace and manages to drag the burnt offering out of the
flames. Of course we don't want to let Skye put it in his mouth so we put it
in a bucket and I place this on a shelf. Soon Skye is climbing furniture in
an attempt to recover the object of worship. We have a new worry—now
we don't want the dog playing with the blackened toy on Michaela's white
carpet. I'm for throwing it out the front door but Faz puts it on top of a
kitchen cabinet next to the dog's ball sling. I have to warn Michaela
that she may have a surprise when she reaches for this object the next
morning.

Sunday, December 16:

The sun is making a breakthrough on another frigid morning, but
Fritz and I make a brave entrance into the park at our usual time—soon
joining up with Georgie, who again has Sparkie and Winnie. At the café
we encounter Janet with Daisy-Mae (also suffering form tummy problems
these days) and Liz with Roxy. A group now forms for a procession over
the top of Mt. Bannister and Fritz enjoys being part of the pack—when
he is not darting off the hilltop on his own mysterious missions. I enjoy
the view from up here, the gulls floating serenely on the surface of Lake
Botham.

At coffee we have Peter, Ofra, Ronnie, Janet, Georgie, and Liz. Fritz
is still nil by mouth out here (he has already had his intestinal formula
breakfast food at home) but he is still deeply disappointed not to receive
further handouts and he spends most of the session in Liz's lap. We
discuss the progress of contestants on *The X Factor* and *Strictly Come
Dancing*. Ronnie, looking backward, says he likes *Columbo* and Peter,
looking forward, begins to worry about the death of the sun in four million
years.

I realize I have a problem; it's bitter cold out here and I have only one glove. My gloves are always falling out of my jacket pocket and I am quite vexed because this is a relatively new pair. With the surviving glove I drink my black coffee. (If you remember your *Of Mice And Men*, you will recall that Curly wore only one glove as well.) On the back passage walkround, therefore, I have everybody on the lookout for the lost object. It's nowhere to be seen anywhere in the park but after I have made my exit I find it on the pavement opposite my building. Much relieved, we scramble upstairs in search of some warmth.

Monday, December 17:

There is a chilling wind blowing across the park as Fritz and I make our first entrance of the week. Yes, the sun is making some effort to emerge, but it might as well not bother. The Rec is unusually quiet—perhaps the schools have begun their break; the only exception to the wonderful calm comes from the voice of the leaf blower over by the café, or the occasional raucous magpie.

Fritz seems to be making satisfactory progress in his recovery from tummy ailments and he does not linger for long on the in-lap. He does manage to take his usual detour trough the café forecourt on his way to the green. Here he is greeted by a well wrapped-up Leila. He might dally even longer but I have spotted Pepper on the green and the mere mention of his friend's name makes my dog manic. Soon there is a recognition scene, amid growls of delighted protest. David the dog sitter is here with Isla and Skye; he complains that the heat seems to have failed in Kate's flat.

At coffee this morning we have Peter (with Holly, Jack and Sandy, the latter two off-lead for once), Ronnie, Georgie, Linda, and Ofra. Ofra is ten minutes late, having kept up a lengthy chatter with Natasha on the green; then she spends ten minutes chatting with Metty and Vicky in the café. The dogs are looking for cozy positions on the laps of the owners. Winnie seems to be in a benign mood (though at Georgie's she barks at James until he gets out of bed) but Daisy-Mae keeps bedeviling poor Sparkie. Then she wants to sit on everybody's lap but she is such a muddy mess that no one will let her do this. Fritz sits on my lap and receives a few pieces of convalescent toast. On the back passage walkround the dogs get into the empty five-a-side pitch and exhaust themselves chasing Sparkie.

Tuesday, December 18:

We have another sunny but frigid morning for our parkland exercise today and Fritz, who seems pretty well recovered from his recent bout of tummy trouble, races ahead between the eerily empty football pitches; just outside the café we encounter Jean-Baptiste and Hercules and do a circuit of the green—still boasting its lakelet, on which the gulls placidly float. Half way around we encounter Christian, who says he has heard a rumor that Tanya the animal warden has been declared persona non-grata in the Rec for objecting too vociferously to the behavior of certain Staffie owners. None of this tale makes *any* sense and I tell him so; unfortunately we see a warden in here so rarely that there is no one to discuss this rumor with.

At coffee we have Hanna, Georgie, Ronnie, Dan (back from New York with a fur-lined tweed pilot's cap), Peter, Ellen, and Nicholas. Georgie reports that Janet has received a worrying text from Cheryl concerning Lola, the younger of her two Pugs, who has collapsed and gone to hospital with a suspected tumor. There is great consternation over this news since Cheryl must be feeling quite helpless in the States and the woman who was keeping an eye on the Pugs is not actually in residence with ancient, mostly blind Ginger. Both Dan and Hanna know that this woman has their telephone numbers (for emergencies) but Dan has been away and Hanna has just discovered that workmen painting her baseboards have unplugged her telephone.

Just as we are about to head up our front stairs I spot Rowena and Timmy in the doggy pen across the street. I have a holiday card for her so I join a large group of dog people who are listening to another disturbing tale. Rowena says (and I later checked these details on the Internet) that there has been an alarming incident in Regents Park. Here too there seems to be a mad desire to pave over paradise in favor of five-a-side courts. Even before planning permission for this act of desecration had been granted the old tennis and golf center in the park was shut down and a 56 year-old coach, unable to find work anywhere else, has hanged himself from a tree that faced the proposed site. (Trees would also have been sacrificed in this madness). A large number of people had joined a protest march some time ago—and these included a number of our dog people, who also use and love Regents Park. Last Thursday, the same day the coach's body was found, planning permission for the project was refused.

Wednesday, December 19:

It's a repeat, weatherwise, as Fritz and I make our usual entrance this morning, though there is very little breeze and so it is not too uncomfortable out here. I find a Schnauzer coming up behind me as I am walking along the cypress trees, but this turns out to be Oscar, much larger and shaggier than Fritz, who just wants a cuddle. Fritz has raced ahead to join a large group of dogs outside the café fence. Then he stops by the early diners to see if there is any toast going and I have to coax him into a little more exercise. We head down the Randolph walkway, then pass behind the tennis courts and return to the green, where my dog can be bribed into crossing the grass by the presence of David the dog sitter. Outside the café there is a chap with two delightful little dogs, a Winnie-like Pug puppy named Cookie and a Japanese Shiba Inu named Kai.

At breakfast this morning we have Ronnie, Ofra, Ellen, Peter, Georgie and Hanna. Georgie is depressed over the muddy state of Daisy-Mae, who spends most of the daytime, while Janet is working, with Sparkie. Bailey, dressed in a red coat, keeps jumping into Ronnie's lap. Fritz is able to participate in the toast handout and then he jumps into my lap to escape the cold flagstones. Holly throws up.

The others are just about to make a move when Linda arrives with Pepper. He and Fritz then take up residence at Hanna's feet, for that lady is about to enjoy a fried egg sandwich. The three of us begin our own back passage walkround—during which Hanna attempts to explain the origins of her Christmas phobia. It was the sight, during childhood, of all those Finnish Santas, who, after being entertained with liquid refreshment at each of the homes they had visited—were now falling down dead drunk—that must have induced the initial disillusionment. Pepper makes a brief visit when we reach the street and later that afternoon he and Fritz have an outing in Regents Park.

Thursday, December 20:

After another bitter cold night frost covers many of the park surfaces this morning, and I decide to put his coat on Fritz, even though the sun is shining brightly. There is little protest, and we are soon underway. Again we pass Pumbaa on our way to a green in which a picket fence continues to surround Lake Botham. (Dan tries to convince us that there is a sign saying "No Swimming" affixed to this barrier, but no one believes him.) Buddy, whom I have not seen in some time, comes up to greet me raucously. David the dog sitter reports that Isla is getting used to his presence in Kate's house. On his first night there she peed on his bed.

Nicholas comes out onto the green and reminds everybody that he has brought a thermos of mulled wine for the group. This is enjoyed after we have made our more conventional orders. At the counter Lurch is handing out greeting cards and a chocolate bar as a Christmas greeting to the faithful from the Park Café itself. Pouring warm wine into paper cups, Nicholas explains in detail the complicated recipe he used to make this concoction last night. Then he tells a filthy Jewish joke.

This morning we have Peter, Ellen, Ronnie, Ofra (who is taking lessons so she can get a license to go with the family's new Smart car), Hanna, Janet, Georgie, and Dan. Janet says that Lola the Pug seems better and is home from hospital. Peter says he is perplexed that they don't sell spirits at Marks and Spencers. Winnie jumps into my lap, since Dan's chair is pushed back from the table and this way she can lean into Georgie's arm as the latter tucks into her well-peppered scrambled eggs. When the food is over she does return to her master's lap but she does manage to head-butt poor Fritz as he is attempting to reclaim my own. He doesn't seem too perturbed but I notice it takes him a while to get up enough courage to attempt a second leap.

Friday, December 21:

I see no frost when I look out the window this morning and this convinces me that Fritz needs no coat. Wrong!

It is bitter cold, in spite of the efforts to the sun to break through, and I am thoroughly chilled almost from the outset. Nevertheless we soldier on toward the green, where David is exercising Kate's dogs and

Buddy is here with his daddy. Fritz wants instant biscuits but when I decline he disappears, literally. I have a look at the café, where Ronnie is seated already, but there is no sign of him. As I scan the horizon I am just beginning to get worried when he suddenly rushes around a corner. When the dog people begin a mass shuffle in the direction of the caff, Fritz starts to follow but, distracted by the arrival of Leila on the green, he disappears for a second time.

Coffee is on Liz this morning, a kind of farewell gesture on the eve of her holiday departure for Falmouth, Massachusetts and Vail, Colorado. She and Ofra have been out clubbing the night before and they are both the worse for wear. Dan presents Liz with a sarong, which he purchased on his last trip to Brazil—a lot of Christmas cards are exchanged as well. The dogs are behaving like spoiled brats this morning. They spit out substandard treats, bark at passersby, and squabble with one another. Roxy sounds like she has just treed a fugitive and Winnie explodes with rage. Only Fritz remains aloof from this ruckus. I am entreating him to jump on my lap, hoping for a little warmth, but he is shivering himself—mollified only by some slow chewing on Liz's toast.

We begin our back passage walkround. Dan says that he is looking forward to New Year's—since, as far as he is concerned, 2007 has been a horrible year. (Tell me about it.) Ofra wants to know when *is* New Year. The others laugh but I explain that in Israel the new year came months ago. Peter notes that today is the shortest day of the year and that it is the official start of Winter—a cheery thought when it feels as though we have had Winter for a long time already. Fritz, who usually starts last but often finishes first on these backstage rambles, manages to delay our return to warmth by making such slow progress that, by the time we have reached our exit gate, he is still last.

Saturday, December 22:

Having learned my lesson, I attach Fritz's coat before we head for the park this morning. The sun is out but it is very cold; at least there is no wind. When we reach the green I can see Georgie and Janet atop Mt. Bannister; they call to Fritz and he rushes up to join Sparkie and Daisy-Mae. Down on the walkway below Dan is trying to discourage Winnie from pursuing joggers, and Fritz is now driving off the one-eyed Humphrey, who is playing with our dogs without the permission of you know who. Gerri, Humphrey's mistress, tells us that yesterday she went to Tesco, leaving her dog outside with her gentleman. Humphrey became so distressed by this abandonment that he slipped his collar, entered the market, and ran up and down every aisle until he found Gerri at check-out.

At breakfast this morning we have Dan, Peter, Ellen, Georgie, Janet, Hanna, Ronnie, Ofra and Liz. Liz, who is leaving for the States this afternoon, brings cards and dog treats for everyone at our table. I remind her to bring her passports this time—she has two for every member of the family. Dan is feeling very rough after a session at a karaoke bar last night. This is a matter of some perplexity since he says he just drank red wine. He orders a huge English breakfast, though the dogs get most of the chips.

We begin a back passage walkround. At the corner of the running track, where the Saturday morning exercise class is at work, I spot Barbara, whose late Hendrix used to be a fixture in this park. I have been carrying around a holiday greeting card for her in my leather jacket; she is rarely seen here these days but I have been trying to provide such cards for everyone who offered me condolences when Dorothy died. Of course I have no addresses for most of the dog people so I need to meet them at least once during the holiday season—Barbara is the last name on my list and when she drops her skipping rope for a moment I am able to make my delivery. It is only when we enter the flat that I can see that Fritz has used my chat with Barbara to steal Daisy-Mae's ball.

Sunday, December 23:

A thick fog lies over Paddington Rec on a quiet Sunday morning today. Georgie is just passing with Sparkie and my first action is to return the purloined ball to her; she *had* been wondering where it had gotten to. Soon we meet Janet with Daisy-Mae herself and dog and ball are reunited at last. I let Fritz run free as far the café, but then I feel I have to put him on lead. In this fog I would have no idea where he was headed for—given his wandering ways. With Janet and Georgie we climb Mt. Bannister. Georgie thinks she spots Skye the Alsatian, whom she is wary of these days, and Janet is worried that Isla must be close at hand and this would mean that the last lingering effects of the haircut that Daisy-Mae received yesterday at Grand Union Pets would soon be destroyed in a monumental wrestling match. But the white Alsatian we have spotted in the mist is not Skye, but Snowdon. At the bottom of the hill I am lead a merry dance by the impatient Fritz, unhappy with the restrains of the lead, and then it is time to go into the café.

At the counter I can see that the picture of Dorothy and me in Paris is displayed along with the other cards received by this establishment—which will now be shutting its doors for the next two weeks. At coffee we have Ellen, Peter (his last day before heading for Leigh-on-Sea), Hanna, Janet, Georgie, Ronnie, and Ofra. Peter says that one of the Sunday tabloids has a recipe for boil-in-the-bag turkey dinner and I say that I'm not trying it until I know that it was recommended by Princess Diana. Ronnie says that just as he was heading for dinner at his favorite restaurant last night Susie reminded him that he was wearing his dog (i.e, park) coat and that he needed to change if he wanted her to accompany him. The dogs are all shivering by now and Fritz spends a lot of time in Ofra's lap. I think we would have gotten up to leave at this moment but Davide now arrives with Winnie and it seems churlish to depart—especially because he and Dan are hosting a party this afternoon.

When we finally get started Fritz continues his intemperate ways. He growls at a Standard cousin, who, in spite of his huge size, retreats into the bushes at the threat. Then it's Humphrey's turn to feel my dog's displeasure. For her part, Winnie is chasing joggers (she likes to pursue these athletes and run just in front of them). I have failed to don my gloves today for some reason, and my hands are stinging again when we finally leave the park.

Monday, December 24:

Yesterday's all-day fog has at last lifted and the temperature has moderated as well, but skies remain gray as Fritz and I head for the park on a Christmas Eve Monday. Inching down the pavement is Spadge, suspended at the end of a lead attached by Hanna to the middle of his back. Inside the park itself my dog's progress is slowed by his penchant for grass shoots and the necessity of seeing Oscar off with a growl. We are overtaken by Nix with Billy the Bearded Collie and even by Spadge. I don't know how to tell Fritz that the café, which we reach at last, is closed.

Off on our right Oscar and Scamp are trying to investigate an Alsatianate bruiser on lead. The owner of this dog takes such curiosity amiss; he seems to have no control over his dog and certainly doesn't trust him off lead. Fritz pokes his nose in here as well, but soon Sabina and I are leading our charges in the opposite direction as we begin a circuit of the green. Fritz insists on admitting himself to the doggy pen on the Grantully side (perhaps because Oscar and Scamp have gone in there as well). Out of the corner of an eye I can see some of our people heading off for Porridge on Lauderdale Parade, so Fritz and I head down Grantully and follow Georgie and Janet across Elgin Avenue.

When we sit down, pulling two outside tables together, we join Ronnie and Dan, with Ofra soon pulling up in the new Smart car. A post-mortem is held on Dan and Davide's splendid Christmas party, which all assembled have also attended last night (Georgie wearing a pair of Dorothy's boots). A meter man is swaggering down the street and Ofra gets up to protect her car, but he passes her by. Janet and Dan trade stories of parking tickets of the past and farewells are said, as Dan is off to Essex and Janet to Kenilworth. It feels a bit like the last day of school as we part on the pavement and I accompany Janet back to her car, parked on a yellow line just outside the Morshead entrance to the park. She has gotten a parking ticket!

Tuesday, December 25:

It's a miserable Christmas morning, rain having ceased only for a moment or two as Fritz and I enter an almost empty park. I have remembered to put his raincoat on and this is needed as a light rain soon returns. We dodge one puddle after the next as we near the narrow fenced passageway between the playing fields. Here we finally encounter other forms of life, half a dozen young men whose language I cannot penetrate (though I would hazard a guess that they are unlikely to have just come from Christmas mass). They discover that the gates to the fields are locked and begin to clamber up a fence that separates them from footy heaven.

Fritz is a bit puzzled by the total absence of activity at the shuttered café but I remind him that I can hear Sparkie charging up the walkway behind us and he immediately retraces his footsteps in order to greet his pal and Georgie. She and I are the only members of our pack present today.

We begin an ascent of Mt. Bannister, the two dogs enjoying the freedom of the park, dashing up and down the slopes into seldom-penetrated foliage and then returning to the walkways when called.

We circle around and Georgie decides to wait at the café, sheltering under the eaves and smoking a cigarette and hoping that Ofra, for whom she has brought some gifts, will show up as promised. I keep an eye on the dogs, who are now climbing the cliff face behind the cricket nets. Soon we begin another circuit over the heights but this time the dogs disappear altogether for an anxious minute or two, emerging where we least expect them and dashing off again in some other direction. It is obvious that no one else is coming to the park on this grey, wet day and so (no hope of a coffee *anywhere*) we head for the gates. Two hours later Pepper arrives for an all-day visit: that is Fritz's Christmas present.

Wednesday, December 26:

The weather has improved immeasurably this morning as Fritz and I have beautiful sunny skies and relatively mild temperatures beckoning us as we reach the park. Unfortunately the Essendine gate, our portal to this lovely prospect, is locked. Not to worry, we just slide down the pavement to the Morshead entrance and make our entry here. Sitting on a low brick wall adjacent to the clubhouse is Ronnie. He gets up to greet us as first Georgie and then Ofra arrive as well. Ofra says that she *was* here yesterday but our distant rambles on Mt. Bannister meant that we missed making contact. She now attaches a miniature silver bone to Fritz's collar, a holiday gift from his Auntie.

Ronnie heads off for his car with Rosie and the rest of us head down the Randolph walkway in order to determine if Starbucks is open. This journey represents a triumph of hope over experience since Georgie has just passed this caffeinated emporium and reported it closed. Nevertheless, as we make our way down the street, that lady is able to report, "They're putting out the tables!" Soon we are seated in the bright sunlight (I get to wear my dark glasses on Boxing Day). Ronnie pulls up as well and soon joins us. He says that yesterday's drive to Bedfordshire in the rain was a bore and the presence of a three year-old at Christmas lunch a chore. Susie's daughter has a pet shop near Biggleswade and (since Ofra is hunting for several items) Ronnie puts through a call. The rest of us are convulsed when we hear Ofra ask, "Do you have fleas?"—the translation for which is, "Do you have a fleece coat?" As we get up to leave Georgie reminds Ofra that she has left her keys on an adjacent table.

We decide to walk back through the park and today there are quite a few familiar faces. We pass the fluffy white Arran, then meet Saffy and Tinkerbelle as we find Albert sitting on a bench in the sun, and finally we reach Pasha the Weimaraner, walking with her entire family. Ofra stops to chat with Tanya and Georgie and I continue toward our exit, a progress not helped by the rambunctious Sparky, who wants to have a tug of war with his lead.

Thursday, December 27:

The skies are much greyer this morning, but at least our gate is unlocked and we make a rapid entry into the park. There are a lot more people and dogs about today and these again include Ofra with Bailey and Georgie with Sparkie. It looks like we are about to begin an ascent of Mt. Bannister when I see that Fritz is heading with great speed toward the Carlton gate. I take off in hot pursuit, arriving just in time to see him squatting next to a bush at the gate to the doggy playpen on this side. I admit the rascal to this safe space while I am doing my cleanup duties. Then, back on lead, we walk through the parking lot and along the back of the tennis courts (avoiding the climb up the mount) and intersect Ofra and Georgie as they are about to head off for Starbucks.

Our table is waiting for us and we settle in for another session facing the traffic of Randolph Avenue. Ofra tells a complex tale involving her latest act of forgetfulness. After some extended hours of shopping with Georgie yesterday afternoon she, Ricky and Bailey went to a party. When they got home she couldn't find her keys—which were, in fact, a set belonging to Ricky. Her children, sleeping over with friends, were called—but they and other friends and associates could offer no help. It was now nearing midnight and the decision was made to see if there might be set at Ricky's office. On the drive Ofra suddenly remembered that she had given her keys to Georgie for safekeeping. Luckily James picked up the phone at Georgie's hourse (Georgie being fast asleep) and some order was restored. I then remind the women that this story actually began when Ofra left the keys on a table at Starbucks yesterday.

We walk back to the park while Ofra shares with us Elian's recipe for scrambled eggs. She says that her sixteen year-old daughter gets

£20 a day spending money, though she has now applied for work at Abercrombie's. Inside the park Bailey spots a squirrel and goes crazy. Fritz rushes forward to see what is going on and, since he is on lead, he bangs my thumb against a post. A second squirrel is spotted atop the tennis court fence and Bailey sets us a howl again. Parked in front of the loos is Lee the animal warden. When he gets out of his van to give me some poo poo bags I can see that he has shaved his head. We now head for the Morshead gate; a large Rottweiler has just elegantly vaulted over the trackside fence.

Friday, December 28:

It is still relatively mild outside, though grey. Fritz makes a slow progress toward the café in the company of Kathy's Paddy—who keeps having to retrace his steps in search of his abandoned tennis ball. In front of the clubhouse we see Georgie, Ofra, Ronnie, and David the dog sitter. David still has Skye the Alsatian and Isla in his care but this has been a mixed blessing since he has had to take the dogs to his mom's house over Christmas—even though his mom has discouraged this. It didn't take too long for them to puke, piss and poop on the alien carpet. (Puke, piss and poop must be the canine equivalent of punt, pass and kick.) I suggest that he needs to ask for a higher fee when sitting Kate's dogs—hazardous duty pay.

We begin a slow shuffle toward Porridge—that is most of us do. Ofra moves her Smart car opposite the eatery and begins to valet her dog with a hairbrush while waiting for the rest of us. I start to pull two tables together, telling our waitress that there will be five of us. Behind me Bailey spots his pals on the pavement and dashes across the street, narrowly avoiding a collision with a speeding lorry. Janet is unnerved by the incident, for which she blames Ofra. Our waitress, seeing the dogs arrive, says, "You mean you need a table for ten."

Soon we are eleven for Hanna is making her slow way toward us on the pavement. We have not seen her in a number of days and this is usually a cause for concern. So it is today for she sits down tearfully and tells us that Spadge has died on Boxing Day. The veteran Schnauzer suffered a massive convulsion and was taken to the vet, where the end came soon. Hanna had to call Spadge's titular owner, Kumar, in India; he says that the dog was sixteen and a half—so old that he knew my Toby. Of course Spadge had been poorly for a few years now, but no animal has ever received such loving and expert nursing care. With George having died only four months or so ago everyone realizes just how empty Hanna's house must be now. It's the end of an era. It's the end of an era in Pakistan as well, with the assassination of Benazir Bhuto. "She was a really nice woman," Hanna says, "she was one of my clients at Valentinos."

Saturday, December 29:

Across the street I can see our gang making a leisurely circuit along our usual pathways—which today they do under bright sunlight on a chilly day. Unfortunately Fritz and I are in pursuit of the ubiquitous window painters and our entry into the park is delayed. Fritz eventually detects the scent of his pals and takes off after them at great speed. I don't catch up with him until I have reached the café.

I can now see that there are some strangers in our midst, for the procession includes not only Janet and Georgie but Cheryl, who has returned to England in the company of two twenty-something sons, Dan and Michael. Introductions are made and Cheryl, knowing my fondness for the college game, presents me with a bright red sweatshirt celebrating the forthcoming Fiesta Bowl in Glendale, Arizona—a contest in which her beloved Oklahoma will participate. As we climb Mt. Bannister she reports that Lola, after three days in hospital, seems quite recovered—the source of her indisposition never fully determined, though a minor stroke is now suspected. Fritz manages to stay fairly close to the pack today but when we descend the hill I put him on lead for the walk to Porridge. On route we pick up Ofra and Ronnie as well.

Dan and Michael end up at a "children's" table of their own when we sit down. Ofra soon complains that her cushion is wet and she can feel the damp rising by capillary action into her trousers. I share with the others a letter I have just received from Joanna Pettet and we discuss plans for my forthcoming birthday. The others are full of advice on what the brothers should see during their visit. The younger of these lads still has a year and a half to go at Southwestern Oklahoma State, where, evidently, the sight of a tumbleweed rolling down the street is an exciting moment. Indeed, we are told that when he and a pal were making their first visit to this isolated location, there was an instant analysis of the cultural landscape of Weatherford, Oklahoma: "Look, there's a steakhouse in case you need a steak." "And look, there's a bridge in case you need to hang yourself."

Sunday, December 30:

Under grey skies Fritz and I wander into Paddington Rec on the penultimate day of 2007. The park is again rather quiet and there aren't many distractions as we make our way out to the green. I can see Georgie and Janet on the opposite side and I head off in this direction across the very uneven, muddy ground, a surface that doesn't do much for my right knee—tweaked again last night when Fritz pulled me over in a sudden spurt on the pavement. In the middle of the green a huge Shar-pei has jumped over the fence in order to have a joyous paddle in Lake Botham. His owner circles this body of water, imploring his pet to vacate the premises—to no avail.

I reach the others at last, Fritz nearby, and now it is Daisy-Mae's turn to become interested in the lake. Fortunately she can't get through the fence and has soon joined a party including Bailey and Sparkie as we head toward the bandstand. Here our dogs disappear into the forbidden rose garden and it takes some time for us to get them out of there. The strange chap in the flat cap and glasses, the one who often talks to himself as he sits outside the café, is sitting near the bandstand and chuckling over the canine antics.

Around the corner we encounter Dan with Winnie. The little pug is having great difficulty placing any weight on her right front leg and Dan is unable to explain the nature of her disability. I suggest that it may simply be a sympathy gesture on their pet's part, for two nights ago Dan pushed Davide through a glass door!

More of this tale is revealed over coffee, where we have a large turnout at Porridge: Dan and Davide, Ofra, Georgie, Janet, Cheryl, and Ronnie. The lads, it is now related by a very contrite Dan, were having a row, but the shove in the direction of the door was not meant to cause a six hour wait in casualty at St. Mary's nor the nine stitches that had to be sewn into Davide's shoulder. (There was a retaliatory kick to Dan's knee, but this did not require hospital treatment.) "You guys need to find some other method of resolving disputes," I suggest. Dan says that since they are both obsessed with money perhaps they ought to fine one another in moments of conflict. (One bone of contention has evidently been whether or not there are still Routemaster buses on London's streets. There *are*, but only for tourists, so both sides win.)

Winnie, meanwhile, is looking more and more miserable and Cherlyl takes the Pug into her lap in an attempt to cheer her up. As they walk back to their car Dan is holding Winnie on his shoulder. The little madam is barking furiously at the world. In this gesture she echoes her pal Sparkie, who, so we have been told, always barks at men in uniform, no, he always barks at men who are working, no he always barks at *any* man—as he does now at some poor teenager who is standing innocently outside the Gustoso deli.

Monday, December 31:

Skies remain gray but at least it is not too cold as Fritz and I make our final appearance for the year in Paddington Rec. We pass Charlie the giant Poodle on our way to the green, where Fritz immediately begins to show a streak of year-end ill-temper. First he has a growling match with the usually mild-mannered Tara the Ridgeback. Then he decides to interfere in a ball squabble involving Sparkie and Pepper. This actually proves to be useful because Pepper is distracted by the presence of his pal and breaks off his tussle with the Yorkie.

We begin to make our way toward the Morshead gate, on our way to Porridge. Winnie is moving much more comfortably today but there is definitely a pink swelling between two toes and Dan says she has an appointment at the vet's at 10:30. As we are rounding up our dogs the rambunctious Jody makes a rare morning appearance. Dan notes that Bailey is cheating on his wife (Rosie) with other dogs. I ask if Bailey has determined which sex he actually prefers and Dan says that Bailey is definitely gay. The dog now gets a ride down to Porridge in the Smart car while the rest of us walk. Today there will be eight of us, including Janet, Georgie, Linda, Ronnie, Ofra, Dan and Hanna.

A chap who has not taken our orders before tries to make sense of all the requests coming his way at the same time, then decides that he better go round the table with his pad. This causes Ofra to forget what she wanted to order. She is in some discomfort in other ways—Guy having smashed her finger in the door back home, necessitating another visit to the emergency room, though this one at the Royal Free. Fritz gets into another growling match, this time with Bailey, who is sitting on Ofra's lap. Winnie is taken off to her appointment. Pepper shrieks at regular intervals.

January, 2008

Tuesday, January 1:

New Year's Day comes at last; after the night we have had in our household, it can't come fast enough. New Year's Eve began pleasantly enough as Fritz and I visited the doggy pen on Morshead Road at about 3:30. Here we were soon joined by Natasha with Leila and Jonesie, by Jo Lynn with Tilly, and by Christian and Reina—who not only have Vito in tow but their once and future pup, Miro. The latter is making his second visit to these shores, having been deported after deficient paperwork and thus spending half a year back in the south of France. Now ten months old, he is a French Bulldog (Vito is a mix between this breed and a Boston Terrier), quite a bruiser of a chap and able to dominate his brother from the outset. He runs around and tries to bully everybody else as well, but he meets his match in Fritz—who sees him off with some spirit.

At home nightfall brought its usual pre-celebration anxieties. Fritz managed to eat his tea without any problems and we even got in a round-the-block walk at 9:45. But as the fireworks began in earnest Fritz retreated to his spot under the bed and the pawing and panting began. I went to bed at about 10:30, hoping for a little nap, and when I got up once shortly before midnight Fritz emerged and I put him under the duvet. He put his nose up on my bare leg and continued his heavy breathing, leaving a wet patch on the bottom sheet. Thereafter, as the midnight ambuscade began in earnest, he retreated to a spot under the bed and for the next several hours he pawed away at the carpet in his distress. It was impossible for me to get any sleep and at 2:45 I got up for an hour. He continued his anxiety rituals long after the last firework had exploded but I was at last able to get some rest.

This morning he seems bright enough and we head for the park at our normal hour. Once again they have neglected to open the Essendine gate and we follow Dan into the Morshead entrance. It sounds as though he is shaking a tube of dog treats but as we near the clubhouse I can see that the scraping noise is coming from a contraption covering Winnie's right paw. Dan says that she has had a cyst lanced between two toes, but that there is even more dire news: the vet says that the Pug needs to lose a kilo in weight. Ronnie, to whom I gave this homework assignment yesterday, reports that Starbucks *is* open today, so with Ofra, Georgie, and Janet the five of us head off toward the Randolph gate (after our dogs have made a spectacle of themselves by barracking a timid terrier on lead).

Ronnie has retreated to his car and when he pulls up in front of Starbucks a few minutes later we see that he has picked up Albert and *his* two dogs. Albert is coming down with a cold (Georgie has one too); as in the park, he now sits down at his own table in the background. Gossip and caffeine follow but soon a light drizzle begins and we decide to head back for the park. Winnie, who has received no treats at all this morning, is beyond cross. It seems particularly cruel that her noisy progress invites the rest of us to snap, "Winnie, pick up your feet!"

Wednesday, January 2:

It is extremely cold again and I have made Fritz don his nice coat before heading for the park on a gray morning.

My dog is trying to settle down for an icy b.m. (ICBM) when he is broadsided by Oscar. This naughty Schnauzer, getting shaggier every day, next manages to end up on the running track (a section of fencing having collapsed altogether) and then, in spite of the urgent calls of Sabina, he stations himself at my feet in an attempt to get a reward out of my pocket. Amazing what memories these dogs have, for I couldn't have given Oscar a biscuit more than one or two times in the past and yet he seems to know that if he jumps high enough there might be something in it for him.

We reach the abandoned café and find Georgie heading our way with Sparkie (who has already managed to lose today's ball) and Daisy-Mae. We begin a slow progress toward the Morshead gate, overtaken by Christian with Miro and Vito. In the last few days Christian seems to have lost confidence in the purity of Miro's bloodlines—others having reminded him that French Bulldogs don't have tails but they do have vertical ears. As we near our gate we pick up Ofra with Bailey and Ronnie with Rosie. Even Albert follows us down to Porridge with Saffy and Tinkerbelle.

We urge the veteran to sit with us and take some hot refreshment but he again finds a chair in the background and says he's not allowed to have a drink. Dan pulls up in his car and produces the still gimpy Winnie; she has a new plastic arrangement, wrapped in green ribbon, on her injured foot. Again she is allowed no treats and this hardly improves her disposition. Every time a stranger exits the café she barks furiously. In spite of the cold I unzip my jacket to reveal that I am the only citizen of Maida Vale to be wearing a sweatshirt with today's date on it—having put on the Oklahoma top given to me by Cheryl, the one that celebrates today's Fiesta Bowl in Glendale, Arizona. Ofra too is wearing an exotic garment—her teenage son's track pants (he is still asleep so he doesn't know about this borrowing). Dan soon announces that Winnie has another visit at the vet's now, and no one else is interested in lingering for long on such a chilly day anyway.

Thursday, January 3:

Another very cold morning greets us as we hit the street today—Fritz in his coat, long-johns providing a little extra protection for me. The school kids have not yet returned to the scene so it is pretty quiet in the Rec and there is not much to distract us as we make our way out to the green. A group of dog owners is gathered at the eastern end of the greensward and we head here. New Year's greetings are exchanged as Fritz insists on a cuddle from David the dog sitter.

I am keeping an eye open for my coffee group and I can just see them standing at the opposite end of the green as they begin their march for the Morshead gate. This means that Fritz and I have quite a job of catch-up, though this is accomplished fairly rapidly; Fritz even stops long enough to go back on lead before we reach the street. By this time I am only a block behind Ronnie, Georgie and Dan (Ofra is moving the Smart car) and I have caught up with everybody by the time we reach Porridge. "Thanks for waiting for me!" I complain—the frigid temperatures having outweighed this civility.

Georgie has a bad cold but Winnie seems better—no exotic footwear today. She is still denied the biscuits and carrots that Ronnie distributes and her disposition is not improved by this denial. Dan spends most of the session answering calls on his mobile phone—having been elected secretary of his building's tenants' association he now has to work on a neighbor's insurance claim. No one has the heart to tell the friendly staff at Porridge that tomorrow is likely to be our last day here: the park's café should be open for business again on Saturday.

Friday, January 4:

A cold grey morning greets us as we move toward the green today. I am back in long-johns but Fritz has been allowed to leave his coat behind. The park remains rather quiet but—hopeful sign—they are working in the café against tomorrow's reopening as we pass the locked doors one last time. There is no problem in my joining the others this morning since the other dog owners are on the western side of the green—which is where we head next.

I can see David the dog sitter, Isla and Skye, but—wait a minute!—I can also see Kate and Bob, which must mean that either David is now looking after the entire congregation, canine and human, or he must be here with another client. This proves to be the case as he is here with the pretty Australian Shepherd Dog, Summer. Some Australians have told him that Summer is not a member of this breed but Internet research has proved *them* wrong. At any rate, Summer has a delightful time running with the pack and then it is time for most of us to head off for our last visit to Porridge.

Here Kate and Bob, whom we have not seen in some weeks, tell us of their recent travels to India and Scotland (from which a large box of shortbread is produced for the table). On their way home from Glasgow they have had another incident involving keys and dogs. At the service exit near Tebay Bob went to pay for petrol, leaving Kate and the keys in the car. Kate then decided to buy some water, leaving the dogs and the keys in the car. Isla, however, managed to step on the locking mechanism in her anxiety and this meant that the doors could no longer be opened from the outside. (We all remember how the Puli managed to turn on the remote control to Janet's TV in an earlier incident.) Fortunately there was already an RAC man in attendance nearby and so the problem was remedied without too much delay. Things happen to Kate (as well as to Ofra and Liz), it would seem.

On our way home Fritz snaffles something from a food container in the street and, as he has already been nibbling at grass shoots, I don't suppose it is too surprising that later that afternoon he vomits in the sitting room. I starve him at night but he compensates for this gesture by seizing on a pork rib on the pavement in front of Leith Mansions during our late night walk. A titanic wrestling match occurs over this prize. I think I have won but he still manages to chomp down some of the prize—which remerges at 4:30 in the morning, when it too comes up in a corner of the bedroom.

Saturday, January 5:

The sun is trying to break through as Fritz and I enter the Rec today; we pass Ellen with Jack and Sandy—she too is eagerly awaiting the opening of the café this morning. I am trying to see if Fritz's tummy troubles have also affected the other end, but it takes him a while to squat (his poo seems solid enough) and by this time we have climbed all the way to the summit of Mt. Bannister. Below us the Saturday morning exercise class is having its first lesson of the year—and the lesson consists of trying to concentrate while Fritz is sniffing the pupils' private parts.

I allow my dog a little refreshment (toast and kibble) when it is time for us to resume our proper positions at a table in front of the café. Winnie, sitting on Davide's lap, is nil by mouth still and she is in a foul mood, as Bailey discovers when he too tries to find room on the same lap. In this case the dogs are trying to get close to Ellen, who is sharing her cheese croissant with the canines. She tells us that yesterday she fell over on the grass when she stepped on a hidden tennis ball. "I felt like a beached whale," she laments, "I saw Ronnie walking past but he didn't see me." "So how did you get up?" Peter asks. "With great difficulty," is the laconic reply. These two now discuss the possibility of snow heading our way. Ellen says she looks forward to it. Not surprisingly, Peter finds snow to be both a nuisance and a menace.

This morning we have, in addition to the aforementioned customers, Georgie, Ofra (who now has the bad cold), Hanna, Kate, Bob, and Janet—with Albert and Faz each operating as a satellite. Kate has brought with her a neighbor's dog, a sixteen year-old hound named (we think) Boise. Boise is partly blind, which will explain why he has walked into a post on the way over here. Hanna, hearing of my dog's latest misadventure, suggests a night-time muzzle, an idea which I think I do have to consider seriously. Fortunately she has brought with her four cans of intestinal formula dog food, property of her former charges, and I walk home with this in a long procession that today includes two buggies, Faz with Scarlett and, coming up behind us, Cheryl with Ginger. Inside the Oklahoma Sooner covered wagon we have today, in fact, *two* Pugs: Ginger and a very lifelike stuffed toy asleep in its own basket!

Anthony Linick

Sunday, January 6:

It's a beautiful golden January morning but there is frost on the ground as well and I have put Fritz into his coat for our visit to the park today. Ahead of us I can see Winnie, Daisy-Mae and Sparkie, and this means that by the time we have caught up with these dogs, just outside the kiddies playground, it is Janet, Dan and Georgie who are the first members of our fraternity to wish me Happy Birthday. I am 70 today.

When we reach the Carlton walkway we turn left and begin to climb Mt. Bannister. I pick up Fritz's poo (it seems to be fine) and notice that there is not a single trash bin up here and that the red doggy poo bin hasn't been emptied in days. After we descend we begin a grand circle of the green, with Cheryl soon coming up behind us with Lola (Ginger has refused to come today).

Near the bandstand we encounter a bouncy Snowdon (the white Alsatian, not the Tibetan Terrier) and then a frisky Akita named Harry. Fritz and I have gotten a bit ahead here because Sparkie and Daisy-Mae have remained behind to penetrate the forbidden rose garden and so we continue on to the café, where Ronnie, Peter and Ellen, already seated, become the next group to offer me their felicitations.

There is a very large turnout on this lovely morning. Hanna arrives and Michaela comes in with a card as well. Ofra arrives with Liz, just back from the States, and a birthday cake on which she has stenciled Happy B-day in silver balls. I have to blow out the three candles and then she cuts the cake with a sharp knife she has brought with her. Everyone has a piece of this wonderful chocolate confection, even me—breaking my month-long Atkinsonian regimen. There are so many of us that Faz and Bob have to start their own table near the front door of the café; conversation is quite disjointed in a setting with much cross chatter and dog barking. "I feel like *I'm in One Flew Over The Cuckoo's Nest,*" Dan says. Hanna says that Dorothy is obviously here in spirit and that we can thank her for the lovely weather.

Albert now arrives with Saffy and Tinkerbelle and John with Ché, though only John agrees to take a piece of cake (the last few pieces are taken inside to the café staff). When we get up to begin our back passage walkround there remains the problem of what to do with the knife—as the sight of Ofra brandishing this weapon is likely to raise an eyebrow or two. So we wrap it in a sack and put it in Janet's purse. A ragged file now

206

heads off between the fences, Winnie having relented in her ceaseless headbutting of Bailey, but Skye the Cairn once again insisting on our kicking his beloved tennis ball.

The goodbyes which I usually receive on being the first to exit the gates are modified today to "See you later," for after only two hours or so our group re-gathers at the Cochonnet for my birthday lunch. We have fourteen at two tables: Dan, Davide, Hanna, Cheryl, Ofra and Ricky, Liz, Ronnie and Susie, Janet, Georgie, Kate and Bob—with Rob making a late appearance after a day of sailing with Linda, who stays long enough for a glass of wine. Roast beef and Yorkshire pud and pizza are the gustatory choices (I stick to smoked chicken and avocado salad), with lots of wine consumed. I receive a polo neck sweater and a 94 proof bottle of Jack Daniels. In my acceptance speech I note that, happily, spirits have no carbohydrates. Dorothy's name is invoked at many moments in the proceedings and I make the point that, lacking any real family in London at this point in my life, the park people now serve as a worthy surrogate. Dorothy is here in more than spirit today: Georgie is wearing one of my late wife's pair of boots and brandishing one of her multitudinous handbags.

Monday, January 7:

Winds are raking the park on another sunny morning, depressing the temperatures and causing complaint among the dog people. Fritz has to see off Oscar and Scamp as we reach the cypress trees, but we encounter them again a few minutes later when we join a procession around the green that by now also includes Georgie, Janet and Liz. When Oscar and Scamp admit themselves to the Grantully doggy area it is necessary for Fritz to follow them and it takes quite a while for us to extract them all. Janet notes that, the broken pipework at last having been repaired, Lake Botham has receded—leaving only a muddy morass still surrounded by its mesh fence.

At the café we hunker down at our usual table, joining Ronnie, Peter, Ellen, Cheryl, and Hanna. Dan soon arrives with Winnie as well and Faz takes up his usual spot near the front door with baby Scarlett. He complains that some of his relatives have given Jasmine two mince pies and that her stomach is still dicky. What hardy souls we are, pretending that we are not sitting in a gale. Peter warns me that I am sitting downwind of Georgie's scrambled eggs and that I am likely to be covered by this foodstuff at the next gust. Ginger has agreed to accompany Cheryl to the park this morning. Her wizened head looks like a cabbage.

I am eager to know how much longer the "Party Hard" contingent remained after I left lunch yesterday at 4:00. Janet thinks it was 6:00 but the partying just shifted to Dan and Davide's then. (I saw Hanna heading for home when I had Fritz out for his late night walk at 10:00.) Dan reports that (without any participation on his part) Davide has cut his head on a kitchen cabinet. His dog, cross over her enforced dieting, now uses her head to see off any other dogs who happen to cross her path. She even goes for Fritz, on my lap, but, thinking better of it, merely head-butts my knee.

Tuesday, January 8:

It's a dark day with gray skies closing in on the brave dog walkers of Paddington Rec. Fritz makes slow progress toward the café, where we can see that Ronnie is already in residence. (He somehow manages to get a cup of espresso out of the staff twenty minutes or so before the doors are opened for the rest of us.) Around the corner Dan is just passing Winnie over to Davide before heading off for work. Coops the Pugalier is rolling Daisy-Mae over in the grass and this crime is immediately a cause for concern because it is the job of *my* dog to police matters on behalf of his "pack"—the result is that he chases Coops off more than once.

It is beginning to drizzle as we head for the café and I end up with a chair on the outside of the circle, with drops soon decorating my leather jacket. Ofra goes in to deliver our orders but she forgets that I wanted a Spartan black coffee and I end with up a cappuccino instead. Peter and Ellen arrive and take seats to my right, that is directly in the flight path of the wet weather. There are ten of us in the end, the café's only customers. Davide says he'll be thinking of us tomorrow when he is lying by the pool in Johannesberg.

Georgie says that she is still waiting for her disabled student to return from holiday before resuming morning duties in ferrying the girl to school. Davide has come up with the idea of the dog people undertaking a round robin of international eateries, organized by alphabet, and he will book a table at an Austrian restaurant in Bayswater for Saturday. Linda says that she didn't get up until 8:30 this morning and then went back to bed.

Ronnie says that he is attending the funeral of an uncle today in Golders Green. Ofra announces that it will stop raining today at exactly 3:00.

Wednesday, January 9:

Sunny skies have brought colder temperatures to the park this morning but we make a lively enough start as we enter to the accompaniment of furious barking in the nearby doggy pen. Georgie is shepherding Sparkie and Daisy-Mae in my direction so I ask her for some information on the canine confrontation that is causing all this noise. She says that Vito is mixing it up with an alien Shih-Tzu and, indeed, I can just see the blonde hair of a woman who has just picked up one of the contestants.

Five minutes later we have reached the café, but by this time I have also lost track of my dog (I blame the bright sun in my eyes) and I turn right, thinking that Fritz has headed this way, but he is nowhere to be seen on the green and Ronnie, Peter, and Ellen confirm that he has not paid them a visit at the café either. This must mean that he has headed left on the Carlton roadway and, sure enough, when I turn my attention to this direction, here he comes, bouncing along as though I have been the neglectful one. We now join a large group of little dogs in front of the loos. Natasha is here with Leila and Jonesie and she has brought with her the blonde woman sighted earlier—Vito's opponent is named Sonny. Sonny is wearing one of Leila's outfits and this may be causing gender confusion since Sparkie insists on mounting the chap. Fritz is introduced by Dan as the boss of the park. Natasha says she has made a New Year's resolution not to be a bad girl until August.

While we are waiting out the queue at the café Dan and I slowly begin to realize that we kind of recognize Natasha's friend—who turns out to be the actress Nicola Stapleton, once well-known for her parts on children's television—though she will be remembered for her roles on *EastEnders* and *Bad Girls* as well. Eventually we join the others, now including Ofra, and the tortuous process of feeding the other dogs (while trying to keep Winnie on the straight and narrow) begins. Dan takes two telephone calls. The first is from Liz, phoning in her breakfast order, which is therefore steaming at her place when she arrives a few minutes later. (There's a lot of toast and Fritz ends up with a piece all to himself.) Dan's second call is from Davide in Johannesberg. The latter reports that he has banged his head again and that it is raining. I suggest that after taunting us yesterday with all that talk about thinking of us while *he* is poolside, there is at least *some* justice.

A lovely dog named Spikey is tied up outside the café's front door. He looks sort of half Corgi and half fox but when he is at last claimed by his attractive mistress he turns out to be another Shiba Inu. As we begin our back passage walkround ("the canine express," according to Jeff, who is trying to get Elvis to walk the other way) we learn of another disappointment for Davide. The Austrian restaurant is fully booked for Saturday and so the search is on for an alternative. No one seems to fancy Albanian cuisine so, as I leave Liz and Dan at the Essendine gate, I hear that the search is now on for something with an Argentine tang.

Thursday, January 10:

Under darkening skies Fritz and I penetrate the precincts of Paddington Park; there are even a few spots of rain, the prelude of something worse to come, or so it would appear. When we reach the café Fritz rushes in to check things out and finds Ronnie, Peter and Ellen already seated. Ronnie introduces me to an attractive young lady from the Czech Republic named Stephanie. She, in turn, is accompanied by a bruiser of a pup, a 10 month-old Standard Schnauzer with a sweet face and a tail. This is Lightning.

Promising to return in a few minutes, we then continue on to the green, where the receding waters of Lake Botham have left a muddy mess. There are quite a few little dogs dancing about, even another Pug. This is Monty, whom we have met before; he is soon joined in the Pug takeover by Lola and Ginger—Winnie is already in residence. Fritz soon wanders off and I follow at a distance, on clean-up duties, as he wanders down the Randolph walkway and then trails behind the tennis courts.

By the time we have returned to the café our numbers have swollen to fourteen, including Ian, who has accompanied Monty, and Stephanie, who, we learn, is preparing for a career as an English teacher in her native country (she complains about all the obscure tenses in our language). The dogs are unnerved by Lightning who, as an intact male, is a rarity in their midst. Bailey, in particular, causes such a ruckus that he has to go onto Ofra's lap. When they are not making a fuss over the newcomer they are baying and barking at any moving object; it sounds like we are sitting in a kennel. A delighted baby toddles around stroking their heads.

Fritz soon sits in my lap, though this means that he is perilously close to the ravenous Winnie, who shares Dan's lap to my left. On his left is Hanna, who has been fussing over Fritz's whiskers for the last few days—since these furry appendages are easily caked with his own food. Dan objects, however, to her picking them apart over his lap. Then Albert chimes in to say that Hanna has made *him* re-do the collars on Saffy and Tinkerbelle. "Well, their little eyes were bulging out," she says.

Albert is a member of the long tail of dog owners who begin a back passage walkround. The kids are back from their Christmas break and this gives Sparkie plenty of opportunity for some of his patented percussive barking. His mad syllable somehow reminds me of Father Jack, "Feck! Feck! Feck! Feck!" Dan tells me that, with the Austrians booked and the Argentinians too dear, that he and Liz are now working on the Belgians.

Friday, January 11:

Not only is it dark outside but it is raining as well, and one look out the window this morning is enough to convince me that I might as well go back to bed. This I do, not arising until shortly before 9:00. This time I bite the bullet, completing my usual pre-park rituals, albeit some fifteen minutes behind schedule, and, placing both dog and owner in appropriate rain gear, I head for the park at about 9:20. Fritz skips along in his raincoat, never completely happy in this outfit—though he has no hesitation in splashing through the many muddle puddles that hours of rain have brought to the scene.

At the café I see that the only members of our group in residence are Ellen, Janet and Georgie. "Now these are stalwart dog owners," I say. "Did you say stalwart or stupid?" Janet replies. I leave Fritz with her while I go inside to order my coffee. Outside we endure a windy, rain-splattered morning under the eaves. Daisy-Mae is sitting in Georgie's lap, trying to intercept scrambled eggs on their way to Georgie's mouth. The latter has Winnie with her today as well, but Dan has given Georgie permission to dump the diet for the day. Janet has brought a towel with her and placed it in her lap; nevertheless Sparkie is so wet that his presence is actively discouraged. In the background Robin is hopping about, hoping for a handout.

No one seems to be in a mood for a back passage walkround and each of us sets off in a different direction.

I have to drop off a prescription renewal form at the Randolph Avenue surgery. So, dog on lead, we begin a long slosh through the rain. Fritz always rushes into the vestibule of the surgery as though he were late for an appointment but I always have to disappoint him—retreating from this spot as soon as I have deposited my envelope in the metal box. It is still raining. I go back to bed.

Saturday, January 12:

The bright sunlight that is streaming into the park on this radiant Saturday is in some contrast to the weather that Fritz and I endured only a few hours before. Returning from an evening out well after midnight it was necessary for me to fasten the dog's hated raincoat into position for our trot around the block—for the rain had returned in force. This morning we trail Georgie and Sparkie on our in-lap, soon turning left at the café and climbing Mt. Bannister with this pair. On the summit we meet Janet and Dan and their dogs. Even with my dark glasses I find it hard to see into the glare below; I *can* see that Lightning has joined the Saturday morning obedience class.

We complete a circle of the green, Fritz minding his manners for most of the time, but when we reach the clubhouse I can see him heading behind this soon to be "improved" structure, and by the time I have headed this way myself the naughty animal has headed through an open gate and onto the running track, where, surprisingly, they have stored a large number of the potted palm trees. (Yesterday we saw others on their way to the bandstand; they were appalled—someone had promised them that they would be repositioned in Rio not Maida Vale.) I manage to extract my dog from the track before he has had much of a run and we soon join the others at our table outside the café.

Today we have Peter, Ellen, Hanna, Janet, Cheryl, Ofra, Georgie, Dan, Liz and Ronnie. Hanna is trying to drum up an interest in the Russian winter festival in Trafalgar Square and Peter is having none of it. Dan is trying to organize tonight's expedition to Belgo in Chalk Farm, but I say I won't abandon Fritz for a second night running. Phoenix rushes up and begins to lick Bailey's privates as the latter sits in Ronnie's lap—Bailey lets him. The others are trying to explain the virtues of free-range chickens to Ofra but she can't get this through her head. Ronnie phones Susie (who has taken Rosie for a haircut in Biggleswade) to find out if they can go to

Belgo tonight. They can't. I announce that I have to be home in time for a delivery and so I head on my own toward the Morshead gate. The park is very busy this morning. Two joggers are discussing Fritz as they cross our path. "Those dogs always look like grumpy old men," one of them says.

Sunday, January 13:

We head for the park this morning under gray skies, but at least there is no rain. Temperatures are also mild enough, that is until a chill wind changes the picture somewhat. Fritz somehow notices that Janet and Georgie are some distance ahead of us on the in-lap, and he rushes to catch up. I can see him far ahead of me, beginning to join the others for an ascent of Mt. Bannister. By the time I have reached the summit myself the others have started down the other side. It has been several minutes since I have seen my own dog but Janet points him out, just ahead of the rest of the party, as we all begin a circuit of the green. All the dogs want to have a brief look into the Grantully doggy area; then, when we get them moving in the right direction, we get as far as the bandstand where they have to touch noses with a white mixed-breed dog named Shaggy. The latter is making his first visit to the park and has been here for such a short time that he is still quite clean.

At breakfast there is again a small turnout, with just Peter, Ellen, Janet and Georgie. Janet has brought with her a sample puppy cardigan in lilac wool and bearing the message "Top Dog," one of a series of canine jumpers knitted by her sister. Georgie tries this outfit out on Sparkie and orders a duplicate in chocolate brown. Janet says she wants one for Daisy-Mae with the legend "Dirty Bitch." They ask me for additional suggestions but I tell them I will have nothing to do with the sissification of our dogs and they are on their own for suitable texts.

One by one the missing persons arrive, first Ofra, then Ronnie, then Dan and Davide. Part of this late arrival can be attributed to last night's partying, for, after Belgo, Dan, Ofra and Liz continued on to the famous gay nightclub in Camden Town, the Black Cat. Cell phone pictures of these festivities are passed around while our dogs are trying out various laps. Fritz is sitting next to Dan, who offers him several fingers full of cappuccino foam. Winnie is sitting on Davide's lap, from where she launches a vicious attack on poor Bailey. Ronnie is charmed by a sweet-faced King Charles named Raffy. Daisy-Mae has to be coaxed away from a nearby table, where she is begging for scraps. Linda arrives with Pepper but doesn't stay for long. With all these latecomers we are at table for quite a while, though at last we begin a back passage walkround, with man, woman and beast repeatedly bundled out of the way by the intemperate joggers hurtling by without so much as an "Excuse me."

Monday, January 14:

A light rain is again falling this morning. Fritz has to wear his raincoat but I decide to brave it out in my leather jacket and wool hat and after fifteen minutes the moisture stops for a while. School groups have stayed away, so it is pretty quiet in the park as Fritz and I reach the green. I am immediately spotted by Buddy, who rushes up, sits at my feet, and waits patiently for his reward from my green biscuit bag. Saskia is a bit unnerved following an incident with Harry the Akita, whom we again see outside the café a few minutes later. I would like to head in for my morning coffee but Fritz needs to explore the Randolph walkway, the tennis courts, and the foliage at the north end of the Grantully doggy area and it takes some time before we can head across the soggy grass.

There is a small turnout today, not surprisingly. Peter and Ellen are at a small table of their own so it is just Davide, Hanna, Georgie and Cheryl at ours. Hanna is a bit the worse for wear, blaming the four strawberry beers she downed at Belgo's on Saturday night. Winnie and Lola take turns barking at Harry. Lola is wearing an "It's raining cats and dogs" rain poncho and this interferes with her balance so much that she falls off the chair that she is sharing with Daisy-Mae. Georgie tells us that today is the first time she has worked since September—the special needs student she usually ferries to school having had a major surgery and then a long period of holiday before returning to the Jack Taylor School on Boundary Road this morning.

The expected upturn in the weather has not materialized as we begin our back passage walkround—Hanna still hidden beneath her capacious maroon umbrella. At the head of the track Sparkie, soon followed by Daisy-Mae, spots the gap in the fence (the problematic bit here having disappeared altogether) and rushes out to accompany a jogger in a barking charge. I decide to delay my local errands for another morning and better weather. "I don't blame you," Georgie says.

Tuesday, January 15:

The strategy of delaying my errands for a better day has clearly backfired since it is again raining when Fritz and I have to buckle on our rain gear for yet another wet morning in the park. Once again the place is almost deserted but this doesn't mean that our progress toward the green is any more speedy. When we finally reach the the spot I can see Peter and Ellen approaching along the Randolph walkway and, behind them, Georgie and Dan in their rain togs as well. For once, however, Fritz does not wander off just when I want to seek the shelter of the café's overhang and we are soon shoving our table closer to the front door.

Hanna and Ofra now arrive as well and Ofra offers the interesting intelligence that she has just spotted a minor celebrity. I have too, though as the lady in question is also buttoned up against the inclemency and intent on her mobile phone conversation, I haven't made the connection. Her small young black dog, Noodle, soon discovers the comfort of our table and here the pup happily remains even when her mistress, though still on the phone, begins to call for her. I therefore go out to the green to report on the dog's whereabouts. I am talking to one of the most notorious personalities ever to make an early exit, as she did just a few weeks ago, from *I'm A Celebrity, Get Me Out of Here!* I am talking to Lynn Franks. The public relations guru fishes her dog out from the ruck under the table and the rest of us discuss the unusual accident of a second celebrity sighting in one week. For that matter, Dan now tells us, he frequently sees Heather Small of M People jogging around the Rec.

As she settles down to her breakfast Hanna wants to know what possessed her to come out on a morning like this. Ofra announces that she is expecting a visit from Israel of her sister and her father. I discuss the photos I have sent off to the folks at *Dog Tails* as an accompaniment to an article I have written about our annual doggy picnic. The rain is driving in at us and no one wants to linger for long over conversation—so we soon begin a back passage walkround. In the five-a-side field a class of maroon-clad hockeyettes is being put through their paces in the rain. "You see," Dan says, "I learned to hate exercise when I was made to run in such weather." I don't need to hate errands (that came about long ago) even though I have to get on with mine as soon as I get home.

Wednesday, January 16:

A marvelous sunrise decorates the southern skies at the start of a far more pleasant day, bright and sunny and not too cold. Georgie comes up behind us with Sparkie and Daisy-Mae and together we walk out to the green, where I soon lose track of my dog in the glare of the sun. I search the horizon with my dark glasses on but I am not successful until I look behind me. There on the summit of Mt. Bannister I observe a file of dogs, including Scamp, Oscar and Rizzo, but, wait, there are two Schnauzers up there and one of them must be my Fritz. As they seem to be heading for the Carlton walkway I head past Ronnie, seated in front of the café, in an attempt to head off my rascal. Sabina, tells me, however, that he has not followed the others downhill, and I have to head back past Ronnie and out to the green again, where, sure enough, Fritz is running toward me as though I were the missing person.

The good weather brings out a large number of dog owners: Georgie, Dan, Ofra, Liz, Nicholas, Faz, John, Cheryl, and Hanna. It is a squeeze getting everybody seated but some of the early comers get up to yield their seats to newcomers. Faz reports that he has finally found a gardening crew worthy of the name, that they worked on his yard without a break and that, most surprising of all, they turned out to be English! Liz, who says she is deferring her interior design studies for a while, adds that she needs the name of these paragons, though at this point John produces *his* business card (as handyman, not shaman). Faz also announces that he is leaving the police force, first to look after baby Scarlett, and then to establish a private security business. This announcement prompts Nicholas to bombard Faz with half a dozen suggestions on what to do next.

I make an announcement. I tell the others that it is time for me to say farewell to those old friends, my park shoes. I have worn the same pair of brown loafers to the park ever since Fritz was a puppy. They lost all tread years ago, holes formed in the heels and trapped an interesting collection of stones, and a succession of replacements had to be found for the rotten laces. But just in the last week they have begun to take in moisture, leaving stains on my socks every time I venture into damp territory. Today, for the first time, I have worn my new park shoes—another pair of brown loafers.

Thursday, January 17:

Gray skies have returned to our Maida Vale scene and it seems that we will be lucky to escape this morning's park session without more rain. Nevertheless Fritz makes an active start to the proceedings and we have soon reached the green, where workmen are fencing off the grass facing the clubhouse—soon to undergo its own modernization. I pause to chat with Sabina and Denise and, of course, this means that I lose track of the whereabouts of my dog altogether.

Eventually I spot him strolling along with two Pugs. I can tell that the one with Dan is Winnie, but the stranger is a burly boy named Freddy. When we reach the Grantully gate we encounter Ofra, Georgie and Liz, walking toward us, and we turn around to join them in the rest of a grand circle of the green. Soon it is Nicholas approaching and Hanna coming up behind. Once again I am so intent on conversation that I lose track of Fritz, who has hived off from the pack in order to crash through the foliage on his way to the Randolph walkway. I slow him down with the bribe of a biscuit and soon we are all heading for the café.

Ronnie is already here and Cheryl is just arriving with Lola and Ginger. Albert is just arriving as well, but he snags his leg on a chair and has to walk it off, leaving Saffy and Tinkerbelle with Ronnie. People are just beginning to complain about the cold when there is an incident. Lola has hopped into Ronnie's lap in order to have a better view of the tabletop scene. The next thing we know the naughty Pug has leaped onto this surface, the better to continue her investigations. Unfortunately she catches a toenail in the wire mesh surface of the table and begins to flail about in attempt to free her paw. Ronnie's cigar butt flies out of its ashtray and a full cup of latte is sent flying in the direction of Georgie and Liz. Hanna manages to free Lola's paw but the cup lies in shards under the table and Daisy-Mae is beginning to lap up the coffee puddle. Cheryl is deeply embarrassed but Lurch soon arrives with a mop and we are able to finish our drinks and begin our back passage walkround.

Friday, January 18:

What a surprise—it's raining again! Fritz submits to the indignity of his raincoat and we are off for another sodden morning in the park. At the café there is already a small colony of dog people sheltering from the moisture—fifteen minutes before the doors are scheduled to open. I pass through with my dog, however, knowing that we have had precious little exercise so far.

At the east end of the green I can spot Hanna heading our way under one of her many umbrellas from the pound shop. Fritz scans the horizon eagerly when I mention her name but he can't locate her whereabouts—even though by this time she is whistling and calling his name. When we at last meet up she says that Schnauzers don't see well, whereas I would argue that their vision is selective, just like their hearing. Hanna now turns around to accompany us on a circle of the green. Workmen are still erecting a perimeter fence around the clubhouse and she manages to snag the head groundsman in order to put in a request for a ramp that will keep walkers from sinking into the grass of the green as they try to get around the building.

There is a very small turnout for coffee this morning. Dan is just about to leave for work with Winnie, Cheryl is here with her two Pugs, we have Peter, Ellen, Nicholas and Hanna, but, unusually, there is no sign of Georgie—who almost never misses a morning session. Cheryl is debating whether to visit the V&A or Hampton Court this morning. Hanna tells me that the episode of *Trial And Retribution* featuring Victoria Smurfit (another former client) on the steps of my building was screened last night (I have recorded it). Then she repeats a Jamie Oliver recipe for a shoulder of lamb that she saw the celebrity chef make last night on TV—but when she notes that he has specified a four-hour cooking time at low temperatures Peter says, "I wouldn't want to pay *his* gas bill." Cheryl has not brought the covered wagon today so Ginger has to walk the back passage on her own four feet. Soon she and the others are so far behind me that Fritz and I leave the park without our customary goodbye from the others.

Saturday, January 19:

There are a few dots of moisture but no real rain as Fritz and I enter a suddenly crowded Paddington Rec on a gray January Saturday. Progress seems slow as we inch toward the green, where a wooden palisade now surrounds the clubhouse—which looks like a beleaguered fort. There is a large party of dog owners and their pets near the little metal gazebo. Present are Franca, Valentina, Frank and Bianca: the humans in this grouping have been in Italy for a month and a half and so we haven't seen them for a while. Another Pug is dancing about here too but I later learn that here is yet another newcomer, Zorro. The Pugs are really taking over the park.

Fritz heads down the Randolph walkway and, as usual, I manage to deflect his attentions before he goes too far, leading him behind the tennis courts where instruction seems to be taking place in a number of the courts. My dog heads for the wall on the Grantully side of the park but here I notice that he disappears not into the foliage at the head of the doggy area but into the bowling green itself. Now I have to give pursuit as I know he doesn't belong in this seldom-used enclave—noting as I approach that there is a gap in the border hedge that makes it easy for small dogs to penetrate. It takes a while for me to get him to exit from the same gap he has used to enter and by this time the others have all gone in for coffee.

This morning we have Georgie, Janet, Dan, Peter, Ellen and Hanna. Dan spends much of his time dandling the delighted Valentina, who seems to be wearing purple jodhpurs and tights. For that matter Winnie is trying on a purple body stocking that Janet's sister has knitted; Sparkie seems a bit miserable in his brown version. Of course Daisy-Mae has a blue creation on; Janet has brought Tilly with her this morning since Jo Lynn has a bad back.

We begin a back passage walkround but it is not easy. A lot of fierce looking women with sticks are looking for the right playing field. Joggers insist on shouldering us aside and the narrow walkways are crowded with junior footballers, some of them with their last names emblazoned on their jerseys—they are about to begin an hour of being yelled at by their dads for not trying hard enough. There is plenty of dog crap underfoot as well and parents have once again brought their pets onto the pitch itself. Sparkie is terrorizing a little girl who has come to watch her brother play and Fritz is growling every time a new dog is encountered anywhere. I am almost happy to return to the peace of an empty flat.

Sunday, January 20:

There seems to have been no change in the weather at all, for we again have gray overcast skies (though with relatively mild temperatures) for our morning ramble in the park. I meet the American woman who owns Lulu the Lurcher almost as soon as I enter the Rec. "There are already crocuses in bloom. Isn't that heartening?" she says. "Unless you take it as a sign of global warming—in which case it is disheartening," I reply. There are far fewer people in the park this morning and Fritz makes quick work of reaching the empty green.

He heads off toward the Randolph entryway but I get him turned around to greet Dan, who is just arriving with Winnie. We begin a circle of the green (after Fritz has disappeared for a second time), soon encountering Janet with Daisy-Mae and Tilly and Georgie with Sparkie. Heading toward us is a tiny version of Leila (if that is possible) named Albert. He wraps himself around Daisy-Mae's neck, where he looks like a giant insect. We have gotten as far as the bandstand when Fritz, much to my surprise, reverses direction and heads at great speed back toward the Grantully gate. The answer to this riddle is soon evident, for he has somehow sensed the arrival of Linda and Pepper from this direction (don't ask me how) and has gone to greet them. In a few minutes the Schnauzers have to be extracted from the rose garden and lead through a break in the stockade as we head for the café.

There is a large turnout this morning, including all of the aforementioned plus Ofra, Ronnie, Hanna, Peter, and Ellen. Winnie launches a vicious attack on Pepper's head—his crime: being fed while she is not. Raffy, the King Charles Spaniel, is again tied to the fence while his mom is inside and when he begins to bark in some agitation Daisy-Mae trots over to comfort him. Sammy, a little black dog with his tackle still intact, arrives to woo Bianca the Boxer and this causes a stir of agitation among the other dogs, especially Frank. Both Pepper and Sammy are collared and lead away and five minutes later they are both back, Pepper in search of food, Sammy sex. It is time to make a move.

Monday, January 21:

The gray weather seems to be with us forever. I meet Cheryl near the cypress trees and tell her not to say anything about the football playoffs in the States (which I have not seen yet); she has not brought the covered wagon today since Ginger has agreed to hoof it with Lola today. These three turn around to accompany us but Fritz is by now racing ahead and I have to follow him out to the green, where I can see that they are painting the bare boards of the stockade—quite an improvement over the raw wood. Hanna, whom we soon encounter, says that the clubhouse conversion is supposed to take three months. As yet there is no sign of the walkway around the palisade requested by the lady.

I can see a group of dog owners on the opposite side of the green and here I head; we are followed by another lively black dog, confusingly called Skye. He is chasing a ball being propelled by his mistress but when we reach the bandstand we encounter Saskia with Buddy and David the dog sitter with Skye the Cairn. The latter is also chasing his ball and the two Skyes get quite confused when they are both being called. Confusion is an understatement if you are measuring my mood (consternation comes closer) because while we are standing on the walkway David tells me that he is retiring from the dog sitting business to concentrate on his photography! He has been such a dependable presence in our midst these many years that he will be sorely missed.

Linda arrives with Pepper again and we round the green while I try to get my head around David's news. At coffee we have Linda, Ellen, Peter, Georgie, Cheryl, Hanna, Ronnie, and Liz. The latter is at her wits end with Roxy, who last night managed to steal four doughnuts off the tabletop—and then threw up and pooped in the house. "So, she's not an anorexic," someone says of the portly Beagle, "she's bulemic." Georgie says that daughter Lynn claims to be bulemic; it's just that she forgets to vomit. One of the park managers stops by to tell us that the fire alarms will go off at 10:00 and Ronnie, who is having computer problems, decides to head for home since Rosie dislikes such noise. Lola, occupying a chair of her own, keeps up a constant woofing commentary on life at her table. She and Fritz both object to the presence of Harry the Akita, chained to a nearby wall. The maroon hockeyettes are shoving one another all over the Carlton roadway as we begin our back passage walkround.

Tuesday, January 22:

Sunny skies have returned for this morning's session in the park and we make a lively enough start—if you don't count the slightly suspect poo deposited by my pet, who gobbled something on the street that he shouldn't have yesterday afternoon. As we work our way through the café we meet a new black Cocker pup named Aoibhe, an Irish spelling for Eva. (Her mom calls her Evie.) Sitting in his van outside the loos is Lee the animal warden and I manage to secure a small supply of green bags.

Fritz then wanders down the Randolph walkway before I get him turned around at coffee time.

I tell the others that I would have greater confidence in the promised three-month duration for the proposed clubhouse conversion if workers weren't adding a second coat of paint to the perimeter fence. Hanna says she preferred the gray undercoat to the lurid green final version we are getting now. Aoibhe is tied to the door of the café and this (forbidden) act causes a good deal of trouble for other customers. Metty himself appears to refasten the Cocker to one of the new hooks in the wall separating our table from the forecourt. Ofra complains that Nicholas has taken *her* chair but it isn't true; he has brought his own to the table and it is Daisy-Mae who has taken her chair.

We have a good turnout today with the aforementioned dog owners plus Peter, Ellen, Georgie, Dan, Davide and Ronnie. I make the mistake of asking Ronnie if his computer has been repaired yet and Peter now jumps in with some persistent but elemental advice that is clearly unwelcome. Unfortunately Peter can't stop his litany and Ronnie is becoming more and more perturbed and it is just as well that Hanna arrives to put a chair between the codgers at cudgel-point. Pretty soon Nicholas, his mobile phone call concluded, is offering advice on any available topic as well. I tell Ronnie that Nicholas and Peter can now contest the title "Mavin of Maida Vale."

Wednesday, January 23:

Well, our day begins a little bit earlier than usual when, at 2:30, Fritz jumps off the bed and vomits on the bedroom carpet. It's mostly his evening meal but when we hit the streets a minute later we get yellow foam and a series of increasingly wet poos. He's sick again. Fortunately it is a mild night followed by a nice morning and at 8:00 we have to answer the urgent calls of nature again; by this time the poo is projectile.

When we enter the park at our usual time I locate the other dog people, but only long enough to wish Dan bon voyage (he, Davide and Davide's parents leave for Cuba tomorrow) and to suggest that Fritz and I will not be joining the group for coffee and treats this morning.

I don't believe it, but I am already scheduled to walk up to Boundary Road for an 11:00 hair cutting appointment and while I am here I slip next door to make an appointment for 4:15 at the Hamilton vets. (Fritz might as well have a standing appointment—he seems to spend so much time here.)

Later in the afternoon we make the journey a second time and while we are waiting to see Frank Seddon I bite the bullet and purchase a black cloth muzzle which my pet may have to wear on the pavements, where his indiscriminate scavenging is becoming chronic (and expensive). I can hear my dog's stomach rumbling as Frank listens in with his electronic stethoscope—evidently a deafening sound. Loaded down with the usual pills and cans we make our homeward journey in darkness; Dan and Davide are both present at the café—where I pause to give a bulletin to the other dog owners before they tuck into a huge plate of chips.

Thursday, January 24:

Fritz begins his day with breakfast, an unusual event for him, but a welcome one—as he has not had any food since the day before yesterday. Fortunately he likes his intestinal formula food (into which I have squeezed his colon medicine and his antibiotic pill) and he seems lively enough as we make our way into the park on another gray morning.

We catch up with Ellen, who is accompanying Sandy and Jack, both with dangling leads dragging on the ground. When we reach the corner of the café forecourt I pause to chat with Denise and Sabina while Tarquin, the eight month-old King Charles, tries to get a rise out of the dowager of this breed in our park—Rosie. The latter will have nothing to do with his advances and Bailey, who is just a larger version of the pup, swats him down with one paw. Out on the green I congratulate a partisan David, whose Spurs have finally beaten Arsenal. Harry the Akita is running loose out here and, though he seems docile enough, the other dogs are spooked by his rambunctious presence. Skye the Cairn begins to bark hysterically and Harry also gets tangled up in Fritz's lead.

I have put my dog on lead because it is time to head in for coffee, though the others have been warned not to give any food to the convalescent. This morning we have Ofra (who is only here to buy croissants), Nicholas (who soon disappears), Georgie, Ellen, Ronnie and Peter (who slips Fritz a forbidden biscuit). Georgie reports that Winnie arrived for a ten day stay last night by checking the food bowl, climbing into her bed for a nap, and then barking at husband James since she can't stand the sight of him lying in his bed. Georgie also has both Sparkie and Daisy-Mae with her and reports that progress is very slow since Daisy-Mae will not leave Winnie alone and the Pug won't move when she is under assault. On the back passage walkround, however, it is Sparkie who is the target; he is a bit miz since Georgie has reloaded the batteries in his collar zapper. When he is broadsided by the Shih-Tzu he retaliates by dragging her along the pavement by the fur on her head, as though she were just another rag doll. For her part, Daisy-Mae has a new trick; she has discovered the string ties at the bottom of Georgie's coat and she likes to grab hold with her teeth. "At least I know she's right behind me," Georgie says philosophically.

Friday, January 25:

Fritz has just nuzzled down the beginnings of his second can of intestinal formula food (and had his face washed soon thereafter) when we enter the park on a chilly but sunny morning. Walking in the opposite direction we find Sabina with Scamp and Oscar and Hanna walking Yoyo and so we decide to follow them so that Miniature Schnauzers can rule. I keep a close eye of Fritz's poo—though I no longer need to shine my torch on the questionable object, as I did last night. Hanna and I make a slow circle of the green, observing that they are preparing the bed for the walkway that will soon be constructed outside the clubhouse stockade.

At coffee we have Hanna, Georgie, Peter, Ellen, Nicholas, Faz and Ronnie. Fritz is still nil by mouth and Georgie is trying to keep Winnie on diet and I note that *we* always end up feeling guilty when we have to withhold food from our pets. Winnie, however, solves the problem by stationing herself at the foot of a stranger's table, where she gets plenty of clandestine treats. Hanna says that she too has been suffering from stomach problems; she has brought her own sachet of fennel tea to insert into the café's cup of hot water.

Shortly before ten Fritz and I head off, painfully slowly, for his check-up at Hamilton Vets on Boundary Road. No sooner has he heard Frank Seddon's voice than he jumps into my lap—"That's the man who uses me as a canine pin cushion" seems to be the message. From this lofty perspective my pet growls at an exiting Bull Terrier and an incoming young Staffie. "Who's making all this noise?" Frank wants to know when it is time to be carried into the examining room. I leave armed with two more cans of food, two more pills, and a supply of pro-biotic powder.

"Let's see if he is still as noisy now that he is no longer in your lap," Frank says. Indeed Fritz is quieter, quieter that is until we pass Elvis as we return through the park a few minutes later. "Ah, the growler," Jeff says.

Saturday, January 26:

It is again sunny and crisp as Fritz and I hit a park bustling with activity on a busy Saturday morning. It takes quite a while for Fritz to find the right spot for his convalescent poo and then there are lots of other dogs that must be sniffed as we slowly make our way out to the green. Here Fritz also has to touch noses with half a dozen pupils—here for their usual obedience class. He doesn't seem to upset the order of this classroom and, satisfied at last, he makes his way down the Randolph walkway. Here we encounter Lightning, with another woman in charge. She is just beginning to understand that her boy is not the *Miniature* Schnauzer they said he was when she obtained her pet.

I get Fritz turned around and hooked and we make our way to the café, where I hand him over to Janet. This task would normally go to Ronnie but there is a pile of carrots at the foot of his chair and I don't want Fritz to eat anything in the park these days. By the time I have returned from the counter Hanna has arrived and Fritz has taken up a position in her lap. When Janet gets up Daisy-Mae hops into the empty seat and nearly becomes a throw rug when Janet sits down almost immediately.

In addition to those already mentioned we have Peter, Ellen, Georgie, Ofra, Albert and Nicholas this morning.

I describe the symptoms of my ailing television set (which no one will actually come out to the house to have a look at) and the others all advise me to get a new set. Bob comes in with Skye and Isla. The latter is now twice Daisy-Mae's size and their wrestling matches are not as even-handed as formerly. Bob says that Isla can now open the car windows—which I consider to be dangerous in the extreme. Natasha comes by with Leila and Nicola Stapleton's Sonny just as we are rising to begin our back passage walkround. With all the soccer moms and the bustling joggers it is not easy getting past the playing fields this morning. Hanna is giving Albert a lecture on what his little dogs are getting up to behind his back.

Monday, January 28:

A thick fog lies like a blanket over the Rec on this quiet Monday morning as Fritz and I head for our rendezvous with canine destiny. I have missed a day in the park, having enjoyed a rare January walk on the Capital Ring. Fritz was here, of course, but I had handed him over to Hanna on my way to the tube stop. He enjoyed a busy day, with lots of long walks. He got to chase Hanna's cat, he got screeched at by the cockateel, he played with a miniature rugby ball in Hanna's hall. Hanna even managed to get most of the nits out of his moustache and would have given him a bath had I not returned before 5:00. She handed him over attached to a green retractable lead once the property of Spadge or George. His usual lead was stripped by this point in time and so it is with this green successor that we begin our walk today.

Behind us I can see Georgie approaching with Sparkie, Daisy-Mae and Winnie. I hang back since Hanna has told me that Georgie's mother has died in Scotland over the weekend and I want to have a word. Georgie's mom had been poorly for years, having had several heart attacks and suffering from some form of dementia. (Nurse: How old are you? Mom: I'll be 52 next week. Jean: You're never 52, mom, you'll be 81 at your next birthday. Mom: I know, but next week I'll be 52.")

A man is approaching with what looks like a miniature Husky. "There's going to be a fight here!" he announces. "Why?" we ask. "There's a lot of growling." "Who's growling?" "This gray one here." He is of course referring to Fritz and we assure him that there will be no fighting. A man on a tractor is raking pellets into the artificial turf and he has left the doors to the playing fields wide open—and here Georgie's dogs end up in a joyous romp. She has the devil of a time getting them out of there and I can't help since I dare not let Fritz out of my sight on such a foggy morning.

Out on the green we meet Ellen. When I tell her about Georgie's mom she says that Aisne, the owner of Jack and Sandy, is also suffering from dementia and that last night she ate so many chocolates and nuts that her blood sugar went through the ceiling and her son had to take her to hospital. This morning she doesn't remember any of this. Fritz has, by this time, wandered up the Randolph walkway, but I get him turned around when we meet Cheryl, entering the park with Ginger and Lola (and no covered wagon).

At coffee we have Peter, Ellen, Nicholas, Ronnie, Ofra, Cheryl and Georgie. Cheryl is just returned from a long weekend in Cairo, where she jumped into a dogfight on behalf of a victimized puppy and got yelled at by her husband for endangering her own health through such a gesture. (She did not get off her camel when a whip was used on a little boy rather than on one of the beasts—but she felt like it.) She now says that she'd be glad to take on Georgie's trio if the latter has to go to Glasgow for the funeral. Other travel experiences are summoned. Nicholas says that when he was 18 he fell in love with the Cinnabon outlets in America—where he went as a camp counselor and where he got lost in darkest Boston and had to be returned to camp by the police. It's time to head for home; the fog is lifting.

Tuesday, January 29:

I lose track of Fritz almost as soon as we enter the park. He disappears into the bushes near the Essendine entrance and I cannot tempt him to rejoin me until Bob, bringing Skye and Isla into the park, elicits a series of growls from my hidden pet. Bob heads toward the green while I manage to get Fritz pointed in the right direction for the cypress trees. Soon we encounter Christian and Reina; Christian is being tugged forward by the twin dynamos of Miro and Vito. He says that the lively boys are being socialized after no fewer than three complaints from other dog owners. One, he adds with a truly injured tone, was because of a fight started by Hercules! "Wrongly accused," he says, "I feel just like Gene Hackman in *Mississippi Burning*."

Out on the green I can see a knot of dog people at the eastern end of the grass and we head here next. Leila detaches herself from the group and rushes over to greet Fritz—who is playing hard to get, as usual. Natasha notes that Leila is one of the few dogs whom Fritz will tolerate without a growl. "He doesn't exactly have super star social skills," she adds. "No," I respond, "he's more like a member of Oasis." The thug in question has rushed down the Randolph walkway to greet Faz and baby Scarlett; they accompany us behind the tennis courts but when Fritz actually admits himself to an empty court (alas, no loose balls) I bid goodbye and try to hustle my dog out of there. He does emerge, but only to rush into the woods atop the Grantully doggy area. This is fox territory and a number of the dogs enjoy having a nose round. Unfortunately mine emerges chewing on something strictly off the diet (and Fritz is technically convalescent as it is) and I have the devil of a time getting him headed for the café.

At breakfast we have Georgie, Ronnie, Cheryl, Peter, Ellen and Hanna. Georgie is bewailing the sodden state of Daisy-Mae, who has been wrestling on the grass with Isla. Fritz, from the lofty prospect of my lap, is objecting vociferously to any canine interloper. Size does not matter, he whines when he sees the large Ché and is equally vociferous when the tiny Yorkie, Cheeky, makes an appearance. Lola is also a lap hooligan, barking at every moving object until Cheryl puts her down. I suppose you could say that the theme for the day is dog naughtiness. On the walkround it is Daisy-Mae's turn as, once again, she squeezes through the bars of the picnic ground—refusing to return no matter how many times she is called.

Wednesday, January 30:

After a night of light rain the sun is making an effort to emerge as Fritz and I begin another day in Paddington Rec. When we reach the green I can see Ofra descending Mt. Bannister. She is wearing white trousers and both Hanna and I remind her that this is a mistake. Hanna, who has come in from the opposite direction, hands over to me another gift from the late George, a nice fleece-lined blue coat for Fritz. The latter manages to stay within reasonable distance while the humans are chatting, though I do catch him rolling in a patch of mud nearby. Then we all turn around and head in for coffee.

There is a good turnout, which one might reasonably expect on such a bright (though crisp) morning. Today we have Peter, Ellen, Janet, Georgie, Hanna, Ofra, Liz and Ronnie, though when Peter and Ellen depart their seats are taken by Cheryl and Nicholas. Before bums can go on seats, however, Daisy-Mae has to try out every one herself, hopping round the table like the Shih-Tzu version of Goldilocks. At a nearby table a mom has pulled in with a toddler and this grouping soon attracts the attention of our dogs for the baby is holding a large croissant in a limp hand and everyone can foresee disaster. Daisy-Mae is at her ingratiating best, Winnie is sniffing for crumbs, but Liz and I are convinced that Roxy (having made off with a muffin at home) will, like a distant linebacker blitzing the passer, pounce.

Over coffee Janet tells us that she is off this morning to have her will drawn up (jokes about the richest Shih-Tzu in the history of West Kilburn ensue) and that she has discovered evidence of a theft in her kitchen. Mice have burrowed into the back of a cupboard and eaten a two-kilo bag of dog food (jokes about super-sized mice squeezing down the hallway). Liz says that her oldest son, having begged for a new ski jacket at Vail a few weeks ago, has lost said object while skateboarding behind Tesco. This now seems like a minor blip on the radar when she adds that one of her boy's classmates in Bermuda has died of a brain hemorrhage at age 15. All of a sudden no one is joking any more.

Thursday, January 31:

Winds are whistling through the park as we reach the end of the month on a gray Thursday. I have not noticed that there is also moisture in the wind as well—Fritz could have worn his new raincoat. As we near the cypress trees I am surprised to see Ronnie coming up behind us with Rosie. We don't usually see him at all on wet days but he has parked his car near the Essendine gate and now he accompanies me to the café, where he takes shelter while I promise to return in a few minutes.

Almost immediately Fritz and I encounter Fritz, Fritz II that is, the now fully-grown Standard Schnauzer whom we have not seen in months. What a wonderful specimen he is—it looks like someone has supersized my dog. Fritz II is walking with Christine, the wind turning his ears inside out, and I join them for a circuit of the green. The two dogs make such a handsome picture running together, they somehow sense an affinity, and if one stops to explore some bushes the other has to stop as well. "Will all Schnauzers named Fritz please get a move on," I say at one point. Unfortunately my version can't get enough of a flowerbed near the Grantully exit and I lose track of Christine and her pet soon thereafter. Ofra is coming up behind me with Bailey and we complete the circle, using, for the first time, a paved pathway around the clubhouse fence. (I hope this doesn't become permanent for it would mean the loss of another portion of the green.)

Only the very brave are present for breakfast this morning. Ronnie has been joined by Ellen and Peter and after Ofra and I take seats Georgie and Hanna arrive as well. The moisture is relentless and we have to move our table closer to the front door of the café. Ellen makes the mistake of letting Fritz know that she has Jack's squeaky ball in her purse and he sits enraptured at her feet for the rest of the session. When someone remarks that Winnie is very quiet Georgie says that this morning she attached the lead to the Pug's collar while the latter was asleep in her little bed, woke her up for the trip to the park and watched as Winnie got out of bed—only to jump into Sparkie's bed for a nap. Ronnie is waiting all this time for some letup in the storm and when he announces it is time to make a move, everyone follows.

February, 2008

Friday, February 1:

Although the sun is shining it provides no evidence of warmth as Fritz and I enter the park on a quiet Friday morning. None of the school kids have arrived yet and, indeed, the place is eerily silent. We do pass a little Toy Poodle in a pink sweater and then Sabina comes around the corner with Scamp and Oscar. The latter doesn't seem to be at all jealous when Fritz approaches his mommy for an extended cuddle. There is a group of dog people hunkered down outside the café as Fritz and I play through (Peter, Ellen, Ronnie and Hanna—with Yoyo in her lap) but we spend a few more minutes on the margins of the green; again not only is no one out on the grass itself but no one seems to be walking around its margins either.

At coffee, a few minutes later, I join the others, and Cheryl, Janet and Georgie arrive as well. Janet has brought with her more of the doggy knitwear made by her sister; orders are taken. Ronnie passes around an ancient photo showing a lot of dog people posing on the green: I can see Michael and Charlie and Joanna Pettet and Jake among others. Janet says that Dan took the picture, that she has a version on her computer and that she will send it to me. Cheryl has brought her camera with her and takes pictures of Winnie, Sparkie and Daisy-Mae modeling their designer jumpers.

The latter stages of our session turn ragged, from my perspective. Georgie (who will soon depart for Glasgow with Sparkie, as she attends her mom's funeral) gets up to take a phone call from Dan, who has just landed at Gatwick. Kate comes by with Skye and Isla but departs almost immediately for the green. Tarquin the King Charles rushes up but Fritz, sitting in my lap, has a fit over the intrusion of a stranger. Tarquin's mom says that she is having second thoughts about preserving the crown jewels of her pet since he is beginning to wander in the park and to molest her daughter's stuffed toys at home. I say that I am getting cold and get up to begin my back passage walkround. Ronnie accompanies me but it takes a long time for the others to follow suit.

Saturday, February 2:

It is brilliantly sunny this morning, though at first it doesn't seem as cold as we were lead to believe it would be. Over on our right I can see that Janet is putting a jumping Daisy-Mae through her paces on the exercise bars—"Do your tricks, Daisy-Mae." These two soon join our party as we make our way behind the playing fields and then up Mt. Bannister. I tell Janet that, seeing no wind, I have not put my long-johns on this morning. She says that she *has*, and is now regretting it. Daisy-Mae is failing to get any rise out of Fritz, a playtime necessity since Winnie has gone home and Sparkie is in Glasgow. Janet confirms that Georgie and James did get seats on the train that took them to Scotland last night. She also admits that Daisy-Mae, who should know better at eight months, is still peeing on the duvet at home.

Down below us we can see a very large turnout at the Saturday morning obedience class—I count a dozen owners. Janet and I begin to circle the green but we haven't got very far before we encounter a young woman from Manchester. The latter is charmed by our dogs, since her mom used to have a Schnauzer and a Shih-Tzu too. Today the visitor has her own Shih-Tzu pup, a six-month old charmer named Oscar. He and Daisy-Mae are soon fast friends and I have had to leave everybody else behind as Fritz continues his circle. When he gets to the Grantully gate he admits himself to the doggy area on this side and we spend a few minutes here before reversing directions and circling the green in a counter-clockwise fashion. I can see that Lightning is practicing his recall: "Look, Fritz, a Schnauzer who comes when he is called." My pet is unimpressed.

At coffee this morning we have Hanna, Janet, Liz and her friend Claire, John, Albert, Peter, Ofra, and Dan. Liz and Claire are on their way to Liz's restaurant, where they intend to do an inventory; Peter is muttering because there has been no sign of Ellen this morning; Albert has a black eye, having fallen over on his wrist two days ago; and Dan is just back after his trip to Cuba. He describes what he has seen there (not much—since he was in a luxury hotel most of the time). Hanna again has Yoyo, but the latter is in disgrace after shouldering the traumatized cat

232

away from her own food bowl this morning. The dogs have all left the cold flagstones for the laps of their owners and even these folk are beginning to complain of the cold and so we begin our back passage walkround.

Sunday, February 3:

Again we have cold but sunny skies for our excursion into the park. As we enter we attract the attention of little Albert, the lively Miniature Pinscher pup; he had been part of a group of dogs in the Morshead doggy pen yesterday afternoon—and I have been taking Fritz here most afternoons in preference to our usual sojourn on the chicken-bone strewn pavements of Maida Vale. In term time and in the afternoon one cannot move half a block without encountering a discarded carton from one of the chippies in West Kilburn and we all know what dangers such items carry for my scavenging and delicate-tummied pet. (At night our route usually carries us away from the boneyard that is Paddington College, though last night there was a new excitement—this time Fritz was able not only to smell but to see a large fox strolling in the roadway at the corners of Grantully and Biddulph.)

When we reach the café now, Ronnie is taking up residence and Dan is here as well. The latter detaches himself, however, for the doors of the establishment will not open for another fifteen minutes, and follows us, with Winnie, out to the green. I have just discovered a pink plastic ball and our two pets take turns chasing this object as we make a slow circle of the green. Dan and some of the others have had a Chinese meal in Soho last night and I promise I will see if there are any restaurants representing the letter D in our copy of the *Zagat Survey* for London. (There is a Danish restaurant in SW7.) By the time we have reached the bandstand we find Janet, Ofra and Liz approaching with their dogs. Daisy-Mae has the devil of a time getting her mouth open wide enough to bite the pink ball.

At breakfast this morning we have all of the aforementioned plus Ellen, Peter and Hanna. Ellen manages to distribute virtually every bite of her cheese croissant to the dogs—though Ofra notes that her vet now says that it is Bailey who is overweight. The lonely gent with the flat cap is sitting next to the front door of the café and talking non-stop to the dogs—"I bet you want to go inside, but you can't." Rob comes by with

Pepper and there are squeals of delight from Fritz (when he is not moaning over the presence of Ché). There is a strong wind gaining strength as the morning matures and once again there are complaints about the cold; pretty soon we are off on our back passage walkround.

Monday, February 4:

I can see that Fritz is standing at attention and checking out the scene behind us—just as we have cleared the cypress trees on our entry into the park on yet another cold but sunny day. This is because he has spotted two dogs coming up behind us and he has to make certain that they know their place in his pecking order. Pretty soon I can hear his barking charge—but this is answered robustly by Rowena's Timmy, who is walking this morning with Rowena's neighbor, Julia. Julia also has with her another dog that she seems to have the care of much of the time, a brown Cocker named Andorra. When I ask about this name Julia says that Andorra's owners had lost a Pyrenees Mountain Dog and wanted to preserve a memory of this pet in the name of its successor. When we reach the café Julia calls for Timmy, who obediently comes ands sits so that his lead can be attached. "I hope you tell Rowena what a good boy her dog has been this morning," Julia says.

Fritz has rushed into the café forecourt and had a nose around the feet of the early diners but there is still ten minutes or so to go before the doors are opened and so we continue on to the green, where Buddy stations himself at my feet, hoping for a handout. And he would get one too if I hadn't forgotten to put my treat bag in my pocket. Saskia, meanwhile, is in conference with the head groundsman, Boyd, and I think at first that this has something to with the park staff, who are repositioning the netting around the perimeter of the lost Lake Botham. Instead the conversation is devoted to another act of vandalism. Kids have stripped all the lower branches off of a Japanese magnolia tree that was planted to honor the completion of Jan Prendergast's tenure as mayor of our borough. As we walk along, Saskia is equally upset by another chapter in the annals of the British builder. After major structural works on their flat (including new underpinning) their builder says that he has underestimated the final costs by £30,000—but that he hasn't the receipts to prove this.

Fritz heads left when we reach the tennis courts and I follow him out to the parking lot on the Carlton side and here he goes back on lead as we circle around to the café a second time. This morning we have Peter, Ellen, Ronnie, Hanna, Cheryl, and both Dan and Davide. Dan has brought with him some tiny baby mittens to go over Ginger's sore feet, though the latter has refused to come to the park today, even in her covered wagon. Lola *is* here and she and a slimmed-down Winnie exchange gutteral utterances. Fritz, as he usually does these days, sits in my lap; this is a mixed blessing since his position means that Aunt Hanna can continue to pick away at the sticky spots in his moustache—it's the sticky spots at the other end that have my attention. We begin a back passage walkround during which Daisy-Mae, Rosie, and Winnie all decide to have a squat at the same time. For once Fritz makes no contribution.

Tuesday, February 5:

I think I might need my sunglasses today, as there is some brightness in a sky from which the rain has just departed but, in the event, the sun never makes much of a strong showing. It seems pretty mild, in fact, as I climb a flank of Mt. Bannister with Dan, who is accompanied this morning by Winnie and Daisy-Mae. Just as we reach the bottom of the hill we encounter Cheryl who is wearing an Oklahoma Sooners number 23 (Adrian Peterson) sweatshirt and pushing a covered wagon at the same time! Ginger is on foot, however, and she and Lola agree to shuffle after us as we continue on a circuit of the green.

We pass the bare stump of the vandalized magnolia tree and approach the Grantully gate, where Fritz and a long-haired Dachshund named Parsley investigate one another's private parts. Parsley's owner is a bit worried, not by the required growls issuing from my dog's throat but by the proximity of the open gate, through which her dog has headed on his own more than once. "I know what you mean," I say, "my dog has done that as well." Fritz and I have gotten well ahead of the others by this time and I succeed in getting him turned around for a rendezvous with a trio of Pugs just in time for Dan to realize that Daisy-Mae is no longer a member of our party. There is no response to his anguished calls and he begins to retrace his steps in the direction of the Randolph walkway. He has just about reached this spot when the little madam emerges from the bushes where Cheryl and I have remained rooted to the spot. Much relieved, we continue forward (Fritz having indeed tiptoed out of the park through the aforementioned gate). We get as far as the clubhouse—Ofra, again with a bad cold, having joined us with Bailey—and we meet up with Oxana, Saskia and Lee the animal warden. Buddy and Rufus are covered in mud. "I want to report a crime," I say, "these two dogs are stealing soil from the park."

At breakfast we have Hanna, Ronnie, Peter, Ellen and all those heretofore cited. Lola keeps up a non-stop colloquy on the subject of the gigantic Harry, who is chained to the fence behind us. He rises up on his back legs in order to embrace Cheryl and the sight of his front paws behind his dance partner's back causes much merriment. Fritz, of course, is not amused. First he has to endure the ministrations of his Aunt Hanna, who is still fiddling with his moustache, then he spots, from the heights of my lap, several strange dogs who do not have his permission to be here. Daisy-Mae remains firmly attached to her lead. Ronnie announces that Rosie wants to walk *now* and even before all the coffee has been consumed we get up to begin our walkround.

Wednesday, February 6:

Cloudy bright skies preside over the park scene as Fritz and I begin the day's adventure in Paddington Rec. There is a bit of a jam up as we enter. A sheepdog named Kayla is the object of the attentions of Harry, who is leaning eagerly over the doggy pen fence, and Kayla's owner is a bit nervous about this. Coming in the other direction is a soft-coated large dog with spots; she seems to be named Lady Tara and her owner, a black woman, is trying to get her away from Kayla. Fritz is not interested in any of this and soon squeezes through a tangle of legs to emerge at the cypress trees and so on to the café.

Around the corner comes Lee the animal warden. He is carrying a cage in one hand and a net in the other and tells me that some crows are attacking a fallen magpie in the picnic area. The magpie doesn't want to be rescued but there is a great ruckus going on in the branches overhead. I follow Fritz along the Randolph walkway and here we encounter Cheryl with Ginger and Lola. As we head for the café a second time we encounter Ofra, Hanna and Georgie. Hanna has discovered a large pile of dog poo (as least we hope it is *dog* poo) artfully piled in a monolith that looks like a miniature Henry Moore. Ofra is urged to take a picture of this sculpture with her mobile phone; Boyd cleans up the mess (this should not be his responsibility). He reports that the park will have to replace the vandalized magnolia tree.

At coffee we have the aforementioned dog owners plus Ronnie, Ellen and Peter. Hanna insists that Ofra send a picture of the poo to Dan and Liz, and Cheryl experiments with the idea of using the image as her screensaver. Georgie reports that on her trip to Scotland a woman in the adjacent seat immediately announced an allergy to dogs—though she failed to move when a nearby Sparkie-free seat opened up. Georgie says she feels a bit rough this morning and that the loss of her mother is finally beginning to sink in. I tell the others that I have spoken to Michael, the former king of Paddington Rec, and that he hopes to pay us a visit on Friday. The temperature has plummeted since our arrival and it looks like rain so there is an early move toward the gates. "Let's see the picture of the poo one more time," Hanna says.

Thursday, February 7:

It seems to be another mild morning in the park, though the skies are certainly grayer than we have seen them lately; somewhat like yesterday, temperatures begin to tumble in the hour or so that we are here. Fritz, who is getting pretty shaggy, doesn't seem to be perturbed by such weather, and marches steadfastly forward to the café. Here, unusually, we find not a soul and so we continue on to the green. There is not much activity here either; somehow the mesh fence in the center of the greensward, by foreclosing the chief gathering ground of the dog owners, has served to scatter our lot to the four corners.

Hanna is approaching and, mischievously, lets my dog know that she has a squeaky toy in her pocket. He is instantly mesmerized and he won't let go of her leg until she produces the object of desire, a blue fish. Thereafter Fritz becomes obsessed by the toy and even heads back through the café and onto a back passage walkround on his own, heading for home with his prize. Janet and Georgie are coming in at this point and Janet manages to snag my dog for me. At coffee he will take no sustenance since he can't figure out how to chew the fish and eat a biscuit at the same time. Eventually he forgets himself and we manage to return the object to Hanna's ownership.

Hanna, Janet, Georgie, Peter, Ellen, Ofra, Ronnie, and Cheryl make up our circle this morning, with the faithful Albert riding shotgun.

Conversation this morning is sobered by the recent discovery of a headless torso behind some shops off the Kilburn High Road. In the morning's *Metro* a local resident complains that this area is becoming very dangerous—"There are a lot of young people, with pit bull dogs, who are dealing drugs. You feel very unsafe." To lighten the mood, Janet circulates a greeting card she has made from the union of two recent snapshots: one of Ofra sniffing something distasteful at the Chinese restaurant and a close-up of yesterday's monumental poo pile.

Friday, February 8:

For once it is not true that twenty-four hours have passed since our last visit to the café, for yesterday afternoon I wandered up here with Fritz on our afternoon walk. We passed Vito and Miro and I paused to chat with Christian. Three lads were entering from the Carlton roadway, each with a thrusting young Staffie. I continued on to the end of the green where I was delighted to encounter Naomi and the famous Tanzanite. I hadn't seen them in about two years and it was a great pleasure to note that they were both well, Naomi now working at the Royal Albert Hall (and thus using other parks most of the time), her hair having turned a lovely shade of purple in the interim.

Soon I spotted Linda coming in with Pepper and I let Fritz off the lead. Linda had a number of complaints beginning with the size of her dog's vet bills, since Pepper too has been making himself sick with street food. She also noted that the young thugs I had encountered were geeing up their dogs for a fight near the clubhouse and that a schoolboy punch-up was scheduled as well. Pretty soon we could see the latter taking place and Linda urged park personnel to call the police as park security guards headed for the tussle. We continued to walk around the green, our dogs on lead, and pretty soon police on bikes and in cars were pouring into the Rec. The Staffordshire trio had just slunk out through the Grantully gate.

Today we enter a quiet park on a beautiful radiant sunny morning. Fritz penetrates the precincts of the café but there is no one about yet and so we continue on to the green, where there is a lively group on the walkway near the metal gazebo. Once again I have to tell Buddy that I have not brought any biscuits with me today. Fritz is bouncing around sniffing all the dogs, especially one newcomer, a delightful sixteen week-old Dachshund puppy named Whisker. The latter is a bit overawed by this new environment and, indeed, has insisted on being carried to the park. Hanna arrives and we head for the café a second time, though before we can enter she spots Michael making his way in our direction from the walkway in front of the clubhouse. In a minute we have the king and queen of Paddington Rec united again at last, though, sadly, neither one of them is in possession of a dog any longer.

When we sit down both Sparkie and Fritz jump into Michael's lap and Fritz has a jealous fit over this. Michael, who looks well, has brought some dog treats with him. I ask him about his current feelings on the subject of the Paddington Academy, knowing that he had great objections to this colossus as it went up across the street from his home. He says that the pupils behaved well enough for the first month or so of the renovated school's life but that thereafter they resumed their old disrespectful, obstructionist and violent ways (the school itself has been trashed by its own pupils) and that not only are there four security guards in residence, as it were, but there is a police presence every day when school comes to an end. Dan, hearing this recital, adds that closer to home Natasha and a gentleman friend were set upon when they objected to the behavior of a brute who tried to kick Leila near the corner of Morshead and Elgin Avenue—and that the police had to be called to arrest the miscreant.

Not everything is doom and gloom. A little boy comes in wearing a Batman suit (though he is afraid of the puppies) and the others are reminded of favorite childhood costumes of their own. "I had a Spiderman outfit," Dan volunteers. "You mean you had a Wonder Woman outfit," Liz retorts. That lady is scheduled to fly off to Boston in two hours but she is obviously reluctant to go. As we get up to begin our back passage walkround she seems torn. "Talk about a fork in the road," I say, "Liz can't decide between Boston and Essendine Road."

Saturday, February 9:

We have a glorious morning for today's visit to the park: bright sun, mild temperatures. The park is already very crowded. Even before 8:00 the lie-in peace of the neighborhood has been shattered by eager hockey players bouncing their balls with great vigor off the wooden perimeter of the playing field on the Morshead side. The usual troupe of footy lads is also streaming into the park and in front of the café a gaggle of comely hockeyettes have dragged their weapons of mass destruction.

Roland also has a large turnout for his obedience class and Fritz has to touch noses with each of the pupils before agreeing to walk with me down the Randolph walkway. I have forgotten my poo poo bags but the sack in which I have brought a lifetime supply of biscuits serves the usual purpose when I tear it in half. There is no sign of any of our lot out on the green so Fritz and I continue around the circle. As we near the clubhouse there are lots of kids, some on forbidden bicycles, some pretending to be menaced by a Miniature Schnauzer.

At the café I find Davide, Ronnie, Georgie, Yasmina and Janet already seated. Ofra, Hanna, Cheryl, Peter, Ellen, and John soon make this a very crowded table indeed. There is a long Saturday queue in the café. I am always taken by surprise when I see moms buying their kids ice cream cones at this early hour of the day—I'm sure this would have been frowned upon when I was their age. There is so much noise and we form such a wide circle that I don't hear a word of the conversation emanating from the other side of the table. We do all hear the interjection of a chap with a West Indian accent who, spotting Winnie, Ginger and Lola, leans in and announces, "Hey, you've got all those dogs from *Men in Black*."

Sunday, February 10:

Our entry into the park this morning is a halting one, for I seem to have pulled a muscle in my right leg. I blame Fritz—only because he had to select his *football* from the array of toys in his basket yesterday, cleverly positioning himself so that every time I walked up or down the hallway (as I replenished my window box watering bottle) I was required to give the ball a hearty kick. It was a few back-heeled passes that did the damage, I suppose. I have already had one application of heat cream on the back of my leg as we make our way along the walkways. At least it is a very pleasant morning and I have put my dark glasses on as I turn in the direction of the café.

There is no one about yet, unless you count Metty, who is scrubbing some ketchup off our tabletop. Fritz heads out along the Randolph walkway as I slowly follow. I sit down on a bench near the tennis courts and wait for him to turn around which, after I have repeated my entreaty to him several times, he finally does. I put him on lead (not the easiest mode of progress for my leg) and we head for the café. I can see a group including Georgie, Dan, Davide, Janet and Ofra along the walkway in front of the clubhouse. We rendezvous at our now spotless table, where we are soon joined by Hanna and Ronnie and even by Jeremy, who has brought in a tethered Cressida—who is suffering today from a hip complaint.

Davide has the Sunday papers with him and this leads to a discussion of the fire that yesterday destroyed much of the Camden market. Peter (who is sitting at a nearby table with Ellen) says that he never goes into Camden Town but that he did yesterday and got caught up in the turmoil there. Also at a nearby table is Franca. When Valentina is unstrapped there is a tussle over possession of the delightful toddler, with Aunty Ofra claiming the prize. Both she and Dan want to adopt the baby and Franca says that she is more than willing. (She also reports that for the second time in a week her sitting room sofa has collapsed, trapping baby, mother and grandmother in its jaws.) At a third small table is the old chap with the flat cap, John; he has learned some of the dog names and keeps up a non-stop monologue, even placing his muffin sleeve on the ground so that they can lick the crumbs. Unfortunately his best customer is Winnie—and she is still supposed to be on a diet. We begin a back passage walkround. I have Fritz's lead in my left hand; my right hand is being manipulated by our resident reflexologist, Hanna, who says this well help with my leg.

Monday, February 11:

My leg is a little better this morning and it is certainly a lovely day for life in the park. Almost immediately Fritz manages to get onto the running track; easy enough to do since one whole section of the fence is missing at the top end—but he answers my call immediately. Some of the local schools are already into half-term mode and it takes a while for the chattering classrooms to show up—so we have only the ominous roar of the leaf blower to spoil our morning.

Fritz gets his usual warm welcome from fellow Schnauzer owner Sabina. She has her little boy with her today but this is because he has a doctor's appointment; his school is still in session. His symptoms are discussed at some length with our local councilor, Jan Prendergast, who is obviously spending some quality time in the park this morning. Fritz

241

begins his usual trot down the Randolph walkway but before getting too close to the gate he meets a Border Terrier whom he really likes and this prompts him to reverse directions and head back toward the café.

There is only a small turnout this morning—just Georgie, Hanna, Dan, Davide, and Cheryl. Dan nags Georgie because she won't move her chair into the sun; she accuses him of jumping the queue with his coffee order in the café. It turns out that this gang did none of the things they had planned to do yesterday; they did not have a walk in Regents Park, they did not crash the French Bulldog meeting in Primrose Hill; they didn't even go to the pub. Instead they had a very abstemious evening at Dan and Davide's, playing charades and eating Chinese takeout. Georgie says she really feels good this morning—an early bedtime last night and no hangover today.

Tuesday, February 12:

A thick fog lies on the ground as Fritz and I make today's foray into Paddington Rec. There is partial visibility and it looks like the sun is trying to break through, so I let my dog ramble off lead. As we round the first corner we pass our head groundsman, Boyd, doing battle with the foliage which overhangs the narrowest part of the pathway. Ronnie is already seated at the café, a fact we discover as Fritz dances through, but there is also a small knot of dog owners out on the grass. David the dog sitter, honoring an old commitment, is here with Skye the Cairn and Dan is kicking a laundry ball around for Winnie. Oscar and Scamp are soon a part of this grouping as well. Fortunately Fritz stays pretty close, because he could easily disappear in the fog if he went any distance.

David joins us at coffee (we talk of *Lost* and the Super Bowl). Today Georgie is not feeling well but her surgery can't offer any appointments that don't conflict with her morning work assignment. Dan announces that he will be 34 in March and that, in Ongar at least, 34 is a really important birthday and the occasion for lots of *very* expensive presents. Ofra announces that yesterday she forgot that an empty plastic kettle was still bubbling away on her hob and that she has suffered a meltdown as a consequence. Daisy-Mae keeps wandering off, Winnie remains frustrated by dietary restrictions, and Bailey jumps from lap to lap in search of tabletop goodies.

Albert sits down for a short while, then departs with Peter and Ellen. It is soon noticed that he has left behind a black mitten and Georgie picks it up for the old chap so that it won't be lost forever. We begin a back passage walkround, during which I notice that the first of the daffodils is now is sunny bloom. Albert is heading our way with Saffy and Tinkerbelle; these two little ladies have tried to pull his arm out of its socket chasing after a squirrel. He is reunited with his lost glove.

Wednesday, February 13:

We have had a cold (and noisy) night and there is still a bit of frost on the playing fields; surprising, therefore, that with the arrival of the sun that temperatures improve dramatically and we now have another wonderful pre-Spring morning. Soon we have caught up with Georgie, who is making slow progress behind the playing fields with Sparkie and Daisy-Mae. Together we head up the back of Mt. Bannister, though Fritz chooses this time to investigate the parking lot on the Carlton side of things. Successfully returned to us, we continue over the top of the hill, where we encounter Nicholas with Monty.

Fritz turns left to head along the Randolph walkway and I have to follow him as he trots along the little paths near the tennis courts before emerging above the green. I spot Saskia and Natasha standing in the frozen grass and head in their direction. Leila comes dashing forward to cavort with Fritz and Buddy advances in hope—receiving a biscuit from my pocket when we meet. Natasha seems to have recovered from her recent pavement contretemps but Saskia has more crime news. The helicopters that we heard buzzing overhead in the early hours were part of a dawn raid on a house on Saltram Crescent in West Kilburn! We can only hope that it was drugs they were looking for and not terrorists.

Fritz and I now head for the café, Dan crossing our path after handing Winnie off to Georgie. There is only a small turnout at coffee: just Ellen (Peter has again gone to Leigh-on-Sea), Ofra, Hanna, Georgie and Ronnie. After a while, however, Tanya comes by with Pasha the Weimaraner and baby Lucca; she sits down and asks for the latest gossip and here is a summary of what she gets. Ben Hull, who was once a regular here with his Boston Terrier Nelson, is now playing a nurse on the afternoon soap, *The Royal Today*, and has gotten married. Vito, who also shares Boston Terrier lineage, has further disgraced himself, according to

Christian, by knocking over a little boy. The little boy, to add piquancy to the tale, has turned out to be the son of Jude Law, who has recently bought a property nearby, and who was evidently quite laid back about the incident. Tanya, for her part, says that the Hungarian housekeeper hired to lend a hand in a household dominated by two babies, has been systematically stealing clothes, household objects and cash and that she will be arrested this week. All these juicy items of gossip and a dawn raid in Saltram Crescent—what more can you ask for? We begin our usual retreat, our way barred by the inquisitive presence of Pippa the Papillion (now there's an instant tongue twister).

Thursday, February 14:

The recent run of good weather has come to an end and today our journey to the park begins under grey skies. Moreover the temperature is depressed and after several days in a baseball cap I have had to return to its woolen cousin. And gloves. Fritz makes a lively enough start to the proceedings and we soon reach the green, where Ronnie is in conversation with Christianne (pregnant I see) and Natasha. Fritz seems quite content to follow these two ladies (and Stella and Leila, of course) as they ascend Mt. Bannister. When we have re-reached the Carlton walkway we meet Dan and Cheryl on their way to the café, where we are soon seated.

We are joined by Ofra, Georgie, Tanya, Linda and Ellen, though Hanna, wishing to eat her breakfast in peace, chooses a little table by herself. Several recent topics are mopped up before we can begin with new material. Yesterday's helicopter-sprouting raid, we now know, was part of a citywide blitz on drug and money-laundering activity. I tell Dan that I have written to the chamber of commerce of Ongar in Essex to ask if it is true that the thirty-fourth birthday of any of its native sons requires the production of expensive and glamorous gifts and that the reply has confirmed that not only is this true but that an equally expensive donation is required to the Ongar Policeman's Ball.

Ronnie now tells us that he and Susie have attended a production of *The Magic Flute* last night, but that Rosie spent the evening at Tanis' house while they were out. Ofra is trying to find a venue for a sweet-sixteen party for her daughter and a number of suggestions are made. I am visited by a long queue of dogs when I begin to pass out the biscuits, but Winnie's disappointment over not being included in this handout is haunting. There is a lot of talk about Valentine's Day ceremonial but this too has a rather melancholy ring for me—the first time in almost four and a half decades that I have nothing to celebrate.

Friday, February 15:

There has been no improvement in the weather, and today very much resembles yesterday: cold and gray. Unfortunately I have to do a lot of standing around as Fritz makes only the slowest progress toward the green. First he has to touch noses with Buddy, then with Andrew the Akita, then with Lancer the chocolate-colored Lab, then with Oscar and Scamp. I learn that Buddy, the charming and docile Golden Retriever, has been recruited by St. Mungo's, a charity that encourages dog visits in its care homes. I think he would make an ideal visitor—as long as the old folks have biscuits in their bathrobes.

When we reach the green I see Dan with Winnie. Dan is talking with Beano's mom and it is always nice to have a visit from any member of that lively contingent of Tibetan Terriers who once made up their own pack in Paddington Rec. Fritz heads down the Randolph walkway but I am only partially successful in getting him to turn around, for instead of following me back to the café, he turns left and follows the perimeter of the green as far as Sabina, who is tossing a nice rubber ball to her own Schnauzer. Naturally Fritz now takes an interest in this object and makes off with it. I have a devil of a time trying to get him to release Oscar's toy, dangling the temptation of a biscuit as a bribe. (Oscar eats the biscuit and Fritz keeps the ball). Eventually I am successful and the ball goes back into Sabina's bag; we are now free to follow the others into the café.

Again there is a rather small turnout: Ellen, Dan, Georgie, Hanna, Ronnie and Cheryl, who warns us on arrival not to pick up Ginger, who has just stepped in somebody else's poo. The blind Pug remains on the ground and her one-eyed sister, Lola, jumps into every empty seat and continues her barking colloquy on every topic under the (absent) sun. Sparkie too is very noisy this morning, especially when Georgie disappears for a moment or two—and Fritz is excited by the presence of the towering Harry, leaning over the garden fence. It is Daisy-Mae, however, who takes more watching than the rest: she is forever disappearing on her own investigations and one after another of the dog owners has to jump up to retrieve her. It is getting colder as the wind picks up and there is universal assent to the proposition that we need our walkround *now*. The last thing I hear as I enter my own building, five minutes later, is a chorus from Georgie and Dan still in the park: "Daisy-Mae, Daisy-Mae, get over here at once."

Saturday, February 16:

The sun has returned but it has not brought any real warmth with it and I am chilled within five minutes. Fritz, whose poo was suspiciously loose last night, begins a morning of ever deadlier deposits and I now have another visit to the vet under consideration. As we near the café we join Janet and Georgie and begin to climb Mt. Bannister. Janet shares some awful news: Angie, the owner of Chelsea, the portly Jack Russell with the skin complaint, is dying of cancer. A mother of two, only 42 years old, the poor woman is fading away alarmingly. The news, with its echoes of my own recent tragedy, sends me into a tailspin of depression for the rest of the day.

We descend. Daisy-Mae, Sparkie and Fritz make up a pack of their own and when one penetrates the bushes the other two have to follow. Thus it takes us a long time to get around the green and when we do, Bailey joins the group as well. Ofra tells us that she has had a delicious meal in a Kurdish restaurant in Stoke Newington (though she has no idea where this village lies) and the others file this suggestion away for the turn of the letter "K" in their alphabetical progress through the restaurants of London. A woman walks by with a young Staffordshire named Rocky. "I can see that in certain parts of London you could no more live without a Staffie than you could survive without a Sky dish on your roof," I say. "Or an anti-social behavior order," Janet replies.

When we sit down for coffee I tell the others that Fritz is again nil by mouth. Janet is worried that Daisy-Mae is getting chunky and Bailey's intake is also being monitored—so Ronnie, his nose out of joint, doesn't have many takers for the biscuits and carrots he has brought with him; at one point he gets up to feed a black Lab who is chained to the fence. Janet passes out information on the Battersea fund-raising efforts being undertaken by Kate's son, who is part of a team tackling the Arctic with dogsleds in March. "Well, I'm not going with them," Ronnie says (purposely missing the point), "I have enough trouble getting to the park." Albert too is into the irrelevant comment this morning. Noting that all the dogs seem to be food-restricted these days, he adds, "In the desert I was so hungry I could eat dirt."

Sunday, February 17:

I have Fritz under close observation after yesterday's substandard poos, but he seems to show no signs of illness. Indeed, when I took him over to the doggy area on Morshead Road yesterday afternoon he participated in a furious round of tennis ball chasing lead by his Aunt Hanna. It was a wild scene since there were lots of other dogs around including a spirited trio of mid-size animals including Hugo the Collie, a Labradoodle named Rocco and a red Chow named Redford. An elderly chap in a Chelsea cap was leaning over the gate and observing all this activity and as I prepared to leave he said, wistfully, "The happiest people in the world are those who love dogs."

Fritz's poo chooses to adhere to an already mucky backside when we reach the cypress trees this morning but it seems solid enough. Dan, Georgie and Janet are circling the green, half of which is bathed in a radiant sunshine, and we join them for a walkround. Fritz wanders into the center to see Skye and Isla but when I call him he rushes back—"I hope you are watching this, Daisy-Mae," Janet says. We then move our table into the sunlight and crowd round, a large group of eleven that soon includes Kate, Bob, Dan, Davide, Janet, Ellen, Ofra, Georgie, Georgie's daughter Lynn and Lynn's husband Sean. Liz has also returned from Boston with George Bush-shaped dog biscuits ("Chomp, Chomp, He's Gone").

We have a jolly session. Kate passes around photos of the recent ski holiday near Chamonix, where painful boots and bronchitis kept her in a permanent *après*-ski mode. Janet is reminded of her own days on the slopes including the moment she was blindsided by an out-of-control skier who sent her flying. She congratulated herself on surviving this collision with no broken bones but when she got up three front teeth fell out. Bob is now trying to get up a field trip to a doggy-friendly pub in St. Albans: "You can count it as the E on your list—English." Kate has brought a tin of jammed-filled biscuits from France. They go down well with this morning's coffee, which is on the house—Metty and his red-clad staff are celebrating the outcome of the Kosovan independence referendum.

Things rather fall apart as we near the end of the session. Fritz, who has been offered only the lightest of food fare (just a few official Channel 4 *It's Me Or The Dog* treats) has been eyeing the sausage sandwiches of Lynn and Sean but, as rude as this might be, it is nothing compared to the behavior of Roxy (puffed up with the news that a Beagle has won the Westminster Dog Show in New York). Our version of this breed now sticks her nose over the parapet and helps herself to half a sandwich. Rosie, meanwhile, has wandered off to the green from the little table that latecomers Ronnie and Hanna occupy. She has to be secured for the back passage walkround but Roxy is still helping the waitress clear our table and she fails to begin this procession altogether and Liz has to go back to the café to fetch her. The line is so slow-moving that Fritz and I get far ahead of the rest of the group and return to the welcoming warmth of our flat without having had a chance to say goodbye to anyone.

Monday, February 18:

There is still frost on many surfaces as Fritz and I begin our stint in the park this morning, but there is also a lovely sunshine that is rapidly bringing some warmth to the surroundings. As I see the bum of my dog disappear down the garden path I have time to reflect on the almighty struggle that has just taken place as I attempted to clean that bottom, which was encrusted with age-old poo, some even requiring the scissors and all of it necessitating an ill-tempered extraction process as I fought it out with Mr. Sensitive.

On the green we find Buddy, Rufus and Winnie and I am soon surrounded by dogs seeking treats. I am trying to restrict these in Fritz's case—since Hanna believes that some of his tummy problems are due to overindulgence in dog biscuits. My dog now heads down the Randolph walkway and when I get him turned around it is time to head in for coffee. Doors are opened late here as much of the crew has been out last night celebrating Kosovan independence. Many are still wearing their celebratory red jumpers.

Considering how nice a morning it is turning out to be it is surprising that we have such a small turnout—just Ellen, Ronnie, Dan, Davide and Hanna, though Natasha eventually arrives and sits down with us in order to re-dress Lelia in one of her many outfits. Natasha too says that she was quite the worse for wear last night—even managing to knock a picture off a restaurant wall when she tumbled down the stairs. I remind her of her New Year's Resolution not to be a bad girl until August but she says that being a drunken girl is not the same thing as being a bad girl. Dan gets up to head for work—he and Davide having one last argument over who is most responsible for breaking Winnie's diet. Ronnie too heads off to wait for his gardener so it is just Hanna and Davide accompanying us on our back passage walkround. (Winnie evidently refused to leave the precincts of the café yesterday afternoon—hoping to hoover up one last crumb, no doubt—and there was great consternation when it was discovered at last that she was missing.)

Tuesday, February 19:

It looks like it should be a comfortable day in the park—since there is no frost anywhere, but after only a few steps I can tell that it is very chilly indeed. The wind counteracts any influence that the nascent sun might have and I am zipping up my jacket almost immediately. Just ahead of us we have Sparkie and Daisy-Mae and we follow them. Sparkie has a small rubber ball and I can hear Georgie encouraging him to pick it up when she is not urging a dilatory Daisy-Mae to move her bum. Fritz manages to steal the ball once but he is not greatly interested. We turn left to begin an ascent of Mt. Bannister. Near the top we are joined by Bailey, who has just emerged from Ofra's Smart car in the parking lot below.

For some reason the dog owners have chosen to congregate on the hillside, though I notice that for the first time all of the netting has been removed from the lakebed of the lost Lake Botham in the centre of the now empty green and thus for the first time in quite a while we could have uninterrupted use of our old haunting ground. Buddy, a trail of his own spit spanning his nose, spots me on the hilltop and reports for his morning biscuit. This scene is soon repeated as all the other dogs, including Pepper, make an appearance at my feet. Dan even permits Winnie to participate in this feast. Eventually the gang starts to move toward the café, which again seems to have opened a bit late this morning.

Today we have Dan, Davide, Hanna, Cheryl, Georgie, Ellen, Liz and Ofra. The latter has again suffered a loss. "The global icecap is melting, the world is on the brink of economic recession and closer to home," I tease, "Ofra has misplaced £6.80 worth of asparagus ravioli." Mention of food sets off a long discussion on where to eat next, though no one mentions the hunt for a suitable "D" eatery. Behind us a black Lab is chained to the fence while his owner is inside the café and the poor fellow is hysterical with separation anxiety, barking without letup. The Pugs, Lola and Winnie especially, take up this challenge by barking back (though just out of range), winding him up even more. Soon a third Pug arrives as well, little Cookie (and her mate Kai). Cheryl and Dan are beside themselves over the presence of this adorable version of their own pets and much cuddling takes place. By this time I am thoroughly chilled and I have to begin a back passage walkround before my teeth start to chatter.

Wednesday, February 20:

The thin fog is just lifting as Fritz and I make it into the park this morning. Georgie is just passing the Essendine gate with Daisy-Mae and Sparkie and I can already hear her begging her dog to pick his ball up. I try to kick it to him as well, but this is hard to do since he attacks the ball with his teeth the moment you try to kick it, and the consequence is that it doesn't go very far. At one point, near the cypress trees, I see Fritz heading in the opposite direction. I wait for him to resume the correct line of march but Georgie says that he is now well ahead of us—and thus I realize that it is Oscar who has just sprinted past, not Fritz.

When we have topped Mt. Bannister again and met up with Ofra and Bailey we can see Cheryl just entering the scene with the covered wagon and her Pugs. At the corner of the green there is a blonde trio of Golden Retrievers including Buddy, Rufus and a new contender, a dog named Lachan, who belongs to an Israeli chap. He and Ofra begin a conversation in Hebrew while Georgie exclaims, "Fritz has got a great big bone!" Sure enough I can see the Schnauzer rushing through the pack brandishing the prize for all the other dogs to see—only once again it's Oscar who is the mischief-maker, not Fritz. Sabina is wondering how she can get this object away from her boy but I have the solution in my pocket, the bribe of a Shapes biscuit. This works very well and I dispose of the bone in a trash bin. In the process I have attracted a crowd and every other dog in the park gets a biscuit as well.

The Israeli chap, who is a music producer, joins us at coffee. He says "Lachan" means musical composition—which, I think, few of us would choose in its English version as the name for a dog. Dan makes arrangements for Winnie to have a sleepover at Georgie's. Ellen, who is having her heart bypass op tomorrow, receives the good wishes of the rest of us. While our backs are turned Daisy-Mae climbs into the covered wagon and plays with Ginger's blanket. Nearby someone lights up a marijuana cigarette. "I saw you breathing deeply," Hanna says to me as we begin our back passage walkround. I am again thoroughly chilled as we reach our front door. I wish I could say that doggy tales are over for the day but that afternoon Fritz is bitten on the backside by Harry the Akita!

Thursday, February 21:

The incident to which I have referred at the conclusion of yesterday's entry occurred like this: I was walking Fritz over to the doggy pen on Morshead Road. Its only occupant was Harry, who began following us with his nose sticking through the iron fence as we made our way along the pavement. There was a lot of territorial growling but this often happens with other dogs; once both are inside the play area things usually settle down rather rapidly. I anticipated that this would be the case now and, with Fritz still on lead, I opened the door of the site and my dog was immediately and viciously attacked by the Akita, who sank his fangs into Fritz's backside. The owner, a well-spoken Balkan chap, immediately intervened, dragged his dog off, and apologized.

I exited the doggy area as soon as I could and ran my fingers over Fritz's back. I could feel no blood, just slobber, and we continued to complete a back passage walkround. Fritz, in a state of shock, didn't want his biscuit when we returned but he did eat his dinner at the normal time and had a lively walk late in the evening. I noticed that he didn't want me to touch the sore spots on his back but otherwise he seemed unaffected by the incident and settled down for a good night's sleep—which is more than can be said for his owner.

This morning I can feel the welts where Harry's teeth had punctured the skin and as soon as it is open I have to phone the vets. We are given a 10:15 appointment. I now take Fritz around the block at an early hour and at about 9:50 we begin to head for the park. Jeff and Jean-Baptiste are walking with their dogs so I can bring them up to date on the incident. The gang at coffee chide me for being so late but they soon realize that there is a good reason for my adopting a new schedule today.

At the vets Dr. Saddiqui has to shave huge lumps out of Fritz's fur so that she can clean his wounds with antiseptic wash. He gets an antibiotic injection as well. She doesn't think that surgery will be required but we have to make an appointment for a return visit on Saturday. I feel so sorry for my poor dog.

Friday, February 22:

Fritz seems to have spent a comfortable night—as other aspects of his routine also return to normal—and we begin a day that also includes antibiotics and septic washes by strapping on his raincoat before we go outside. It is chilly in the park but the coat provides some protection for his wounds as well as disguising the shaved patches on his backside. He is as mobile as ever and we soon reach the green where, for only the first time in half a dozen attempts, I have to explain what has happened to Fritz. Dan is just passing Winnie's lead on to Georgie, for tonight his little Pug will be having a sleepover. Georgie says that by the time her hubby has had his Friday night cans she'll have snoring in stereo when she goes to bed.

We go in for coffee: Georgie, Janet, Cheryl and Hanna. To my surprise Ellen and Peter also come in, and I tell the former, "That's the fastest recovery time I've ever seen." Of course it turns out that her operation has been put back a week or so after a test was misread and the original procedure cancelled. Fritz now camps in front of her chair, convinced that she must be carrying a ham sandwich in her purse. He gets his morning biscuits again these days and there are a few other goodies in which he shares.

When we begin our back passage walkround we pass Pippa the Papillion and Janet tells me that when this little dog is wearing her coat we are not to distract her since she is working—as a guide for her hearing-impaired owner. Next we meet the American woman who not only has her Border Terrier, Artemis, but a small black dog, Jeffrey, who belongs to an elderly neighbor. Jeffrey has his foot in an improvised boot after the removal of a dewclaw. We manage to reach our gate without a sighting of Harry the Akita but in the early afternoon I see him prancing around the abandoned doggy area. He is still unmuzzled.

Saturday, February 23:

Under grey skies Fritz and I make our entry into the Rec; temperatures are mild enough, however. We pass Ellen with Jack and Sandy—all three of them are sitting on a bench at the head of the running track and Fritz gets an early food handout. The park is very crowded, mostly with little boys undergoing their Saturday morning footy lessons, but out on the green Roland has a class for the doggies of the park as well; I see that Pippa the Papillion is a member of this circle. Fritz checks out the pupils and then heads for the center of the green, where Buddy comes to a smart halt in front of me, waiting for his biscuit handout. While I am chatting to Rhiann I can see Fritz heading off toward the bandstand where Bailey, Winnie, Daisy-Mae, and Sparkie are completing a grand circle of the green. By the time I have made my way over here Fritz is nowhere to be seen, though this is only because I am looking at the ground and he is several feet above this, getting a cuddly lift from his Aunt Hanna.

Because of all the people in the park there is a long queue in the café and it takes a long time for our orders to arrive. I ask Georgie how Winnie's sleepover went. "She's no trouble," is the response, "all she does is eat, sleep, fart and snore." "Just like James," Janet adds. (It is true that Winnie has also taken exception to the visits of that gentleman to the loo, standing outside and barking until he re-emerges.) There is some interesting news at breakfast this morning: Saskia is pregnant and Kate and Bob are engaged! Kate is brandishing a magnificent ring on her finger and a date for the wedding has already been set for May 6. We toast the happy couple with our late arriving coffees, indeed I can only get through half of mine before it is time for Fritz and I to head over to Boundary Road for a check-up.

Frank Seddon has a close look at my dog's wounds, marveling at the imprint of Harry's jaws on poor Fritz's backside—"This could be used for forensic identification." He also notes that Akitas are famous for their aggressive temperament. (Linda and I had passed a young thuglet with an Akita puppy in the five-aside pitch yesterday afternoon. I had observed that the Akita is becoming the Staffordshire Bull Terrier of this generation. She said, "Bring back the Staffie!") Fortunately there are no medical complications and I just have to continue to the end of the antibiotic pills and pink antiseptic wound wash with Fritz. The gang have dispersed by the time we return to the park but for once Fritz is anxious to get home. He had parked himself below a shelf in Frank's shop and whined until I bought him a rubber bone and now, at last, I can take it out of my pocket.

Sunday, February 24:

The sun is making a fine effort this morning and it seems somewhat nonsensical to strap the raincoat on old Fritz, but I want to make sure that his wounds are still covered while we are in the park. Temperatures are also mild, adding to the cognitive dissonance, but we persevere in our journey to the park, where, just inside the Essendine gate, we encounter Rocky the Staffordshire puppy. Progress is fairly rapid until we begin to encounter the legions of football junkies who are streaming toward the pitches. So single-minded are they that three lads head our way walking abreast and not one of them has the courtesy to step aside so that traffic moving in the opposite direction can get by. The problem is particularly acute in the narrow fenced walkway between the fields, something John now calls Colditz Alley.

I can see that our group has foregathered at the eastern end of the green and I get Fritz moving in this direction too. Buddy is always the first to spot me, rushing forward with a number of small dogs in his wake, in order to be first in line for the biscuit bestowal. Today we have the lively presence of Zorro, another tan Pug, who is bustling about with a row of bells jingling on the halter that crosses his chest. Bob has brought his hairbrush and is trying to comb through Skye's thick fur; then he has a go at any other dog in his vicinity. Faz arrives with baby Scarlett and Jasmine. He announces that he and Dianah have bought a five-bedroom house in Walton-on-Thames and that their own flat has been sold as well. This is sobering news for the other dog owners, who will miss this contingent keenly.

There is again a long queue at the coffee counter but Bob agrees to place my order when he arrives. Today we have all of those already mentioned plus Peter, Ellen, Ofra, Liz, Janet, Georgie, Ronnie, Hanna and Dan. The latter has the group shout out a mobile phone greeting to Davide, who is at Heathrow. "Ooh, he's swearing," Dan says. "Swearing at who?" someone asks. "Swearing at you lot," is the answer. The gang discuss last night's field trip to the Ethiopian restaurant on the Harrow

Road, a non-English "E." Dan is enthusiastic but some of the others have their doubts—evidently diners were not offered silverware at this venue. "I suppose it's French next?" I inquire. This is confirmed by Janet but that lady has a unique suggestion in this regard—"I'll see if there are any special offers on Eurostar. Then we can have lunch in Lille."

Monday, February 25:

It is another lovely, spring-like morning in Paddington Rec and we enter briskly enough, getting as far as the second bench before Fritz can growl at Oscar and Scamp. When we reach the green we ignore the collection of large blonde dogs over at one corner and I follow my dog toward the Randolph gate; soon he encounters Spikey and I manage to get him turned around in time for a second meeting with Sabina and her dogs. She tells me that Harry's willful behavior has had an earlier instance when he jumped the doggy pen fence in pursuit of some enemy, went missing for two hours and throttled another dog before he could be corralled.

At breakfast this morning we have Peter, Ellen, Albert, Georgie, Ronnie, Cheryl and Hanna. Georgie says that she has lost her mobile phone but it has been found in the taxi she uses to ferry her disabled student to school. A woman walks by with an unknown black Lab and all of our dogs begin to show signs of agitation—even Peter's Holly. For his part, Fritz brings a chuckle to the assembled owners when *his* protest takes the form of a high-pitched song. Someone notes that Angie, the owner of Chelsea, has died—and this rather casts a pall over proceedings.

Out of the corner of an eye I see that Harry the Akita is being lead into the garden and this means that I have to let his owner know just what damage his dog has caused and to suggest the use of a muzzle in the park. The initial response is defensive (Fritz bit his dog first; I shouldn't have brought my dog into the pen) but I point out that such spaces are for *all* dogs. I present to him my bill from the vets for £50 (I have paid an additional £12 on the return visit) and resume my seat. In a minute he presents himself at our table and, to his credit, peels off £60 from a wad of bills—"Money is nothing to me; I have a million pounds." The incident is unnerving at best and I am just as glad to start for home soon thereafter.

Tuesday, February 26:

The rain that has lashed the streets overnight has lifted and we now have sun and bright skies for our entry into the park on a quiet Tuesday morning. There seem to be no school groups in residence today, only a parade of endlessly lapping dogs circling the walkways. I follow Fritz along the Randolph roadway, struggling to get him to turn around when he gets too close to the gate on that side. Cheryl is just coming in with her Pugs and after I have hooked my dog we begin a slow progress toward the café. A little girl in Wellingtons is jumping into every puddle and pulling behind her a Beagle, a toy Beagle with little mechanical legs pumping away. As we pass she picks up the toy and brings it over to Lola first and then to Fritz so that all the dogs (real and not so real) can have a good sniff.

At breakfast this morning we have Peter, Ellen, Ronnie, Cheryl, Ofra, Dan, Georgie, Hannah and John. Cheryl is full of good cheer, having discovered a source for cheap golf balls. Ginger sits in her lap, accepting with good grace the pieces of buttered toast that Hanna passes across my lap for the senior Pug. Lola, meanwhile, is having a set-to with the irascible Winnie; she soon has to retreat to Ellen's abandoned chair in defeat. Winnie then turns on Sparkie, in the next lap, and Dan not only has to restrain the angry Pug but, after he has calmed her down a bit, he has to take her over to the naughty corner to cool off. Angie comes by to announce that today is the funeral for the other Angie.

In spite of the need for dark glasses I am chilled by a strong wind that is cooling the park down and just as happy when someone announces a back passage walkround. As we get up I notice that Harry's owner has a muzzle attached to his dog's lead—a really good idea. Fritz attempts to find a good spot for his second poo of the morning; unfortunately, Sparkie manages to wedge his rubber ball just below my dog's bum and for a moment I foresee an awful tragedy; Fritz, however, wants a little bit more peace and quiet and moves off to find another spot. We meet Saskia who tells us that her Buddy jumped off a seven foot balcony yesterday; the flying Golden Retriever seems none the worse for wear; we don't know about the cat that was passing just then.

Our progress is not at all tidy. Way out in front we have Ronnie and Albert. Behind us we have Cheryl and Hanna. I eventually catch up with a middle group that includes Georgie and Dan. Sparkie is having a mad moment, running in great circles at great speed, pausing only now and then to crash into Daisy-Mae.

Wednesday, February 27:

A beautiful and crisp sunny morning greets us as we make a mid-week visit to Paddington Rec. We haven't taken many steps into the park before I realize that I have forgotten both biscuits and my poo-poo bags. I can forget poo-poo bags and still have a biscuit bag as a spare, but to forget both is a tragedy. Before Fritz has decided to squat, however, I pick up an empty crisp bag from the walkway and a small bit of branch. I am still carrying these objects when we reach the green and, though Sabina and Denise offer me a real bag (having noticed the strange objects in my hand) I am determined to persevere with my improvisation. "Watch this," I say as Fritz backs up against a tree. In a dazzling display of slight of hand I push the poo into the empty bag and deftly deposit all objects in an adjacent bin. *Then* I accept two real bags from Sabina.

Fritz and I follow these ladies—and Scamp, Oscar, and Rizzo—around the green. Oscar is caught rolling in something but he responds to an instant intervention. By the time we have reached the clubhouse I have hooked Fritz in anticipation of the visit to our table outside the café doors. Ronnie is already in residence and Peter, Ellen, Hanna, Dan, Georgie and Ofra soon arrive. Hanna moves Peter since she wants a chair that sits in the sun. Beneath Peter's new chair is Noodle, the young black dog who belongs to Lynn Franks. When that lady shows up Hanna tells her that the café is always the place to look for straying dogs in this park. Dan later complains that the celebrity public relations lady should have been invited to have coffee with us and adds that he will be very cross if this omission occurs again.

Peter suggests that the community hall which he manages on his estate on Greville Road might serve as a proper venue for the birthday party that Ofra is trying to organize—but it turns out that twelve is the upper age limit for such gatherings and Lee is sixteen (and in need of a far more glamorous setting). Rhiann comes by to complain that she has gotten a parking ticket for an "improperly displayed permit," whatever that means. She is livid and her distress elicits a long series of complaints from wounded drivers who have been unjustly ticketed. Ronnie adds that people are always parking in his disabled spot and that it takes about

twenty minutes to have them towed away. The other owners are surprised
at the swiftness of this response but then there is big money to be made is
lifting some vehicle off the street. Fritz has spent most of this gripe session
in Hanna's lap but we depart after only twenty minutes (I haven't even
ordered a coffee this morning) as I need to get home for a delivery man.

Thursday, February 28:

Grey skies have returned as Fritz and I begin our walk in the park on
a chilly Thursday morning. When we reach the green I can spot Georgie
and Liz out on the grass and we head here first. Georgie has Sparkie
and Daisy-Mae with her, though neither dog pays any attention to her
commands. "I blame James," she says, "they can see that he doesn't do
anything I ask *him* to do either." Liz has a very bad back and has needed
the assistance of her eldest son just to get a foot placed on the floor
when she arose this morning. Roxy, for her part, is barking at any man
in a brightly colored vest and there are quite a few of them around this
morning, though most of them take this noisy objection to their presence
in good part.

At breakfast this morning we have the aforementioned ladies plus
Hanna, Ofra, Dan, Davide and Cheryl. Ellen has gone into hospital for her
bypass operation and Peter (having left Holly with Ronnie) has gone off
to give Sandy and Jack some exercise. Dan offers to share his expedition
to Sainsbury with Ofra but that lady says she prefers to undertake such
expeditions with the eagle-eyed Davide. There is much discussion of the
earthquake that was felt in these parts night before last. Quite a few of
those present did feel the shock; others slept through it all. Hanna says
that her bird went crazy. Cheryl announces that she now has her own
blog, though the only person she sends it to at present is herself.

We have been at table well over half an hour and there is still no
sign of Peter. He at last returns, dogless, and announces that he is late
because Harry has attacked Jack in the Morshead doggy pen! Ronnie
says that Harry is being trained as a guard dog and, if so, he has done
a good job of defending his turf against the predations of a timid Jack
Russell. (Peter is not certain to what extent Jack has been injured at
this point.) Franca arrives to give a version of the incident, including
the intelligence that Harry doesn't bite other dogs—which will be news
of especial interest to Fritz. She doesn't realize that right behind her is

the owner of the dog in question, listening intently to this recital without offering any commentary himself—Harry (at last) muzzled at his side. By this time the temperature seems to have dropped several degrees and there is universal agreement that it is now time to get a move on.

Friday, February 29:

Grey skies continue to dominate on a chilly morning that marks the end of an extra-long February. Soon after we enter the park Georgie comes in behind us with Sparkie and Daisy-Mae. Sparkie has his ball on a string and the object of the game is to tease Daisy-Mae into a tug-of-war and, when he has triumphed, to abandon the toy until the next time she tries to pick it up. We follow this party up to the top of Mt. Bannister and down the other side. Here Georgie heads for the café but Fritz continues forward at great speed. I never figure out what has excited his interest but when I do catch up with him I place him on lead and continue my own progress toward the café, dodging through a party of kids in yellow tops who have stopped off to use the loos.

This morning we have Hanna, Ronnie, Liz, Dan, Georgie, Cheryl and Peter. Peter reports that Ellen's heart op seems to have been successful and that little Jack seems to be fine as well. I ask Liz how her back is; she says that last night she, Janet and Dan went to see some Pinter plays and that she fell down the stairs so that today her knee is the troublesome spot and her back feels better by contrast. I too visited the theatre last night to see *West Side Story*, the inaugural production in ASL's new performing arts venue. What they hadn't told me (not even Angie, who had seen an OAP version two days earlier) was that the production had been dedicated to Dorothy. I now pass around a copy of the program so that all of Dorothy's park friends can read the dedication.

The dogs, meanwhile, are going crazy over the presence of so many plates of scrambled eggs on the table. Roxy gets her jaws around a piece of toast on Liz's plate before I drag her back. Tara, the Rhodesian Ridgeback, almost takes someone's hand off when offered a treat from this groaning board. And Buddy, after putting on a demonstration of eye-mouth coordination while wolfing down some of Winnie's pellets lofted in his direction by Dan, now stations himself at my elbow. He accepts his usual morning biscuit, wipes his slobber all over my jacket sleeve, and then it is time for him to leave.

March, 2008

Saturday, March 1:

Our part of the world has been raked by high winds for hours and Fritz and I get up somewhat groggily on the first day of March. The noise has been so upsetting that the dog has slept in the well next to my side of the bed and I have had to turn the lights on several times in an effort to read until drowsiness had once more overtaken me. It is 8:00 before we get up and it is still windy outside when we reach the park. Fortunately it is also sunny and bright; it would be a perfect morning if the breezes would go away.

At the café I encounter Georgie and Janet and we accompany these ladies and their dogs over the top of Mt. Bannister. Janet has just been to a performance of *Buddy* (Holly that is); the park's Buddy is nowhere to be seen this morning. Dan is at the bottom of the hill where a svelte Winnie is chasing her laundry ball. By this time we can head for the café in earnest, finding Ronnie and Hanna already seated. As early customers they have managed to get their orders in; now there is a long queue, peopled by all the parents of the footie lads on adjacent fields. This is bad news for Ofra, who will have difficulty jumping this queue. Bob, who comes in with Kate, Isla and Skye, notices this problem and says, "She just has to imagine she's invading Egypt." Evidently the staff are also in a teasing mood—"We always serve you first to get rid of you as quickly as possible," one of them tells Ofra.

An elderly Lab named King is tied to the fence this morning. Inside the forecourt two kids are kicking a football about and on several occasions it sails over the low wall and bounces up against our table. Bob is still trying to organize an expedition to St. Albans but Janet reports that it will be too expensive to take the Eurostar to Lille for lunch. Dan wants an "F" cuisine that is not French anyway, but Hanna says there is no Finnish restaurant in London. Fijian? Ronnie accepts a cigar from Bob, who offers a choice of two packets. "You have your choice between this one, labeled 'Smoking Kills,'" I say, "and this one labeled, 'Smoking can cause the cessation of all meaningful life.'"

Jan Prendergast comes by to begin a surgery session inside the café. As earlier we dog people had addressed a petition to her on the subject of dogs running free in Paddington Rec so now she circulates a petition attacking the decision to close the Formosa Street Post Office. (To me there is no greater symbol of the decline in our civic life than the closure of local post offices; they closed the Clifton Road post office some time ago as well.) I go inside the café for a chat with our councilwoman. She has heard the sad news of the demise of the Japanese magnolia tree that was planted to honor her year as mayor of our borough and she hopes that its replacement will have strong roots. "I want to have some of my ashes scattered at its feet," she says. She is a woman with strong roots in this community.

Sunday, March 2:

Except for an occasional cooling gust of wind we have lovely spring-like weather for our session in the Rec this morning. I need to wear my dark glasses, of course, but there are moments when I can put my wool cap in my pocket. Surprisingly, there isn't much activity out on the green and it takes me a while to spot Dan, Georgie, Ofra and Janet as they complete a grand circle. I lead Fritz across the green so that we can intercept this party. Ronnie, I now see, is coming up behind them and so we are soon seated in front of the café and ready for our morning coffee.

Liz has her scrambled eggs and toast and some of the women share a panini. Dan, who has joined his dog in a bout of dieting, even disdains sugar in his coffee. The old chap with the flat cap, John, is trying to enjoy a quiet croissant next to the front door but, for some reason, Roxy objects to his presence and we have a long chorus of barking. Liz puts her pet on lead but now the Beagle has now a new objection—a worker is emptying a bin behind us and this is the cause of yet more percussive barking. Liz says that Roxy has knocked over a carton of chocolate milk at home, lapping up its contents of course, but that her tail is down today, usually a sign of distress. "Perhaps she prefers plain milk to chocolate," I suggest helpfully.

There are quite a few interruptions to our learned discourse this morning as a number of people drop by for a chat, without actually sitting down. First we have Peter, who needs help with a computer formatting problem. Then Kate comes by in the middle of a doggy exercise session with Skye and Isla out on the grass. Michael the Pirate, wearing multiple hats, comes by for a chat and so does Rhiann, who arrives with Otw. Today she is holding a second session of dog portraiture at her studio and several members of our group are planning on making a visit. Behind us a damaged teenaged boy, obviously in the company of a health care worker, gets frightened by a loose dog and begins to whine in a high-pitched moan. Meanwhile, Raffy the King Charles, suffering from terminal separation anxiety while his mom is in the café, takes up the job of hysterical barking abandoned by Roxy.

Monday, March 3:

A new week begins under bright skies; it is sunny but crisp. Often, as today, I can see Harry the Akita prancing around in an empty doggy pen as Fritz and I cross Morshead Road. They say that his owner has taken to wrapping his leash around the entrance gate so that no one will accidentally penetrate this space dedicated to temper and teeth. This is an improvement on the accidental encounter that an open door might invite but there is something unacceptable in this unhappy compromise—since it says that this space is for the private use of *my* dog; others can piss off. I can't help noting that this gesture is too often the paradigm of immigrant arrival on these shores: I now claim this portion of your space but don't expect me to share it with the rest of you or respect your ways in any meaningful sense.

Behind us, as we advance on the cypress trees, I can see Sparkie and Daisy-Mae advancing. When they catch up Georgie tells me that there has been another bedroom accident and that she has tripped over the wires of a redundant television on the floor and cracked her ribs on the set. She has had some breathing difficulties (Jean's arthritis pain killers help) and now manages to ascend Mt. Bannister. Here two black dogs rush up the hill to see what ours are up to and a little black dog, Sam, has to be chased away by Fritz. Cheryl and Dan are also waiting at the top of the hill and Lola now dons a lurid red, yellow and black jumper knitted by Janet's sister; she looks like a Watford supporter. We descend and head for our table, where Ronnie is already sitting. Georgie repeats the story of her fall. Ronnie says, "You always wanted to be on television anyway."

We are joined by Peter, again walking Jack and Sandy, and Albert. Dan says that a whole chicken breast was lying next to a bin in front of his house this morning and that an almighty struggle ensued when he tried to wrest it out of Winnie's mouth. The three Pugs soon surround Cheryl as she tucks into her scrambled eggs and none gets a proper share—I'm sure they would all say. Dan adds that he's waiting for a delivery of Winnie's special diet food and that, in the interim, his pet *is* allowed to join in the share-out. Saffy and Tinkerbelle do well this morning too, though one pellet lands just out of reach and there is a titanic tussle to reach it against the restraints of their lead. "I hate to see a grown dog scrabble," I conclude.

Tuesday, March 4:

Gray skies dominate as Fritz and I head for the park on a frigid Tuesday morning. Around the first corner we encounter Dan in conversation with Christianne. The latter has Stella on lead but soon she will be accompanying another creature into the park—for she is due to give birth on the 14th. Georgie now comes up behind us as well and we see how she is coping with her sore ribs. The three of us and our dogs continue past the cypress trees but on the far side they have been doing some clean-up work in the little square meadow that has been fenced off for the last half year and one after another of our dogs have to rush through an open gate and check out the place. Winnie manages to lose track of how she entered this space and can't get out. There are no school groups in the park this morning and it is blissfully quiet.

We turn left at the café and climb Mt. Bannister. The others head for coffee when we reach the bottom on the other side but Fritz has to check out the pristine white Arran and then Lola and Ginger are encountered on the Randolph walkway as well. I meet up with Saskia, who says that Buddy, who survived his fall without injury, was discovered to have a burst ear drum when he was taken to the vet (he had been scratching his ear) and now, with the threat of deafness hanging over the fellow, he is all doped up; indeed he fails to ask for a biscuit so you know something is wrong. I ask how the cat, whose presence occasioned Buddy's flight in the first place, has survived this incident. Saskia says that not only did the cat survive but that it now positions itself in the same spot—daring Buddy to have a second go.

There is only a small turnout at coffee, just Dan, Georgie, Hanna, Ofra and Cheryl—with Peter and Albert hovering in the background. I notice that Ofra is wearing Dan's pilot's cap, the tweed creation with fur accents. There is a lot of fashion chatter this morning as some of the dog people have been watching a program on fashion fakes recently. I sort of zone out but Hanna is in her element. She has been absent for several days and the rumor is that she has gone to attend the funeral of an aunt. As we get up (leaving behind not another café customer inside or out) I ask her if she has been in Finland. "No," she replies, "only Chorleywood."

Wednesday, March 5:

Though still crisp, the temperatures have risen considerably as Fritz and I head for the park on a beautiful, sunny morning. Far ahead of us I can see Georgie and Dan walking with Sparkie, Winnie and Daisy-Mae, but there is no chance that we can catch up with them for Fritz wants to make very slow progress indeed, sniffing every bush and sampling a few grass shoots on the way. We pass Saskia with Buddy and Denise and Sabina with their dogs but by the time we have reached the café I know that Dan and Georgie have long since climbed Mt. Bannister.

Ronnie is already seated in front of the café as we play through on our way to the green. By this time the others are well into a grand circle and again I attempt to catch up. It's no use, though I do notice that only Georgie is nearing the bandstand; Dan must have turned Winnie over to her as he exited for work via the Grantully gate. When Fritz and I reach the bandstand we pass a black woman in a turban who is reading aloud from some religious text. We also encounter the Schnauzer, Gus, whom I have not seen in the park in some time.

At coffee we have Ronnie, Georgie, Ofra, and Hanna, with Peter and Albert making up the numbers. Ofra is trying to fill in her social calendar, with quite a few trips to New York in the offing. Ronnie announces that he and Susie will be flying to Marbella the last weekend in May. Georgie says that the taxi driver has had to help her with the wheelchair of her disabled student since she herself is suffering these days with her cracked ribs. Hanna says that she has had a wonderful halibut from the Grimsby fish man who brings his van to our streets weekly. I announce that Fritz is not wearing his coat today so that he can start to get used to the colder temperatures he will have to endure when, at 11:00, he gets delivered to St. Johns Pets for his long-overdue clipping.

Thursday, March 6:

When we hit the park on an overcast gray morning Fritz is, for the first time in two weeks, able to prance along without the imposition of his hated raincoat—for yesterday Karen was able to work her wonders, reducing the length of his shaggy fur to that of the sleek patina that had been revealed when two giant patches had to be shaved at the vets in order to expose his war wounds. The latter are still visible, but not disfiguring, and he seems to be half his size as we make our advance onto the green. Liz and Ronnie are already sitting at a table in front of the café but we continue on for some more exercise on the walkways before settling in for our morning coffee.

Today there are nine of us at table, including Liz, Ronnie, Hanna, Dan, Davide, Georgie, Janet, and Ofra.

Davide has brought with him a baseball magazine that I asked him to pick up for me in the States. Dan has also brought an unusual object, a stuffed toy octopus belonging to Winnie. He has done so because he needs some help in interpreting the strangled message (followed by the unmistakable sound of water splashing) that this toy utters when squeezed. He thinks the voice says something about a bloody asshole. Others interpret it as, "Lets build a castle," and another version is, "That's really awesome." Saskia comes by with Buddy and she is asked for her interpretation. "Very well," she says, "but I hope it's speaking in Latin which, as you all know, is my second language." Her rendition of the message is, "That Buddy's awesome." Fritz, in the meantime, has fallen in love with the toy and, since his devil doll has recently lost *its* voice, I ask Dan to order one for me too.

We begin a back passage walkround, though today there is a surprising amount of counter-traffic. First we meet Jeremy, who is just arriving with Cressida, then Cheryl with Lola and Ginger, and finally Rowena with Timmy. While we are chatting an incident occurs. Timmy has admitted himself to the running track through the wide space offered by the absent fencing and is pursuing a jogger at great speed, barking maniacally all the while. The jogger, fortunately, is more amused than anything else and he ignores Rowena's attempts to get *him* to stop. Meanwhile Roxy has penetrated the gap as well and is lumbering around the track in lane two. Timmy gives up and the dogs are ushered off the track at last. Fritz has overtaken all of them—perhaps he would just as soon get out of the cold (which he must really feel after his recent adventure with the barber's clippers) and get back into some indoor warmth.

Friday, March 7:

A rainstorm has just cleared as Fritz and I make our way downstairs at the outset of another expedition in Paddington Rec. At our feet on the doormat is a pile of leaflets inviting neighbors to have a look at the plans for the new environmental area, which park officials hope to begin work on soon. Already there are plans for new pathways, hedgerows, diverse plantings, benches and a loggery, whatever that is. Whether dogs will be allowed into this new space is uncertain, but I have my doubts.

The sun is now shining brightly on a morning that began in such gloom and Fritz skips along in a lively fashion, encountering no other souls, human or canine, until we have reached the green, where he spots Dan coming in with Winnie. He often heads directly for Dan since the later usually kneels to give him an extended cuddle—Winnie dancing around nervously in the meantime. Dan is left talking to Peter as I accompany Georgie over the hill. At the bottom there is quite a collection of dogs including an alien Shar-Pei. The latter is a most unusual specimen, with a nose that seems to cover half of his face. "He looks like a hippopotamus," Saskia concludes. The bustling chap seems friendly enough and everyone has a sniff at the newcomer before heading in for coffee. Or I attempt to head in for coffee; Fritz has other ideas, running through the café forecourt and out along the Carlton walkway before I can retrieve him.

Discouraged by the early morning rain we have only the smallest of turnouts this morning—just Dan, Georgie and Peter at our table. Dan is full of social plans, past and future. He reports a grand time at the Pigalle club last night and announces that a party of eight dog owners is heading for Southwold for three days of hijinks in mid-April. Hanna is evidently a member of this party and there is some discussion of her recent attack on park gossiping. Even to have such a discussion, however, requires a certain amount of gossip at its heart—and so I'm not certain if we have adequately censored this crime or just committed a new one.

Saturday, March 8:

A gray and chilly morning awaits us as we hit the park on a busy Saturday morning in the park. Just ahead of us I can see Janet and Georgie and around the corner come Linda, Sabina and Denise. There is a grand junction of dogs at this point. Rizzo, Scamp and Oscar continue against our flow but Linda reverses direction and joins the incoming party. Unfortunately Fritz is frequently behind everyone else and it is not until we reach the café that we are able to add ourselves to the group now climbing Mt. Bannister. It will underline the slowness of our movements this morning if I add that crossing our paths at the top of this eminence we encounter Rizzo, Scamp and Oscar a second time. They have made a grand circle of the park in the time it has taken Fritz to reach the daffodil patch at the top of the hill.

Below us we can see Roland's Saturday morning obedience class and a few of our number have to integrate this grouping in an attempt to see who really *is* obedient. When we get to the doors of the café we discover that there is already a long queue waiting to be admitted. To speed matters along Dan gets a pad from the staff when the doors are at last open and takes down every order himself. (Liz offers him a job at her Italian restaurant.) By the time our orders eventually surface we have a huge turnout at coffee: Dan, Davide, Liz, Ofra, Janet, Georgie, Hanna, Cheryl, Albert, Kate, Bob, Ronnie, and Linda. Rhiann also comes by with Otw, who, when food is on offer, dances on two legs and even does whirling circles on her back toes in return for a treat. Liz is in the process of making arrangements for Rhiann to take pictures of Roxy *and* her kids.

Fritz is obviously unhappy with the cold weather (in his shorn state) and spends much of the session first in Cheryl's lap and then in mine. I try to cheer him up by letting him lick my cappuccino foam; Pepper is scandalized (that he didn't get any of this treat himself). Isla and Skye keep up a cacophony of barking entreaties, though Isla is at least quiet when she is chasing Daisy-Mae. The Pugs, Lola and Winnie, gang up on poor Sparkie and Winnie manages to snatch a piece of toast from Hanna's hand. For this she has to sit on Dan's naughty lap; however we discover

Dan in a naughtiness as well—the eight dollars I gave him yesterday to repay Davide for my baseball magazine has gone missing. It takes a while for everyone to get their proper change back after our group order and Ofra leaves a pound and a half as a tip. This reminds Ronnie of the time an officious waiter presented him with the bill and the injunction, "You'll notice that service has not been included." "I noticed only too well," was Ronnie's response.

Sunday, March 9:

A period of rain has come to an end when it is time for us to head for the park today but temperatures are mild enough. There is no way we can catch up with Georgie and Sparkie and even the sight of Dan heading up Mt. Bannister with Winnie comes too late for us to join the front runners. We climb the hill anyway and then, while Fritz rushes down to check out his pals, I tiptoe gingerly down the steep walkway. At the bottom we encounter Linda with Pepper and there is a joyous reunion. The others head in for an early coffee at the café, Fritz in pursuit, but when they turn right he continues on his own past the clubhouse and out along the Morshead roadway. From a great distance I can see him greeting Albert and the girls, then veering left in the direction of the bandstand. Fortunately, as I start to cross the grass in pursuit, he answers my whistle, speeding toward me (and the proffered biscuit) at the end of a long run.

An article that I wrote several months ago on the dogs of Paddington Rec for *London Dog Tails* has at last appeared and it is the sensation of our breakfast session in front of the café—indeed a picture of us at coffee accompanies the article (perhaps taken by Suzanne) as does a picture of Janet cuddling Daisy-Mae and a large picture of Fritz, taken either by myself or by Rob. Unfortunately the magazine, which is a free sheet, is distributed via vets and pet shops and so far only one copy (found by Kate at Village Vets) has found its way into our midst. There is a great demand for it. Ronnie wants to take it home to show Susie, and Albert wants to know where he can buy a copy. There is also a minute critique of everyone's appearance in the group photo. Hanna thinks her face is too red, Ofra thinks she looks like a man, Dan has his nose out of joint because his back is turned to the camera, and Liz (among others) is upset because she wasn't in the park when the photo was taken.

Fritz receives many compliments on his photo. He has chosen another comforting lap, that of Liz today, and here he basks in the attention, licking the foam from my cappuccino cup and growling at any strange dogs wandering through, especially at the bruiser of a young Pug named Zorro, who not only has bells across his chest but pennies embedded in his harness. (Zorro later joins us for our back passage walkround during which Fritz is quite content to have the company of the newcomer.) Peter comes by to report that Ellen, home after only four days in hospital, is suffering considerably from the after-effects of her bypass surgery. It is a sobering thought; Dan says we had better get used to it—as many of us will face the same procedure some time in the future.

Monday, March 10:

We begin today's adventure in the park under stormy skies indeed. We are on the edges of a volatile frontal system that has brought gale force winds to other parts of Southern England and high winds and lashing rain have been raking us for the last few hours. There doesn't seem to be too much moisture coming down at departure time and so I disdain my own rain jacket, though Fritz gets his—amid the usual protests.

As we hit the street I am carrying a bag of paper for the recycling chaps who visit our streets on Monday mornings. A pile of chicken bones appropriately guards the Essendine entrance as we enter a very lonely park indeed: no school groups, no other dogs, just the isolated mad jogger and the workers who are beavering away on the clubhouse extension. Birds are singing sweetly in the trees and I am taking this as a sign of better things to come when, just as we reach the cypress trees, a fresh shower descends. Fritz seems somewhat puzzled by the return of high winds but we persevere as far as the still shuttered café, where some (Filipino?) chaps are huddled under the overhang. I can see Georgie in front of the clubhouse itself but she seems to be retreating rather than heading our way and so we turn along the Randolph walkway. We have an errand—the delivery of a prescription renewal request at the Randolph surgery.

We are not there long (just long enough to see that the medical cadre is undergoing yet more changes—the inevitable consequence of staffing a surgery with child-bearing female doctors only). We return to the park and I have a look into the café (the Filipinos have lined up at the counter)

269

but not one of the dog people is in place. So, uncoffeed, we have a solitary back passage walkround. At least there are bright patches in the western sky. Indeed, by the time we have ripped off the raincoat from my dog's back the sun has emerged briefly. Then we have a day of showers; we both get soaked on our afternoon walk.

Tuesday, March 11:

It's time to return to the park and, though it is gray, windy and chilly, at least there is no rainfall this morning. When we reach the green Cheryl is chatting with the owner of Charlie the Cocker—Ginger's covered wagon by her side. From around the fence corner in front of the clubhouse we can see Sparkie, Winnie, Roxy and Daisy-Mae heading our way and Fritz crosses the green to join them. The others head in for coffee but Fritz has to be corralled half way down the Randolph walkway before I can get him moving in the right direction as well.

This morning we have Dan, Georgie, Liz, Ofra, Albert and Peter. Liz reports that *half* of her work as a parent is done, with her older son coming home absolutely inspired by the appearance of Al Gore at the American School and her younger son asking, "How can one man be *so* boring?" A puzzled Cheryl, who provides the needed lap refuge for Fritz this morning, says, "Are we sure that global warming *is* a bad thing?" Bless her heart. A medium-sized black dog is chained to the fence behind us and, while his owner is inside, he barks unceasingly for ten minutes. Perhaps this unwanted noise sets off a doggy reaction in our group for I notice that Winnie is definitely perturbed by the intrusion and at one point she leaps off Dan's lap to attack Roxy, who is quietly munching on a stick. Not satisfied with this unprovoked attack she then has a go at Sparkie, who is innocently sitting in Georgie's lap—dreaming of just how nice it will be to spend the day sleeping on the sofa. Someone says that dogs have an aural vocabulary of 200 words. I respond that Fritz has a special affinity for "C" words: Chicken, Chocolate, Cheese, Chinese Food—it's just that he fails to recognize Come.

Georgie asks if it isn't time to walk round back. Our progress across the Carlton walkway is interrupted, however, by the arrival of a tribe of Francis Holland hockey maidens in maroon. Unlike other school groups, the members of this fierce body are *enchanted* by all of our dogs; they begin cooing and petting and they are charmed by Ginger's covered wagon. Once past this peril we can continue en masse between the fences, Roxy almost felling poor Albert as she, Sparkie and Daisy-Mae race by in tandem. For some reason Fritz is very slow this morning and the others have passed our exit long before we draw near.

Wednesday, March 12:

Another night of high winds has unsettled sleep; unfortunately—though there is no chance of rain—fierce breezes continue to thrash their way through the park as Fritz and I make our usual entry. As we turn the corner after clearing the cypress trees we meet Rizzo, Scamp, and Oscar—Fritz can't resist chasing Oscar for old time's sake but then he settles down to schmooze with these familiar canines while I chat with Sabina and Denise. Fritz soon grows bored and takes off at great speed for the café, though I am gratified to see that he pauses after rounding a corner to see if I am following him. Thirty seconds later, no longer gratified, I have lost track of the rascal.

Ronnie is sitting alone outside the still closed doors of the café and I ask if Fritz has played through. He has not, and so I return to the Carlton roadway, calling for my missing dog, and heading up the hill to see if he has followed two gents who were walking ahead of us. This must have been the case for I find my dog in the company of Dan and Winnie, who are sitting on a windswept park bench at the top. We join them for a while; our view encompasses a green where netting has again surrounded the dry bed of Lake Botham. All of a sudden both dogs leap from our laps to object to the presence of Noodle, the black dog on the lead of a startled Lynn Franks. "Well," I say to Dan, "at least our dogs are not overawed by celebrity."

Georgie soon joins us with Sparkie and Daisy-Mae and we head down the hill and so on to the café, where I hand my watch to Ronnie since it still thinks we are on the 10th of the month. We are joined by Hanna and Ofra as well—our teeth chattering as stories of the effects of the high winds are exchanged (Dan seems to have lost his TV antenna). Ronnie starts to choke with laughter as he remembers how a shop awning once engulfed two passersby and the spluttering causes a shower of croissant crumbs to rain down on the dogs—his napkin and paper plate having gone airborne a long time ago. The Philippine contingent have three dogs chained to the fence behind us and these animals keep up a barrage of barking while their owners bask in the warmth of the café. "Let's all do this with our dogs," I suggest. Ofra complains that her tea has gotten cold and, winding her up, Dan suggests that she complain that she wants another cup. She gets up to do this and Dan and Georgie follow a minute later to say that *their* coffees have gotten cold and they want new ones too. I can see Bouzha having a good chuckle at this demonstration but no one gets a free refill, nor do they expect one.

Thursday, March 13:

Temperatures have moderated a bit this morning, though the skies are grey and carry with them the promise of more rain. Fritz makes very slow progress along the back passage (no hope of catching up with Dan and Winnie) before emerging at the fence outside the café. Soon I can see Georgie and Ofra walking in front of the clubhouse and Fritz can see them too, rushing forward to join his pals among the canine fraternity. While *they* are milling about in front of the café *he* continues on past the loos and around the corner.

I am about to follow him when Sabina and Denise emerge from this direction and I am surprise to see that both Scamp and Oscar are on lead. It is soon obvious that Sabina is in an agitated state for, at the top of the hill behind us, poor Scamp has been attacked by the Springer Spaniel, Mungo. Both of the ears of the Westie have been bitten and they are turning pink with blood, which Sabina washes off with some tissue from the ladies loo. No one can explain such aberrant behavior from a member of a breed not known for its aggressive nature but since Mungo (though now on lead) is still with his mistress on top of the hill the other ladies choose another route for their escape.

At coffee this morning we have Liz, Dan, Georgie, Hanna and Ofra. Our dogs spend most of the session leaping from lap to lap. I have Sparkie in mine on three or four occasions, I have Bailey several times as well, and even Winnie arrives here the better to observe Liz's disappearing scrambled eggs. Fritz too spends some time on my lap (after a long session on Ofra's). As ever, he is keen to spot the presence of any interlopers and this is the status awarded Monty, who arrives with Nicholas after weeks away from our table. Georgie is still complaining about her sore ribs and the rest of us are encouraging her to get an x-ray at the emergency room at St. Mary's. That famous hospital seems to have outsourced its blood sampling facilities, or so we learn from Ronnie, who arrives late after a visit devoted to this task at a new center on the Harrow Road. He has had to fast and so is quick to order his morning croissant. Peter comes up behind him and the two have one of their usual cross-purpose quarrels, this time on the subject of the freedom pass. Ronnie says that he never uses public transportation but he'd be happy to stick a pass on his forehead if it would please Peter. Peter says he would be happy to stick one on Ronnie's head. We begin a back passage walkround. When I get home I see that *my* surgery now wants me to report for a blood test at the new health center on the Harrow Road.

Friday, March 14:

Milder temperatures have returned but the sun is having a hard time making much of an appearance today. Fritz skips along briskly enough, though when he reaches the Carlton roadway I again have some difficulty figuring out which direction he has taken. Today he has headed directly for the green, whose eastern end is dotted by dogs, the same animals who might congregate in the center of this area were it not again fenced off. I head for the owners who are gathered in the corner because I want to see how Scamp is doing today. Sabina says he rather made a meal of his invalid status yesterday but that he seems fine today. Buddy reports for his morning biscuit; he now offers a paw in return for his treat.

At the other end of the green I can see Georgie heading this way with Janet and Jean, who is visiting from Glasgow. The latter is accompanied by her Billy, but Mozart has been left behind in Scotland, mostly because he insists on biting the ankles of Georgie's James—that is when he is not sitting at these same feet waiting for handouts from the dinner table. We discuss Georgie's sore ribs and Jean says she will make certain that medical assistance is sought. Janet says that she will be heading to the dentist at the end of this morning session: two teeth have to come out.

We are eight at table this morning as we have Davide, Cheryl, Georgie, Jean, Ronnie, Janet, and Hanna. The latter hands me for safekeeping the airline ticket she will use next month to fly to Finland for her aunt's funeral. Cheryl says she is nearing completion of her autobiography and fretting over which self-publishing outfit will offer the best royalty. I tell her that she is unlikely to sell so many copies that this will become an issue and that she needs to choose a firm that will produce an attractive copy that will be a treasured keepsake for family and friends. The gang discuss tonight's get-together venue. Earlier in the week they seem to have chosen the Warrington pub (now an outpost of the Gordon Ramsey empire), but now they seem to have switched their allegiance to the Ordnance Arms in St. John's Wood.

Saturday, March 15:

Again temperatures are on the mild side, though skies are still gray on a Saturday morning in which the park is buzzing with very young people practicing their football on every available surface. Fritz jumps into a bed of pansies for his first pee, don't ask me why, and it takes me a while to get him going in the right direction. When we reach the green we continue on along the Randolph walkway, soon encountering an entering Ronnie with Rosie. Fritz turns right at the tennis courts and a minute later a woman, watching a friend who is receiving a tennis lesson, says, "What's he eating?" I have no idea: "Something he shouldn't be," is my reply. When we re-emerge on the green the mistress of Jasper the Springer Spaniel is sitting by herself on a bench listening to Abba on her radio.

Saskia has stopped by the previous day with almost a dozen copies of *London Dog Trails* and I can now make sure that everyone who wants one can have a copy. Soon Hanna comes in with another ten copies and we have gone from dearth to surplus in just a day. I take a copy inside to share with Bouzha and the staff and Peter, Ronnie, Jean, John, Albert, Georgie and Liz all take copies as well. I will send some to friends in the States, many of whom have visited the scene pictured in the Paddington Rec article.

There is a brief post-mortem on last night's field trip to the Ordnance Arms. I did not attend but the venue is well known to me as the site of many an end-of-term party for ASL faculty and staff. Ofra evidently tried to give everyone a ride home at the end of the festivities but Hanna, who seems cheerful enough this morning, refused to cram in. A good deal of food is consumed this morning and the dogs are wild with anticipation. Roxy takes a bite out of Ofra's hand (well it had a panini in it, right?) and Winnie (with a bandaged paw after yet another cyst has been spotted between her toes) and Sparkie have several furious growling matches over who gets the next mouthful. Soon I see the ashen face of one of the waitresses, who has been cleaning the tables in the forecourt. I can also see the source of her consternation: Roxy has climbed on top of an empty table, the better to snaffle for crumbs. From my perspective she seems to be airborne but I'm sure this is an illusion.

Sunday, March 16:

Rain has been the predominant weather factor since the wet stuff first made an appearance in the early evening yesterday. Fritz and I, indeed, seem to have had a rare piece of luck as we timed our late night walk during a brief break in the downpour at 10:30—but there is no escaping the drizzle this morning. This means buckling on my dog's raincoat and even stretching an old pair of rubbers over my tennis shoes before we hit the sodden streets. The park is rather quiet for a Sunday, just a few lads playing football and a dedicated jogger or two on the track or along the walkways.

When we reach the green I can see Georgie and Janet sheltering from the rain under the little metal gazebo. Sparkie is wandering along the Randolph roadway, ignoring Georgie's demands that he return at once, and, though he needs no encouragement is such matters, Fritz has to see what the little Yorkie is up to and they spend some time together in the bushes behind the tennis courts. By the time they have both recovered the green Sparkie has headed for the clubhouse, where Ofra is just arriving with Bailey—and Fritz has to head here too. I get him to return with the bribe of a biscuit and we take our places around our usual table—where Peter is in residence with Holly and Wendy's Corky as well.

Outside the café window poor little Raffy has been tied to a chair, moaning pathetically until Daisy-Mae arrives to keep him company. Ofra, saying that she is not in the mood for a gossip, does not enter the café today, indeed she takes no refreshment. Her strategy works only in part because before long Bouzha appears at the door to tease her—"These seats are for customers only; if you don't order something I'll have to call security." (They say that Bouzha is studying cosmetology though I think she should be running some corporation.) Ofra and Janet have been to the West End to see *Jersey Boys*, a show featuring the music of Frankie Valli and the Four Seasons. Janet says she had a really good time but Ofra says that their seats were so high she was dizzy for the first fifteen minutes. Janet calls Dan to twit him about his failure to brave the downpour but he claims that Winnie's bandaged foot needs to be protected from the wetness. There seems to be no chance that the rain will lift at all this morning and so we now brave the elements for our back passage walkround.

Monday, March 17:

I am carrying a heavy shopping bag with me as Fritz and I head for the green; its contents (more of Dorothy's shoes) are for Georgie and, indeed, we encounter her and Jean almost as soon as we enter the park. They tell me that Harry the Akita is back and that he has already flattened poor Charlie the Cocker, who was saved from further damage since the incident took place outside the doggy pen and Harry was on lead. The three of us reach the café and turn left for a climb up Mt. Bannister. Dan is just ascending this precipice from the other side; Winnie is scheduled for a visit to the vet at 10:30 and she is wearing a plastic bag over her foot sock and it makes a scraping sound with every step. Once again one is tempted to say to the poor Pug, "Winnie, pick up your feet."

When we descend there is a brief rendezvous with Gus and then we all head for the café, which has just opened—Ronnie and Hanna are already in residence. Hanna has been following the fortunes of the Finnish drivers in the first Formula 1 race of the year, in Melbourne, and seems quite pleased by the outcome. Peter comes by and sits down. He tells us that the other night the police stopped to ask him what he was doing ambling about at this late hour. He explained that he was walking with Holly, though, unfortunately, just at this moment his ancient companion had disappeared. Peter is wearing his own version of Dan's Flying Aces pilot's cap and there is speculation that the police stopped him because of his ugly headgear. This leads to a discussion of Jean's Peruvian peasant hat, the one with dropping wool attachments—something the others refer to as her "care in the community hat."

I get up once to deliver a copy of the recent issue of *Dog Tails* to the front desk, just as a courtesy, since I assume the management would like to know what is being said about Paddington Rec in publications other than their own. Truth to tell, our morning session is less comfortable than it should be. Harry is chained to the fence behind us and everyone needs to be on guard lest our dogs wander that way (this precaution is lost on the other Peter, a newlywed now, who comes by with Gypsy, Jody and two other dogs). Then we also have the intrusive barking of the black dog belonging to one of the Filipino chaps, comfortably ensconced inside the cafe; it rather spoils things to have your cappuccino filtered through ten minutes of hysterical barking.

Tuesday, March 18:

My efforts to get Fritz to catch up with some of his pals are usually unavailing, but today, a chilly and gray morning in the park, I succeed in reminding him that just ahead of us we have Billy, Winnie, Daisy-Mae and Sparkie. We have drawn level with this grouping by the time we have cleared the cypress trees. I am happy to see that Winnie is bandage-free today, though the vet says that she could still lose another kilo. Dan kneels to give Fritz a cuddle, a gesture that produces a blood-curdling chortle of delight. Then we all head up the hill, having picked Liz up on our way.

That lady and her boys are off on a ten day-trip to Hong Kong and Japan at 6:00 this evening and everyone wants to know their precise itinerary as we settle down to coffee in a group that contains all of the aforementioned as well as Ofra, Jean, Georgie, Hanna and Ronnie—with Peter and Albert hovering in the background. Fritz spends most of the session in my lap; he doesn't seem to mind it when Bailey joins him here, finding that my legs give him a much better insight into just how far Jean has progressed in the consumption of her own scrambled eggs.

Dan is making plans for a birthday dinner tomorrow night at Tziakos on Marylands Road. There also ensues a complex discussion on the best time to leave town on April 11th, when the group is heading for Southwold for a long weekend in a dog-friendly house belonging to a friend of Dan's. The others want to leave in mid-afternoon, as soon as Dan is off work, but Dan says, that with the start of school holidays on that date, the traffic will be horrendous. The dogs in question are having a riot of a time chasing one another in circles around the table and out onto the green, which means that one of the owners is always getting up to go off in pursuit of a wayward pet. Overhead, as we get up to begin our back passage walkround, two low-flying helicopters are passing over the park. "They must be attending a road traffic accident," Albert concludes. I ask him if he was here when one of these machines actually landed on the green because of an accident on Elgin Avenue. "No," he says, "but I sure would have like to have seen *that*."

Wednesday, March 19:

The sun is making a real effort this morning but there is no chance that it will be able to warm things up on a chilly, breezy day. Between the pitches I pass Denise and Sabina; they have been asking after the article in *Dog Tails* and this morning I have brought copies for them with me. I pass through the precincts of the café, where Ronnie is already unwrapping the carrots. Fritz disdains so early a treat and heads out to the green. I leave the last bag of Dorothy's shoes on Georgie's chair.

To my surprise I see David out on the grass with Summer, the Australian Shepherd Dog. This, two cats, then Skye and Isla, constitute the last of his animal-sitting assignments. He says that he is taking a course in web design and keeping very busy with his photography. Fritz is delighted to see him, but my dog is soon exploring the bushes at the eastern end of the green. Hanna, inspired by David's mention of cats, says that many years ago, when she was walking her Bruno, that the family cat, Sooty, used to follow them all the way around the park, hiding in the bushes. Now a spirited female Bull Terrier comes out to run with Summer; Fritz chases Oscar.

David joins us at coffee this morning, where all of the aforementioned plus Jean and Ofra arrive to celebrate Dan's birthday. The café staff cut up a number of little cakes as an additional treat and we have a jolly time. The Bull Terrier is chained to the fence behind us and here Daisy-Mae plants herself, the tease. We also have the noisy black dog barking away behind us as well. Guy comes by with his Hootch, plus Franca's Bianca and Frank. He has been vacationing in Thailand and has had to endure a power failure forty minutes before the recent play-off between Chelsea and Tottenham, a club that both he and David support. The wind is picking up speed and it seems to be getting colder so, somewhat earlier than usual, we begin a back passage walkround.

Thursday, March 20:

Carrying the garbage with us, Fritz and I head for our usual entrance on a cold gray Thursday morning. As usual, there is an almighty struggle as we near the black bin at the end of Essendine—for my dog is discomfited by these devices and tries to pull in the opposite direction as we near the gaping maw of this useful object. Once we are safely inside the park

Janet comes up behind us with Daisy-Mae and we continue all the way to the top of Mt. Bannister.

As we descend I can see a small knot of dog people gathering at the eastern end of the green (which is having an early mow administered by a chap on a tractor). I would like my dog to join this grouping but he has other ideas and soon he and I are heading toward the Randolph exit. This is always a worrying moment, for I don't want Fritz to exit off-lead. He is distracted momentarily by Arran and then he has to be bribed with a biscuit. Both of David's charges, Summer and Buddy, come rushing up to receive a treat as well.

At breakfast this morning we have Dan, Davide, Hanna, Ofra, Janet, Georgie, and Jean. These people were all present last night for Dan's birthday celebrations, first at the Greek restaurant on Marylands Road, then at Dan and Davide's—where Dan has a new karaoke set-up that rates the performance of each participant. (I would have turned out for these gatherings too, but I had been out of the house for five hours yesterday and I couldn't abandon Fritz a second time.) Some leftover cheesecake is produced and this goes well with our coffee. Peter and Albert are hovering in the background and Angie soon arrives with Trouble; she too gets a piece of cake. When it is time for us to depart I accompany the Scottish sisters past the huge presence of Bo the Rottweiler and as far as the Nosh store on Castelaine Parade—so that I can hand Fritz over to Georgie while I dart inside to buy the *Radio Times*.

Friday, March 21:

After a wild night, one that had Daisy-Mae barking at the wind, we enter the park on a sunny but frigid morning. The aforementioned Shih-Tzu is a member of a party that also includes Billy and Sparkie and together we make our way toward the cypress trees. It is Good Friday and there are no school groups about; indeed, the park seems a bit empty this morning. The chill winds must have something to do with this as well. Ironically, it is the first day of Spring.

Fritz is the first to reach the café but I get him turned around since there is no one on the green, and we head up the hill with the rest of the dogs. At the top I encounter Richard with Fritz II, the Standard Schnauzer who is enjoying himself amid the daffodils and grape hyacinths that grow on the hilltop. While I am chatting with Richard my own Fritz disappears but he has rejoined the party by the time we begin our descent. A dark Alsatian, Tyson, has come up to check out our dogs and all of these animals end up in the bushes above the tennis courts.

When we reach the café there is only Tara the Ridgeback in residence, though I do note that Albert must be in the loo since Tara's owner has Saffy and Tinkerbelle in tow. Our own table is empty; no Ronnie to hold our place, and no need for anyone to do so today—only these mad dog owners would brave hypothermia on such a morning. Janet announces that she is wearing a "care in the community" ski hat as well; asked where she got it, I suggest that the social worker must have brought it. Janet has to get up several times because Daisy-Mae keeps wandering off to the green; the little madam has been playing with two Border Terriers who, it would appear, somebody has erroneously died orange.

We would just about have survived our session in the cold were it not for the late arrivals, first Hanna, then Ofra (fresh from a night at Bungalow 57), finally Dan. The latter arrives at about 10:00 and this means that, in order not to disappear immediately, the rest of us, not wishing to be considered rude, have to wait for all the latecomers to finish *their* drinks before we can thaw out. Poor Fritz is shivering in my lap (none of us have thought to put coats on our dogs today), whining whenever any strange dogs make an appearance at our feet. Finally I announce that I have to make a move and this is the signal for a mass exodus. We have been sitting in the icebox for forty-five minutes and I have to spend the first few moments after our return under the covers.

Saturday, March 22:

The same covers referred to above are hiding Fritz, who has buried himself deep in the bed this morning; unfortunately I don't know this and *sit* on the poor chap while I am pulling on my long underwear. Obviously we are still in the grips of an icy spell in the weather and memories of yesterday afternoon are not very far behind us. No sooner had Fritz and I returned from a visit to the doggy pen then the heavens darkened, the lightning began to flash, thunder shook the house, hail hit the windowpanes, and my dog disappeared under the bed. Fortunately he emerged in time for his puppy supper and I had prepared an extra comfort-sausage for him as well. Now I have dressed him in a blue coat that Hanna has passed on—and we head into the morning's gale.

There is moisture lashing away at us but some of the sleet contains a bit of white thrown in for good measure. Coming up behind us almost immediately are Georgie and Jean. Janet is also waiting for us at the beginning of the cypress trees. She is wearing a tufted bobble hat today, as is Jean, but I suggest that we'd all be classified as "care in the community" types if anybody could see us out for a stroll in this weather. Dan is now waiting for us between the playing fields, Winnie in tow. The others make it no farther than the café overhang but Fritz continues on for a while along the margins of the green before he too can be redirected. I meet a departing Cheryl in the coffee queue while snow flurries eddy outside. She says that she was in a gondola of the London Eye when the storm hit yesterday afternoon; she had quite a view for quite a while as they froze the service—with already boarded passengers left dangling in mid-air.

Franca is here with quite an assemblage this morning—no Valentina, but two little black boys, her own nephew, Bianca and Frank. The latter (hairless) has to be kept moving since he is shivering so. Another little boy arrives with a long-haired Jack Russell named Trixie. At our table we have the aforementioned ladies plus Ronnie and Dan. I suggest that we need to have a pact this morning since our desire to be nice to latecomers yesterday meant that we had to endure forty-five minutes in this cold and so latecomers today can drink their coffee alone. Sure enough Hanna and Ofra soon arrive; at least no one orders a big meal today. Ofra is carrying a hot water bottle. Georgie places a sorry-for-himself Sparkie in her lap; Daisy-Mare has been pulling on his jumper with her teeth.

There is some discussion of which bobble hat outranks the other, since both Janet and Jean are sporting intricate versions of the Peruvian peasant look. Janet's tuft is much grander but she has only two dangling bobbles to Jean's four. Ronnie says that Jean seems to have two pairs of testicles hanging from her head. Dan waspishly adds, "Well there's a first time for everything." However he doesn't escape a good kidding himself. I suggest that his fur-lined tweed pilot's cap can be classified as a care in the community chapeau as well—as long as the community is Mayfair. One of the others tells him that there is a new nickname for his intemperate pet: Win-Laden.

Sunday, March 23:

When I part the curtains on a grey Easter morning I can see that Fritz and I will be making our morning entry into Paddington Rec under the cover of a light snowfall. Snow has, indeed, settled on many of the artificial playing surfaces, but the walkways are still clear—though there is not much activity thereupon. We pass Denise, out with Rizzo, several times—the first encounter taking place in the fenced defile between the playing fields; the footy-obsessed lads have used a trash bin to climb into the locked central field, scattering all the trash, including piles of wrapped dog poo, all over the walkway—and breaking the rim of the bin in the process.

Denise remarks that there is no one about but I can hear the distant rattle of Sparkie's hysterical barking. When we reach the green I discover Dan with Win-Laden, sheltering under the little metal gazebo and chatting with Gerry, whose Humphrey is wearing a green hooded raincoat. Fritz takes off on one of his solitary rambles and I have to follow at some distance. We pass the tennis courts, which are unplayable this morning because of all the snow. Eventually Fritz spots Jean, Janet and Georgie on top of Mt. Bannister and rushes up to greet his pals. When they descend it is time to head in for coffee; we are the only customers, inside or out.

Ronnie, wearing a flat cap, is already seated and Ofra and Hanna soon arrive. Hanna is a bit cross because she has missed the 7:00 start of the Malaysian Grand Prix but she has managed to make two snowballs with which to pelt Jean and Ofra at close quarters. While we are seated a major snow shower begins and the wind blows the huge flakes all over our table—with the newly arrived coffees each getting a sprinkling of the white stuff. Dan tells us that he has had a dream in which he and Gordon Ramsey have not only fallen in love but have had to break the news to Mrs. Ramsey—who was not best pleased. David the dog sitter comes by with Summer and joins us for a back passage walkround. Fortunately I have forgotten to turn the heat off before leaving the house and it is so nice and toasty when we return from our morning adventures.

Monday, March 24:

There are still bits of white floating through the air as Fritz and I make our entry into the park. They melt as soon as they collide with any object, walkway, grass or nose, but it is gray and chilly nonetheless. Coming in behind us we have Georgie and Jean with their dogs; I am anxious to get Fritz moving in the opposite direction because looming over the fence of the doggy area is a curious Harry. When we are all pointed in the right direction we have Janet coming toward us from the cypress trees with Daisy-Mae and Dan coming up behind us with Winnie. There are lots of little footie boys at play on the pitches this morning; their older brothers, on bikes, pretend to be scared of our dogs.

The latter turn left on the Carlton walkway and ascend Mt. Bannister, where they meet up with Corky, Holly and Foxy. On the other side I meet up with Bob, who has brought Skye and Isla with him, He says that he and Kate have just returned from a skiing holiday in Bulgaria (Kate again poorly) and that they are continuing the excitement with a day in Essex. Fritz is lofted for a cuddle by his Aunt Hanna—who is delighting in the fact that two Finns have earned podium places at the Malaysian Grand Prix. My dog then begins one of his worrying rambles along the Randolph walkway but I get him turned around when it is time to head in for coffee.

Our group, which also includes Ofra, is a second sitting, in fact, of the personnel at a party at Janet's the previous afternoon—and the dogs are still enjoying a sack of leftovers that she has brought with her. Hanna teases Fritz with the whistle that has fallen out of one of the many squeaky toys he played with at the party. Dan also wants to pursue a serious topic that was first introduced at the gathering yesterday: if we died and no one was there to discover our bodies, would our dogs eat us? Georgie says that Sparkie would never eat her. Jean says that Billy would *not*, but Mozart *would*. Dan says that Winnie is not above sampling a finger when he is not even dead, just asleep. The next question is, what part of the body would they eat first? "Whatever part we last buttered," is my suggestion.

Janet has brought a leftover cheesecake with her and pieces are passed around. Hovering atop a brick pillar (in the warmth of an electric light) is Robin, and Hanna makes certain that a plate of cheesecake crumbs is placed atop the low wall for the little fellow to feast on. After we have been in the cold for half an hour Ronnie toddles in with Rosie, but I offer him my seat. I have to get home to prepare for a visit from Pepper.

Tuesday, March 25:

The sun seems to be shining brightly—which will explain why I haven't bothered with a coat for Fritz—but almost as soon as we enter the park I begin to regret this decision. Temperatures begin to drop almost immediately and the sun becomes less than constant. The park is quiet at this hour and Fritz has only a solo journey to make over the walkways, at least until we reach the top of Mt. Bannister—where we can see Dan and Winnie descending the other side.

Fritz takes off at this point, trying to catch up, and he is rewarded with a treat from Dan when he arrives. Out on the green we can see a dog who appears to be a miniature version of Hootch. Just at this moment Guy arrives with the giant Rottweiler-Alsatian cross, his mouth agape at the same discovery. The newcomer, only five months old, is Toppler. It looks like Hootch has had a puppy but, when the little fellow tries to make off with his senior's tennis ball, there are words.

At coffee this morning we have Ronnie, Dan, Georgie, Jean, Hanna, Ofra and Cheryl. The dogs are unable to keep still and on several occasions either Georgie or Jean has to get up and go off in search of Daisy-Mae, Billy or Sparkie. We decide that it's the dog borstal for Sparkie, who has even gone up to the top of the hill on his own. Georgie can't find her gloves because Jean is sitting on them. Soon that Scottish lady also has a shivering Fritz in her lap. Indeed we are all shivering and our departure is almost fifteen minutes earlier than usual. Dan notices that the park has new eco-friendly lanterns atop the lighting poles—very retro.

Wednesday, March 26:

Temperatures have moderated since yesterday and the only reason that Fritz has his coat on is that it is spitting a bit as we enter the park. Sabina is heading toward us with Scamp and Oscar, very excited by the presence in the park of Ziggy, the *Big Brother* luminary. Just at this moment Miro and Vito are passing and I tell Sabina that we can thank Reina for Ziggy's celebrity, since she works for Endemol, *Big Brother*'s production company. My problem is that I don't know what Ziggy looks like—and I have to rely on others to inform me of sightings.

Fritz and I reach the Cartlon roadway and I am about to turn right when there is almost an accident. One of the many vans that speed through our park during all this construction is about to turn off the Randolph roadway into the one on which we are standing (blind corner when it comes to toddlers and dogs) and there is a great shout of protest at its driver because a mid-sized blonde dog is running straight for this corner as well. Breaks applied, there is no tragedy and we continue forward to the walkway in front of the clubhouse, where Dan is talking to Peter. Dan has also witnessed the recent incident and tells me (too late to do any good) that the protesting dog owner is the aforementioned Ziggy. I ask Dan if he said anything to the TV personality and he admits that he is a bit embarrassed to do so since, in another recent outbreak of road rage, he has yelled at Ziggy over the way he has parked his car.

I have a lot of trouble turning Fritz around—he has to check out Noodle while Lynne Franks (this is our day for realty TV stars) is intent on her mobile phone. Dan has been waiting for the Scottish ladies, who will have the care of Winnie today, but they are late and Hanna ends up with the Pug—or I do for, as Hanna goes in to order our coffees, Winnie jumps up in my lap and moans unhappily since there is not a scrap of food about. Eventually Jean and Georgie arrive and we are soon joined by Nicholas, Ofra, Peter and Kate. Bob, dressed in his office best, has gone off to work wearing an elegant black overcoat. "Doesn't he scrub up nice," I say. "Yes," Kate replies, "but his coat is covered in Skye's dog hairs. I have told him that if he cheats on me it has to be with a blonde."

Kate agrees that one week in Bulgaria was quite enough; she has now been on two skiing holidays and not skied once. ("Maybe it's snow you are allergic to," I suggest.) Her son has started his fund-raising Arctic adventure this week and Isla has welcomed her mom home by chewing on all of the fat-busting pills and a nose atomizer. (She can get away with any naughtiness, however, for she can do no wrong in Kate's eyes.) It takes forever to get Fritz moving homeward; this is at last accomplished but soon I have to return through the park with Hanna—as we are off to Kilburn to buy shoes.

Thursday, March 27:

We have a lovely sunny morning in the park as Fritz and I make our usual entry. There are no other dogs about but a chap with a very ancient specimen is soon trailing in behind us. Fritz will not move until he has had a sniff; the other owner, observing this scene, says, "Dogs are such strange creatures." At least my version of the species has not spotted the bread, which someone has scattered on the grass for the birds, and we are able to make our way forward without further incident until we reach the Carlton walkway. Here Boyd, his heart breaking as it must for park-keepers everywhere, says to a pissing Fritz, "No, not on the bushes; that's what kills them!"

Cheryl and Ronnie are already seated outside the café, ten minutes early. After a few minutes on the green, where there is a good turnout because of the handsome weather, I return briefly to the café to anchor my dog to Ronnie's chair while I disappear for a few minutes. My mission is to walk over to the Randolph surgery and make an appointment (for next Monday) on behalf of my sore right knee. When I return to the café I make sure that Hanna is sitting on my right so that she can, as she did yesterday, apply some reflexology moves to my right hand: my knee did feel a bit better after yesterday's treatment.

At breakfast today we have Hanna, Georgie, Jean, Ofra, Dan, Cheryl, Ronnie, Peter, and John. Ofra has brought a hairbrush with her and Bailey gets a tableside grooming; then Sparkie is smartened up and Winnie gets a lick as well. Dan says that he and Jean have had another karaoke sing-off and that he has again triumphed. Peter, hearing that a female pilot has landed the first plane at the new Heathrow terminal five, says he wouldn't want to be on any plane piloted by a woman—"Have you seen the way they park their cars?" This brings an angry reaction from an injured reflexologist.

Meanwhile a loose Staffie with a pink lead and a huge chain collar has suddenly appeared beneath our table and almost turned it over thrashing about in play with the other dogs. Another interloper is a Bull Terrier puppy named Geisha, who is soon attached to the fencing behind us while her owner gets his coffee. When it is time for us to begin our back passage walkround Sparkie, Billy and Daisy-Mae discover than someone has left the gate to the newest pitch open and they enter this empty space for some wild circles before we can get them moving in the right direction again. The sun has gone in and the temperature has dropped by several degrees.

Friday, March 28:

I can see that it is spitting a bit as we make our preparations for departure this morning, and so I wrestle his coat onto Fritz. What I have

286

not anticipated is just how cold it is outside; almost immediately I am regretting that I have worn my baseball cap instead of my woolly chapeau. The park is rather quiet this morning—just brave dog walkers and their pets. We encounter Sabina with Oscar and Scamp on several occasions as Fritz seems to want to join their party. We follow them up the hill, down the other side, along the Randolph walkway to the tennis courts and back to the green.

Here Fritz pushes ahead, reaching the precincts of the bandstand where I notice that he has discovered a pile of ketchup-soaked chips abandoned on the ground yesterday by one of the scholars from the local college. As I rush after my dog, hoping to prevent any further ingestion of this fast food, I slip on the greasy paving stones that surround the bandstand and give my back a considerable wrench. My knee, at least, seems to have survived this slide without further damage. At any rate I am able to catch up with the chip-inhaling Schnauzer and get his lead reattached. To this point I have not seen any of the gang but as I near the café I meet up with Hanna and I can see, much later than usual, Jean, Georgie, and Dan descending Mt. Bannister with their dogs.

We five are on our own on this frigid morning, Jean's last visit to the park before her return to Glasgow later in the day. (The cousins, Sparkie and Billy, celebrate this departure by having a furious quarrel on the subject of whose ball is this anyway beneath our table.) Most of the conversation this morning is a remembrance of things past, with Dan (Winnie peeking her head out of his protective jacket) telling the story of the day he skipped school by hiding in a rug in the rafters of his dad's garage, and Jean and Georgie reminiscing about all those times they were strapped for coming late to school. Georgie then remembers the day her niece put her auntie's false teeth into her own mouth and got them stuck there—with everyone else in a state of panic over the discomfiture of the permanently grinning scamp. We begin a back passage walkround with a lot of synchronized pooing. Jean gets to celebrate her last day in the park by mopping up three piles with one bag.

Saturday, March 29:

The sun seems to be shining brightly so Fritz and I head for the park in our spring outfits (no coat for the dog; a baseball cap on my head). Georgie is coming up behind us and so are Bob and Kate with their dogs. Janet, as she often does, comes out to greet us from the cypress trees and together we head for the café. On the Randolph walkway we encounter a lively charcoal-colored Schnauzer named Zig-Zag. I point out to Bob that in front of us we are witnessing a scene not encountered in some months, a green without any fencing. To celebrate we near the long-forbidden cricket crease and then Fritz begins a grand circle of the green in reverse. The Saturday morning obedience class is also gathering on the greensward. Yellow balloons, celebrating an open day at the gym, are flying from trees and bushes.

I hand Fritz over to Janet while I join Georgie in the queue; I can see that my dog has taken advantage of Janet's good nature and has hopped aboard her lap while I am away. For quite a while we three are the only customers at our outdoor table and this seems a surprise since it is a pleasant Saturday morning, but eventually we are joined by Dan, Hanna, Ofra and her Ricky, Nicholas, even the Israeli chap who owns Lachan (and whose name not even Ofra remembers). Daisy-Mae, seeing Fritz in her mommy's lap (and a panini aloft as well) jumps into the lap as well, inserting herself between Fritz and Janet. This looks adorable; then Fritz, fighting for room, sits on the Shih-Tzu, who eventually gives up and pursues Winnie—whose tail she likes to grab in her teeth. For her part, the disgruntled Pug wanders over to tease an embarrassed looking elderly Lab who has been chained to the fence.

Ofra has been driven to the park today because she has been busted for driving without a proper British license. The others tease her mercilessly, suggesting all forms of burdensome community service and or interesting episodes behind bars—in which she would obviously become the queen of all proceedings. That lady is outraged to discover that Dan has attended the opening night of the Gay and Lesbian Film Festival without her, even partying in the after-premiere presence of the stars of *Love And Other Disasters*, Gwyeth Paltrow, Orlando Bloom and Katherine Tate. Then, as skies darken and temperatures drop, he has to go home to clean the house in anticipation of the lunchtime arrival of his mom.

Sunday, March 30:

Rain has just cleared as Fritz and I make our way into the park on the first day of British Summer Time. I never know what to expect on such a day, for more than once some of our dog owners have not remembered to change their clocks properly and are, hence, a long way from achieving our usual meetings time. I am surprised, therefore, to see that some of my pals are indeed circling the green shortly after 9:30. Fritz has spotted them as well and heads off along the stockade fence in front of the clubhouse, hoping for a rendezvous with Dan, Georgie, Janet and, returned from her holiday in Hong Kong and Japan, Liz.

I think we are about to head in for coffee but my dog has other ideas, for he bypasses the café entrance as the others head in, choosing instead to ramble down the Carlton roadway. Okay, I can see he has to do a second poo, but, this task completed and tidied out of existence, he persists in heading in the wrong direction, climbing up Mt. Bannister to touch noses with Charlie the Giant Poodle and continuing over the top of this eminence as though he were on a mission. I struggle up after him, hooking him at last after our descent and handing him over to Janet while I go inside to order my cappuccino at the café. Here, again to my surprise, I encounter Ofra, who usually manages to miss most clock changes. Perhaps she has had some assistance in this matter because she has again arrived with the assistance of chauffeur Ricky.

Liz gives us a thorough debriefing on her holiday and turns over to me several English language newspapers picked up in the Orient. Japan, she says, was immensely expensive (she had to veto the Kobe Beef order of one kid since the price tag was $200), but on the whole everyone had a good time until they flew back into the chaos of Heathrow's just opened terminal five where, after waiting for four hours for their luggage, they had to go home without it. Here they discovered a new slimmed down Roxy, walked for three hours a day in their absence, and looking very fit, very fit, that is, until, the Beagle discovered that the boys and their pals had secreted a box of doughnuts in the upstairs bathtub, whereupon she had to eat nine of them. As this tale is being told to us Roxy, sensing the need for a better balanced diet, leaps up and snatches a slice of tomato out of Liz's panini. All the dogs, for that matter, are making pests of themselves in their relentless search for treats and Davide has to stand up to eat his sandwich out of the reach of snapping teeth.

Monday, March 31:

It is rather gray this morning, but not too chilly at least, and Fritz and I make a timely entrance into the park. Almost immediately we encounter

David the dog sitter strolling along with Skye the Cairn and Nix with her Billy. As soon as Fritz realizes that his old pal is present he goes into transports of joy, emotions that David has to quell gently in the services of his pristine gray trousers. The same kind of joyful reunion takes place a minute later when Dan kneels to give Fritz a cuddle in front of the loos. Electrical engineers are at work at this spot and they are blasting hip-hop over the sacred precincts of the green.

Fritz continues along the Randolph walkway but I point out to him that Hanna is entering from our right and he rushes off for another rapturous greeting. Then he gets interested in Tarquin the King Charles, who is supposed to be exiting at the Randolph gate. I don't have any trouble getting my dog to turn around this morning for a gent is just entering with little tan Coco and Pip the Jack Russell and both Fritz and Tarquin (ignoring the entreaties of his mom) follow these dogs back toward the green. Exiting from the little enclosed garden is a dad pushing a baby in a stroller, a little girl (also pushing her dolly's stroller) and a black dog named Mowgli. All five dogs begin a sniffathon while the dad explains that this is why his family won't kiss Mowgli on the nose.

Dan, Davide, Hanna, Nicholas and Georgie have turned out for coffee this morning. Nicholas has brought some redundant knitting needles and wool for Hanna and Dan claims that he can make pom-poms—and that this is an extremely intricate task that few can master. Not having seen Ronnie is some time Dan now dials our pal on his mobile phone. Unfortunately, this is answered by Ronnie in St. Mary's where an MS episode has hospitalized our friend for several days. Davide, meanwhile, is fuming because the council have warned him that there is a heavy fine coming his way if he doesn't remove his satellite dish from the front elevation. Georgie has to abandon her scrambled eggs on toast because Sparkie, once again, has gone wandering. I pass around an announcement, dropped through my letter box by the ever-efficient Jan Prendergast, to the effect that on Wednesday there will be a major pre-Olympic road show in the park—with music, story telling, archery and other activities that our civic bureaucrats have thought to keep a secret from the actual neighbors of Paddington Rec, who, so far, have not heard a word of this. "They're bringing in their own people," Hanna concludes, "they don't want us to know."

April, 2008

Tuesday, April 1:

Rain has just cleared the region as Fritz and I make our first April visit to the park. Skies are brightening and temperatures are moderate enough but perhaps the early inclemency has discouraged people from coming to this place because the Rec has a kind of Mary Celeste feel to it—Fritz and I do not encounter a single soul until we reach the café, where Liz and Georgie are already taking their places. I return the Mandarin Oriental Hotel cloth bag that Liz had used to turn over to me the Asian newspapers, and then we continue on to the green.

I can see that Ofra is making her way down from the hilltop on my left; she has walked to the park this morning since she has become, perforce, a non-driver these days. Georgie, remembering Davide's difficulties with the council over his satellite dish, wants to make a "Free the Paddington Two" sign. Hanna is also at coffee this morning but we five are the only outdoor customers.

The dogs make a real nuisance of themselves, using their wet paws to climb onto our knees in search of treats. When they are not doing this they are off in search of sustenance around the corner near the café's bins. Liz and Georgie frequently rise in order to see what the animals are up to now.

Liz is in despair over the behavior of her Beagle, who is food-obsessed. In her Bermuda youth this naughty lady applied all her energies to escape, disappearing so many times that Liz spent a thousand dollars having a fence installed, only to see her dog dig a hole under it and escape again. Now, every time she comes in from the outside, Roxy rushes upstairs and canvasses every room searching for any leftovers that might have fallen through the cracks. Hanna says that Liz needs a kiddy gate to prevent access to certain rooms, but Liz says she *has* one and, if deployed, Roxy just howls down the house in protest. Hanna then suggests that Liz needs to keep a water pistol at the ready in order to squirt her dog when she is naughty. "I can't live like that," Liz says, "if I have to squirt my dog like that in my own house then I'd have to find her a home in the country." Georgie says that she tried the water pistol on her mischievous Sparkie, who *liked* being squirted so much that he made a game of biting the water stream.

Wednesday, April 2:

I have not placed the raincoat on my dog, even though it is spitting a bit as we enter the park on a gray Wednesday morning. Almost immediately we encounter Georgie with Sparkie and Daisy-Mae; these two animals admit themselves to the empty five-a-side pitch for a few joyous circles. Georgie says that, in response to a relentless canine scolding, Boyd has pretended to chase Sparkie this morning—and the little Yorkie has rushed from the scene, the tail between his legs. Now our group climbs to the top of Mt. Bannister and down the other side.

Here I can see David with Skye the Cairn and Saskia with Buddy. The latter is still under treatment for his ear problems and so I don't require him to shake paws when he gets his usual biscuit. Around us there are a number of tents and other structures housing the attractions that go with the pre-Olympic roadshow. (Hanna says that Leith Mansions did receive flyers on the subject of this event, but I know that other nearby mansion blocks did *not*.) In the background Harry the Akita is hovering and Fritz is a bit reluctant to take his place at our usual table but I leave him with Georgie while I go into the men's loo to wash my hands. For the first time in living memory the hot air hand dryers work! I feel like washing my hands a second time.

At breakfast this morning we have Georgie, Hanna (off to Finland tomorrow), Dan (enjoying a day off), Ofra and her half-term son Guy. Guy eats a plate of scrambled eggs on toast, with Bailey hovering over his shoulder. Winnie decides that she wants that seat and the two dogs have a furious exchange over who gets to stare at the food first. Hanna says that she has visited Ronnie in hospital and that he is doing better. Dan reports that Christiann has had a little girl and Georgie says that Celine (of Celine, Christopher and Ziggy fame) may have given birth by now as well—we haven't seen any of them in quite a while. Finally, as we get up to begin our back passage walkround, we see Peter walking along the Carlton roadway with Ellen, making her first venture outside (helped along by a cane) since her bypass operation. It is still spitting (Harry has had to be moved since he doesn't like the rain, evidently) and the park certainly doesn't seem to have much activity—unless you count the teenaged girls in black and yellow who are at the head of the track and trying to put the shot more than five feet.

Thursday, April 3:

The sun is making a real effort today as Fritz and I head for the park. We don't have many distractions as we head for the café, passing only Sabina (on her mobile phone), Scamp and Oscar. There are a lot of vans about and it is somewhat tricky getting the dog through the hazards provided by these interlopers. Out on the green we have David, still with Skye the Cairn, Saskia with Buddy, and Rufus with both of his parents (Oksana is evidently pregnant as well). Fritz lingers only for a little while and then he is off on his usual Randolph walkway ramble. When we return five minutes later I find Dan in an intense mobile phone conversation of his own—in this case with the TV antenna men who are at his house, wrestling with the windblown aerial and pondering the problem of repositioning Davide's dish.

Dan has to go off and attend to these chaps soon after a quick cup of coffee and so we have only the small grouping of Georgie, Ofra and Guy. Elian chooses this morning to reward our dogs with the gratis treat of a plate of sausages. They are shared out, even though we know he really has a soft spot only for Winnie—who has been turned over to Georgie for the rest of the day. Tanya comes by with a sleeping Lucca and the Weimaraner Pasha. We haven't seen her in a while, perhaps because the family has been on holiday in Dubai. This venture seems to have been a great success, with much to occupy children, furious construction for the adults to watch, Russians as the principal visitors and Indians as the bulk of the work force. As I dislike hot weather, beach holidays and shopping I shall probably give the place a miss.

We get up to begin our back passage walkround, but not before Spikey arrives to touch noses with our dogs. Georgie now has Daisy-Mae, Winnie and her own Sparkie, so her progress is slowed, especially because one of these animals is always playing tug of war with his or her lead or leaving a treasured ball behind. On a park bench at the head of the track we pass Peter (of Peter and Gypsy) who has brought five dogs to the park with him today, including Jody. The black and yellow-clad lady shot-putters are still at their labors, though how this counts as exercise I couldn't tell you—since we have a dozen kids sitting around watching *one* of their number shuffle about before plopping down the famous object only a few feet in front of her own toes.

Friday, April 4:

We have a lovely Spring morning today and I don't mind it that Fritz dawdles among the grass shoots at the head of the running track. We are approached by Christian and Reina, who get Miro and Vito to jump onto a park bench so that they can be hooked prior to their departure. Christian asks me if I am looking forward to the weekend and I have to answer that since retirement there isn't actually much difference for me in the days of the week. Fritz and I continue on to the green, where I spot a knot of dog people at the eastern end. Here we have David with Skye and Nix with Billy but my dog does not linger for long and I have to follow him along the Randolph walkway. Dan is turning Winnie over to Georgie; he has formally recognized the change in season by sporting shorts today; I have recognized it in the presence of ants in my kitchen sink.

The Nila truck has missed its usual delivery port and is blocking the entry to the café as we return (I notice that they have changed their slogan from "Crackers!" to "Cheesy?"). Our numbers are very much reduced today with Hanna in Finland and Ronnie in hospital—just Georgie, Ofra and Nicholas. Georgie has three dogs with her again and Daisy-Mae teases me by jumping into every empty chair that I approach. Sabina comes by with Oscar and Scamp but when she goes into the café Scamp becomes very anxious about her whereabouts and starts the back passage walkround in a panic. Winnie, Sparkie, Bailey, Monty and Fritz profit from Georgie's sausage sandwich.

Nicholas is pondering the order of priorities in the life of newlyweds. The couple wants a baby, a new house, Edwina wants to resume her career, should they have an *au pair* or a live-in nanny? Ofra has a lot of advice, much of it involving the superiority (in service and expense) of Philippine maids and I have to remind her that we are surrounded by such ladies as we drink our coffee. Nicholas, meanwhile, had sold his flat and is moving into his wife's flat nearby. The subject of moving leads naturally to one of those sad subtractions that always arises in the

ever-changing personal landscape of the Paddington Rec dog crowd:
Georgie says that Faz and Dianah have moved to Walton-on-Thames and
that we are unlikely to see them or the Shih-Tzu Jasmine again.

Saturday, April 5:

A short shower has cleared away an hour or so before it is time for
us to resume our place on the walkways of Paddington Rec. Ahead of us
I can see Janet and Georgie but Fritz makes such slow going of it that
there is no chance of catching up. Instead he gets to growl at every other
dog encountered, beginning with a sharp-faced tan dog named Rocca,
who enters with a hockey ball in his mouth (it soon gets forgotten in
a flower bed). By the time we have reached the green we can see the
aforementioned ladies coming down from the top of Mt. Bannister. Two
Shar-Peis are bouncing around among our dogs but they seem friendly
enough; Fritz gets to growl at them too.

At breakfast we have Janet, Georgie, Dan, Ofra, Rickey, Liz, Kate and
Bob. Dan says that he has had a dream about the forthcoming wedding
of the latter two, one which took place in the Houses of Parliament and
Westminster Abbey, and that in the dream Bob wore a tan kilt and that
the cast of the *Vicar of Dibley* and several zombies were among the guests.
Peter (of Peter and Holly) comes by to complain that a café customer,
hearing a dog owner order a sausage for her dog, has declared that he is
not going to order food from any establishment that also serves *dogs*. Even
though our lot has long since ceased putting in such orders this news
elicits the expected outrage. Whether dogs are invited guests at tonight's
party at Liz's house in St. Johns Wood is the next topic of conversation.
Liz is quite agreeable but after Kate and Bob leave there is some worried
afterthoughts about the effects of Skye's tail on vulnerable wine glasses
and Isla's penchant for household naughtiness.

At 7:15 that evening, therefore, Fritz and I wait outside for a ride to
Liz's party in Janet's Fiat Panda. Fritz is beside himself with excitement,
climbing up onto the back seat with Daisy-Mae and exploring every
inch of Liz's house soon thereafter. The guest list also includes Ofra and
Rickey (with Bailey), Dan, Davide, Winnie (and a visiting Sardinian
dentist named Gianni), and Kate and Bob (no dogs after all). Roxy is a
very benign and laid-back hostess, even falling asleep in her bed while
the others continue to race about. Once Fritz gives us all a scare by

running out to the street when the door is opened for a new guest, but on the whole he seems to enjoy himself and he behaves well. The food, supplemented by goodies from Liz's Italian restaurant, is excellent and plentiful. Dan has tracked down a copy of *Best in Show* and the others start to watch this after I walk home with my dog at about 10:45—but they can't stop chattering and never finish the film.

Sunday, April 6:

All week long they have been talking about a return to winter on the weekend and, sure enough, a glance out of the window this morning reveals that much snow has fallen; indeed, large wet flakes are still descending. This means that special preparations have to be made (coat for Fritz, long underwear and hiking boots for me) before we can venture forth this morning. Fritz has been in snow before but there is quite a bit on the ground this morning and I am anxious to see how he takes it. He loves it—rushing at steady speed over the surface, his nose acting like a snowplow. We catch up with Janet and Georgie (who missed last night's festivities with a cold) just as Sparkie and Daisy-Mae are beginning to battle over an empty plastic bottle in the snow-choked five-a-side pitch.

Fritz actually joins them for a bit in this forbidden site but soon enough we get them all moving to the top of the hill.

The view is like a Currier and Ives print. Every tree has a lacey tracery of snow clinging to bare branches and below us we can see small groups at work on snowmen. (I don't quite approve of the little girl who breaks off a tree branch to make an arm for her version.) When we get to the bottom we can see a small but familiar group out in the middle of the green (which is white today, not green) including Saskia, Kate and Bob. Some of the dogs are encrusted in white frozen pompoms, Daisy-Mae and Fritz among them, but no one has more snowy adhesions than the all-black Isla. Buddy approaches me for a handout and I try to put him off (not wanting to remove my gloves) but I know that his limpid eyes will haunt me for the rest of the day if I don't produce the desired biscuit.

Dan and Ofra join us at table this morning, a brave group and their shivering dogs waiting for their coffee. It is not possible to strip the legs of our dogs free of the encrusting snowballs, the ice just becomes more compacted as we try, and so it is agreed that we will not dawdle this morning. Fritz, given the option of a snow-free footpath, nevertheless returns to the snow this morning and his feet are covered in more pom-poms by the time we get home. I have a solution that works well—a trip to the bathtub where the warm water from the shower spray attachment immediately melts the offending matter. A vigorous application of his warm orange towel and the crisis is over.

Monday, April 7:

The snows of yesterday have long since disappeared, except for an isolated lump or two, but temperatures are still depressed as Fritz and I head for the park on a mostly gray morning. Almost immediately we encounter Lisa with Zara and Dash and David the dogsitter with Yoyo. The latter, her coat more gray than black, takes jealous exception to Fritz's insistence on a cuddle from David and there are angry words. "It's nice to be loved," I tell David.

There now begins an extensive period of Schnauzer naughtiness. First Fritz seems reluctant to head in the right direction and only turns around when a Phoenix-like dog stops for a sniff. Then my dog admits himself to the running track (a fence panel is still missing) and I get him turned around here only when a woman in a burkha comes plodding by and he decides to follow her. Then, when we get to the five-a-side-pitch, perhaps remembering yesterday's adventures in the snow, he enters this forbidden area, where a chap on a tractor is spreading rubber pellets. I get him to exit from another open gate. We cross the green, where Dan is just taking Winnie off and Andrew (the acceptable face of Akitadom) is inching along with Linda the dog walker.

We join David with Yoyo again but Fritz manages to exit the Grantully gate and then to join his cousin in snaffling down some bread left for the birds. As we round the green and reach the Randolph walkway my dog heads for this exit too. I can see out of the corner of my eye that another cousin, Gus, is waiting for an opportunity to slip by while Fritz isn't looking. Eventually he does so at great speed, Fritz managing only a disapproving growl when he spots Gus rushing by. Noses are touched with Tay, the long-haired Jack Russell with the half-white, half-black face, and then it is time to go in for coffee.

To my surprise only Cheryl, just back from Athens, is sitting at our table. Ofra and Georgie soon arrive as well and Peter sits down with Holly, Jack and Sandy. There is much discussion of yesterday's snowfall.

Peter says he was amazed at how rapidly the snow melted from his car, taking this as yet another symbol of global warming. "Everything is blamed these days either on global warming or George Bush," Cheryl says petulantly. "There *is* a connection between the two," I reply. Ginger, on anti-inflammatories and painkillers, is pretty well spaced out but Lola, Daisy-Mae and Sparkie are soon scrapping with one another and Fritz has let out an almighty bellow at the sudden appearance of Humphrey. It's time to make a move.

Tuesday, April 8:

A lovely spring morning greets us as we hit the streets this morning; the grass is green, the birds are singing and Dan is having a furious text row with Davide as we enter the park. Nevertheless we follow him and Winnie as they make slow progress along the walkways and up to the top of the hill, where a park keeper on a tractor is mowing the greensward. Down below us we can see Georgie with Daisy-Mae off to one side and a larger group containing Saskia with Buddy in the middle. A Frenchman is having a meltdown over the recent performance of Arsenal as he leads his dog onto the Randolph walkway—while the rest of us head in for coffee.

Saskia announces that she is joining us for a hot chocolate; this morning our table includes Dan, Georgie, Liz, Cheryl, Suzanne and her friend Sue—who has brought with her the King Charles named Sidney and another Phoenix-like medium-sized senior citizen named Milly. Suzanne tells us about her recent trip to Peru and we discuss plans for the alumni reunion at ASL next month. Cheryl sums up her trip to Greece and more plans are made for the weekend's expedition to Southwold. Rebel crashes the party and begins to lick Sunny's bum—with all of the other dogs voicing their disapproval.

Saskia's cell phone rings and she has to rush home to let in the builders. She has left us all something to ponder, a story she picked up from her mother, one set in Spain where the son of a friend has a girlfriend who is also a pet lover. The pet, in this case, was not a dog but a boa constrictor, and the animal just wouldn't eat. The girl took the snake to the vet and he couldn't find anything wrong with the reptile. He asked if there had been any signs of unusual behavior. The girl thought a bit and said there hadn't, though recently she had awakened to discover the snake stretched out vertically on top of her. Hearing this, the vet said, "I think the snake needs to go back in its box *now* and then it has to go *directly* to the zoo." He then explained that what the boa was doing was sizing up its next meal, stretching out to see if it had room to swallow its own owner. Cries of horrified anguish greet Saskia's tale. I tell her that the moral of the story is, "Take this snake to the zoo, and the girlfriend too."

Wednesday, April 9:

Again we have a lovely spring morning in the park and again I am content to let Fritz take as much time as he wants during our first moments. There are a lot of people taking advantage of the sunny weather, though, this being half term, there aren't that many school groups. Eventually Fritz begins to pick up some speed, enough to make me a bit concerned about the arrival of the Nila truck on our left (back in its Crackers! livery) but this vehicle stops at the kitchen gate and Fritz is free to wander along the Carlton runway and out onto the green.

Here he spots Dan walking with Georgie in front of the clubhouse and he is in pursuit before long—Daisy-Mae is chasing Winnie's tail again and I must say Winnie puts up with this indignity with better humor than one might expect. Sparkie is only interested in his ball. I follow this group on a grand circle as Dan, who has been quite anxious of late, brings us up to date on his work situation, where everyone had received a letter threatening redundancies. Three of his colleagues have been dismissed but Dan has survived and even been given a promotion and a rise. It means that he will now be responsible for three box offices but he will be asked to work on a more regular nine to five basis and will move from his own theatre to an office on Neal Street in Covent Garden. He is obviously relieved at much of this but apprehensive as well; working nine to five means no early morning appearances in the park, except on the weekends. I tell him that even if things don't work out the new position will look good on his CV.

When we settle in to our morning coffee is it noted that there is still a very small turnout here, given the improvement in the weather—just the three of us, Peter and Ellen. The latter has to remind the dogs not to jump on her sore leg. Peter says that he was the cause of a traffic accident this morning when a car, which had stopped to let him cross near the Marriott

299

Hotel, was rear-ended by a careless pursuer. He also shares with us the unhappy news that Denise, whom I had seen earlier with her Rizzo and Sabina and her two dogs, actually witnessed the fatal knife attack on a local youngster a few weeks ago, and that she has been in considerable shock ever since. Reflecting on the dark times in which we live we begin our back passage walkround.

Thursday, April 10:

An instant replay, weatherwise. And again Fritz makes slow work of our forward progress. But standing surrounded by flowers (even bluebells) and birdsong is so pleasant that I am content to lean up against the running track fence and let my dog take his time. Likewise, a minute later, I am not at all perturbed when Fritz disappears behind the cypress trees—I just wait while the joggers pound by and when he at last emerges we can round the corner and continue between the playing fields. For some reason this stretch galvanizes my pet at last and he dashes forward without stopping until he has reached the Carlton Roadway. The park is much quieter this morning, but I can see a knot of dog owners out on the green and so here is where we head next.

The owner of Aoibhe (Evie) and her thirteen year-old daughter, I soon discover, are in a state. Their small black cocker has been savaged by, yes, once again, Harry the Akita. The incident took place near the doggy pen next to the parking lot (Harry burrowing under the fence to attack Aoibhe)—with the Akita (not in the care of his owner this morning) again unmuzzled. "At least he doesn't bite other dogs," Franca again says, but she is soon corrected by some of the rest of us. Aoibhe's owner says she is going to report the incident to the front desk while Franca says she will have a word with Harry's owner. Meanwhile baby Valentina, who can now get up to quite some speed on her little legs, is wandering off just like one of our wayward dogs. And so is Fritz, who somehow decides that it would be nice to follow Dan to work this morning.

I have a brief chat with Sabina about Denise's recent discomfiture and when I report for coffee only Georgie is present. She watches Fritz (along with Winnie, Daisy-Mae, and Sparkie) while I go in to order my cappuccino. There is a security guard at the counter and I tell him about the morning's incident. I can't tell if he can understand English; under any circumstances he shows no interest in the matter whatsoever. Outside

Franca, taking pity on the Paddington Two, sits down at our table, sharing out her toast with the dogs and the baby (who manages to chew on the same bread that Frank and Bianca have just had in their mouths). Cheryl comes by with her Pugs (Lola has to be ejected twice from the interior of the café) and Peter sits down with Holly, Jack and Sandy. Franca tells us in great detail about the purchase of a used car over eBay, a method of buying a vehicle that Peter clearly disapproves of. Valentina, in her stroller, waves goodbye to the rest of us and we begin our back passage walkround.

Friday, April 11:

Temperatures have dropped a bit as Fritz and I enter the park on a sunny morning in April. Almost immediately we encounter Humphrey with Billy the Bearded Collie (Little and Large); they are sniffing out something important in the bushes and Fritz has to lend a nose. Re-started, we next encounter Suzanne with Sunny and Saskia with Buddy. Even though we are not in the middle of the green Buddy rushes forward to sit at my feet—I'm just the biscuit man to him.

When we do reach the green Franca is just leaving with Frank and Bianca (no Valentina today). "Don't take this personally," she says, "I just need my coffee." Fritz shows no interest in any of the other dogs and I soon find myself pursuing him on a grand circle around the green, one that even includes an impromptu visit to the Grantully doggy pen. Thereafter I try to get him back into the center of the grass, where Sunny is having an hysterical time of it, barking at her own shadow. Sabina is carrying a plastic bag and Fritz is certain that it must contain something useful, so she lets him have a sniff. It doesn't. At this point I put him on lead so that we make some orderly progress toward our own coffee.

Cheryl, Georgie and Janet are already seated and eventually we add Liz, Bob, Suzanne and the latter's friend Tammy. Tomorrow is Cheryl's birthday and she has put some money behind the counter as a way of treating her friends. Fritz is still her friend, even though he has been warned not to piss on the covered wagon, and he spends some time on her lap—when he is not on Janet's lap. When he is returned to the ground he begins to whine and it takes me a while to figure out what it is he wants. Peter and Ellen have taken their old corner in the forecourt, the spot with benches on two sides of a table and, more importantly, they have just

301

taken delivery on a plate of toast. So I unhook my dog, who rushes forward only to discover that both of the gates are closed. Everyone pays close attention to his problem-solving skills and he somehow remembers (not having used it in months) that there is a back passage over on the right; the missing fence section on the Carlton roadway has been replaced. In a very short time he has presented himself for toast eating duties; he is joined by Daisy-Mae, who has been admitted after experimentally *pushing* on the gate—shown up by a Shih-Tzu! Then Liz, Georgie and Janet head for home and some last minute packing, for this afternoon they, and others, begin the expedition to Southwold.

Saturday, April 12:

The dog's day begins with an unusual incident. He has been snuggling under the covers, as he often does even after I have risen, and from my study I can hear the strangely muffled but unmistakable sounds of vomiting. I rush into the bedroom where there is the large projection of a standing Schnauzer under the bedspread. He is somewhat embarrassed but there is not that much mess and I get it cleaned up pretty quickly. Soon he is whining near the front door and, at about 7:40, we begin our morning in the park about an hour and a half early.

I cannot say that I am entirely surprised by these developments since yesterday's poo was decidedly substandard and matters were made worse by a thunderstorm that sent the poor fellow under the bed for a few hours. In fact this morning's efforts are better than yesterday's, consistency poor, color still acceptable. I decide to wait and see if this episode requires yet another visit to the vet. It is a lovely morning in the park and, at this early hour, the place is almost empty, just a jogger or two and some dogs we don't usually see. Fritz makes his usual lively progress, not forgetting to sample a few medicinal grass shoots and we complete a grand circle of the green before heading for home. Of course there is no point in thinking of coffee; we are far too early for that and, anyway, most of the usual coffee drinkers are having their cuppas in Southwold this weekend.

Our afternoon walk produces another substandard specimen, sort of slime covered. It's too late to get an appointment at the vet's so I'll have to wait and see if we can get in tomorrow morning. Today is Fritz's fifth birthday and what a way to spend it—no coffee hour, no pals about, no food, just a dicky tummy.

Sunday, April 13:

There is no improvement in my dog's health, indeed at midnight last night we had a session of yellowish vomiting in the hallway. We complete an early morning walk in the park, poo still a problem (with a touch of pink) but at least Fritz chooses a short route around the club house and out the Morshead roadway. We are again early, in this case by some half an hour, and the only dog we recognize is Billy the Border Collie.

An hour or so later I am calling the emergency number of the Hamilton surgery, where they hold a short session on Sunday mornings, and we soon have an appointment at 11:00 with Sara. Skies are full of activity as we depart a second time and there are some ominous dark clouds as we take the well-remembered route to Boundary Road. Fritz can't seem to go longer than three months between bouts of tummy trouble; this time it has been just two and a half months. It is just beginning to rain as we arrive.

Dr. Sara discovers that Fritz has a temperature and she gives him two injections and then she sends him home with antacid medicine, antibiotic pills, colon medicine, and intestinal formula food. I have to get my umbrella out as we pass through the park on the return journey and we also dodge the drops on our afternoon walk. Still, I feel a little less helpless now that a regime has been established and Fritz is about to get his first food in 48 hours.

Monday, April 14:

Fritz seems to have spent a much more comfortable night and we are able to depart for the park at our usual hour this morning. It is very beautiful outside, a Spring gem, and I realize I could have gone walking had it not been for the invalid at home. Fritz now growls out a welcome at several dogs as we continue along the walkways, though he has nothing to say to Keith Millman, my long-time colleague at the American School, who charges past us at a jog—his walkman chugging insistently. I spot Boyd inspecting his own handiwork in the picnic area and I pause to tell him how lovely the elliptical flowerbed surrounding a lone tree looks. "It does look nice, doesn't it?" he says with justifiable pride.

Fritz takes a left turn at the Carlton roadway and we are soon climbing Mt. Bannister. At the top he does a convalescent poo—sometimes it seems to take days before he is able to do this. As we begin our descent I spot Hanna, whom I have not seen in some time. First she was in Finland, then she had the flu, then Fritz had to adopt a most unusual morning schedule because of his tummy.

We are about to get started on a catch-up when Franca approaches with a question for Hanna: would she be willing to foster a miniature Yorkie who is in the care of the Mayhew home after some sad experiences at home? Hanna is a bit uncertain whether she can take on this responsibility but agrees to give the matter some thought. The dog comes from a home in which the wife was abused and the dog himself hurled out of a window—so there are lots of problems. Hanna now heads in for coffee but I decide to get Fritz home so he can have his prescribed breakfast.

Tuesday, April 15:

Another gorgeous morning greets us as we enter the park today. Fritz is making his usual slow progress along the back walkways when he veers off to investigate the grass behind the bushes that surround the parallel bars. I wait a long time for him to emerge and then I notice that he has admitted himself to the running track (there are two missing fence panels now) and that he is rushing around in lane three. I get him to turn around just as he reaches a corner but it is touch and go whether he will choose to answer my whistles and bribes ("Biscuits!"). Eventually he decides to comply with my wishes but when he discovers that I am not carrying *any* treats (because of his convalescent stomach) he is mightily perturbed and I can't get him going again in the right direction. He is distracted by Arran and Andorra briefly and then by a stick I have found and then by a lone tennis ball, but he just wants to go back the way we have come in. I have to comply but I put him on lead, since I don't trust him, and in this fashion he has to remain stationary while I chat with little Fix's owner, Barry.

We continue toward the green and pass the clubhouse—here I can see Cheryl entering the café forecourt with her two Pugs. I am happy to see that Ronnie is back in his old seat; it has been some time since he has been well enough to make the journey to the park. He lights up his first cigar in three months. Also present today we have Georgie, Ofra, and Janet (all returned from the long weekend in Southwold), Suzanne,

Nicholas, Ellen and Peter. The Southwold expedition (which also included Dan, Davide, Liz, Kate and Bob) seems to have been a great success. All the dogs enjoyed the beach (Daisy-Mae distinguishing herself by trotting along with a starfish and then a crab in her mouth and Bailey by scaling the cliffs in a daredevil fashion). I ask which dog was the best behaved and Janet says it was definitely Daisy-Mae. I ask which dog was the naughtiest. She says that would be Daisy-Mae as well.

Fritz is again nil by mouth and he is quite cross about this. Daisy-Mae keeps jumping into every empty chair. Sunny is keeping up a litany of forbidden woofing and Lola is barking out a running commentary as well. "How unusual," I say, "that Sparkie is the quietest dog here today." Georgie beams with pride over this—but, alerted by the sound of a leaf blower starting up, Sparkie begins to bark maniacally. We are about ready to leave when Ginger goes missing, but she waddles back from the green before panic sets in. Rosie is also hard to spot as we begin our procession but soon we are underway.

The back passage walkround in full of incident. Tanya comes by with baby Lucca and Pasha and stops to tell me that she has just learned of Dorothy's passing. We are chatting when two youths riding bikes charge through, complaining about all the dogs in their path. This enrages Ronnie, who reminds them they are not allowed to ride *their* vehicles in the park. One of these lads actually wants Ronnie to move out of his way and there are words. I miss what happens next, since I am still talking to Tanya, but evidently one of the bike riders snags Suzanne with a handlebar and there are more words. The bike riders retreat but a large number of lads in the five-a-side pitch (where signs for the "Unity in the Community" League are prominent) are laughing at Suzanne's protest and Cheryl makes the tactical error of reminding them, "If we were in the States you'd be sued for an incident like this." "We're not in the States" is the politest of the barracking responses that follow this remark and a teacher now intervenes to ask the lads to show some respect. Suzanne remains behind to plead her case with this chap while the rest of us, in small groups, gradually continue our slow progress toward the exits.

Wednesday, April 16:

Fritz, who seems to have survived yesterday afternoon's check-up well enough, finishes his convalescent breakfast before we head for the park this morning. I have been fearing the return of showers but the sun is now making a breakthrough and I have high hopes for a continual improvement in the heavens. Just as we enter the park a party including Janet, Georgie and Dan, are heading for the cypress trees and Suzanne, coming toward us, reverses direction to accompany this group as well. My former colleague has asked me about my current proofreading chores—as I labor to complete my stepfather's biography. We are discussing the vexed question of the difference between a hyphen and a dash when I notice that Fritz is not following us.

As yesterday, my dog seems reluctant to continue in our usual direction (was he spooked by the explosion of a cannon shot of a soccer ball against the fence recently?). I have to abandon Suzanne as I follow my dog in his retreat; it is soon obvious that he is going to reach the green from the right rather than the left-hand route. I pause to chat with Jan Prendergast and while I am doing this I can see him squatting for a distant poo. When I finally reach this spot I can't find it anywhere. Next he admits himself to the forbidden rose garden and then heads off to the bandstand, where Denise has chained her bicycle to a lamppost. It has a flat and the tire has come off the rim and she is not looking forward to pushing this home with Rizzo in the basket. We meet up with Suzanne again but Fritz is soon rushing across the green and out along the Randolph walkway and so I have to head here too, at last putting the willful animal on lead (is this rebellion a reaction to the dietary restrictions he is enduring due to his illness?).

At breakfast this morning we have all of the aforementioned humans, minus Dan (who has gone to work) plus Hanna and Ofra, who is now planning a trip to New York. Georgie, Hanna and Janet all seem to have the flu and Janet says that she was so poorly last night that she had to ignore all of Daisy-Mae's bedside attention-getting antics. This morning, reaching out to stroke her dog she was surprised by the velvety texture of her pet—realizing all too late that she was petting the dead mouse that Daisy-Mae had been trying to get her to look at last night. Peter and Ellen come by but Ellen is warned that our table is contagious and they take their own table. So do Winnie and Daisy-Mae, who have taken their own seats at a table abandoned by Yasmina and Franca. We begin an uneventful back passage walkround. Winnie is in a sulk (having found nothing edible at her new place setting) and she manages to complete the exit walk at a turtle's pace.

Thursday, April 17:

It has stopped sending hailstones into my window boxes by the time we hit the streets this morning but it is still very cold. As has been his habit of late my dog finds lots of excuses not to make the proper progress toward the cypress trees. He has to sample a few grass shoots, he has to go behind the bluebells to examine the back fence, he has to touch noses with Lancer the Labrador, he has to disappear behind the parallel bars again. I manage to get him to rejoin me by shaking my tube of "It's Me or the Dog" baked treats but he escapes before I can get his lead attached and the next thing I know he has admitted himself to the running track and is heading down the straightaway. I have to duck under the bar and follow him this time; he races all the way to the starting point and out an open gate onto the Morshead roadway, returning cheekily once to see what's keeping *me*.

I try to get him to head directly for the green, where I can see a circle of dog owners, but even this is not easy to accomplish. When we do reach the spot we find Dan with Winnie and Daisy-Mae, Bob with Skye and Isla and Saskia with Buddy. Daisy-Mae looks like a sodden floor-mop and her condition is not improved by her contact with the little whippet-like black dog named Fly—who likes to drag the ragmop through the wet grass with his/her teeth. Saskia says that the woman accompanying Fly is, in fact, the celebrity model Jasmine Guinness, but she is too far away for us to get a close look. Fritz, meanwhile, has headed across the green to join up with Oscar and Scamp at the eastern end; when he continues on to the tennis courts I at last get him on lead since it is time to go in for coffee.

This morning we have Georgie, Dan, Bob, Hanna, Ofra, Cheryl and Suzanne—who thinks she is coming down with the collective cold. Dan blames the absent Kate for introducing this infection to the group—this is adding insult to injury as she has just broken a toe at home. The dogs are very noisy this morning, with a lot of ill-tempered barking. A wet Daisy-Mae is shivering so she is wrapped in Dan's scarf and then placed in a plastic bag. I suggest that the next step is to put her on Valentina's lap and lower the plastic hood on the baby's carriage. In fact Valentina is removed from her buggy and placed on an empty chair and tickled by Ofra and Dan. Franca says that a man in a white van has been casing the dog scene and that there is considerable concern over a dognapping threat just now. A chill wind is also blowing down our necks so we begin to make a move somewhat earlier than usual. Dan gets a call from Janet, who wants her dog back—God knows why.

Friday, April 18

The park comes to join us this morning, that is a circular from the City of Westminster drops through the mail chute at an early hour describing an event scheduled for a week from Saturday, when the park will reveal yet more development plans in the café. I am pleased that there has been an attempt to communicate with the park's neighbors this time, that there is some recognition of the need for retaining the Rec's "parkland setting" and that an attempt is to be made to make "the best use of the space in the park whilst ensuring that the tranquility remains for those who want quiet relaxation." What this actually means when we also hear that the plans are to benefit "the whole city community" and that there are to be "further development works" is unclear.

Fritz and I begin another chilly morning in the park, first passing Christian and Reina, who is being tugged forward by Miro and Vito as though she were on water skiis, then Arran again. I am keeping a close eye on my dog, having noticed that a third panel is missing in the trackside fence, and wondering if I can get him to move past the cypress trees this morning. He is beginning to turn tail at this point when Georgie comes up behind us with Sparkie. Fritz follows them into the danger zone and in this way conquers his phobia. We continue on to the top of Mt. Bannister where we encounter Janet and Dan chatting with Fix's owner, Barry. This group is left behind as I follow my dog along the Randolph walkway. Boyd pauses to greet Fritz and suggests that he has ordered some taller and hardier curbside plants in hopes of their surviving the inevitable shower of puppy pee. There is a large school group huddling around their teachers in front of the loos and Winnie, to everyone's amusement, manages to insert herself into the center of this intimate circle.

At breakfast we have Hanna, Janet, Georgie, Ofra, and Dan. Janet circulates a draft of an account of the doggy weekend in Southwold, one that she wants to submit to *London Dog Tails*. Ofra is about to hand over the care of Bailey to Georgie as she departs for a week in New York City this afternoon—a handover complicated by the fact that Bailey is going to the beauty parlor this morning. Dan teases Ofra by suggesting that a stranger could walk in, say Bailey is in *his* care, and sell the King Charles at the Portobello Market for £10.00. "Notice that I say £10.00. If it were Winnie the price would be £400.00." The famous Pug, meanwhile, is displaced—Fritz having decided to spend most of the morning shivering on Dan's lap. She sits on my lap and for a while I have both dogs there. When she regains a place on Dan's lap she is suddenly far too close to Sparkie for anyone's comfort and the spooked Yorkie recoils in barking horror. We are about to leave, thoroughly chilled, when our resident clairvoyant, Katherine McCormack, suddenly takes a seat at our table with her bottle of pear juice, has a sip or two, and, when no one has anything to say to her, gets up and goes to another table. But then, again, she would have known this would happen.

Saturday, April 19:

It is still very chilly and quite gray as Fritz and I head for the park on a busy Saturday morning. I am keeping a close eye on my pet, who has to be discouraged from wandering too close to the yawning gaps in the running track fence, but in the event he does manage to continue along the path next to the cypress trees and, fighting his way through the crowds of parents and siblings who are here to watch the boys play, on to the café. We pass Liz with Roxy and continue on to the green, where I can see Janet, Dan and Georgie descending from the hilltop—just as Davide is coming up behind me from the clubhouse. The others head in for coffee but I accompany Fritz on further rambles (Randolph walkway, tennis courts, back to the green) before joining them.

Hanna is also present this morning and other park characters are hovering in the background. It is not quite as cold as yesterday but no one would call it pleasant sitting out here in the chill breeze. Dan and Davide quarrel over which one of them has had the more glamorous vacations this year (they go to Hong Kong later this week) and I tell them that neither is going to get any sympathy from the rest of us. Janet, who can barely talk, is also getting ready for travel, as next week she flies off to Naples and Ischia. There are still a lot of Southwold stories in circulation and Liz, who had major clean-up duties, says she loves cleaning other people's houses—the cue for Georgie to hand over the keys to her flat.

Fritz is allowed real biscuits by now but when I take out my bag all the other dogs report for a treat as well. Daisy-Mae sits on hers and when

Fritz tries to winkle it out later she attacks him with some spirit. Bailey, Roxy and Winnie travel from table to table cadging treats. I note that no one has spirited Bailey away yesterday or sold him for £10.00 at the Portobello market but Janet says she did try but was only offered £5.00. Then she gets up to mop up some vomit—as poor Daisy-Mae is feeling a bit under the weather.

Sunday, April 20:

Gray skies persist but at least there is no wind to depress temperatures and we can make our entrance under comfortable enough conditions. Fritz seems to have gotten over his tummy troubles and his paranoia and we are soon dancing along with Humphrey behind the cypress trees. Indeed my dog gets well ahead of me here and I don't catch up with him until I have reached the middle of the green, where Bob is exercising Skye and Isla. Janet and Georgie are seated at the top of Mt. Bannister and Fritz decides to pay them a visit; soon a procession is climbing the hill—Davide with Winnie coming up as well. Janet has an almighty cough, Dan is at home with a temperature and Suzanne, her voice lowered by several octaves, comes struggling up the hill with Sunny; it is the first time she has been able to give her dog much of a walk since Wednesday.

When we descend to take our places at the usual spot in front of the café we make up a party that includes all of the aforementioned minus Bob plus Hanna. Peter sits down for a while but gets up when we spot Ellen, still using her cane, making a slow passage in front of the café with Sandy and Jack—the first time she has been able to resume her dog-walking duties since her operation. Chained to the fence behind us is Raffy and his hysterical barking contributes to putting us all on edge—and we are about to endure an incident. In the forecourt some boys are playing football and, given the restricted nature of this space, it is not surprising that the ball flies over the low stone wall on a number of occasions. When it actually hits Hanna that angry lady picks it up and storms off with it, intending to put it on the green, where it belongs. Janet, perhaps not knowing that the ball has caused actual injury, chides Hanna for over-reacting and these two ladies have words—finally agreeing to disagree over a matter of opinion.

A second incident is brewing. The dogs, not satisfied with the offerings at our table, have been making a nuisance of themselves at other tables—Daisy-Mae, who is getting to be as defensive about food as Winnie, snaps several times at Fritz and then goes off to visit a small table where there is a 20 week-old Lhasa Apso puppy named, of all things, Bailey. John, the chap with the flat cap and the cotton stuck in his ears, is giving a running commentary on all this; Janet takes his picture when Daisy-Mae takes the empty seat at his table. Davide, meanwhile, has taken delivery on a bacon sandwich whose toast is buttered (he had asked for dry). He eats it anyway, Winnie sitting in his lap with intense interest as every mouthful is consumed—then Bouzha (who doesn't like to leave the café interior because of the dogs underfoot outside) hands out a plate with the dry toast as originally requested. Davide, who asks her for his espresso now, doesn't know what to do with the extra bread but he is about to have this problem solved definitively since, just as Bouzha leans out of the door with the coffee, Winnie makes a sudden leap, knocking this liquid all over her daddy, his neighbors and over the plate of once-dry toast. Hanna decides to tear the latter into tiny pieces for the birds but it is these delicate morsels that Sparkie wants to eat. "He likes bird bread," she says, and I, who have just been told that he has lost yet another ball in the bushes, add waspishly, "To go with his bird brain."

Monday, April 21:

There is some evidence of recent showers as Fritz and I head for the park on a cold, gray morning, but the moisture is no longer falling in any appreciable amounts.

Fritz makes a lively enough progress toward the café, where I find Ronnie, making only his second visit to the park since his recent hospitalization. This is good news for me since I rely on the former jeweler to make all the adjustments on Dorothy's Swatch watch—which is still on winter time. I leave this timepiece with him and continue on toward the green, hoping to make contact with my dog, whom I have not seen in several minutes.

I spot him in front of the clubhouse, where he is checking out Peter and Ellen with Jack, Sandy and Holly. Soon there is quite a whirlpool of dogs in the center of the green, with Oscar, Scamp, Ginger, Lola, Bailey, Winnie, and Daisy-Mae all present. Buddy rushes forward to offer both paws in exchange for a biscuit. The others soon head in for coffee but I expect Fritz will want some more exercise so we follow his usual pathways for the next ten minutes or so and then I put his lead back on so I can make my own progress toward the café.

This morning we have Hanna, Georgie, Peter, Ellen, Davide, Cheryl and Ronnie. I hand my dog over to the latter (who also has Sparkie in his lap) when I go in to order my cappuccino. Cheryl is wearing another Oklahoma Sooners sweatshirt and I wonder what would happen if one morning she looked in the mirror and noted that she was now wearing one from Oklahoma *State*. She and Hanna are planning an expedition to Kew Gardens today. Hanna again prepares a feast of breadcrumbs for the birds, directing Peter in the precise placement of this feast atop the dividing wall. "Yes," he says, "I know what a wall looks like." Tara the Ridgeback comes by for a handout but our dogs create no fuss. Toast is distributed to all and then we begin a back passage walkround.

Tuesday, April 22:

The sun is making some effort this morning and temperatures are mild enough. Fritz begins his day by scaring the wits out of the postman, who is just entering the building as we are departing it. In the park it is quiet enough (no school groups) and we make rapid enough progress toward the green. Here I can see that Fly has once again decided to treat Daisy-Mae as a furry pull-toy, dragging her through the grass using only teeth. I'm sure it looks worse than it actually is, and Daisy-Mae keeps coming back for more, but seeing her pet treated in this brutal fashion is extremely distressing to Janet—who keeps trying to intervene in this ritual.

Fritz checks out the scene on the green and then takes off for a distant corner, meeting up with his cousin Gus as he nears the Randolph walkway. Fritz has always chased Gus off before this, but today they decide to be pals and spend the next five minutes sniffing in the bushes together. The others have gone in for coffee by this time and so I hand Fritz over to Davide while I am inside, waiting for my coffee. Hanna, Cheryl, Georgie, and Janet take their places at our table. Cheryl is wearing *another* Oklahoma Sooners sweater—pink accented with coffee stains.

Davide reports that Dan is well enough to go to work but may miss the trip to Hong Kong. He also missed last night's theatre expedition, when Liz and I and her friend Corinne went to the Old Vic to see Jeff Goldblum and Kevin Spacey in David Mamet's *Speed The Plow*. I have to give a report on this excellent production and then we turn to other topics: news reports that you can pick up MRSA from your dog if you let him sleep in your bed; Hanna and Cheryl's trip to Kew Gardens; Daisy-Mae's bullying of the other dogs in Georgie's house; a promised mini-heatwave, with temperatures in the 60s! Behind us someone has chained up a Westie in a harness while a breakfast order is placed inside. Daisy-Mae tries to keep the anxious fellow amused but he shrieks with all the intensity of a set of fingernails on a chalkboard.

Wednesday, April 23:

A light but penetrating rain is falling on our heads as we head for the park on a sodden Wednesday. Fritz is wearing his raincoat and I am in my rain jacket, but soon the moisture is soaking through my shoes and adding to the misery of the morning. We pass Sabina with Oscar and Scamp and, five minutes later, Denise with Rizzo. Now at last we have a real use for the mobile phone—for these two ladies can use their own versions of this instrument to discover where the other is walking and thus plot a rendezvous. Oscar, as usual, would really like to make friends with my dog, but Fritz isn't having any of it. At least he doesn't chase the chubby Schnauzer away.

In front of the café there is a small knot of brave dog owners occupying the dry half of our usual table: Dan, Ronnie, Peter, Ellen and Nicholas. Ronnie and Peter are having one of their usual arguments; Nicholas has beaten the queue by phoning in his coffee order; Dan, feeling much better, still can't decide whether to go to Hong Kong this afternoon. Georgie is absent—but with Bailey, Daisy-Mae and Sparkie all in her care these days, the rain may have discouraged her visit this morning. Hanna arrives under her giant maroon estate agent umbrella. She says that one domestic crisis has been averted (she no longer needs a screwdriver to get in the front door of her building) but that out back the actor Julian Rhind-Tutt, who owns property on Elgin Avenue, has been driving his noisy motorcycle up and down the alleyway at unsocial hours. She reports that yesterday she went to an African store on the Harrow Road and treated herself to a take-out coconut water, the top of the nut macheted off by the proprietor so that a straw could be inserted.

Saskia comes by, raindrops clinging to the tummy bulge that will one day produce a sibling for Buddy. That lucky dog sticks his nose into my lap just as I am about to offer a biscuit to Fritz. A look-alike cousin of Buddy's, Bessie, is also hovering about today. Hovering might be a good word to describe the crowds of saturated schoolgirls who are hanging about on the roadways, waiting for Miss to direct them toward some nearby playing field. As we begin our back passage walkround Dan points out that only girls have braved the inclement skies today. I suggest that you know you are making slow progress when the caravan is lead by a purposeful Ronnie, up ahead. I wish Dan a tentative bon voyage as we part at the Essendine gate.

Thursday, April 24:

Although I actually went to the park yesterday afternoon without a jacket, something tells me that winter is about to stage a comeback and I am wrapped up again as Fritz and I head for the entrance gate this morning. Almost immediately Georgie comes up behind us. She says that she did get as far as the Morshead gate yesterday and then, defeated by the rain, she returned to the comforts of her parlor. Her problems were exacerbated by the responsibility of caring for three dogs, her own Sparkie, Bailey (Ofra is still in New York), and Daisy-Mae (Janet left for Ischia yestrday). At least Winnie wasn't added to the menagerie because Dan has decided *not* to fly to Hong Kong after all.

Daisy-Mae now rushes up to greet me, and so does Bailey—who now comes forward to vomit a gout of grass-flavored spittle at my feet. As we round the corner, making very slow progress, Denise is having problems with the other end of Rizzo, who has a dirty bottom that needs attention. When we reach the café we head for the top of Mt. Bannister amid darkening skies. Fritz and I are the last ones left on this precipice and before long I put him on lead so that I can follow Georgie into coffee. The park is quieter than usual as today we have teacher strikes throughout the nation and fewer groups have made it to the park.

I sit down between the grumpy old men, Ronnie and Peter, though the insults continue to fly over my knees.

Ronnie has seen a program about dockers, one of whom was nicknamed Eighteen Months because he had lost part of an ear and thus was remembered as an 'ear and a half. Cheryl now arrives with her

Pugs; she tells us that her husband has just called to remind her that a band of rain is heading our way. Ronnie wants to know if the bacon she has ordered for the dogs is kosher. (Fritz eats far too many of Ronnie's scattered carrots.) Dan arrives twice since he has forgotten his mobile phone on his car seat and has to go back to retrieve it. Winnie now jumps into Cheryl's lap. "She just kissed me," Cheryl says delightedly, "unless it was only a head butt." Hanna arrives and we wait for her to finish her coffee before beginning our back passage walkround. It is beginning to rain.

Friday, April 25:

A weak sun and mild temperatures greet us as we enter a very quiet park this morning. We pass through the café and out onto the green where I can see that Dan and Saskia are in conclave on the hillside beneath the (new) magnolia tree. Saskia is just one of many dog owners who are anxious about tomorrow's consultation event at the café—where we are scheduled to learn just what it is that the developers have in store for us at Paddington Rec now. Her anxiety is augmented by the fact that she won't be here (many regulars are going to be absent tomorrow) because she is about to fly off to Austria to visit her family. Fritz has long ago taken off for the Randolph walkway and I can see him checking out the two Shar-Peis before touching noses with Arran. We walk behind the tennis courts and then cross the green, as it is now coffee time.

Peter and Ronnie have been sitting at our regular table for twenty minutes by now and they are well into their largely good-natured quarrelling. Hanna complains of a sore throat and Ronnie says, "Just give your symptoms to Peter and he'll be happy to worry about them for you." Peter answers that Ronnie's jokes are as tired as those of Bruce Forsythe. "But he got knighted," Ronnie says. "Get knotted would be more appropriate in your case," is the response.

Lurch arrives with our coffee orders, complaining that he has to walk to the far side of the table in order to find an empty space for his tray. "That makes us your personal trainer," Georgie says. "Did you order food today?" he asks that lady, "well you're not getting it." Dan, meanwhile, is telling Vicky that she ought to have a special doggy menu, but when she replies that the dogs prefer to eat the same food as their owners everyone agrees that no special menu is needed after all. I tell Georgie that there is a sign on the window advertising the need for additional café staff and since, with her long history in the pubs of our locality, she is the only one here with behind the counter experience *she* ought to apply. Everyone chuckles at this notion; then someone adds, "But suppose you had to serve *Ofra*," and it's no longer funny. Dan, casting Winnie in the Joan Crawford role, says that Daisy-Mae is beginning to look more and more like Bette Davis in *Whatever Happened to Baby Jane*. Our two ladies are squabbling as we begin our back passage walkround.

Saturday, April 26:

I am correct in anticipating much warmer weather today—for I have abandoned my jacket this morning, something I haven't been able to do in a long time. The park, reflecting the resplendent sunshine, is full of activity, beginning with a woman who is standing at the head of the track, her boxing gloves and flying feet resounding with thuds and thwacks against the leather targets supplied by her instructor. Joggers abound. Kids are streaming toward the pitches for some seven-a-side contests this morning. Fritz manages to weave through all these feet and to pass the front door of the café, where Ronnie is already sitting with Hanna. The latter has a visiting Yoyo on her lap but we do not stop yet, continuing on to the green, where Dan and Liz are just turning a corner with Barry. Fritz spots some dogs he knows at the top of the hill and so he has to go up and have a visit; eventually I can corral him as we head in for our morning coffee.

Today we have, in addition to those already mentioned, Cheryl and Georgie. (Peter and Ellen—just having been given the discharge by her doctor—are at their own table.) Liz says that a little dog has rushed from its garden in St. Johns Wood and bitten Roxy on the tail. Yoyo thinks that the plate of scrambled eggs and toast delivered to Hanna is just for her, and even manages to lick the toast before she is placed on the ground. Unfortunately this puts her next to an equally greedy Winnie and we soon have a food fight. There is considerable alarm when a sports car tools in to drop off someone at the clubhouse, and on its return journey a woman has to scream to get it to stop—since her dog is just crossing the Carlton walkway. Dan is outraged and doesn't know whom to complain to; the walkways seem to be open to all drivers now that we are in the middle of construction.

Today is the park's "consultation event" and I am soon nominated to go inside the café to find out what it is that the developers have in store for us. I have a nice chat with a chap from Westminster. He confirms the demise of the bowling green (with more tennis courts scheduled for the site)—which would be a shame—but he says that there are no changes that would involve the loss of additional green spaces. He seems pretty cool with dogs off lead, and remembers well our efforts in this matter. We talk about the need for additional visits by the animal warden, replacement of the missing fence panels outside the running track, and refurbishments to the café building—which should include a community center. I am given a form to fill out and, indeed, he later comes out to distribute more of these to my sedentary chums. The latter have the devil of a time getting their dogs moving toward our back passage walkround; the animals have exhausted the food scraps at our table but there are lots of other tables where people are still eating.

Sunday, April 27:

I make two entrances to the park this morning, since Pepper, who has been our overnight guest, seems to need to go out about an hour earlier than his cousin. The two dogs have had a pleasant enough night, with both of them on my bed, and at 9:10, our usual starting hour, I return to the park, keeping Pepper on lead and letting Fritz wander at will. He demonstrates the superiority of his position by heading in the opposite direction from the one we usually take—and we end up doing a complete circle of the green. Up ahead of us we can see Hanna, again on Yoyo duties.

I can see other members of our party descending from the top of Mt. Bannister and we have caught up with them by the time they approach our usual table. Dan, however, objects to our sacred spot this time—since there is some sticky substance underfoot, and we choose an empty picnic table in the forecourt instead. Here we have Liz, Dan, Ronnie, Natasha (whom we have not seen since Valentines Day) and Georgie. Hanna takes another table because she doesn't trust Yoyo in such close proximity to other dogs and because she is somewhat upset over queue-jumpers at the café counter. Ellen is around the corner at her bench table, though she does have the company of Daisy-Mae at her side. The café, indeed the whole park, is crowded this morning; three little girls, each with a dolly, are atop the low stone wall, though they do climb down periodically to pet all the dogs.

I tell the others that thunderstorms are expected today and this remark, to the amazement of all, is accompanied by a distant rumble. Natasha says she is angry with a friend for giving away one of her dogs. Georgie reports that outside the Neald pub on Shirland Road yesterday afternoon there was a terrible incident during which a man with two Staffies was attacked by a gang who hit him over the head (and perhaps stabbed him as well) and made off with a four month-old Staffie puppy. (I heard the hovering helicopter without understanding the import of this noise.) Winnie now jumps up on the bench between Ronnie and Liz, trying to be appealing as Liz finishes her scrambled eggs. Dan, charmed by the antics of his pet, puts Winnie is his lap, squeezes her bottom and ends up with teeth marks on his finger as a consequence. I am very popular with my biscuit bag; it's the only thing that shuts the chirping Pepper up.

Monday, April 28:

Temperatures are a bit cooler this morning but I am still comfortable enough without a jacket. Under any circumstances it is a beautiful spring morning in the park, the leaves coming out on the tall trees and resplendent blossoms turning corners of the Rec into splashes of pink and white. Behind us I can see Georgie making slow progress with Sparkie, Bailey and Daisy-Mae. When they at last arrive Georgie has a tale to tell. It seems that Simon the Cocker has found something interesting, a befouled set of men's boxer shorts which one of our park users has abandoned (in preference to actually reporting to the loos) in the bushes. Simon, to the horror of his owner, now refuses to part with this prize and for a while Georgie is afraid that Daisy-Mae might be impelled to have a tug on this specimen too. At last all dogs, without contraband, are heading in the right direction.

Fritz is out front today and it is he who takes the initiative in turning left at the café and heading up to the hilltop. It is reported that Ofra has at last surfaced but that Georgie will still be heading home with three dogs anyway—as she is about to take delivery on Winnie from a work-bound Dan. Indeed this handover takes place in front of the loos as we descend, and now the only question is, will the painters who noticed that she was leaving her house with a Spaniel notice that she has returned with a Pug?

When we get to the café there is a haze of disapproval descending in a mist over our table: dog owners have been told to keep their dogs on lead in the precincts of the café. Of course I have long done just this with my Fritz (more because he is a wanderer than a menace or a pest) but some of the other dogs (this means you, Daisy-Mae and Winnie) lay siege to every other table if there is food on offer and other dogs uniformly block the café entrance, to the consternation of many a dog-phobic customer. Amid much grumbling most of our dogs now feel the restraint of their leads, though Ronnie insists that Rosie is fine beneath his chair and Peter says Holly is on an invisible lead. I remind the others that, like all the other park rules, this one will be forgotten in a few weeks.

This morning we have all of the aforementioned owners plus Ellen, Nicholas (who leaves after the obligatory business calls on his mobile), Hanna (still with Yoyo), and Valentina, who eats part of Ronnie's croissant while her mother sits at another table. After a few minutes Ofra at last returns and there is a wonderful reunion scene as Bailey climbs all over his mommy. To no one's surprise, Ofra has forgotten one of her suitcases on the carousel at Heathrow Airport. (Not to worry, Davide has assured her, they just blow such luggage up.) I feel guilty about teasing her since she has remembered to bring me a bottle of super-sized Tums from New York and some mint-flavored industrial strength tennis balls for the dogs.

Tuesday, April 29:

A light rain is just ending as Fritz and I reach our entrance gate this morning; we are both in raingear though *I* didn't try to hide when it was time to put my jacket on like someone else I know. Almost immediately we encounter Denise and Sabina; they are looking decidedly uncomfortable and staring off into the distance apprehensively. Soon they share with me the source of their anxiety—a very large Staffie, whom they clearly don't trust. "Scamp would be okay," Sabina says, "but Oscar would run right up to it." Denise says, "I can just see its jaws hanging on to Rizzo." They seem ready to reverse directions but in the end they persevere on their original line of march.

The wet weather has certainly depressed attendance in the park this morning—not a single school group is present. Fritz continues without many pauses and we reach the green, where Dan and Cheryl are in conversation with the owner of the aforementioned Staffie. He is, in fact, a Staffie-Mastiff mix, his name is Max, and he is on lead—so there is no cause for alarm. I follow Fritz over to the tennis courts where we encounter Saskia, just returned from Austria, and her Buddy. Buddy can't make up his mind where to part with his gift this morning and keeps circling around on the grassy hillside. Saskia and I discuss the Austrian story of the moment, the revelation that a chap has kept his own daughter in a cellar for 24 years, fathered seven of her children, and kept his wife upstairs ignorant of the whole matter. Saskia says that she has a great aunt, who, hearing all this, has concluded, "Well, he doesn't sound normal to me." We encounter Boyd, who is supervising the installation of some new bedding plants on the Randolph walkway. We are in agreement that it would be a shame to lose the bowling green to more hard surfaces and Boyd, fantasizing, proposes that there might be an ornamental doggy garden on the site, complete with a wading pool for the dogs. Buddy, having just baptized one of the new plants, agrees.

At coffee this morning we have Ellen, Peter, Linda, Hanna, Dan and Cheryl. The latter is getting ready for a visit to the States tomorrow and discusses the details of the dog-sitting arrangements she has made for Lola and Ginger. Ellen says that Sandy has a tumor on her back and that she is scheduled to undergo surgery. Dan reports that Roxy is not at all well and that further investigations are needed at the Hamilton Vet Clinic. Peter and Hanna quarrel when Peter takes exceptions to one of Hanna's brainstorms. "Now children," Ellen say and both sides of the debate require the other side to "grow up." We discuss Bob and Kate's wedding, scheduled for a week from today. Many of the dog people think they are invited and want to attend—but no one has actually seen an invitation or been given any details about when or where this event is coming off, and Kate has been absent from the scene for some time. "Maybe they've eloped," I suggest.

Wednesday, April 30:

Well April is famous for its showers and so, true to form, we again begin our day by strapping on our raingear. Off in the misty horizon I can see Saskia with Buddy and Sabina with Oscar and Scamp but we have the walkways pretty much to ourselves again. There are no school groups about this morning as we make rapid progress toward the café, where Peter and Dan are already stationed. I continue on to the green with my dog, and we spend a further ten minutes at our usual morning rituals—though, as Fritz seems to have fallen in love with a patch of tasty grass, I lose patience and put him on lead. It has not stopped raining all this time.

I hand Fritz over to Dan as I seek the comforts of the café. With my cappuccino in hand I return to a table that also has Ellen and Hanna—that's it, just the fearless five.

Dan reports that Roxy has passed through extensive medical tests without any discernible problems—perhaps just a muscle strain. Hanna reports that in the few days that she has had Yoyo in her care that little madam has put on weight—since the black Schnauzer is food-obsessed, hoovering in the gutters, cadging for treats, even licking the cat's dish clean. A Parcel Force red van comes speeding along the Carlton roadway. "Some day," an outraged Dan observes, "someone or something is going to be killed."

The conversation shifts to Kate's mysterious wedding. Dan has heard from the lady by phone, with an email to follow. When Dan reported later that he had received no such email she checked her computer and realized that she had sent the message off to another Dan (and one whom she had *not* intended to invite). The inescapable conclusion is that Kate doesn't know most of our last names, so how is she going to leave a guest list at the door of the club on Shaftsbury Avenue—where the nuptials, dinner and party are due to take place? And are guests invited to all three, two out of three, one out of three? There can't be any good reason, for that matter, why Kate needs to invite all of the doggy people of Paddington Rec. I, of course, will not start out for any of these events without something more formal by way of invitation—not that I need to be physically present to wish the couple well. Dan also reports that Kate has finally gotten around to buying some material for her wedding dress and has delivered it (a week ago) to a recommended seamstress. Asked for the date of the wedding, Kate has supplied the information—only to see this recorded as May 6, 2009—because that's how much time this lady needs to complete such an assignment.

May, 2008

Thursday, May 1:

The rains have at last lifted as Fritz and I make our way into the park on a brisk Thursday morning, May having taken over at last from a very wet April. The walkways remain relatively quiet and we do not encounter anyone we know until the green has been reached. Here I can see Natasha with Leila, Georgie with Sparkie, and Janet—just returned from Ischia to reclaim her Daisy-Mae. Leila rushes forward to greet her "boyfriend," and the two do run in tandem for a while, but my dog has other fish to fry and soon we are on a solitary ramble around the eastern edges of the park in search of important smells. By the time we have returned to the green the great space is empty and I know it is time to head in for coffee.

Janet abandons her place in the queue to get my order (and later refuses to be compensated for this generous gesture). Peter, Ellen and Ofra (still on foot) soon join us as well. When we are seated I turn to my left and say, "It's great to have you back—Georgie," since that lady has two unexcused absences to 'splain. Sparkie, seated on his mommy's lap, has a dot of pink paint on his nose after sniffing the work of the laborers in his home hallway. Janet tells us about her Italian holiday and passes around the famous email from Kate. Ofra then passes around a text she has just received, one promising the return of her forgotten case from Heathrow. Bekki comes by with her sister's dog, the huge Boxer Bounce, whom we have not seen since November. Fritz, who is mightily bored, sets up an angry diatribe over this intrusion and he isn't mollified when the next head to intrude between our knees in that of Buddy. Saskia urges her dog to return to the green and I think she says, "Come on Buddy, before they call us 'Fuckers,'" but Georgie, who has heard it better over all the barking, reports that what Saskia actually said was, "Come on Buddy before we cause a fracas."

We begin a back passage walkround. Someone has left open the gate to the central playing field and before we know it Sparkie has begun a series of speedy circles, pursued by Daisy-Mae and Bailey. They manage to let themselves out once but they quickly return before we can get the gate closed. Georgie says that Sparkie is just acting as the personal trainer for the other dogs and he should get paid. As we clear the cypresses I see an unusual sight: a magpie (who is usually content to battle it out with the crows) is pursuing a squirrel—who has come too close to the nest. In the tight confines of the braches the bird can't open its wings so it is hopping from branch to branch in pursuit of its foe—hopping mad. As I exit the park I meet Rowena with Timmy. She is pumped with excitement (which none of the other dog people seem to share), sensing a Tory victory in today's mayoral election and having just come from the polling booth at the Essendine School—where she has no doubt helped send Ken Livingstone on his way.

Friday, May 2:

There are still a lot of clouds about and temperatures are depressed but at least the sun is making an attempt at some kind of comeback—indeed I *was* finally able to walk to Sainsbury's yesterday morning after staring at an empty fridge for several days. As so often happens, however, I have managed to leave the house without something needed for the park. I have my sack of biscuits, my poo poo bags, my sunglasses and my keys, but I have forgotten a trifecta of money, sweetener and watch.

Fritz is on a lonely, independent quest this morning and that means he doesn't have much time for socializing. He skips by the metal gazebo where Saskia and Oxana, both heavily pregnant, are seated on the metal bars while the blonde duo of Buddy and Rufus duke it out. He then climbs Mt. Bannister to sniff Holly's bum, descending to the tennis courts and returning to the Randolph walkway. Then it's a stroll toward the bowling green, but no, he has to disappear several times into the bushes before emerging to greet Jack and Sandy and the drooling black Chow, Chin. By this time the others have gone in for coffee. I take a seat as well, but as I have forgotten my money, my only refreshment this morning consists of a few Lemoncello biscuits that Janet has brought back form Italy.

This morning we have Ronnie, Hanna, Janet (who is feeling poorly again), Peter, Ellen, Georgie and Nicholas. Behind us, on the Carlton

---

roadway, a worker is creating a din as he installs another of the many new white signs that are going up all over the park and at its entrances. Hanna doesn't like them because they *are* so white and because she is sure that they will soon be covered in graffiti. There is still no word on who has won the mayor's race in yesterday's election, though Ronnie says Ken *should* have a third term, a third term of imprisonment. If Boris wins, I tell him, he has to buy the coffees tomorrow in celebration of the event.

Saturday, May 3:

The sun is shining purposefully this morning and I am not certain how many layers I may need for our adventure in the park. In the event I decide to leave my scarf behind; I could have abandoned my jacket as well. For some strange reason Fritz decides to follow a jogger who is racing by us as we enter. He has no designs on this chap's ankles, indeed he soon overtakes his human competitor—not slowing down until he has cleared the running track. As usual we have a large turnout of Saturday morning footie lads gathering for this morning's matches but Fritz manages to weave his way through these ankles as well and the next time I see him he is crossing the green.

He seems to be heading past Dan and Bob and toward Suzanne, who is standing on the hillside near the Grantully gate. A lively Jack Russell named Snoopy comes out to jump on my dog's back but Fritz does not seem at all perturbed by this. Instead he admits himself to the doggy area on this side and, in isolation, has a nice sniff on its meadow-like surfaces. I can see that several slats are missing in the fence that separates this area from the foxy jungle at the northeastern end, and I have visions of Fritz disappearing into this space, but fortunately he doesn't see it and we have soon returned to the green. I put him on lead and we pass in front of the clubhouse on our way to morning coffee.

Suzanne and her math department colleague Ray are playing backgammon at one little table and Peter and Ellen have also headed for their spot in the forecourt—just as well because this morning we have an even dozen people at our table: Janet, Georgie, Dan, Davide, John, Ofra, Hanna, Liz, Ronnie, Bob and the latter's older brother Michael. These chaps order the full English as antidotes to the pre-wedding hangovers they are suffering from this morning. The news: Ronnie agrees that both Ken and Boris have made gentlemanly speeches at the final count in the mayoralty race—concluded at midnight in Boris's favor; Ofra's forgotten bag has been returned to her by airport officials who have been so careless of late that they think the misadventure was *their* fault; Liz has completed successfully a computer graphics course in interior design; Dan will now be in charge of the box offices of the Phoenix, the Fortune and The Duke of York; Janet feels a lot better today, though she is still on peppermint tea. Sparkie likes mint as well, which explains why he is still very possessive over the battered tennis ball that his Auntie Ofra brought back from New York. He had better be possessive since Fritz steals this object twice. No sooner have I reached home base than Dan calls to say that Bob really wants me to come to the wedding party on Tuesday night.

Sunday, May 4:

We have overcast skies on a rather humid Bank Holiday Sunday and I am warm enough in my sweatshirt only today. Fritz skips along in a lively fashion, completing the long straightway at the back of the central pitch by following a hidden tunnel behind the cypress trees. When he at last emerges he is quick to reach the café, and, passing through, to reach the green and continue his wanderings. First he has to chase off Fritz II, his much larger cousin. Georgie and Janet are descending Mt. Bannister and Bob is coming in from the Randolph entrance with Skye and Isla. We chat (he repeats the invitation to the wedding party) while Fritz nibbles on nearby grass shoots.

At the far end of the green we can see Dan with Winnie, Liz with Roxy, and Saskia with Buddy. Skye, seeing her large friend, begins to slink across the grass, waiting to pounce. Buddy does the same thing but finally Skye breaks into a speedy lope and the chase is on. Out of the corner of my eye I can see Suzanne with Sunny and Sunny's alternate owner, Richie from Horsham. I haven't seen him in some time but he has come to town, in part, because of a computer problem. The machine in question has been left with a neighbor and she now comes in while we are getting seated at a metal table in the forecourt. This is the lovely Danielle Cornelius, and I haven't seen her in some time either. After she leaves the machine with its owner I tell the others that twenty years ago this mother of two was a student of mine in a high school social studies class.

We are eleven at breakfast this morning: Dan, Georgie, Janet, Suzanne, Richie, Bob and our bride-to-be Kate, Ronnie, Ofra and Liz. (I know this makes only ten names but I make the eleventh diner, don't I?) Ronnie and I discuss this weekend's edition of *Have I Got News For You*, an edition so blue it would never have been broadcast in my native country. Suzanne discusses an unforeseen hiatus in the reconstruction of her kitchen. Kate tells us what really happened on Bob's stag night. We begin a back passage walkround. It is quite obvious that, her tail furled, Roxy is still not feeling well. "Maybe she voted for Ken," is my diagnosis.

Monday, May 5:

Mexican Independence Day coincides with a Bank Holiday Monday this year and, though there is no Chihuahua in sight, we have lovely warm sunny weather for our day in the park. Fritz moves along fairly swiftly in the company of a longhaired Dachshund and we have soon arrived at the café, where Ronnie and Suzanne are already settling in. Fritz disdains the doggy activity on the green and leads me his usual merry chase: along the Randolph roadway, behind the tennis courts, back to the green, around its perimeter as far as the bandstand and, finally, back to the hub of canine activity outside the café.

There are only six of us today and a rickety metal table in the forecourt is chosen for Ronnie, Janet, Georgie, Hanna and Dan—though Ray and Suzanne have resumed their backgammon battle at another table (he is trying to win back the £24,000 pounds he owes her) and Peter and Ellen occupy a bench behind us. We begin by discussing the news (true or not is yet to be definitively established) that the caff won't serve single sausages to dogs anymore—since such an order is not on the menu (and such a gesture has outraged one or more of the stuffier customers anyway). I propose we try a variation on the famous scene in *Five Easy Pieces* in which we order a sausage sandwich (which *is* on the menu) and ask them to hold the toast. The irony is that these days none of us order sausages for our dogs, this treat being seen as too rich a diet for their delicate stomachs, but the rule, if true, is still another assault on our liberty and there will be repercussions.

While we are on the subject of food Dan holds forth on a barbeque he went to yesterday. He says he brought a box of Krispy Kreme doughnuts with him, one which none of his health-conscious friends would touch until *one* guest at last reached out a hand, the body's insatiable craving for trans-fatty acids taking over, and a feeding frenzy among the other guests ensued. Winnie was also a guest at this picnic and did very well at the feet of the head barbequer. When that source dried up she stalked a rug rat named Freddie and licked out the interior of his mouth (well, it must have contained food once). Dan is still pursuing the food theme when he concludes the proceedings by organizing another doggy people field trip today—one that will include a visit to the Little Venice canal cavalcade and a picnic in Regents Park.

Tuesday, May 6:

It is quite warm outside today, with lots of strong sun warming the walkways and green spaces in Paddington Rec. When we reach the green, however, Saskia shares the news of a darker patch: yesterday afternoon at the café a Pit Bull/Staffie cross, a snappy dog who accompanies a chap in a mechanized wheel chair, attacked a Golden Retriever named, of all things, Fritz. Her own version of this same breed is soon alerted to the arrival of his pal Rufus and off he goes for a reunion, soon to be become a threesome as Skye the Alsatian is charging this way as well. Her presence is also an indication of the arrival of today's groom, Bob; the condemned man receives congratulations from a number of us.

I tell Ronnie that I will see him in a few minutes but Fritz and I now have an errand to run, our bi-monthly visit to the Randolph surgery, where I place my prescription renewal request in the appropriate box. Randolph Avenue is a bit of an obstacle course this morning since there are piles of recycling bags along the pavement. Near the precincts of the surgery there are several cats and one, protected by an iron railing, has a staring contest with Fritz. Neither blinks, though Fritz, at last figuring out that this is the enemy, begins to bark. We return to the park, following the seldom seen Fonzi, and, my dog still on lead, makes it as far as the café.

Still utilizing our table in the forecourt we have Ronnie, Georgie, Ofra, Davide, Janet and Nicholas this morning. Ofra has hurt her shoulder and is out of sorts. She has brought with her a dress she wants Georgie to wear to tonight's wedding party, though Georgie claims it is too short. The café staff bring out a bowl of water and the dogs help themselves; perhaps this is the first time this year that such a ritual has been played out. Beneath our table Monty and Bailey have a tussle over a scrap of food, then Monty poos on the flagstones and Nicholas has to clean it up. Ofra says her shoulder may be sore because of all the pulling it receives when she is walking her dog to the park so Winnie's harness is detached and fitted over the King Charles to see if it will fit. "What is this," I say, "Bailey tries cross-dressing?" The others then point out that he has enough gender identity problems as it is. Nicholas complains that they have forgotten about his toasted ham and cheese sandwich but Georgie reminds him that they were calling out numbers while he was on the phone. "It was number 17," I add. "That's my number!" he explodes. He goes in to retrieve his food but by now we have been at table for so long that he has to eat his sandwich on the march as we begin our back passage walkround.

Wednesday, May 7:

I am expecting quite warm weather today and I'm down to two layers only as Fritz and I enter the park on a sun-sparkling day. Things go well enough as we approach the cypress trees but here I am separated from my dog, who seems to have double-backed. I lose track of him momentarily as I answer a greeting from an obviously pregnant Mary McCartney, walking my way with her Paddy, and when I begin my investigations I discover that my scamp has admitted himself to the running track again (there are now four missing fence panels) and is off. He completely ignores my calls (did I listen to *his* request that I *not* go out last night?) and I am soon in pursuit as he makes a multi-staged passage to the head of the straightway and thence out an open door onto the green. For the next few minutes, having learned my lesson, I follow him about as he pursues his own agenda but at 9:30 I manage to collar the beast and we head in for coffee.

This morning we have Dan, Ofra, Georgie, Ronnie, and Suzanne. The first three (and I) attended the wedding party of Kate and Bob last night (hence my suitably punished defection from my own house) and so naturally there are a lot of post-mortems. Someone says that there was an ex-England footballer in the party but they can't remember which one. I say that, after all these years, I have actually met Georgie's husband, James, and that I came home from the Century Club on Shaftesbury Avenue with Saskia and her husband Patrick.

On other topics, the conversation is more general. Dan, who never has to take the short-haired Winnie to the groomer, has had to do his own job on her dew claws. He says that the rest of her nails get worn off on the cement and I say, "I thought they got worn off on the refrigerator door." Daisy-Mae is rapidly becoming Winnie II. She scraps with Fritz over a morsel of food beneath my chair and snaps at Ofra's fingers when Bailey is getting a treat. That lady is wearing sandals and has to be told by Dan not to call them slippers. There follows a discussion on the origin of the name flip-flop and I add, trying to out-Ronnie Ronnie, that they call them Birkenstocks because they only keep them in stock for berks. We begin a back passage walkround, our progress slowed by Ofra's insistence that we view yesterday's wedding ceremony on her mobile phone.

Friday, May 9:

I have missed a day in the park while completing, with my friend Tosh, a section of the Capital Ring in suburban Lewisham and leafy Bromley. Fritz has *not* missed a day in the park since Linda added him to her Pepper and, according to Suzanne, he quite enjoyed himself on four circuits of the place. (Linda adds that she had to wrestle a chicken bone out his molars during one such circle.) It was quite warm yesterday and Fritz did drink a lot of water but today it is more overcast and considerably cooler in the morning. We make slow progress toward the green—as many a grass shoot has to be sampled.

The park is very noisy this morning. To the usual cacophony of construction sounds we have the chatter of dozens of entering student athletes, the intrusion of a lawnmower that is being driven in circles on the green outside the café, even the lorry of the Star caterers is running its engine for no good reasons as goods are unloaded. We settle down at a wire table just inside the forecourt, one which Dan prefers because it means that the dogs are not hovering near the front door of the café.

There are eight of us today including Dan, Ronnie, Janet, Georgie, Ofra, Suzanne and Leslie—the owner of Suki the Vizsla.

Bouzha arrives with the food, carefully placing it on top of the stone wall so that she won't have to be too close to the dogs and offering some gratuitous beauty tips on the subject of Ofra's hair. That lady has a huge black and blue bruise on her leg but, of course, she can't remember how she got it. Her Bailey is jumping from lap to lap, often with little warning; finally Ronnie makes him get down. Sparkie and Winnie are active beneath our feet, though yesterday afternoon, so I understand, they had a major fight here. Janet leaves early with Daisy-Mae since they are visiting Janet's mother today. The rest of us follow along soon thereafter. Footie fans have dumped a large pile of sunflower seed husks on the walkway between the pitches. Bailey has found something to roll in at the head of the track.

Saturday, May 10

The warm and muggy weather persists and I am in short-sleeved shirt again as Fritz and I enter the park on a busy Saturday morning. Progress is rapid enough toward the green and while I am washing my hands in the loo (the dryer is still alive) Fritz is working the green, where a number of our pals have gathered. Thereafter my dog heads for the east end of the greensward where I can see a Filipino corner that somehow also includes the American chap who owns Cristal (Tagalog Tagalong).

I don't want Fritz to tire himself out too much on such a warm day and so I put him on lead here and follow the others into the café.

Our new table is soon accommodating a party of ten, including Hanna, braving the pollen on another hay fever day, Janet, Georgie, Dan, Ronnie, Ofra, Liz, and the newlyweds. There is a good deal of wedding chatter, though it makes little sense to those who were not present in whole or in part, and Janet passes around a Photoshopped print of the dogs of the favored five wearing wedding hats.

The café soon has a long queue inside and families at every table outside. Hanna has me open her bottle of water and pours some of it into a saucer for the dogs. Fritz soon has his wet mouth dripping all over my shirt.

Both Bailey and Winnie sit in my lap when Fritz is not there himself; this is only because they can get closer in this way to Ofra's scrambled eggs on toast. A woman comes by with a Shih-Tzu puppy, one whom we believe to be the chap also called Bailey, but it turns out to be the latter's sister, Molly—just an adorable creature who is soon getting cuddles from everyone. A little boy passes by our table on the way to the loo, shying away from an innocent Winnie, who just happens to be standing near the gate. "Don't do that," the boy's fire-plug shaped dad says sternly, "if it gets in your way just give it a kick." Such are the lessons of child-rearing in the land of the Chavs.

Sunday, May 11:

It is again very warm as Fritz and I make our way into the park; I'm sure my dog could already benefit from another haircut. Coming our way is Charlie, the Giant Poodle, but he and Fritz seem to co-exist in harmony as they do some sniffing in the bushes. Georgie comes up behind us with Sparkie and together we walk toward the green, Sparkie taking exception to some chap in shorts who is innocently watching a football match. Out on the grass we can see that Dan has brought his blanket and he has been joined on it by Janet and Liz. Fritz plays through and continues on his wanderings, though, fortunately for me, many of these are in shaded areas. The new magnolia tree already looks like it needs water.

Hanna comes into the park and we check out the details of this afternoon's Turkish Grand Prix while heading for the café. It will be another crowded day here, with queues already forming inside.

Much of the morning's conversation is devoted to cars. Both Liz and Hanna have had to tell off other drivers, who, perhaps maddened by the heat of the moment, have acted in a dangerous fashion recently. From here it is not much of a stretch to go on to the subject of mini-cabs. Although it is agreed that it is a courtesy to let them know when you are bringing a dog with you, several of our ladies have encountered hostility from the largely Asian driver force when the latter have made nasty remarks on actually seeing the dog in question. Georgie says that she recently told the dispatcher three times that she had a small dog but when her driver showed up and he wouldn't stop scolding her she ordered him to remove her bags from his boot. Liz says that she has twice been scolded as "one of those people." (Yesterday I teased her that her coffee order could be remembered because she too was a medium-sized Americano. Today we notice that her receipt bears the legend, "strong, white.")

Dan reports that, after some fighting at the café yesterday (unwitnessed by any of our group) there has been an urgent request to keep dogs on lead. This works for a while but Ofra doesn't have a lead for Bailey, who ends up sitting on the bench of a nearby table at feeding time. The human at this table, who has brought in a lovely large Vizsla named Duke, doesn't seem to mind, but Liz does jump up when Roxy approaches some toddlers who are also in the vicinity of food. (Roxy's tail is beginning to approach its normal angle and she does wag it often, so she must be getting better.) Winnie tries to jump in Hanna's lap when the scrambled eggs and toast arrive. Fritz has just vacated this spot, crossed my lap, and seated himself in Janet's lap. Hanna says that Fritz is getting chunky again (an allegation I deny) but this doesn't stop her from offering tidbits of toast.

Monday, May 12:

We have another lovely morning for our session in the park today, though it looks like things will again get rather warm by noon. (Fritz is waiting for the next cancellation at St. John's Pets, for I do think he would be more comfortable with less hair—and certain people would stop saying he is getting fat.) When we reach the green I can see the nucleus of a lively scene in the middle and so we head here too. It is like the good old days, eventually, with some ten dogs and their owners in a tight circle at the heart of the greensward. We have the blonde trio of Buddy, Rufus and Sasha, Michaela is making a late appearance (for her) with Skye the Cairn, Bekki is here with Bounce, Davide with Winnie, Peter with Holly, Nicholas with Monty, Georgie with Sparkie—there is even a Boxer pup with a tail who wants to jump on everybody until Fritz puts him in his place. Surprisingly, Fritz remains in touch with the group for most of the time spent in conversation, and when he starts to get restless it is time for us to head for the café anyway.

The café is experiencing some Monday morning hiccups. The bread man has failed to show up and all the toast eaters are soon offered ciabatta rolls only. This leads to great confusion and hurried conferences have to be held at the door to see if this is okay with those who have specified toast. When Nicholas gets his ham and cheese on ciabatta he sulks a bit and won't eat much, but the others manage to help him out, particularly the ravenous Winnie. Ronnie has requested some water for the dogs but this doesn't arrive either. "Imagine," I say, "the café is out of bread *and* water!"

Nicholas now has extra time on his hands and, after putting away the mobile phone, he starts to tell a complicated joke with lots of obscure gestures, something involving the Pope and the Grand Rabbi of Rome. Unfortunately, he can remember the punchline but not the intricate detail that precedes it and so he has to pause a number of times in the middle of his recital to see if he can recall any of the missing information. The rest of us are in an agony of boredom and Ronnie gets up to put out his cigar, arriving back several minutes later to discover that the joke is no further along. There is still no sign of the bread truck either.

Tuesday, May 13:

Temperatures have again dropped just a bit and there is quite a breeze reducing the warmth; still, it is a lovely Spring morning and Fritz makes a reasonable progress along the walkways. I notice that he turns left when we reach the Carlton roadway, not his usual direction these days, and soon we are climbing up the hill under a bower of overarching trees. Down below us I can see Saskia with Buddy; she points to me but it is a while before her dog realizes that he can lope to the top of the hill and receive a biscuit. We begin a descent, though soon Leila is gamboling up and Fritz has touched noses with Gus at the bottom. Oscar, Scamp and Rizzo are at the crossroads and Georgie is just reaching this spot with Sparkie, Daisy-Mae and Winnie; the latter almost manages to trip up a woman from the Middle East, who dances away in panic.

The conversation again turns to crime. Saskia says that yesterday afternoon violence spilled out from the college on Elgin Avenue, with a mob of boys, egged on by their female counterparts, chasing others of their ilk, headbutting their victims and whipping them with belts. Cheryl says that by accident she witnessed this scene as she and her husband were returning from the airport—and that one of those in flight was almost hit by a bus. Saskia, who says that she will be phoning the college later today, adds that two of her workmen rushed out to intervene—even though one was far too old to make a difference and the other far too fat. At breakfast the crime theme continues as we discuss the death of a sixteen year-old boy on Sunday, the thirteenth murdered teenager in London this year. I mention that two days before this incident Tosh and I had walked past his school in Eltham on our Capital Ring walk.

Peter arrives, dressed in shorts and cardigan, an outfit that amuses Ronnie no end. We get up to leave shortly after the chap in the wheel-chair arrives with his intemperate Staffie. (Come to think of it, this vehicle may not be motor-driven; the dog seems to provide the motive force.) Cheryl (just back from seeing a child graduate from the University of Oklahoma) has brought her vehicle too, the famous covered wagon—though both Lola and Ginger are walking today. We pass the pair of Bo and Bubbles, Rottweiler and Jack Russell, though, ironically, it is Bubbles who has to be muzzled. Rounding a corner of the running track I wait for Georgie and her ball sling, for just over the fence is a loose ball which she can now pluck as an addition to Sparkie's vast collection.

Wednesday, May 14:

I am back in a sweatshirt as temperatures have definitely cooled off this morning and skies have gone gray for the first time in a number of days. Barry is entering the park with Fix just as we arrive at our gate and we walk around together. Fix is even slower than Fritz, though he has an excuse, since the elderly little fellow is almost blind and, indeed, runs into stationary objects on a number of occasions. Fritz turns left again at the café and this means another ascent of Mt. Bannister. From here I can see that workmen are scraping away at the top of the little metal gazebo below, preparing it for a new coat of paint. Fritz turns left when we reach the bottom ourselves and I have to follow him toward the Randolph walkway.

He turns around to follow Jonesie back in the right direction and at this point I put him on lead and we head in for coffee.

It is a rather quiet morning, at least as far as the dog people are concerned, and our table has only Ofra, Georgie, Peter, Ellen and Hanna. There is a discussion of some important football fixtures, since Glasgow Rangers are playing one championship match against a Russian team in Manchester and Chelsea and Man U are playing one another in Russia (go figure). Ofra tells us that she has transplanted her bargaining skills, honed in the Old City of Jerusalem, to New York and that the "I Love NY" sweatshirt that she is wearing today is evidence of her success. Bekkie hooks Bounce to the wall behind our table and all our dogs go crazy at the presence of a newcomer.

My friend, the photographer Richard Dunkley, wheels his bike into the café (at least he knows the rules) and I excuse myself from our table in order to chat with him at a second one. He recommends the new coffee shop at the top of Castellaine Parade, Plan 9, where, I know, the dog people have gone for milkshakes. While we are chatting a brigade of chair-bound visitors is wheeled into the park by their carers and there is a second unusual sight as Richard and I exit the park. The running track is being circumnavigated by dozens of youngsters, every one of whom has disdained running in favor of forward progress by scooter.

Thursday, May 15:

A light rain is falling as Fritz and I prepare for our departure. This means rain jacket for me and rain coat for the dog, but this morning (not counting the initial struggle common to all such moments) I have trouble getting this garment adjusted and twice we have to stop in the park for repositioning. It looks like the fish man has dumped a lot of leftover whitebait on the entry planter (there is even a block of ice nearby) and I have to work hard to get Fritz to bypass this temptation. In spite of the rain progress is very slow and I am suspicious that my dog either wants to get onto the running track or return to the fish so I put him on lead for a while as we get closer to the green. Not surprisingly there are not many people about this morning.

Just as we near the café the first Paddington Academy lads come jogging down the path, with the obligatory convulsive sidestep when they spot danger in the form of a Schnauzer in a raincoat. (Fans of school integration will be saddened by the fact that there is not a single white face in this grouping.) As Fritz and I complete a grand circle of the green, passing a chap with a circular saw who is putting an end to the life of the old Grantully entry sign, we encounter the gym class a second time. Their teacher is leading them to an exercise bar for some chin-ups but a few minutes later, when I am stationed at the café, the whole lot penetrates this once quiet spot and, taking stacked chairs off the pile, they are soon seated in their own grand circle while their teacher attends to Amir, who has hurt himself on the apparatus—with Miss summoned from school and forms to be filled out in the office. Sodden and bored kids are soon lining up for snacks at the café counter.

Only Peter and Ellen, who have their own table, and Hanna and Cheryl, who are seated with me, have braved the elements this morning. Cheryl is full of complaint over the renewal of waterworks on Elgin Avenue, an interruption to normal traffic patterns that has made it impossible for her to leave her cleaning off at 123 Cleaners on the corner of Shirland Road. Hanna says that they have broken the mouth mold she left at the dentist last week and she now has to return to Chorleywood for a second impression. She seems to have reflexology designs on my feet, which she knows I plan to use on an extensive walk in Wales in a month's time. The rain intensifies so we delay any movement home, but at last I sense a return to brighter skies and, on my own for once, begin my back passage walkround.

Friday, May 16:

The dour weather persists as Fritz and I begin our Friday ramble in the park. Almost immediately we encounter the burly, bouncy presence of Miro, the advance guard for a group that includes Christian, Reina, and, bringing up the rear, the wiry Vito. Christian is full of complaint about the return to colder temperatures. I tell him that I had hoped that my leather jacket was finished for the year but that I am glad it is out of the closet one more time.

Fritz follows the inner passage behind the cypress trees, bumping noses once with a female Staffie who is heading in the opposite direction. When we reach the café I leave my coffee money off with Ronnie and continue on to the green, one half of which is in the possession of rounder-playing lads from Paddington Academy. Georgie is crossing the green with Sparkie and Daisy-Mae, while the latter is fending off the charging attentions of Kai. Fritz continues along the Randolph walkway; we turn right at the tennis courts and eventually return to the green—where I can see that Davide has arrived with Winnie and that he and Georgie are heading in for coffee.

When I join our table it seems as though we have only a small turnout today but before long Hanna, Suzanne, Cheryl and Ofra have arrived as well. The latter attempts to give her order directly to Lurch, but he says she has to join the queue like the rest of his customers—much to the amusement of the rest of us. One of his customers is the owner of Kai and Cookie; the latter, a delightful little Pug, manages to rush inside whenever there is a crack in the door. Ronnie drops a pile of carrots on the ground and these are soon consumed. When the cooked food arrives there is the usual scramble for attention among the dogs; Sunny gets told off for percussive barking at Suzanne's elbow. After only a few minutes I tell the others that I hate to drink and run but that I need to get home to take delivery on some of the liquids that these people and others will be consuming at a social gathering on Sunday.

Saturday, May 17:

Gray skies and cool temperatures continue to prevail as Fritz and I make our entry into a busy park. Behind us I can see Barry with Fix and Suzanne with Sunny and, indeed, this party eventually overtakes us as my dog makes very slow work of his progress toward the Carlton walkway. At the café they are just putting out the chairs and tables and we play through, turning left in front of the loos and climbing over the grass to the top of Mt. Bannister. There is a lively scene up here today with a chocolate Lab, also named Bailey, in the mix. My dog doesn't need any encouragement but today he is lead astray by Sparkie, who descends to the parking lot, then marches along the walkway behind the adjacent tennis courts—emerging at last to run at great speed in huge looping circles, hoping that someone will chase him.

A table in the forecourt is selected for morning coffee, though at least this one has chairs. Eventually we are nine: with Dan, Davide, Cheryl, Hanna, Ronnie, Liz, Ofra, and Janet making up the numbers. Peter is hovering in the background and Franca is seated at a table behind us. She has her own dogs, Frank and Bianca, with her, but she also seems to be minding a Yorkie named Boysie. She does not have the delightful Valentina, who is with her mother in Italy while mom studies for this week's psychology exams. Franca says that Valentina likes to go out on the balcony, call all the neighbors out onto their own, and, with the audience in place, dance and sing for them in a tongue unknown to the western world.

Our conversation this morning seems to have a lot to do with Ofra's expectations in the cleaning department—since the Brazilian she has working for her now doesn't seem to measure up. Everybody wants to advise her on what to do next, particularly Hanna, but when Ofra seems not be taking these suggestions on board there are sore feelings. The sorest of feelings, however, belong to none of these today, but to Winnie, who is in a rage. It starts before the food has arrived when she jumps out of a lap to dispatch some pigeons—but it intensifies when it is obvious that there is still uneaten human food on the table and nobody is offering any of it to her. She also doesn't like the look in the eyes of some of the other lap dogs, particularly Sparkie ("You looking at *me*?), and she has to be restrained on several occasions. When she bites Davide Dan gets up and takes her into the naughty corner where, tethered to a fence, she continues to bark at us. Released at last she is dosed with scrambled eggs by Auntie Liz, which may rather defeat the purpose.

Monday, May 19:

I have missed a day in the park, though Fritz has not, for yesterday morning, just when I should have been heading for green pastures, my dog (having been delivered by the ever thoughtful Linda) was having his beauty treatment at St. Johns Pets. This meant (after he and Pepper had made a late entry into the park) that he could be brought home in splendid shape, just what was required to greet his many guests at an afternoon party which I staged for my many friends—whose kindness and many acts of hospitality have been so welcome this last year. Fritz was in his element, having minor hysterics every time a new guest arrived, and dancing on the landing in the hopes that I would have to bribe him back inside with a biscuit. He was the only dog present and I'm sure he ended up with quite a few wonderful snacks in the course of the afternoon. Dog people included Dan, Georgie, Liz, Hanna, Janet, Ronnie, Suzanne, and Ofra (the latter brought a wonderful raspberry cheesecake).

This morning it is again on the cool side (I wish I had brought my jacket) as Fritz and I make slow progress toward the green. Charlie, the little black Poodle, is barking at a workman inside the doomed corner meadow and his owner says that this is because Charlie dislikes fluorescent orange. We meet Hanna crossing the green but Fritz has other excursions on his mind and I have to follow him almost all the way to the Randolph gate before I can get him turned around. Ronnie has taken a table in the forecourt, perhaps in the hopes of getting a little sun, but it rarely makes an appearance.

We are joined by Georgie, Hanna, and Ellen, and the appearance of the latter is Fritz's clue to try and winkle a Shmacko out of her purse. An unnamed black Cairn keeps unwinding its long lead in order to see what is going on at our table while a black Chow is suffering from separation anxiety and barking at the café door. One topic of conversation dominates this morning, and it is a melancholy one. David, the Chinese man who owned Hugo the wild Collie, has died. Only in his late forties, David evidently collapsed at home from a heart attack. Here he remained, Hugo quietly at his side, for the better part of three days before a nephew became alarmed. The door had been bolted from the inside and it was a struggle to gain admission. Hugo is being looked after in the interim by Angie, but his ultimate fate is unknown.

Tuesday, May 20:

I am still trying to be optimistic about the temperature—which means that again I am slightly chilled as, jacketless, I make my way into the park with Fritz on a quiet Tuesday morning. My dog makes quick work of his progress toward the café but here, to his surprise, he has to go back on lead. This is because I can see, staring out at us from a perch inside the forecourt, the giant unmuzzled head of Harry the Akita. I keep Fritz on lead as we work our way along the Randolph walkway, passing Peter with Holly, Ellen with Jack and Sandy, and Cheryl with Ginger and Lola. By the time we have returned to the green there is a knot of dog owners discussing the sad fate of David and the future of Hugo the Collie.

At breakfast this morning we have Hanna, Peter, Ellen, Cheryl, Georgie, Ronnie, Ofra and John. The latter says that Ché would really like to play with Harry, but that he finds the prospect of such an encounter a bit worrying. Much of the morning conversation is devoted to recent television programs on China and Russia—with Hanna still upset about the latter's appropriation of Karelia from Finland all those years ago. A giant crane is swinging its hook behind the clubhouse. "At last," I say, "we can tell Janet that we have discovered a way of getting that new sofa into her flat."

When we get up to leave somebody notes that Winnie is not following us. This is because, unusually, the Pug has not made it to the park this morning at all—or Davide has not, however you look at it. The slowpoke in this morning's procession, therefore, is Ginger, who repeatedly puts the brakes on. Cheryl, who has announced that she has brought her books to read in the park today (never mind that it is freezing) now gives Lola her freedom and picks the senior Pug up. Cheryl won't be doing any reading anyway—as she has just discovered that she has forgotten her glasses.

Wednesday, May 21:

For the first time in several days I feel comfortable enough in just a sweatshirt; it is a lovely fresh morning in the park and the sun is bright in the spring skies. Fritz makes a lively progress along the back walkways and out to the green where Fly is dragging Daisy-Mae around by the teeth and Georgie is having a devil of a time trying to prevent the Shih-Tzu from going back for more. I follow Fritz on his usual perambulations and this means, today, a stroll along the Randolph walkway, a trip behind the tennis courts, a return to the green for a complete circuit (meeting little Gomchi near the Grantully entrance) and finally a visit to the café.

Ronnie, Georgie and Dan are getting settled at our table in the forecourt and I hand Fritz over to Ronnie so I can get into the queue behind John. The latter is trying to sell the park manager on the virtues of comfry as Hanna comes in and asks me to get her a cup of black coffee in a glass and a plain croissant. This is fair enough, as usually it is she who orders my cappuccino—but Metty has to give me a tray when it is time to take all these objects outside. We are ten at table today, all of the aforementioned figures plus Davide, Peter, Ellen, and Ofra.

There is much talk about tonight's football match between Chelsea and Manchester United in Moscow and John is convinced that Chelsea will have bribed their way to a win. Dan, who worked late last night (hence a rare weekday appearance for him today) says that he has to see the musical version of *Gone With The Wind* tonight, a show that is closing soon after a less than stellar run. Ofra is again having passport complications; she has to remove a blob of lipstick from her dog and I say that he has enough gender identity problems as it is. Fritz seems to want to sit on my lap but, once arrived, he really wants to sit on John's lap. Ché doesn't seem to mind and Fritz doesn't make his usual protest when that giant Alsatian head makes an appearance below the table. We begin a back passage walkround and first Sparkie and then Jack penetrate the empty five-a-side pitch for some ecstatic circles.

Thursday, May 22:

We have a wonderful warm Thursday morning for our visit to the park today and I am quite content for Fritz to laze along as we make only the slowest of progress. Eventually he speeds up, but this is now a problem, for I can see that he is heading for a Carlton roadway junction where Metty is driving his car to work in one direction and a tractor is chugging along in the other. I distract him long enough for this menace to pass. He doesn't exactly come at my call, not even with the promise of a biscuit, but his attention is at least sufficiently diverted.

340

At the roadway itself I pause to chat with the owner of Artemis, the Border Terrier, and while I am doing so my dog disappears. I have a vague sense that he went left and so I ascend Mt. Bannister next, finding him on top of the plateau with a lot of other dogs who are heading our way. When we have at last returned to the green I put him on lead, delivering him to Ronnie while I go inside with my coffee order. Hanna is discussing last night's football match in Moscow with Lurch, who is very pleased with himself, as he is a Man U. supporter and Chelsea have lost the competition during a rain-soaked penalty shootout—in spite of any bribery. At breakfast discussion of the game continues; the consensus is that penalty shootouts are not the way to end contests like this.

Today we have Davide, Hanna, Ofra, Georgie, Ellen, Cheryl and Ronnie. Winnie is seated in Davide's lap, just back from the vet after having received some drops for an eye problem. Ofra wants to know if Davide, Cairo-bound, ever returns the same day he flies out. "That's short-haul," Davide says disdainfully, "I'm long-haul." Cheryl is planning her next golfing adventure. She says that her scores were much better before the grass started to grow—since it takes more effort to get a ball out of the rough now, *if* you can find it. Fritz spends a good deal of time in Hanna's lap, then jumps down to lick the foam from my cappuccino cup. I can see that Rosie is eyeing this process greedily and so, after Fritz has had a go, I let her complete the process. During our back passage walkround Hanna starts to apply reflexology pressure to Davide's hand (something about an ear problem) and he complains of the pain. "That's all right," Hanna says, "now give me the other hand."

Friday, May 23:

It is rather overcast this morning but temperatures are mild enough as we make our way into the park. The first of innumerable school groups soon rounds a corner of the running track, though, unusually, these are toddling tykes—some of whom look as though they had just learned to walk. Fritz meanwhile is active on the grass margins of the walkways, munching away at the longer shoots while a curious magpie stares down at us suspiciously. Every now and then I have to push my dog along with the tip of my shoe—for it appears that he is impossible to budge this morning.

When we reach the green there is the usual game of rounders at one end, the sound of the aluminum bat echoing over the grass. A large group of yellow-clad youngsters is entering from Randolph Avenue and they note that Fritz has a beard. Davide has brought Winnie with him but it is little Monty the Pug who bustles over to greet me. On the flanks of Mt. Bannister I see the unusual sight of two bums, one super-sized, one original recipe, rising like rockets pointed at the sky; this is not a position of prayer (at least these bums are not positioned in the right direction needed for worship in any of the world's foremost faiths)—it's just a stage in some sort of exercise. We walk beneath these projections and pass behind the tennis courts where Fritz pauses to throw up all of that grass he has been eating.

At breakfast we have only a small turnout, just Davide, Ofra, Ronnie, Hanna and Georgie. Hanna wants to have another go at curing Davide's blocked ears but he is resistant. She has been to the Body, Mind and Spirit show and purchased a new therapeutic wire ring which she now uses to surround each of my fingers in turn, rolling the ring up and down in the process. It is not to escape any more treatment that Ronnie and I are the first to begin a back passage walkround. He has cleaners at home and I have a houseguest, here to attend a major alumni reunion at the American School.

Sunday, May 25:

It would appear that I have missed another day in the park, though this is only partially true—for I was here yesterday, though half an hour earlier than usual since I had to get ready for a trip up to the school and a ceremony honoring my houseguest, Gavan, and my walking partner Tosh. As often happens, just a small change in the schedule meant that all sorts of dogs not normally encountered in our usual time slot were in evidence, though I did see Denise with Rizzo and Liz with Roxy. The alumni reunions means that Fritz has been having to adjust to a change in his schedule as well—though it was no hazardous duty for him to spend Friday night in Hanna's backyard.

This morning there is really bad news for him: the rain is pelting down and this means that we both have to don our raingear. My dog is most reluctant to move forward into the deluge and I keep him on lead just in case he decides to go home. The park is largely empty, though

Kathy Andon does come up with Paddy—who keeps leaving his ball behind in the odd puddle. There is one group of stalwart footie lads in the five-a-side pitch and when we reach the café I can see an equally brave group of dog people assembling at a table under the overhang.

I hand Fritz over to Janet and join Georgie and Dan in the queue. You would think (as we are the only customers this hour) that service would be pretty swift but Dan and Bouzha are deep in conclave about the results of last night's Eurovision Song Contest and this requires Bouzha to provide a detailed political analysis of why the various Balkan states voted the way they did. The conclusion is that the Contest is now a political rather than a musical event.

Hanna joins us and the owner of Sid as well. The other dogs set up their usual protest when a stranger is in their midst but they soon settle down and make room at the feeding stations for the fellow—who seems to be a cross between a long-haired Jack Russell and a Fox Terrier. His owner says that she is supposed to be participating in a boating party today and the others suggest that she may not have to move very far to climb aboard—as the rain continues to lash down. Dan reports that members of the group attended a performance of *Fat Pig* last night and that when Liz asked the author of this play why all the British actors had assumed American accents he replied peevishly, "Well, you wouldn't want to see *Death of A Salesman* in British accents, would you?" I congratulate Georgie on Rangers having finally won the Scottish Cup (albeit against lowly Queen of the South) and she says that her James would have killed himself if they hadn't. This leads to an intriguing conversation (as we rise to take advantage of a brief lull in the downpour) on just how James *would* commit suicide. Georgie suggests it would begin with, "Run me a bath; I want to drown myself." I suggest, "Georgie, I forgot, how do you turn on the gas?"

Monday, May 26:

There has been no improvement in the weather as Fritz and I make preparations for our adventure in the Rec—Bank Holiday-style. This means the usual evasive tactics from my dog before I eventually corner him so that I can slip on his raincoat. He is much better, however, when it comes to braving the downpour; where, yesterday, I had to drag him along the sodden walkways, today he trots along resignedly. Rain is lashing down and the paths are covered with leaves and branches. I have told

Gavan that if there is no one else waiting for coffee outside the café that I will be back quickly today. To my surprise, however, the dog owners have once again come through.

Janet and Georgie are already in place as Elian unlocks the doors. Janet has brought a paw-print towel on which Daisy-Mae is drying herself; it is lying on the ground so Sparkie sits on it in preference to the wet paving stones. Then it gets placed on the conjoined laps of the two ladies—who look like they have just come to observe some doggy football match from the stands. Ellen arrives with Jack and Sandy and Dan comes in next, also surprised to see he is not alone—though he is *carrying* Winnie so that the latter will not have to get her paws wet. Full marks to Hanna, who arrives next, since she doesn't even have a dog who needs a morning walk, though she will inherit Yoyo later this afternoon. Fritz seems to be quite miserable, though he does manage to get down some biscuits and some cappuccino foam. Winnie and Daisy-Mae get into a food scrap under the table. Metty, in another admirable gesture, surprises each of us, again his only customers, with a gratis piece of pastry each.

Hanna and I discuss yesterday afternoon's Formula 1 race in Monte Carlo, an exciting contest even if a Finn did not win. Georgie says that James is still in bed, twiddling the dials on the TV set and Dan says that the same is true of Davide, who has already sent back his morning coffee because it had gone cold. (Dan also admits that he has committed the serious domestic crime of warming the old cup up in the microwave rather than making a new one, as expected—even humming loudly so that the ping of the oven would not give the game away.) Ofra, meanwhile, has gone to Israel for a wedding and Ronnie and Susie are off to Marbella for a week. This means that Georgie will soon have Bailey, though Tanis will look after Rosie. Georgie seems somewhat relieved at this disposition of animals as Ronnie's dog evidently snores up a storm. Our local storm pauses for breath and I announce that I am going to make a move. Dan and Janet have both parked as close as they can get to the café and so today I walk alone.

Tuesday, May 27:

Every one of yesterday's walks had to be undertaken in a persistent rain and therefore it is with some relief that I can lead Fritz into the park without having to dress him in his raincoat first. It is still gray and humid this morning, but at least there is no moisture, that is there is no moisture falling on our heads—there is plenty of wet in the grass—which I must cross in order to catch up with my dog, who has rushed out to the center of the green to greet Daisy-Mae and Sparkie. The former is being pursued (with amorous intent) by Thomas the Lhasa Apso. Fritz soon spots Ellen walking with Jack and Sandy and he joins them for a while; by now it is time to head for the café. A leaf-blowing park person is creating a din outside this structure and a lady actually stops *me* to complain: "It's just like this every Sunday where I live. People have gardens the size of postage stamps but a broom won't do—they have to have leaf blowers too!"

This morning we have Georgie, Cheryl, Ellen and Hanna—Davide having taken Winnie off early so that he can complete an errand. Cheryl says that she got into a spirited verbal altercation yesterday with a woman who chided her for letting one of the Pugs poo on the green—even though she had picked up the offending matter. Ginger is snuffling about at our feet this morning but Lola has hurt a paw and is a bit out of sorts. Georgie tries to make her lap available to Sparkie and the scamp responds by suddenly jumping into my lap—though he has mistimed his leap and falls off immediately. A wet Daisy-Mae now leaps into Ellen's lap—which is nice and dry. Recipes and TV watching remain the chief topic of conversation; Hanna says that the Somali warlords she saw on last night's program all own property in London.

We get up to begin our back passage walkround. As usual Sparkie has dropped his ball near the exit gate and when Georgie admonishes him, "Pick up the ball!" a little girl, just entering, thinks *she* is being addressed and almost bursts into tears. We meet Wendy with Corky at the corner near the cypress trees and Fritz issues an obligatory growl, then pisses on Daisy-Mae's head. Sparkie now drops his ball under the track fence and Georgie has to climb under the rail to retrieve it. A few minutes later a lively Jack Russell prances into the park and Fritz growls at him too. I deposit my dog and head out to pick up the laundry. Growls turn to howls, howls of protest over this dastardly abandonment.

Wednesday, May 28:

As we get ready for our trip to the park I reflect that yesterday only got worse for my dog. As we were out for our late night walk it began to rain again and soon after we had gone to sleep Fritz retreated beneath the bed in order to paw the carpet in anxiety over the approach of a major thunderstorm. I can't tell whether he simply senses the change in atmospheric pressure or whether he can actually hear distant thunder before the rest of us but, as so often proves the case, he is quite right. We are soon engulfed in a storm, one that hurls lightning bolts and resounds to the explosion of accompanying thunder. Throughout much of the night I can hear him pawing away, though he usually stops when I tell him to do so; I can only wonder what the people downstairs think about the strange sounds coming from their ceiling.

He does not get up when I do, indeed he makes no appearance until Cathy arrives for her weekly dust-up. Now he is full of beans and ready for more mischief in the park. For the latter I blame Oscar the Schnauzer, who uses a gap in the fence to penetrate the running track, thereby giving my dog a really good idea. For a while Fritz follows a lone jogger in a counter clockwise direction but after I have made my own appearance on the track he turns around, passes me on the straightaway and exits onto the Morshead roadway where Georgie (with Sparkie and Daisy-Mae) and Davide (with Winnie) are just beginning a grand circle of the green. Sparkie is chasing after a man on a tractor who is mowing the grass. Fritz, fortunately, shows no interest in this vehicle, but he does abandon the others for some solo time in the Grantully dog pen. When we exit I put him on lead and complete the circle (pausing only once to chide Oscar), reaching the café at last.

This morning, which continues to be gray, humid and threatening, we have only Georgie, Davide and Hanna at breakfast. Georgie, as if two dogs weren't enough, notes that Bailey, whom she expects to look after as well, has yet to show up at her house. Sparkie has an hysterical fit when a man with a green fluorescent vest walks by and Winnie, growing increasingly anxious over the way humans keep eating all the food, suddenly has a go at him—with Davide having to snatch his pet out of harm's way, her little legs flailing furiously. Because of the darkening skies we decide to make an early escape from the park. We pass Farrah's Poppy, who has had a summer haircut, and several other unknown dogs who have to be sniffed carefully. Sparkie has again lost his ball.

Thursday, May 29:

The sun is making an effort this morning and temperatures have again climbed as Fritz and I cross the street to enter the park. My dog completes the earliest portion of our travels in a business-like fashion and I am quite relieved that he has shown no interest today in the gaping entryway in the track fence. He has sprinted well ahead of me as we approach the Carlton roadway, and I can just see that he has turned left here. His focus is on a party made up of Janet, Georgie, Sparkie, Winnie and Daisy-Mae. He has lost interest in me completely and I don't see him again until I have reached the top of Mt. Bannister. We begin our descent, amused at the sight of a seated Rizzo far below us. He has something stuck to his leg and he won't budge until Denise returns to remove it for him.

We still have time for a circuit of the green and so we are soon off. I can see Fritz again making a left turn at the Grantully gate but this time he has neither admitted himself to the doggy pen nor exited the park altogether (which is the chief concern here)—he has just pissed on the gate and resumed our line of march. Sparkie has again lost his ball, but Georgie has brought a small collection of these objects today. Janet also throws a ball to Daisy-Mae, not having noticed that this will place her dog directly in the line of an advancing cyclist, who has to put the breaks on as the Shih-Tzu heads off after the toy. On the next toss it is Fritz who fields the ball, completing one of his patented over the shoulder grabs without breaking his stride.

At breakfast this morning we have only Hanna, Georgie, and Janet. The latter is working from home today—and has already discovered a £38,000 discrepancy in the account she has been scrutinizing on her computer screen. Rising fuel bills are an important topic for this morning's conversation and Hanna says that she is thinking of using one of her fireplaces for heat. Ellen is sitting by herself on the bench next to a corner table in the forecourt and, as the arrival of toast comes ever nearer, she soon attracts a crowd; even Fritz sets up a howl so that I will let him off lead so that he can get himself into position. In this free-for-all no one is more purposeful than Winnie, who somehow manages to jump up from the bench onto the top of the stone wall behind Ellen's head, the better to observe the scene below. Janet has her camera with her and manages to get a good photo of the canine vulture. Meanwhile Daisy-Mae has found some bird poo on the paving stones and rolled enthusiastically over the mess. There is real warmth in the sun as we begin our back passage walkround.

Friday, May 30:

It is rather grey and humid this morning, but at least there is no rain—Fritz and I did get slightly wet during our afternoon walk yesterday. A smooth and rapid progress is made along the back walkway, where a very pregnant mom is pointing out everything that Fritz does for the benefit of her accompanying toddler. Between the playing fields we pass Franca with Frank and Bianca and an Italian woman who has a little dog and a large one, in the latter case it is the burnished black Lab named Dylan. These two ladies are discussing mortgage rates in Italian as we pass in the opposite direction, soon reaching the green—which Fritz crosses to check in with Suzanne and Sunny. A group of us, including the abovementioned plus Barry with Fix and Georgie with Winnie, Daisy-Mae and Sparkie, soon begin a clockwise walkround.

At one point my dog makes one of his darting left turns and I think he must have gone into the Grantully dog pen but Georgie soon spots him in the middle of the forbidden street! He does sit when I command him to do so but he has to spend the rest of the morning on lead and in disgrace. For that matter his nose is covered in the chalk they have used to paint the cricket boundary. When we reach the area of the bandstand we can hear some nasty-sounding barking off to our left and when we get to the Morshead roadway we can see a cluster of dogs and a park keeper in conclave nearby. I am standing in front of the café a little bit later when the Italian woman comes by to announce that a white Pit Bull has attacked Dylan and that she is on her way to the office to report this incident. Soon someone is filling out a report. I tell Georgie that I won't be staying for coffee this morning but could she please get me a napkin from the café so I can clean off my dog's nose.

I can't stay because Fritz has an appointment at Hamilton Vets for his booster shots—and so here is where we march a few minutes later.

He gets a clean bill of health (weight 9.55 kilos) and behaves himself well at injection time. On our return journey we meet up with Hanna and Georgie, who now volunteers to keep an eye on Fritz tomorrow, when I expect to undertake a country walk. The thought occurs to me that, if so, *today* is not only the last day in the park for this month but the end of another volume in the chronicle of Paddington Rec and its dog people.

As I like to do at such a watershed I search my records when I get home to see just how many dogs I have encountered this year during my hour or so in the park: 230. Among these were four dogs named Monty (Lab, Pug, Schnauzer and Cocker) and five named Charley or Charlie (Cocker, Bichon Frise, Beagle, and both Toy and Giant Poodle). Whatever their names, these friends of mankind, the dogs of Paddington Rec, continue to give so many of us delight—save for the odd Pit Bull or two.

INDEX: THE DOGS OF PADDINGTON REC

In the following list I have tried, by date, to note every time one of the dogs of Paddington Rec has been mentioned in the text. If they have *only* been mentioned, though not actually seen by me, I have recorded the date in italics. Of course many dogs share the same name, so I have tried to indicate (in parenthesis) which animal is being referred to. Apologies for the occasional misspelling of a dog's name—but this is inevitable in our world. Dates begin with June, 2007 and conclude with May, 2008.

Bianca: June 2, 9, *15*, 27, August 1, 8, October 23, December 4-5, January 19-20, March 19, 22, April 10-11, May 17, 30
Billy (Bearded Collie): June 3, December 24, March 31, April 4, 11, 13
Billy (sheepdog): June *20*, 22, 25-26, July 2, November *15*, 19-27, March 14, 18, 21, 24-25, 27-28
Blake: June 2, August 13, 23, October 23
Bo: March 20, May 13
Boise: January 5
Bonito: July 2-3
Boo: October 26
Bounce: November 30, May 1, 12, 14
Boysie: May 17
Brea: July 1, September 22, December 2
Bruce: October 10, 13
Bubbles (Jack Russell): May 13
Bubbles (Yorkie): June 12
Buddy: June 6, 16-17, 19, 22-24, July 6, 16-17, August 6, 12, 21, 23, 29, September 9, 11-12, October 2, 13, 15-16, 21, 23, 25-26, 28-29, November 7-8, 14, 22, 26, 28-29, December 5, 20, 21, January 14, 21, February 4-5, 8, 13, 15, 18-20, 23-26, 29, March *1*, 4-6, 14, 20, April 2-3, 6, 8, 11, 17, 21, 23, 29-30, May 1-2, 4, 6, 12-13
Buster: August 16, October 8
Cain: November 27
Campbell: June 24, October 20, 27, November 3, December 5
Carly: June 26
Casey: July 4
Charlie (Beagle): November 25
Charlie (Bichon Frise): October 3
Charlie (Cocker): June 18, July 6, October 25, November 5, March 11, 17
Charlie (Giant Poodle): December 31, March 30, May 11
Charlie (Toy Poodle): June 11, May 19
Ché: July 7-8, August 11, September 30, November 3-4, 24, January 6, 29, February 3, May 20-21
Cheeky: January 29
Chelsea: June 8, 19, October 5, November 7, February *16*, *25*
Chica: June 7, 12, 18-19, 22, July 2, September 4, 6, 11-12, 18, 24, October 4-5, November *30*

Chin: May 2

Coco: March 31

Cookie: December 19, February 19, May 16

Coops (Cooper): September 23, November 25, January 8

Corky: November 26, 28, March 16, 24, May 27

Cosmo: June *22*, September 10, November 5

Cressida: August 21, September 10, February 10, March 6

Cristal: August 14, October 11, November 1, 28, May 10

Daisy: September 15, October 29

Daisy-Mae: June *1*, 2-3, 9, 10, 11-12, 15-17, *18*, 19, 22, 25, 28, 30, July
    3, 4-6, 8, *16*, 17, *18*, 19, 25, 27-31, August 1, 3, 5-8, 12-17, 19-20,
    22-23, 25, 29-30, September 1, 3-5, 7-12, 16-19, 22-23, *24*, 25-28,
    30, October 2-4, 7-8, 12, 14-15, 22-26, 30, November 5, 7, 9, 11-12,
    15, 17-19, 25-26, 28-30, December 2, 4, 9, 12, 15-19, 22-23, 30,
    January 2, 6, 8-9, 11-14, 16-17, 19-20, 22, 24, 26, 28-30, February
    1-5, 12-13, 15-18, 20, 23, 26, 28-29, March 1, 3, 5, 8-9, 11-12, 16,
    18-22, 24-25, 27, 29, April 2-11, 15-17, 19-22, *23*, 24-25, 27-28,
    May 1, 7, 9, 13, 16, 21, 26-30

Dash: November *3*, April 7

Domino: September 4

Duke: May 11

Dylan: May 30

Elvis: November 20-21, January 9, 25, February 21

Fenway: November 8

Fix: April 15, 18, May 14, 17, 30

Flash: July 30, August 4

Flea: June 12

Flo: September 15, October 29

Flossy: October 15

Fly: April 17, 22, May 21

Fonzi: November 18, May 6

Foxie: July 11, March 24

Frank: June 2, 9, *15*, *27*, July 27, December 4, 5, January 19-20, March
    19, 22, April 10-11, May 17, 30

Freddy (Dachshund): October 17

Freddy (Pug): January 17

Fritz: June 1-13, 15-20, 22-26, 28-30, July 1-8, 14, 16-19, 25, 27-31,
    August 1, 3-8, 10-23, 25-27, 29-31, September 1-12, 14-19, 21-30,

October 1-17, 19-31, November 1, 3-30, December 1-31, January 1-26, 28-31, February 1-29, March 1-31, April 1-30, May 1-7, 9-17, 19-23, 25-30

Fritz (Golden Retriever): May *6*

Fritz II (Standard Schnauzer): January 31, March 21, May 4

Geisha: March 27

George: June 1-2, August 1, 6, *14-16*, *19-21*, January *5*, *28*, *30*

Ginger: October 11-12, 15-17, 19, 22, 25, 27, 30, November 1, 6, 21, *27*, 28, 30, December 3, *18*, January 5, *6*, 7, 10, 17-18, 21, 28, February *4*, 5-6, 9, 15, 20, 26, March 3-4, 6, 11, April 7, 15, 18, 21, 24, 29, May 13, 20, 27

Gomchi: May 21

Gracie: November 8

Gus: March 5, 17, April 7, 22, May 13

Gypsy: June 5, July 3, August 29, September 15, October 29, March 17, April 3

Harry: January 6, 14, 21, 24, February 5-6, 15, 20, *21*, 22, *23*, 25-26, 28, March 3, 17, 24, April 2, 10, May 20

Hendrix: August *3*, December *22*

Hendrix (Poodle): August 16

Hercules: June 4, *15*, 19, July 14, 17, 19, 25, September 4, October *4*, 8, 11, 31, December 18, January *29*, February 21

Holly: June 1-2, 16, 19, July 14, August 1, 14, 31, September 3, November 27-28, December 17, February 25, 28, March 16-17, 24, April 5, 7, 10, 21, 28, May 2, 12, 20

Honey: June 28

Hootch: June 6, September 25, March 19, 25

Hugo: November *16*, February *17*, May *19-20*

Humphrey: August 21, September 5, October 3, 15, November 30, December 22-23, March 23, April 7, 11, 20

Isla: September 3, 10-12, 16-17, 19, 21, 25, October 6-8, 12, 14, November *12*, 17-18, December *5*, 11, 13, 17, 20-21, *23*, 28, January 4, 26, 29, February 1, 17, March 1-2, 8, *19*, 24, 26, 29, April 5-6, 17, 20, May 4

Izzy: June 11-12, October 26

Jack (Bichon Frise): November 14

Jack (Jack Russell): June 1, 18, 29, August 1, 11, September 3, November
    20, 27-28, December 3, 12, 17, January 5, 24, 28, 31, February 23,
    28, *29*, March 3, April 7, 10, 20-21, May 2, 20-21, 26-27
Jack (Yorkie): June 22, July 3, August 1, September 4
Jackson: June 3
Jake: September 4
Jasmine: June 1, 5, 8, 17, July 28, August 27, September 8-10, 28, 30,
    October 7, 23, November 21, December 7, January 7, February 24,
    April *4*
Jasper (Patterdale Terrier): June 26, November 20
Jasper (Springer Spaniel): March 15
Jeffrey: October 15, February 22
Jess: June 4
Jody: December 31, March 17, April 3
Jonesie: June *22*, July 27, November 1, January *1*, 9, May 14
Kai: December 19, February 19, May 16
Kayla: February 6
King: March 1
Kiva: June 12
Lachan: February 20, March 29
Lady Tara: February 6
Lancer: September 10, November 7, February 15, April 17
Leila: June 6, 9, 12, July 4, 27, August 17, September 27, October 2,
    17, 29, November 1, 8, December 17, 21, January *1*, 9, *20*, 26, 29,
    February *8*, 13-14, 18, May 1, 13
Lightning: January 10, 12, 26, February 2, 13
Lola: October 11-12, 15-17, 19, 22, 25-26, 30, November 6, 21, 23,
    26-28, 30, December 3-4, 6, *18*, *20*, 29, January 6, 10, 14, 17-18,
    21, 28-29, February 4-6, 9, 15, 19-20, 26, March 3-4, 6, 8, April 7,
    15, 21, 24, 29, May 13, 20, 27
Louie: June 11
Lulu (Coton de Tulier): September 27
Lulu (French Bulldog): August 12, October 21
Lulu (Greyhound/Lurcher): June 3, November 20, 25, 30, December 4,
    8, January 20
Luna: July 5
Mack: October 30

Maddy: July 28, September 2, 8
Max (Mastiff): November 28
Max: (Staffordshire/Mastiff): April 29
Max (Weimaraner): September 27
Milly (mid-sized back): April 8
Milly (Staffie): June 10
Miro: January *1*, 2, 29, February *8*, March 26, April 4, 18, May 16
Molly: June 28
Molly (Shih-Tzu): May 10
Monchhichi: June 19, July 1
Monty (Cocker): August 15, September 25, October 8, 11, 31, November
    28, December 2, 12, February 13, March 13, April 4, May 6, 12
Monty (Labrador): November 23, December 4
Monty (Pug): November 25, January 10, May 23
Monty (Schnauzer): September 24
Mowgli: March 31
Mozart: June *20*, 22, 26, July 2, November *15*, 19-20, 24, 26, March *14*,
    24
Mungo: September 15, March 13
Nemo: September 29
Noodle: January 15, February 27, March 12, 26
Oscar (Schnauzer): June 9, 11, 18, September 1, 10, 19, 22, 24, October
    2, 4, 9, 11, 16, 30, November 1, 30, December 1, 5, 10, 19, 24,
    January 2, 7, 16, 25, February 1, 12, 15, 20, 25, 27, March 5, 8,
    12-13, 19, 26, 28, April 3-4, 9, 17, 21, 23, 29-30, May 13, 28
Oscar (Shih-Tzu): February 2
Otw: August 15, September 1, 7, November 21, March 2, 8
Paddy: September 15, December 28, May 25
Paddy (Irish): December 7, May 7
Parsley: February 5
Pasha: September 25, 27, December 26, February 13, April 3, 15
Pepper: June 3, 10, 28, July 2, August 4, 8, 10, 13, 15, 17, 19, 29-31,
    September *1*, 4, 7-9, 17, 21, 24, 27, October 1-2, 4, 7, 14, 17, 26,
    28, November 1, 3-4, *5-6*, 21-22, *23*, December 7, *12*, 14-15, 17,
    19, 25, 31, January 20-21, February 3, *8*, 19, March 8-9, 24, April
    27, May *9*, *19*
Phoenix: October 5, 17, January 12, April 7

Pickle: July *16*
Pip: March 31
Pippa: February 13, 22-23
Polo: September 1,15
Poppy: May 28
Princess: June 16, September 2
Prune: October 27
Pumbaa: December 14, 20
Raffy: January 13, 20, March 2, 16, April 20
Rebel: June 29, November 7, April 8
Redford: February *17*
Rizzo: August 29, October 9, November 30, January 16, February 27, March 5, 8, 12, 23, April 9, 16, 23-24, 29, May 13, *25*, 29
Rocca: April 5
Rocco: February *17*
Rocky: February 16, 24
Rosie: June 1, 18, August 16, 27, September 1, 10, 15, October 31, November 3, 6, December 2-3, 26, 31, January 2, *12*, 21, 24, 31, February 4-5, 14, 17, March 15, 24, April 15, 28, May 22, 26
Roxy (Beagle): June *7*, 16, July 14, 18-19, August 25, 27, 29, September 6-7, 12, 16, October 28, November 17-18, 24-25, December 16, 21, January 21, 30, February 3, 17, 28-29, March 2, 6, 8, 11, 15, 30, April 1, 5, 19, 26, *29-30*, May 4, 11, *25*
Roxy (Dachshund): September 12, 30, October 17
Roxy (Brown and White Staffie): October 14, 17, 28
Ruby: October 14
Rufus: June 12, July 1, 5-6, 16, August 29, September 4, 11, November 28, February 5, 18, 20, April 3, May 2, 6, 12
Saffy: June 3, 12-13, 20, 25, August 4, 11, 17-18, September 5, 16, 27, October 5, November 5, 11, December 9-11, 26, January 1-2, 6, 10, 17, 26, February 12, March 3, 9, 21
Sam: March 3
Sam (King Charles): August 20
Sammy: January 20
Sandy: June 1, 18, 29, August 11, September 3, November 27-28, December 3, 12, 17, January 5, 24, 28, February 23, 28, March 3, April 7, 10, 20-21, 29, May 2, 20, 26-27

Sasha: June 7, 17-18, 20, 22, 24, July 30, August 29, September 11-12, 19-22, October 2, 9, 30, November 1, 30, December 5, May 12, 26-27

Scamp: June 18, September 10, December 5, 24, January 7, 16, 25, February 1, 12, 15, 25, 27, March 5, 8, 12-14, 26, 28, April 3-4, 9, 17, 21, 23, 29-30, May 13

Shaggy: January 13

Sid (Boxer): June 7, 19, 22, July 5

Sid (Cairn Terrier): June 26

Sid (Jack Russell/Fox Terrier): June 5, May 25

Sidney: October 3, April 8

Simon: June 4, September 2, April 28

Skye (Alsatian): June 1-2, 4, 6, 23-25, 30, July 3, 16, 19, August 3, 6, 21, 23, 29, September 3, 10, 16, 19, 21, October 7, 13, November 10-11, *12*, 17-18, 22, December *5*, 9, 13, 17, 21, *23*, 28, January 4, 26, 29, February 1, 17, 24, March 1-2, 8, *19*, 24, 26, 29, April 5, 17, 20, May 4, 6

Skye (Cairn): June 9, August 6-7, 12, September 5-6, 8, October 26, November 1, 6, December *15*, January 6, 21, 24, February 12, March 31, April 2-4, May 12

Skye (small black): January 21

Snoopy (Dachshund): July 28

Snoopy (Jack Russell): May 3

Snowdon: December 23, January 6

Sonny: January 9, 26

Spadge: June *18*, July *5*, 17, 19, *31*, August 6, 19-20, September 3, 16, 18, 22, 24, *25*, October *9*, December 3, *6*, 24, *28*, January *5*, *28*

Sparkie: June 1, 3, 5, 8, 10-12, 20, 22, 26, 28, 30, July 2-3, 8, 17, 25, 27-30, August 5-8, 12-16, *17*, 23, 25, 27, September 1-2, 7-9, 11, 15-19, 27, 30, October 5, 8, 14, 19-20, 22, 24-25, 29-30, November 1, 8, 10-11, 13, 15, 17-22, 24-25, 28-30, December 2-4, 9-11, 15-17, 19, 22-23, 25-27, 30-31, January 2, 6, 9-14, 16, 19-20, 24, 28, 31, February 1, *2*, 6, 8, 13, 15-16, 19-20, 23, 26, 28-29, March 1, 3, 5, 8-9, 11-13, 15-16, 18, 21-25, 27-28, 31, April 1-4, 6-7, 9-10, 15, 18, 20-21, *23*, 24, 28, May 1, 3, 9, 11-13, 16-17, 21, 26-30

Spikey: January 9, February 25, April 3

Stella: October 4, 30, November 5, February 14, March 4

Storm: September 3

55

55555

.55

55

Suki: June *22*, August 8, May 9

Summer: September 29, January 4, March 19-20, 23

Sunny: July 28-29, August 1, 8, 15-16, 21, 25, 31, September 2, 7, October 3, November 6, 9, 23, April 8, 11, 15, 20, May 4, 16-17, 30

Sweep: September 23

Tanzanite: February *8*

Tara: June 22, August 13, December 31, February 29, March 21, April 21

Tarquin: November 8, January 24, February 1, March 31

Tay: November 23, December 4, April 7

Taz: June 6

Thomas: July 30, May 27

Tia: June *22*

Tilly (Border Terrier): July 8, September 10, October 7, 30, November 23, January *1*, 19-20

Tilly (Shih-Tzu): October 26

Timmy: June 9, 25, September 9, December 18, February 4, March 6, May 1

Tinkerbelle: June 3, 12-13, 20, 25, August 4, 11, 17-18, September 5, 16, 27, October 5, November 5, 11, December 9-11, 26, January 1-2, 6, 10, 17, 26, February 12, March 3, 9, 21

Toby: June 9, 25, October *25*

Toby (Yorkie): June 26

Toppler: March 25

Trixie: March 22

Trouble: September 16, March 20

Tyson: March 21

Vito: August 17, 29, September 4, 6-7, 10, 12, 16, 18, 21, 24-26, October 5, 12, 15, 24-26, 30-31, November 1, 5, 7, 9, 12-13, 21, 26-28, December 12, 14, January *1*, 2, 9, 29, February *8*, *13*, March 26, April 4, 18, May 16

Whisker: February 8

Winnie: June 1, 5-6, 8, 12, 17, 19-20, 22-23, July 3, 5-8, 17, 27-28, August 1, 4, 6, 8, 12-23, 30-31, September 1, 4-5, 7, 11-12, 18-19, 23-25, 27, 29-30, October 3, 5-7, 11, 14, 16-17, 19, 22, 25-28, 30, November 9, 11-13, 17-18, 20-21, 25, 28, December 3-6, 11-12, 15-17, 20-23, 30-31, January 1-3, 5-14, 17-20, 24-25, 28, 30-31,

February 1-5, 9-10, 12-15, 18-19, 22-23, 26, 29, March 1-9, 11-13, 15, *16*, 17-18, 22-29, April 2-5, 7-10, 16-21, 24-28, May 4-7, 9-13, 16-17, 22-23, 26-30

Winston: December 2

Wisley: December 14

Yoyo: September 28, December 11, January 25, February 2, April 7, 26-27, 30, May *26*

Zara: November *3*, April 7

Ziggy: June 2-3, *4*, 8-9, *12*, 13, 16-19, 23-24, 28-29, July 1, 5-8, 16-17, April *2*

Zig-Zag: March 29

Zimba: September 15

Zorro: January 19, February 24, March 9

ABOUT THE AUTHOR

Anthony Linick was born in Los Angeles in 1938 and educated in the city's schools, including Alexander Hamilton High School. In 1955 he entered the University of California at Los Angeles where, majoring in history, he completed his BA in 1959 and his PhD. five years later. While still an undergraduate he began work on the little magazine *Nomad* (1959-1962)—which he co-edited with Donald Factor. This background also contributed to his choice of doctoral dissertation topic, *A History of the American Literary Avant-Garde Since World War II.*

In 1964 he and Dorothy were married in Los Angeles and the following year they moved to East Lansing, Michigan, where Anthony took up a post as Professor of Humanities at Michigan State University. He taught a variety of courses in Western Civilization, literature and contemporary culture here, and published a number of articles on popular culture topics, American and British. Indeed, the Linicks began to spend more and more time in England, including a sabbatical year begun in 1979; in 1981 they moved to London.

Here Anthony began a twenty-year teaching career at the American School in London, in St. John's Wood, offering many courses, first in the high school social studies department and then in the English department—where he served as department head from 1994 to 2002, the year he retired. Dorothy also worked at the American School as a special projects coordinator; she had also held the post of director of student services at the American College in London. She died in July, 2007.

Since his retirement Anthony has been at work on a number of writing projects, including three earlier volumes in the Dog People of Paddington Rec cycle, *Strictly Come Barking, Have I Got Dogs For You!* and *DSI: Dog Scene Investigation*—as well as *The Lives of Ingolf Dahl,* a biography of his stepfather, and *A Walker's Alphabet, Adventures on the long-distance footpaths of Great Britain.* All of these books are available from the publisher at Authorhouse.com or Authorhouse.co.uk—or from any of the other online booksellers. The author can be contacted at anthonylinick@compuserve.com.